ADMIRAL BRADLEY A. FISKE
AND THE AMERICAN NAVY

BRADLEY A. FISKE
October 1912

Admiral Bradley A. Fiske and the American Navy

PAOLO E. COLETTA

THE REGENTS PRESS OF KANSAS
Lawrence

To all others who also served the navy

920
F54/CO

Library of Congress Cataloging in Publication Data

Coletta, Paolo Enrico, 1916–
Admiral Bradley A. Fiske and the American Navy.

Bibliography: p.
Includes index.
1. Fiske, Bradley Allen, 1854–1942.
2. Admirals—United States—Biography.
3. United States. Navy—History. I. Title.
V63.F57C64   359.3′31′0924 [B]   78-16525
ISBN 0-7006-0181-3

2/8312

CONTENTS

FOREWORD

On the broad veranda of the Bay View Hotel in Jamestown, Rhode Island, Bradley Fiske sat with other retired naval officers enjoying after-dinner talk and cigars, while they looked out over Narragansett Bay's calm water during a summer evening. He was both leader and listener in those frequent sessions during the 1920s. Here Fiske would escape the summer heat of New York City and intersperse busy days of reading and writing with watching ships of the navy's Scouting Fleet anchored off the Jamestown shore. This is where I remember him—a slight, mustachioed, and meticulously dressed gentleman who had only an occasional word for the grandchild of one of his fellow officers. What did those old gentlemen, rocking and smoking on the Bay View's veranda, find to talk about? In those days I was mystified. Now, over fifty years later, Paolo Coletta's book has changed mystery to wonderment. How did Fiske and his friends ever say good night and turn in?

This biography covers the life of one of our navy's most intellectual and inventive officers, one whose active duty spanned forty-six years and whose retirement years covered another twenty-six. Paralleling these seventy-two years of Fiske's life is a large part of the history of the United States Navy, from its post–Civil War nadir, when he entered the Naval Academy, until its truly "second-to-none" status during World War II, when he died. During this period there were few major naval projects, problems, or plans with which Fiske was not involved or upon which he did not comment.

The navy was being neglected quite completely by Congress and the public when Fiske graduated from the Naval Academy in 1874. The year before, the threat of war with Spain had brought a brief spurt of interest as a worried administration concentrated ships from the North and South Atlantic and Mediterranean squadrons off Key West. This fleet of wooden steamers and hastily mobilized Civil War monitors, boasting a four-knot fleet speed, was quickly disbanded after Spain agreed to American demands with respect to the *Virginius* affair.

Over the next few years the navy's operational capability sank even lower. Fiske appeared just as the age of steam and electricity took hold of our navy, then ranked eighth in the world. Young officers were thinking ahead and Fiske quickly joined them. To a man with his inventive capabilities, the navy failed to provide a promising career, and Fiske thought several times about resigning. Fortunately, he sought advice, and each time he was counseled to stay in the service. We can be particularly grateful to Park Benjamin, the young retired Naval Academy graduate serving as editor of the *Scientific American*, for keeping Fiske in the navy and thus enabling the navy to profit from his varied talents.

Fiske at one time figured that he would be fifty-nine years old when he became a captain and that he then would have only three years left to wear four stripes and hoist his flag as a rear admiral before retirement. But he beat that timetable: only five years elapsed between the time he assumed his first command in 1906 (of the cruiser *Minneapolis*) and 1911, when he became commander of the Fifth (armored cruisers) Division of the Atlantic Fleet. During his last tour of active duty, as aide for operations to Secretary of the Navy Josephus Daniels, Fiske made his greatest administrative contribution to the service: writing the legislation which created the Office of the Chief of Naval Operations. This tour of duty also brought Fiske and the controversial Daniels into continual conflict. From this time on, most of Fiske's undertakings were tinged with politics: he worked to prepare the navy for war and to counteract administration policies that opposed preparation.

Long before the terms *specialist* and *subspecialist* were used to identify a naval officer's qualifications, Fiske made a subspecialty of research and development. By resigning from the navy, he could have become a specialist and worked in the expanding field of engineering. Instead he maintained his line officer qualifications and duties, but was still able somehow to find time to work on a great number and variety of inventions. With few exceptions these were created to improve the capabilities of ships of the "new navy"—ships authorized after 1883. Fiske's maritime inventions, emphasizing electricity, included turret turning and ammunition hoisting apparatus, sounding devices, an electric log, and electrical controls and visual indicators. Many of these, such as the engine room telegraph, are still used in modern combat and merchant ships. In the optical field he developed the stadimeter (which is used today to measure the distance from a ship to a target), produced several versions of the range finder, and designed the basic sighting telescopes used by all navies to aim guns. Fiske applied Alexander Graham Bell's telephone system to shipboard use and experimented with wireless communications between ships. In all of these areas he was the forerunner of today's naval specialists in ordnance, communications, and sound engineering. His inventions were basic to the ship- and gun-control system of the fleet for many years. Traditionally in the naval service, forward thinkers must overcome senior conservatism. Fiske was no exception, for his inventions had to pass through the navy's bureau system while they were at the same time being reviewed by the Patent Office. He received relatively few patent rights for his many devices; and as a career naval officer he was at a distinct disadvantage in competing with civilian scientists backed by corporate research and development facilities.

Bradley Fiske thought in system-wide terms. His last and perhaps most important combat invention, the torpedo plane, is an excellent example. His ideas for this system, first described in 1912, developed into a major weapons system for the world's navies. It is ironic that his system was finally employed with devastating effect on 7 December 1941 by Japanese torpedo planes at Pearl Harbor. Victims of that attack included some of the American ships that Fiske, as aide for operations, had recommended in testimony before various congressional committees. After his retirement, Fiske spent a great deal of time and effort to secure patent rights for the torpedo aircraft. He was unsuccessful, and as time went on he became almost paranoid on the subject. As with many weapons systems, Fiske's original idea, born long before the value of naval aviation was understood, was improved upon and amplified by others for later use.

In 1915, Fiske lost his battle with Secretary Daniels to prepare the navy for war and also to establish a naval general staff. Thus, he never occupied the post of chief of naval operations which he had done so much to create. Instead he spent his last year of active duty in isolation at the Naval War College. Upon his retirement in 1916 Fiske started a new career writing articles and books. He had always been a prolific writer while on active duty and had contributed articles to professional journals, notably the *U.S. Naval Institute Proceedings*. His early articles concentrated on his inventions and shipboard techniques; in later years Fiske drew on his Naval War College background and long years of experience to write on military strategy and world problems. He became an apostle of Luce and Mahan, emphasizing that naval officers must understand all aspects of war. He was not a saber rattler, but he believed that the United States could not survive without armed power. Fiske was not pro-German, but he admired the efficiency of the German army and navy; he was not an Anglophile, but he never failed to point out that the Royal Navy far surpassed the U.S. Navy in fleet operations and training.

Fiske was not recalled to active duty during World War I. He had become president of the U.S. Naval Institute in 1912 and continued in that post until 1923, a rare honor for a retired officer. After the war much of his time and energy was taken up with what became known as the Daniels-Sims controversy. This dispute between the Navy Department and Adm. William S. Sims, commander of U.S. Naval Forces in Europe, had simmered during 1917 and 1918. After the armistice it boiled over, receiving wide attention in Congress and in the press. At a lengthy congressional hearing, Fiske supported Sims, who was highly critical of the support given him during the war by the department.

Fiske continued to write and speak on naval and international problems until his death in 1942 at the age of eighty-eight. Although he lived at the Waldorf Astoria, on New York's Park Avenue, he summered in Jamestown and occasionally traveled to Washington. He had worked well with Franklin D. Roosevelt when Roosevelt served as Daniels's assistant. It must have warmed Fiske's heart to watch the navy expand under President Roosevelt from 1934 on. Shortly after Fiske's death, his name rejoined the fleet in the destroyer escort U.S.S. *Fiske* (DE-143). This little ship joined the anti–U-boat campaign in the Atlantic during World War II and after less than a year of operations was sunk in combat. Two years later a second *Fiske*, a 2,200-ton destroyer, was commissioned. Today that ship still operates with the Atlantic Fleet, on occasion steaming by the admiral's old haunt, the Bay View Hotel. Although now the *Fiske* is outdated, the admiral would be proud of its thirty years of service—in action off Korea and Vietnam and in steady deployments with the Second and Sixth fleets in the Atlantic. He argued, wrote, and worked hard for a strong navy; during the *Fiske*'s duty such a U.S. Navy existed.

The story of Bradley Allen Fiske is not only the story of an inventive and intellectual U.S. naval officer; it is also the story of the navy during Fiske's long lifetime.

John R. Wadleigh

Newport, R.I.

Rear Admiral, USN (Ret.)

PREFACE

In writing an essay on Josephus Daniels, secretary of the navy, I found Bradley A. Fiske the stormiest naval petrel Daniels had to endure throughout his eight-year tenure. As aide for operations from 1913 to 1915, Fiske disagreed with almost everything Daniels tried to do and was particularly obstreperous in demanding additional preparedness not only before the Great War began in 1914 but thereafter, even though the United States was neutral.

My interest aroused, I read Fiske's memoirs. From them I learned that he had a long and good record as a seagoing officer, that he was perhaps the greatest inventor of optical and electrical mechanisms ever to serve the navy, and that he was in the forefront of those progressives who worked to reform naval organization and administration. But were the memoirs, written from diaries, reliable? Were the diaries written, as some are, to prove that sublimity is predestined? Was he merely a self-seeking publicity hound? I checked the memoirs for accuracy against archival and manuscript data and found them to be utterly correct factually. Questions of interpretation are more difficult to assess; for example, ample room remains for an analysis of the differences of opinion which separated Fiske and Secretary Daniels.

Since Fiske intended to end his memoirs with 1913, when he became aide for operations, it is clear that he did not want to publicize his quarrels with the administration and did so only at the behest of his publisher. By so doing he revealed the classic dilemma of a highly placed military man: should he remain silent, live within the system, and retire with the plaudits of all ringing in his ears; or, should he resign on the grounds that his advice was rejected and thus appear to be a monumental egoist? By resigning, Fiske demonstrated his ethical absolutism. Moreover, because the advice he offered finally was accepted soon after he left office, it is entirely proper to consider him the father of the Office of the Chief of Naval Operations, of the Naval Research Program, and of the National Security Council.

During the twenty-six years of Fiske's retirement, he continued his work on various inventions, wrote copiously and spoke in favor of maintaining the nation's military guard, and was regarded by his generation as the successor to Mahan—a philosopher of sea power. The torpedo plane he invented came of age during the Second World War; his work on the radio control of distant objects is still used in missilery; and the naval organization he supported is still largely in use today. Although he failed to please Daniels, he should be remembered as a loyal and patriotic man who served the navy extremely well as an officer, inventor, progressive reformer, author, and philosopher of sea and air power.

Many persons deserve my gratitude for making this study possible. The grant of sabbatical leave by the superintendent of the U.S. Naval Academy permitted me to concentrate on research for an academic term. Prof. Richard A. Evans, librarian; Miss Antoinette Delisi, head of the Circulation Department; and members of the reference staff at the Academy Library were indefatigable in making available or acquiring needed references. Miss Alice Creighton, head of Special Collections, and her assistant, Pamela Evans, aided my search in publications within their purview. Dr. William W. Jeffries, archivist, and Mrs. Jane Price, assistant archivist, provided archival records. Dr. Paul T. Heffron, assistant chief of the Manuscript Division at the Library of Congress, steered me to the papers of naval officers and others whose careers had touched Fiske's. Dr. Dean C. Allard, head of the Naval History Division's Operational Archives Branch in Washington, D.C., Mrs. Katherine Lloyd, and Bernard Cavalcante provided the Records of the General Board of the Navy and various collections of correspondence, and William Heimdahl called my attention to Fiske material in the Old Navy Records. Data on Fiske and the navy at the National Archives were ferreted out with amazing expertise and unfailing affability by Dr. Robert Krauskopf, Mr. Harry Schwartz, and Dr. Gibson Smith; John Pontius, archival technician, proved very helpful in the Central Search Room. Mr. Anthony Nicolosi, archivist at the U.S. Naval War College, furnished information on the presidents of the college. Mr. James Cheevers, curator of the Naval Academy Museum, lent me a Fiske diary. Comdr. R. T. E. Bowler, USN (Ret.), secretary-treasurer and publisher of the U.S. Naval Institute, and Mrs. Jean Ellinger made available the Record of the Minutes of the Meetings of the Board of Control from 1911 to 1923, while Fiske was president of the institute. Mrs. Robert Maddocks, reference librarian at the Naval Institute, furnished much important material. And Mrs. Young Hi Quick, historical research librarian at the Western Electric

Company in New York City, furnished manuscript materials and books that helped define Fiske's relations with the company.

Rear Adm. John R. Wadleigh, USN (Ret.), read the entire manuscript, which benefits from his keen critique and constructive suggestions. Dr. Jack Sweetman, my colleague at the Naval Academy, commented on Chapter 11. My longtime friend and also a naval biographer from whom I have learned much, Dr. Gerald E. Wheeler, dean of the School of Social Sciences at San Jose State University, provided sustaining encouragement throughout the project and gave substantial advice on Chapters 12 through 19. With great ingenuity, Mrs. Marjorie Whittington transcribed my often illegible hieroglyphics into a polished manuscript.

Last, I must thank my wife, Maria, and our children, Bernarr and Paula Maria, for their love and patience whenever I seemed to live more for Fiske than for them.

Paolo E. Coletta

ADMIRAL BRADLEY A. FISKE
AND THE AMERICAN NAVY

1

"MISTER" FISKE, 1854–1874

Bradley Allen Fiske was born 13 June 1854 at Lyons, New York, the son of an Episcopal minister, William Allen Fiske, and his wife, Susan Matthews Bradley. To improve his financial lot, Rev. Fiske moved to Cleveland, Ohio, in 1860 and to Cincinnati in 1866. There young Bradley attended first the public schools and then a private military school, enduring his first taste of military discipline. He suffered from the fact that, although he had the spirit of a fighting gamecock, he was physically small and delicate. Indeed, he was told by his doctors that the gymnastic exercises he did to strengthen himself had already damaged his heart.[1]

His maternal uncle, John Bradley, a midshipman at the Naval Academy, proved to be the stimulus that convinced Fiske to be a naval officer rather than to enter the ministry or law, the two other careers he had considered. Bradley did not change his mind even after his uncle was killed in the line of duty during the Civil War.[2]

In 1866, when the Fiskes moved to Cincinnati, Bradley began to exhibit an interest in inventing things—for example, extracting fresh water from salt water by evaporation. By the time he completed high school, Bradley was well acquainted with George H. Pendleton, a vestryman at his father's church and a former Democratic representative from Ohio. Through Pendleton's influence, Fiske obtained an appointment to the Naval Academy and arrived in Annapolis on 20 September 1870. He not only passed the academic entrance examinations, which 30 percent of all applicants failed, but the Medical Board (in standard phraseology) found "Bradley Allen Fiske free from deformity and disease and imperfection of the senses and otherwise physically qualified, according to the Regulations, to enter the academy."[3] He then signed articles binding him to serve the navy for eight years.

Fiske's instructors followed the principle that civilian boys were immediately transposed by their entrance into the academy into responsible gentlemen as well as officers of the government. Every midshipman was addressed as "Mister," and discipline was strict but just; the qualities of honor, courage, thoroughness, application, and truthfulness were inculcated at every turn.[4] The day began at 6:00 A.M. except during the winter months, when reveille was at 6:30. Bugle-calls regulated all activity between reveille and 10:00 P.M., with a break before supper (from 5:00 to 6:30 P.M.) and again after study hall (from 9:30 to 10:00 P.M.); then it was "lights out" followed by bed check. September was leave month; holidays were observed at the academy but leave was not granted, even for Christmas.

Fiske's officer instructors insisted upon teaching their charges well because their students later might be their subordinates. To the narrow and heavily technical curriculum the instructors added what they had learned in actual service; they taught as much by example as by precept. The grades they gave were important, too, for these and certain other factors determined class standing, which in turn determined where the graduate would be placed—and most likely remain with respect to seniority—on the navy list.[5]

Among the officer instructors whose careers would affect Fiske's were Robley D. Evans, Henry C. Taylor, Willard Herbert Brownson, Winfield Scott Schley, William Thomas Sampson, and Charles Stillman Sperry. Among the civilian instructors were William Chauvenet, who taught mathematics and navigation, and James R. Soley, who taught English and later became a well-known author, a lecturer in international law at the new Naval War College, and an assistant secretary of the navy.

Of midshipmen at the academy during Fiske's days from 1870 to 1874, those whose careers would intertwine most closely with his were Frank Friday Fletcher (1875), William B. Caperton (1875), Washington Irving Chambers (1876), William Freeland Fullam (1877), Thomas B. Howard (1873), Austin M. Knight (1873), William C. Cowles (1873), Charles J. Badger (1873), Albert Abraham Michelson (1873), Henry Thomas Mayo (1876), and William Sheperd Benson (1877).

In Fiske's day admission requirements to the Naval Academy were easy: candidates had to be between fourteen and eighteen years old, of good moral character, and able to pass an examination in reading, writing, spelling, arithmetic, geography, and English grammar.[6] Each midshipman took courses in eight departments: Practical Seamanship, Naval Gunnery, and Naval and Infantry Tactics; Mathematics; Steam Enginery; Natural and Experimental Philosophy; Ethics and English Studies; French; Spanish; and Drawing. The greatest emphasis was placed upon practical seamanship, taught on training ships moored to a wharf in the Severn River.

The Department of Natural and Experimental Philosophy offered courses in the mechanics of solids, liquids, and "aeriform fluids" and in acoustics, optics, electricity, heat, chemistry, and meteorology and climatology.

Texts were quite elementary, reflecting the current state of knowledge in these fields. Little was known of the vast possibilities of either electricity or steam engineering: the steam turbine and superheated steam were still to come, and radio, of course, had not yet been invented. However rudimentary the subjects, the rigor of midterm examinations is shown by the fact that more than half of Fiske's class "bilged" them and were sent home, leaving Fiske to compete with only about fifty men.

Independent of spirit, Fiske nevertheless had to submit to hazing by upperclassmen. Occasionally he lost his temper. Shortly before Christmas 1870, while lining up as usual for supper, a classmate stepped on his foot. When Fiske exclaimed, "Get off my foot," the offender replied, "You're a liar." In the fight that followed, Fiske was thoroughly thrashed.[7]

Through a miscalculation, Albert Wegman of New York, not Fiske, stood first in the class at the end of their plebe year. The fact that Wegman had only 150 demerits and Fiske 200 (with only thirteen others in the class having more) no doubt counted against him.

Following his first summer practice cruise, Fiske returned to Annapolis in September 1871 feeling that those four months had been the worst he had ever experienced. The midshipmen were embarked in two famous old sailing ships, the *Constellation* and the much smaller *Saratoga*. Fiske, one of the sixty midshipmen on the latter, slept in a hammock (from which he fell once while having a nightmare). Reveille was at 5:00 A.M., although breakfast was not served until 8:00 A.M., after the decks had been scrubbed. Fiske found the food monotonous and the facilities inadequate. Sixty men, many of them seasick, washed in nine washbasins in an unventilated room. When not attending recitations or studying their lessons, they handled the ropes that controlled the sails or attended gunnery and other drills. Fiske attributed the retention of sailing warships to the fact that Americans felt that the Civil War had been the last of all wars and that the only function of a navy was to "show the flag."[8] His analysis, made at seventeen years of age, fell short, but he had to live under conditions as he found them.

Fiske had entered the academy just as the navy reached its post–Civil War nadir. At the end of the war, the navy included 700 ships displacing half a million tons and mounting 5,000 guns. By 1870, it consisted of 50 commissioned warships; by 1871, there were only 29, and the navy ranked eighth in world strength. In 1874, when Fiske graduated, only 5 of the 26 sailing ships and only 73 out of the 137 steam-powered cruising ships were considered useful. Moreover, the necessity of filling vacancies with qualified volunteers (beginning in July 1866) had swelled the number of junior officers who were all approximately the same age. In 1873 Congress extended the midshipman course to six years, with the last two years to be performed with the fleet. Since Congress did not at the same time retire officers in higher grades or otherwise speed up the promotion system, midshipmen and junior officers had to suffer the consequences.

Fiske's second year at the academy was rather uneventful. Wegman again finished first in the class and Fiske second, but Fiske was elected class secretary and treasurer, positions he held until graduation. At the end of his third year Fiske again finished second: Wegman had fallen to third, and George Peters had finished first.[9] Otherwise the year was marked by a fight with fellow student Albert A. Michelson over a most trivial incident. Both Fiske and Michelson were sergeants, or "double diamonds," in the battalion's cadet officer hierarchy. As Michelson lined up the battalion, Fiske dressed his company. Before his men had formed perfectly, Michelson sang out, "Dress back, Mr. Fiske." Affronted, Fiske promptly challenged Michelson to a fight even though Michelson was the academy's welterweight champion. Fiske took his pounding uncomplainingly for ten minutes before the referee, noting that Fiske could not see out of either eye, stopped the fight. Fiske remained on the binnacle list for eight days before his contusions healed, and thereafter he and Michelson became fast friends.[10]

In March of that year Fiske went to Washington for the inauguration ceremonies marking Ulysses S. Grant's second term. It was a very cold day, and the wind was so strong that Fiske, a color sergeant of the battalion, could not carry the flag against it. As a result, he had to relinquish the flag and take a place at the rear.[11]

During his senior year, feeling that both Peters and Wegman were far ahead of him in academics, Fiske failed to bestir himself and often spent his time dancing with the belles in "Crabtown," as the midshipmen called Annapolis. It was a decision he thereafter lamented. For "Frenching out" —taking unauthorized leave—of the academy to meet a girl, he was stripped of his double diamonds and reduced to private. With sardonic pride, he and four others who also had been "busted" organized the "Privates' Club," which required that its members not attend dress parades. Caught while absent from a parade, Fiske was placed under modified arrest, was required to attend all exercises and recitations, and was marched to the academy "brig" ship every evening and back to breakfast every morning for the entire month prior to his graduation.[12]

Fiske's punishment encouraged him to make a renewed academic effort; as a result he finished second in his class and could have been first, he confessed, had he had more self-discipline. When the diplomas were given out, nevertheless, it hurt him to see Peters stretch out an arm that had a double diamond and four stripes on it while Fiske's own sleeve showed where his stripes had been removed for misconduct.[13]

Fiske left the academy in June 1874 with a technical education comparable to that offered by any good engineering school of the day. In his diaries and memoirs he never said whether he liked or disliked the academy, nor did he assess its value as an academic institution. Knowing that its discipline was designed to eliminate unsuitable officer candidates, Fiske refused to transfer to the navy any resentment he may have felt for punishments he received for violating discipline. In later years he praised the academy for its success in building character and teaching leadership. Fiske had done extremely well academically and had proved his courage by challenging stronger men to fights. In addition, during his many months at sea, Fiske had mastered the rudiments of sailing and acquired self-confidence from exposure to heavy weather, hard work, vile living conditions, and poor food. He had learned the need for teamwork and discipline and had become imbued with the qualities expected of a good officer. The objectives—to lead an honourable life, spurn mere material gain, live a life worthy of the navy, and become a good officer—were highly appealing to him. The navy promised a challenging career and guaranteed honorable employment for a lifetime. It was more than civilian college graduates could expect and a particularly important consideration during the depression years of the 1870s. And there was the invitation offered by an old hand on a practice cruise: "I don't think it's hard, Mr. Fiske, to be a naval officer; but it must be awful hard to be a good one."[14]

2

FROM MIDSHIPMAN
TO MASTER—AND MARRIAGE, 1874–1882

Fiske had to serve two years as a midshipman before taking his examinations to become an ensign. After graduation and a visit in Cincinnati with his parents, he received orders to report to Rear Adm. John J. Almy, commander in chief of the Northern Pacific Station, who flew his flag on the sloop-of-war *Pensacola* which was then being repaired at the navy yard at Mare Island, California. The *Pensacola*'s midshipmen served as assistants to the officers; they had the lowest seniority, were given the most onerous, least important duties, and had the poorest living accommodations on shipboard. For five months Fiske helped overhaul the *Pensacola*, but the work day was so short that he had ample time to call on the ladies at the Barnard House in Vallejo. Noticing how much hard liquor naval officers drank, Fiske decided to drink only wine and beer, a resolution he did not keep.[1]

On 23 January 1875, Capt. Bancroft Gherardi inspected the ship and crew. Four days later they began making passage for Honolulu, carrying King Kalakaua as a passenger. He had been touring the United States and was using the *Pensacola* to return home and, on the way, to visit the most important ports of his dominion. For quick work during a storm which broke the mainmast of the *Pensacola*, bringing down the maintopsail yard and parts of the other two masts as well, Captain Gherardi sent a good conduct report on Fiske to Admiral Almy.[2]

While his ship was in Hawaiian waters, Fiske tasted the rigorous discipline of a man-of-war, including infantry maneuvers ashore and shipboard drills. From headquarters in a rented cottage that he and some convivial colleagues named the "Whiskey Ranch," Fiske visited as many historic places as he could during the four-month stay. The *Pensacola* hoisted her anchor on 25 September and headed for La Paz in lower California; she frequently held gun practice during the month of passage. After calling at Mazatlan and at Acapulco (not yet tourist attractions), the *Pensacola* reached Mare Island on 27 January 1876. During the cruise, which had lasted a year, Fiske lost his natural temerity during gales—thanks in part to his particular responsibilities as "midshipman of the foretop." By working in close contact aloft, on deck, and in boats, he came away with a knowledge of the enlisted men's customs and ideas—knowledge vital to a leader.

Fiske worked hard when he had to, but he also played hard with little thought for the morrow. Orders to go home, received in July 1876, suddenly sobered him, for they meant he must take promotion examinations. A second sobering thought concerned his prodigality, for he was in debt and was even forced to borrow money for the return trip. He resolved henceforth never again to get into debt—a resolution he followed for the rest of his life. After studying at home, Fiske went in October to Annapolis and took a rigid examination in all branches of the naval profession. Although he didn't feel he had done well, he got the second highest grade in his class.[3]

Fiske's interest in inventions had lain dormant while he attended the Naval Academy and took his midshipman's cruise. At the age of twenty-two, however, the spirit of investigation was reawakened, and he developed into the most innovative, inventive, and scientifically minded naval officer of his generation.

In 1876, although the revolution caused by coal and iron continued, the United States was still largely awaiting technological transformation. Fiske came to maturity during the second industrial revolution—that of steel and electricity. The era of electrical lights and power had just begun; the telephone was not yet a proven instrument. Neither private nor public systems of research and development existed; no university offered a formal course in electrical engineering; and naval ships lacked electrical power. In time, Fiske would devise electrical and gunfire-control systems that transformed naval ships from poorly lit platforms whose guns might hit a target at two thousand yards to bright vessels in which most of the heavy work was done by electrical power (rather than by hand or steam) and whose projectiles could hit a ship before its hull was visible. Though he assumed all the duties of a line officer, Fiske used private industry to help him develop instruments that would improve the habitability, efficiency, and particularly the fighting capability of naval ships.

Fiske knew about optics, prisms, induction, generators, electric motors, and electromagnetism as a propulsive power. He knew his trigonometry, calculus, and geometry, too; he could sketch well enough to enable a mechanic to give body to his thoughts; and he learned how to write patent applications. If an invention consists of two parts, the idea and its execution, Fiske was primarily the idea man, one who intuitively noted that something was needed and set about providing it. He was a scientist in the sense that he would investigate, build, test, and finally prove that an idea worked. Only then did the idea become an invention. Throughout his life Fiske extracted a tremendous amount of energy from his thin, wiry frame and revealed, moreover, a dogged industry and immense enthusiasm in pursuing ideas until they had resulted in inventions.

While on "waiting orders" in 1876, it occurred to him that it would be better to telegraph in printed letters than in dots and dashes. Would an electromagnet exert enough force to print on paper? Without waiting to survey the literature in the field, Fiske built a typewriter and obtained two patents on it. Only then did he learn that both the typewriter and a telegraph machine—like the ticker-tape on Wall Street—had already been invented and marketed.[4]

During the spring of 1877, after being ordered to the USS *Wyoming*, Fiske heard about the work of Thomas A. Edison and began to study electricity with the help of George Bartlett Prescott's *Electricity and the Electric Telegraph*. In the meantime he thought of a new arrangement which would enable a soldier to hold a musket more steadily. He sent the drawing of it to the Bureau of Ordnance and for his pains received from its chief the comment that it was "neither novel nor useful"[5]—the first in a long series of rebuffs his ideas would receive from those in authority. But for a machine gun which Fiske had put together in two weeks, the same chief, Commodore William M. Jeffers, asserted that he was highly pleased that "a young officer should turn his attention so seriously and so intelligently to the development of an arm much needed in the service."[6]

Before receiving orders to attend the four-month summer course at the Naval Torpedo Station at Newport, Rhode Island, two other ideas came to Fiske. He nearly perfected a "boat-detaching apparatus" which would allow a boat to be lowered from a ship and hoisted in again quickly and safely. He also submitted to the Bureau of Ordnance an improvement over the spar torpedo; but his suggestion—firing six mortar shells electrically when a rapidly moving small boat got within a thousand yards of its target—did not strike the bureau as a particularly good one.[7]

In addition to studying electricity, explosives, and fuse-making, the students at Newport experimented with both torpedoes and explosives. Torpedoes were still so new that there were no texts on the subject. But because all maritime nations were giving serious attention to mobile torpedoes, Jeffers recommended "liberal appropriations for experiments to develop the capabilities of this most important means of offense and defense."[8] According to Adm. David D. Porter, torpedoes were simple, easy to operate, and posed no danger to those who worked with them.[9] Fiske found out differently.

The torpedo station excited Fiske in two ways: first, there were lectures on electricity delivered by a civilian professor, Moses G. Farmer; and second, there were training exercises in which half of the class in one ship would try to pass a towed torpedo beneath another ship carrying the rest of the class. In an accident during these maneuvers, a 330-pound torpedo came into Fiske's ship, threw him heavily to the deck, and put him out of action for a month.[10]

From the torpedo station Fiske was ordered home and then to the USS *Plymouth* (a ship of thirty to forty guns), which left from Norfolk on a Caribbean cruise. Bolstered by the captain's extremely favorable report on his boat-detaching apparatus, Fiske requested permission to continue work on it on shore. On 6 March 1878, he was ordered to report to the New York Navy Yard. On the way he called on Commodore Robert W. Shufeldt, chief of the Bureau of Equipment in Washington. Shufeldt suggested that Fiske have his apparatus built by a private firm; that way he might enjoy some royalties and stimulate other officers to invent things.[11]

In Brooklyn at the New York Navy Yard, Fiske found both the shore establishment and the fleet "almost comatose."[12] Ships were being reduced in number, but there were many more officers than were needed. The ships' crews contained many who were not American citizens; they spoke a dozen foreign languages. Breech-loaded rifled guns, armor plate, and torpedoes were purchased in England, brown powder in Germany, and armor-piercing shells and smokeless powder in France—all because the equipment could not be produced in the United States. The fleet had no submarines, range finders, or battery-control systems, nor was there a naval war college.

Crossing the Hudson to New York City, Fiske found a firm that would make his boat-detaching apparatus for the Bureau of Equipment. Within a year, however, upon finding that inferior metal was being used, Fiske terminated the contract and gave his patent to the bureau. During this period, while on a coast survey ship, Fiske invented an "electric log": a small propeller and an electric wire towed by a ship would indicate each turn and every tenth of a mile covered. With funds supplied by the Bureau of Navigation, he continued experimenting with this log for several years.[13]

One evening Lt. Arthur Allen Boyd, who was also stationed at the navy yard, invited Fiske to dine at his home in New York. One of the other guests was Park Benjamin, a Naval Academy classmate of Boyd's who had resigned in 1869 and was now, at twenty-eight, editor of the *Scientific American*. Benjamin was extremely well informed, particularly about electricity and patents, and completely captivated Fiske. Several days later Fiske called on him and told him that he wished to resign from the navy because he saw no future career in it. Fiske said he wanted to get a fresh start at something, even by being an office boy at *Scientific American*. The knowledgeable Benjamin replied that Fiske already had a good job and that he should hold on to it with both hands. Fortunately, Fiske took the advice.[14]

The forerunner of a sounding machine came to Fiske when he noticed that a small metal plate secured to a towline at a particular angle could be made to signal an alarm in the ship when it struck bottom. As with many other ideas he had during his lifetime, Fiske was unable to develop it, but the scheme was perfected by others and used until radio sounding machines, or fathometers, were perfected during the 1920s.[15]

Another problem on which Fiske spent a good deal of time was finding a way to measure the altitude of the sun when the horizon could not be seen—an idea about which more will be said below. Inventions did not keep Fiske from social activities: he was asked by the daughter of the medical inspector at Brooklyn Hospital to lead a New York cotillion. There he met an extremely pretty red-head, Josephine Harper, a daughter of a director of the publishing firm Harper and Brothers.

By February 1879, when he was ordered to the USS *Powhatan*, at Norfolk, Fiske had become interested in visual signaling. The principal means of nighttime communications between ships—waving an oil-burning lamp back and forth according to a code—was virtually useless at sea. Nor was the recently invented "Very signals" system much better, for it was quite slow and inaccurate since the "stars" shot from pistols were subject to misinterpretation. Why not, Fiske asked, place a lamp behind an aperture which could be opened and closed by a shutter? By pointing the lamp and then opening and closing the shutter according to a code, the sailor could send a number of flashes to be read just as a telegraph operator read the "clicks" on his telegraph-sounder. The "flashing light," whether fixed or hand-held, eventually became an integral and important part of naval communications.[16]

After an extended visit to New York, the *Powhatan* made passage to Port Royal, South Carolina, then visited Guantánamo Bay and Santiago de Cuba before returning to Port Royal and New York. Her log for the forenoon watch of 26 August 1880 noted that "Ensign B. A. Fiske was this day detached and placed on waiting orders."[17]

After three months at home, Fiske requested sea duty and got a billet on the *Colorado*, the receiving ship at the New York Navy Yard. While he invented and patented three types of mechanical lead pencils—simple affairs in which lead in a tube was released or clamped by a spring pushed by the finger—he also experimented with his electric log during a voyage on the *Tallapoosa* from New York to Portsmouth, New Hampshire, and back.[18]

Shortly after his return, Fiske was given a ticket for the Charity Ball in New York; there he again met Josephine Harper, whom he asked frequently to dance. He then proceeded to Washington for his promotion to the grade of master (later, lieutenant junior grade); he had no trouble with the academic and professional examinations but was told by the doctors that he had organic heart disease. Although the doctors passed him, they warned him not to take violent exercise or become excited. Considerably sobered by the warning, Fiske returned to the *Colorado*. He saw "Jo" Harper frequently, inviting her to a series of dances. He then received an invitation from her to call at her Fifth Avenue address. He found a beautiful house and tasteful decorations bespeaking wealth, a very attractive father, and an extremely pretty, if somewhat nervous, mother. Fiske postponed requesting actual sea duty so that he could call often at the Harper home; on St. Valentine's Day 1880 the two became engaged.

She knew nothing of the value of a dollar; he was broke, with no prospects for the future other than slow promotion, poor pay, and an alternating duty of three years ashore and three years at sea. The situation, however, improved considerably when, two weeks after their engagement, he received a royalty check for $1,000 from the sales of one of his mechanical pencils.[19]

Fiske missed seeing his fiancé when he was ordered to the old sailing ship *Saratoga*, on which he had made his plebe cruise. But it was only a three-month stay. Moreover, he was more than repaid by renewing his acquaintance with the *Saratoga*'s captain, Comdr. Henry C. Taylor, who had been his mathematics teacher at the Naval Academy. One day Taylor mentioned the word *foresight*, which Fiske confused with *prophecy*. Taylor corrected him, saying that men do not have the gift of prophecy but react quite similarly to given situations. Foresight was based on the ability "to tell the probable course of events if we can find some set of conditions in the past like those present now." In the light of experience, he who had foresight, Taylor said, could then determine what measures to adopt under given circumstances. Taylor's words engraved themselves on Fiske's memory and, by his own admission, constituted an important influence on his life.[20]

On 17 November 1881, Fiske reported for duty on an old steam frigate, the *Minneapolis*. Taking leave from her on 15 February 1882, he married Jo Harper in St. Thomas's Episcopal Church in New York City. Many naval officers attended the wedding ceremony and the reception that followed in the Harper home. After a brief honeymoon, Fiske returned with his bride to Newport and reported back to his ship.

3

THE BUREAU OF ORDNANCE
AND THE "ABCDs," 1882–1888

Even if Fiske might have been happier in a laboratory than on a ship, he managed to be a naval officer and a master of electro-mechanical contrivances at the same time. For want of a better one, he used his ship as a laboratory.

In 1882, as he wrote in his memoirs with a touch of egotism, Fiske considered the navy "an extremely uninteresting place for a man who had already learned virtually all there was of the naval profession, and who could see no prospect ahead except a tiresome alternation of monotonous cruises at sea and profitless tours on shore."[1] Just then, however, two inventions in electricity—the electric light and the telephone—promised a future to anyone who had listened to what Harry Taylor said about foresight. Fiske sought out Park Benjamin, who had resigned from the *Scientific American* and had opened a New York office with his brother as scientific consultants. Fiske confided in Park Benjamin, and Benjamin encouraged him, saying that it would benefit him to know about electricity whether or not he stayed in the navy and that if he began right away he could show the navy how to use electricity.[2] Fiske immediately applied for a six-month leave to study electricity. Fortunately for him, the assistant to the chief of the Bureau of Navigation was Bowman Hendry McCalla, who had been the executive officer of the *Powhatan*. Once McCalla had said: "Mr. Fiske I do not approve at all of a good deal of your conduct while you have been in this ship. At the same time I recognize in you a mind of considerable originality, and if I can ever do anything for you, you will do me a favor if you will request me to do it." Fiske told McCalla about his desire to study electricity; he also applied directly to the bureau chief, John G. Walker, for leave. When McCalla asked Walker to approve Fiske's request, Walker replied, "Tell Fiske that six months isn't enough, tell him to ask for a year." Fiske did so, got his leave, and began work at once.[3]

Both British and American electrical engineers saw mechanical engineering as basic to their work. Given his excellent engineering training at the academy, Fiske had the chance to become a pioneer by learning about electricity. It was at this time that the cruiser *Trenton* became the first warship in the world to be equipped with an Edison electrical plant powerful enough to light 250 incandescent lamps.

After Fiske had worked out of the Benjamins' office for about three months, he set himself up at the old Astor House as a "consulting electrical engineer." Though he barely earned enough to pay his rent, he received his reward in the love he found for electricity. It was a busy and productive time. His frequent periods of extreme discouragement ended when the *London Electrician* reprinted an article he had published in an American newspaper. Moreover, together with a draftsman who had worked for Thomas Edison, he devised the Fiske-Mott insulator. By increasing the resistance between telegraph wires and insulators as they were secured on telegraph poles, leakage was reduced. The insulators were being marketed by a Chicago company when it came time for Fiske to return to duty, so he sold the patent to the company for a mere $100. Meanwhile he had begun work on a textbook entitled *Electricity in Theory and Practice; or, the Elements of Electrical Engineering* that would bridge the gap between mathematical studies dealing with electricity and manuals for constructing electrical apparatus. Rather than submitting it to Harper and Brothers—the thought made him uneasy—he sent it to D. Van Nostrand, who published it in 1887. It contained eighteen chapters and 180 illustrations. Fiske's discussions of the magnetic field that lies at the heart of the dynamo, of the construction and operation of batteries, of electrical measurements, and of the operation of electrical motors were important scientific contributions.[4] The book went through ten printings and sold for twenty-two years. It could have done even better had Fiske ever found time to revise it, but he never did.

In September 1883 Fiske again had serious doubts about whether he should remain in the navy. He decided to stay because both his family and his wife's family advised him that with the precarious state of his health, the navy at least would give him some pay if he were forced to retire for physical reasons. On 1 October, with McCalla's hand evident in his new orders, Fiske reported for duty as inspector of ordnance to Commodore Montgomery Sicard, chief of the Bureau of Ordnance; Fiske was sent to supervise the manufacture of 6-inch gun forgings at the Midvale Works.[5]

Fiske's decision to study electricity coincided with congressional authorization to build the first ships of the "new navy"—three steel cruisers and a dispatch boat. The first cruiser would displace 4,000 tons and have two-thirds full sail power; the other cruisers would displace 2,500 tons and also have two-thirds sail power. The 15-knot dispatch vessel would be built of iron. Once funding for these ships had been provided in 1883, the downward swing of the navy's fortune, following the Civil War, was finally halted.

The construction bids for the ABCDs—cruisers *Atlanta, Boston,* and *Chicago* and the dispatch boat *Dolphin*—went to John Roach, whose yards were at Chester, Pennsylvania. The contracts, signed on 23 July 1883, called for completion of the *Dolphin* first, within one year, then the cruisers, in eighteen months or by the end of 1884. Soon Fiske would be supervising the installation of the ordnance on the *Atlanta.*

Although Fiske, as directed by Sicard, designed electric primers to fire the new cruisers' guns,[6] he wondered whether the success of his book on electricity didn't warrant his resigning from the navy and going into electrical work. To further prepare himself for the outside, he spent his evenings studying electricity; nevertheless, his navy work continued to hold his interest. On 3 August 1883 Fiske suggested to Sicard that the plans for the *Chicago* ought to include dynamo rooms in well-protected spaces below the waterline, capable of supplying ample power for searchlights, electrical testing instruments, lighting, training guns, hoisting ammunition, firing the batteries, and the like. He warned that if sufficient space were not allotted, "the Bureau will be hampered in the future by an inability to take advantage of the numerous convenient uses of electricity which are rapidly increasing." He also offered numerous suggestions about the construction of the *Atlanta* and the *Boston.*[7]

With Sicard's approval, Fiske experimented with megaphones as a means of communicating between ships. He built one instrument ten feet high and three feet wide, only to find that, along with the messages, it transmitted unintended noises such as the sound of the wind. In the end an Edison megaphone was placed on the *Atlanta.*[8] Fiske also designed for the fleet a system for propelling, steering, and firing a torpedo boat by electricity—all done by an operator using only one wire.[9] Then Sicard sent him to Philadelphia to display the bureau's wares and to learn what he could at the International Electrical Exhibition, held under the auspices of the Franklin Institute from 2 September to 11 October 1884.[10]

The exhibition included discussions of foreign and domestic production of electricity, electrical conductors, measurements, applications of electricity, and terrestrial physics. Meeting concurrently were institutes of mining and electrical engineers, telephone people, railway telegraph superintendents, electricians, and electrical engineers. Among the displays was the Fiske-Mott insulator, deemed 200 percent better than any rival. At the National Conference of Electricians, Fiske rubbed shoulders with Alexander Graham Bell,

Simon Newcomb, Elihu Thomson, Sylvanus P. Thompson, Samuel P. Langley, Edison, naval officers Theodore F. Jewell and William T. Sampson, and former naval officer Frank J. Sprague.[11]

With a number of learned professors, Fiske prepared a report on the exhibition for the Franklin Institute; among other things, they recommended the establishment of a federal Bureau of Standards. Fiske reported to Sicard on developments in storage batteries, signaling by electric light projectors, dynamos and motors, incandescent lighting systems, electrical conductors, telephones (which he suggested be adopted to naval use), "electric signaling without wires between ships," and velocimeters. Furthermore, Fiske suggested that electric rather than steam motors be used to steer ships; hoist powder and projectiles from the magazines; work winches, yards, and stays; fire machine guns; and operate an engine-order telegraph.[12] Meanwhile, at the request of *Popular Science Monthly*, he wrote an article entitled "The Electric Railway" which pointed out the tremendous possibilities for such a mode of transportation. In an extensive article entitled "Electricity in Warfare," published in *Electrical World* late in 1885, Fiske dealt with the use of electricity in mines, torpedoes, telegraphy, telephony, gun-firing from a central fire-control location, shipboard lighting and signaling, and even predicted electrically driven submarines.[13]

Fiske had joined the Bureau of Ordnance just as it was designing armament for the new cruisers. Each ship would carry four 8-inch, eight 6-inch, and two 5-inch guns in the main battery, along with mixed secondary batteries and electric searchlights. After he completed the 6-inch forgings at Midvale, Fiske was made responsible for adapting electricity to the ordnance of the cruisers. He later confessed that he had floundered around, for there were no practical guides to follow; he had to learn by experience. He found, for example, that on a cruiser heeling over only ten degrees it would be impossible for the two men at the training gear to move their gun "uphill" because they had only hand power. He solved the problem by retaining the gun carriage gearing and running a shaft from it down to an engine placed in a compartment below. The gun captain could thus remain at his station and still turn his gun. But should the engine be steam powered (as Sicard preferred and the British used) or pneumatic (as various other officers desired)? Or should it be an electric one, as he preferred? Fiske decided to use an ordinary steam engine and drafted its specifications; the four engines he then had manufactured successfully turned the 8-inch gun mounts of the *Atlanta* and the *Boston*.[14]

Impeded by poor wiring insulation and fragile electrical apparatus, Fiske failed to adopt electricity to the firing of guns. He persisted in his experiments, however, and on 9 December 1885 suggested to Sicard that electricity be used for aiming heavy guns—in both elevation and azimuth—and for firing them. All this was to be done by one gun captain using merely a pistol grip, the wiring of which Fiske sketched. Although the new cruisers were not equipped for electric firing, later ships were.

While looking over the ordnance plans of the *Atlanta*, Fiske wondered why she had no range finder. Upon learning that no shipboard range finder existed, he decided to invent one[15]—a decision that kept him hard at work for many years and involved him in controversies with unbelieving ship captains and bureau heads.

On 29 December, Fiske began to supervise the installation of the ordnance equipment on the *Atlanta*, commanded by Capt. Francis M. Bunce.[16] After Secretary of the Navy William E. Whitney took the ABCDs from Roach Shipyards and ordered their completion in navy yards, the eight months required to build them stretched out to twenty-two. They were small and weak when compared with the newest European ships of a similar type, but the navy had come a long way in a short time. When completed, the United States ranked second in the world in commerce destroyers. Equipped with modern ordnance, searchlights, and a protective deck, the *Atlanta* was, moreover, the first U.S. warship with the improvements in naval design, construction, and ordnance adopted by foreign navies over the last twenty years; and Fiske was proud to have been one of the team that built her.[17]

While on the *Atlanta* Fiske took and passed his examinations for promotion to lieutenant and again saw doctors shaking their heads as they listened to his heart. They said that he had organic heart disease but that it had not progressed far enough to warrant rejecting him.[18] Returning to the *Atlanta* with this cold comfort, Fiske immersed himself in experiments with electricity, especially in wireless telegraphy—or "signaling by induction." Captain Bunce helped by obtaining some funds from the Navy Department with which to build needed electrical apparatus. By wrapping wire about the 3,000-ton *Atlanta*—thereby making her the largest electromagnet in the world—and similarly wiring a tug and placing a telephone in the circuit, Fiske was able to hear "makes and breaks" at the telephone, but only over short distances. He then tried to signal through the water by putting a telephone in a circuit made up of wires connecting immersed copper plates placed ahead and astern of the *Atlanta*. The first experiment delivered a signal over a distance of fifty feet, the second over two hundred yards, but this was still not enough to be of any practical value.[19]

By order of Rear Adm. Stephen B. Luce, who commanded the North Atlantic Station, Fiske tried to learn how using mirrors in the bows of torpedo boats would screen them from discovery as they approached a ship.

Fiske experimented with mirrors fitted at various angles and reported that they did not do well either in daylight or when they came within the rays of a searchlight.[20]

While the *Atlanta* made a four-month cruise to the Caribbean, Fiske proposed to Sicard a new method of governing the motions of guns moved by electric power. He wrote (enclosing a sketch): "The plan is an application to the electric motor of the principles which govern the actions of the following lever in steam engines, the electric motor being made to go ahead or back following the motion of the operator's hand in both direction and speed."[21] Interested, Sicard asked for details.[22] Fiske complied, adding that Frank J. Sprague had said that the plan should work well.[23] Two weeks later, Fiske suggested to Sicard that his plan for controlling the motions of electric motors for training guns could also be used advantageously for other purposes such as hoisting ammunition, shells, and coal ashes.[24]

After the *Atlanta* had returned to the navy yard at Brooklyn, Fiske conceived of an improvement to the stock ticker; he sold it to the Western Union Telegraph Company for $700 along with another (for which he received $100) even before he had obtained a patent.[25] By early August Fiske had come up with the idea that it would be better to train and elevate a 6-inch gun on a moving target simultaneously than to train first and then wait for a favorable time of roll; "and I beg to suggest," he wrote Sicard, "that gun captains be taught to fire in this way."[26]

In a letter to Sicard dated 16 November, Fiske recommended certain changes in the sight bars which would allow quick adjustments to any change in range and enclosed a sketch. Another letter the same day contained his further improvements for sight bars. On 28 November Fiske wrote Sicard requesting permission to test on the *Atlanta* an electric shell hoist manufactured by the Sprague Electric Railway and Motor Company.[27] Sicard approved the request. As for the sight bars, however, Sicard had anticipated him; the changes Fiske suggested had already been adopted for all new secondary battery guns being manufactured in the United States.[28] Feeling encouraged, Fiske wrote a ten-page letter on 8 December detailing his plans for "pointing and firing guns with automatic mechanisms." On a rod attached to a sight bar he placed a spirit level; to this he fused two wires. The rod followed changes made in the sight bar sightings. When the bubble assumed the same angle as the gun, the liquid drained away, thereby breaking the circuit between the wires and firing the gun. Another sketch which Fiske sent Sicard concerned an electric primer that would fire automatically when the gun reached the correct elevation. This mechanism, he concluded, would overcome two major errors in firing: "the delay of the gun captain in actuating the firing mechanism after being aware that the target is on the sights, and . . . the time required to fire the primer after the gun captain has done his part." The time it took for the projectile to leave the gun and minor errors introduced by the "jump" of the gun also had to be taken into account. Fiske's design would obviate these errors and permit firing at any point in the roll of a ship. According to Fiske, Sprague called it "the most feasible scheme for adapting electric motors to gun carriages that he had ever seen."[29]

Fiske's superiors took his efforts seriously. Bunce always forwarded Fiske's letters on to Sicard, and Sicard tested those ideas that showed promise. For example, he sent the electric primer plan to Lt. Austin M. Knight, inspector of ordnance in charge of the Naval Proving Ground at Annapolis. Knight thought Fiske's proposal for lateral train was feasible, but he had reservations about using the spirit bubble, for spirit levels subject to concussion divided into two or more parts and varied in length with the temperature. Moreover, if a gun were trained nearly ahead or astern, the rolling of the ship might throw the bubble to one side of the electric terminals and prevent firing altogether. Nevertheless, Knight suggested that Fiske continue his experiments by the inexpensive method of using primers only.[30]

In acknowledging Fiske's suggestions on 5 March 1888, Sicard questioned the spirit-bubble plan but noted that "the plan proposed by you is being examined with interest, and seems feasible." He added a personal note: "The Bureau would be pleased to hear from you again upon this or other subjects."[31]

In his autobiography, Sir Percy Scott recounts how in May 1896 he fixed a telescope to the sight bar of a gun and added a sight setter to the gun crew; with practice he was able to work the elevating wheel so quickly that he could keep his sights on a target, notwithstanding the roll of his ship. A good sight setter thus made continuous-aim battery firing possible.[32] Scott's account begs comparison with Fiske's plan—devised ten years before—in which Fiske would provide electric motors for both training and elevating guns, thereby removing both the pointer and trainer from a gun crew while making continuous-aim battery fire possible.[33]

Fiske matured rapidly between 1882 and 1888. Though only a lieutenant in 1888, at the age of thirty-four, he had shown his mettle as an investigator and propounder of plans for improving the navy. Although Fiske was a much better draftsman, like Scott, he rarely looked at a mechanism without thinking about how he could improve it. Fiske was knowledgeable enough to have written a textbook on electricity; he had suggested a number of ways in which electric power could be used in naval ships. If an adequate central electrical power plant were installed, Fiske reasoned, electricity could be used for communicating between ships; for training, elevating, and firing guns; and for powering motors that would take much of the physical drudgery out of shipboard work. Yet he had much to learn about the broader aspects of a navy.

When the *Atlanta* visited Newport in November 1887, Fiske spoke with Alfred T. Mahan, the first president of the Naval War College. Reluctantly, Fiske listened to the lectures that Luce ordered the officers of his fleet to attend; Fiske could not see how lectures on strategies used in old campaigns would help one handle the myriad details of contemporary shipboard existence. He slowly realized, however, that Luce, like Harry Taylor, was a man of foresight if not of prophecy. Luce, Mahan, and others showed him that weapons were merely tools, just as a hammer and chisel were to a sculptor or paint and brushes to a painter, and that there was an art of war with certain principles.[34]

Fiske greatly admired Luce, the only flag officer since the Civil War who drilled a fleet in tactical exercises he himself had drafted. Luce, however, by noting "the crass ignorance of naval officers . . . and the imbecility of our Navy Department as a director of . . . operations during war" in a lecture before the U.S. Naval Institute in 1888,[35] provoked his own downfall. His ships were gradually taken away from him and he was detached from command of the fleet. The reason was that Luce had dared to suggest that the department, as long as it remained divided into separate bureaus each concerned with its special tasks, could not prepare for war (or direct war if it came) except under the supervision of a civilian secretary, ignorant of strategy. For saying the same thing more than twenty-five years later, while he was the aide for operations to Secretary of the Navy Josephus Daniels, Fiske too would be similarly punished.

4

REVOLUTIONIZING NAVAL GUNNERY, 1888–1895

Fiske was detached from the *Atlanta* on 30 November 1888 and ordered to special duty as a member of a board established to conduct the acceptance trials of the "dynamite cruiser" *Vesuvius*. Built by William Cramp for the Pneumatic Dynamite Gun Company, the *Vesuvius* carried in her bow, at a fixed elevation of eighteen degrees, three pneumatic guns. Each was fifty-five feet long and fifteen inches in diameter; they had been developed largely by E. L. G. Zalinski, a Polish-born lieutenant in the U.S. Army. Different ranges could be obtained either by using projectiles of different weights or by varying the escape of compressed air kept in reservoirs below deck. Fiske found the *Vesuvius* interesting because unlike other ships, which used a flat trajectory, she used a high trajectory. (It was Zalinski's hope that any "aerial torpedoes" that fell short would continue underwater toward their target.)[1]

In May 1888, the Bureau of Ordnance arranged for the *Vesuvius* to test fire nine shots at three ranges established in Chesapeake Bay, but the bureau declined what appeared to be a generous offer by Edward Wickes, president of the American Range Finder Company. Wickes would place a range finder specially designed by Fiske on the *Vesuvius*, another one on the *Chicago* which would work on both sides of the ship, and still another on a ship with a very small base line, "the condition being that if their performance is satisfactory to you—you will purchase them at $1,500 each." If they failed to perform satisfactorily, the company would remove them at its own cost.[2] At the request of the chief of the Bureau of Ordnance, Montgomery Sicard, Fiske explained "the plan of my range finder" using trigonometry; Fiske promised that he could obtain the range on a target in five seconds.[3] On 20 February, Sicard agreed to Wickes's request to send an officer to examine the range finder Fiske had designed for the *Vesuvius*.[4] On 1 May, satisfied with the report, Sicard ordered two range finders, one for the *Baltimore* and one for the *Chicago*, established conditions under which they would be tested, and pledged to pay Wickes $2,000 for every instrument approved for purchase.[5]

During the *Vesuvius* test on 26 January 1890, eight shots were fired; five hit their target. The next step was to see if each of the guns would fire with the speed stipulated in the contract—at least once every ninety seconds. Following nine months of preparation, the tests took place on 9 October. The guns were a complete success, and the navy accepted the ship; Seaton Schroeder was placed in command. Fiske saw possibilities in her gunnery system but most naval officers disliked the *Vesuvius*, and the failure of the Pneumatic Dynamite Gun Company ended attempts to build others like her.[6]

While on the *Vesuvius*, Fiske got the idea of making a machine gun that would operate by compressed air. He cut a hole in the rear end of the barrel and used the force of the air that escaped to actuate the gun. He also saw that gases from other sources of power, such as powder, could be used. Fiske applied for three patents, one covering the idea of using gas which escaped from a hole in the rear end of the barrel, one covering the application of the plan to pneumatic guns, and the third covering its application to powder guns. All three patents were granted. Foolishly, Fiske then abandoned them all rather than pay the required $60 in "final fees" to the patent office. Browning's later Colt automatic gun and its improved version, the Browning gun, were based squarely on Fiske's idea.[7]

While still on the *Atlanta* Fiske had received patents for an apparatus whereby the motions of an electric motor could be made to follow those of an operator's hand both in speed and in direction and for three applications of it—hoisting ammunition, training guns, and steering ships. He assigned the patents to the Sprague Electric Railway and Motor Company, which quickly built an ammunition hoist that operated perfectly on board the *Atlanta*. The company then made an electric training system for one of the 8-inch gun carriages on the *Chicago*. This also worked well. Fiske was thus the first to demonstrate the practicability of using electricity to hoist ammunition and train guns.[8]

Although the newest American naval ships paced the fastest merchant ships, their accuracy of firing rarely exceeded a thousand yards when the projectile followed a practically flat trajectory. To have a projectile hit a target depended not only upon the eyesight of a gunner but also upon the amount and quality of the powder charge, the quality of the gun itself, and atmospheric conditions. A pointer looked through the rear sight of his gun (which was about fifteen inches from his eye) and the front sight (which was about fifty inches away) to a target anywhere from hundreds to thousands of yards beyond. Even the best pointers erred a minimum of 15 percent, and sighting arrangements for turret guns were even more complicated than for open mounts.[9] Nor had anyone improved on spotting the fall of shot to make corrections or devised a method of providing gunners with the target's relative speed. No wonder captains held their fire until they were within about five hundred yards of the enemy.

Hopeful inventors of a highly desired single-position, or single-instrument, range finder had tried mechanical, stereoscopic, and prism systems to solve the gunnery triangulation problem. All had failed.[10] The problem was complicated: ships converging at twenty knots changed their relative positions by about 680 yards a minute; guns of different sizes required different elevations; and the rolling and pitching of the ship also added to the problem of sighting the guns. Fiske saw that what was vitally needed was, first, knowledge of the enemy's range at the earliest possible moment so that he could be kept under constant fire and, second, a way to calculate every change in relative position. In 1890, by means of a range finder Fiske installed on her, the *Chicago* fired on targets over fifteen hundred yards away with an error not exceeding six-tenths of 1 percent over the entire distance. Thus, she could put a projectile within nine yards of her point of aim at a distance of three quarters of a mile.[11] A range finder on the *Baltimore* did even better—and all of this with no need to make any calculations. The range finder did the measuring instantaneously and automatically whether the target was moving or stationary. But it took Fiske several years of hard work to achieve these results.

To construct the range finder, Fiske had "to find the sum of two angles included between two observers and lines drawn from those two observers to a target."[12] One side of the triangle would be the length of the ship (base line); the two angles would be those made between telescope sights located forward and astern on the ship and the target. Fiske arranged it so that when tracking a target, the telescopes moved along wires, with the distance they traveled representing range to target. A galvanometer dial (based on the principle of the Wheatstone Bridge) then pointed an arrow along a range scale denoting yards to target. The whole process was completed in a few seconds, and the gunners would be informed of the range. A ship with this apparatus would be able to choose the distance at which to open fire and to fire on an enemy long before the enemy could land a shell. Such a finder could also be used between guns located in forts, and its utility for piloting was self-evident.

The first range finder Fiske built—for the *Vesuvius*—failed because, he asserted, it was the first of its kind and the base line, only twenty-six feet, was too short. He then arranged with the American Range Finder Company of New York to seek patents on his apparatus in foreign countries and also to try to secure a contract from the Bureau of Ordnance to install one of his range finders on the *Chicago*. The patents were obtained and, as already noted, the contract was also obtained, but Sicard obdurately declined to put range finders on other ships until those on the *Chicago* and the *Baltimore* had passed their tests.[13]

Fiske encountered great difficulty in installing his gear on board the *Chicago*. It was essential that the telescopes, placed at the bow and stern about three hundred feet apart, be perfectly parallel so that their convergence from a target could be measured. He also was the object of bantering by the ship's officers, who said that a seaman's eye was good enough and that no gear should be added to a ship unless it was absolutely essential.[14] Fiske breathed easier after November 1889 when the first test of his equipment was successful; he then went on to develop an improved version.

The gear Fiske placed on the *Chicago* could be used only on one side of the ship at a time; it had to be shifted to the other side if needed there. Moreover, its wiring was stretched along the deck, rather than being permanently secured.[15] One of the two models he placed aboard the *Baltimore* measured distances ahead and astern; the second, on the fore-and-aft line, measured distances to either side. It is a wonder that these also passed their tests because only temporary wires were used and the instruments and tripods on which they rested were made of heavy iron. The testing board's report also noted that "there is no means of communication between the observers other than word of mouth or preconcerted visual signals" and that the centerline range finder could not be read directly. (The operator had to move a pointer along some resistance wires until the needles of a voltmeter came to zero and then read what the pointer indicated.) Fiske, therefore, invented a direct-reading instrument, and additional refinements made it possible to read ranges on targets that were as much as forty-five degrees away from the perpendicularity of the base line. At the time, Fiske's range finder was the best ever produced for reading short ranges, and the electrical community and some naval officers took notice.[16]

Firing at ranges greater than three thousand yards was considered useless because the errors of sighting were so great that ammunition would be wasted. In fact, in 1890 two thousand yards was considered to be about the limit of accurate range. If, however, extended ranges could be obtained, then more powerful guns with high trajectories could be used. Then, of course, topside ship armor would have to be increased, tactics would change, and increased ship speed would be called for.[17]

During its required year of testing on the *Baltimore*, Fiske's range finder demonstrated its practicability. But the road ahead was not an easy one. On 20 May 1890, another testing board reported that at distances from thirteen to seventeen hundred yards, "the accuracy of fire was excellent." The report concluded, "In our opinion, the Fiske range finder is fairly accurate, with the baseline of the *Baltimore* 276 feet, for all distances under 3,000 yards, provided the bearings are taken between 45° forward and 45° abaft the beam."[18] Capt. Winfield Scott Schley forwarded the report via the chain of command to the Bureau of Ordnance.[19] On 28 May, the chief of the bureau, William N. Folger, blasted the reporting board because of what he called "the slight amount of information which the report conveys." Folger "requested that the commanding officer of the *Baltimore* . . . be directed to repeat the tests. . . . [and provide] a complete set of data upon which the Department may base an opinion as to the value of the device. . . ."[20]

On 21 July, Fiske, newly detailed as inspector of electric lighting at the Cramp shipyard in Philadelphia, suggested to Folger that "for sea gunnery there would not seem to be any necessity in having the range finder accurate beyond 2,000 yards, since there would be no use, and much waste of ammunition, in firing at longer ranges." Fiske continued, "But it would seem very important to note the instant when the enemy reached the distance of 2,000 yards, in order to know when to open fire." Folger snapped back that Fiske's method was "inaccurate." But since "no better method is known," Folger ordered the tests to proceed.[21]

The second report on the *Baltimore*'s range finder, submitted on 23 July, crossed Folger's angry letter to Fiske. The report stated that Fiske's gear "is now in such a condition as to be of no practicable use, owing to the fact that its mechanical construction is entirely inadequate to the demands of the sea, and ship's usage, and it would require considerable repair to put it in working shape." The board held neither the system nor the principle at fault, and suggested such improvements as better wiring.[22] On 13 August, Folger sent Fiske a copy of the report, adding that the improved model would be transferred to the *Yorktown* and that Fiske should forward recommendations on how to install it as a permanent fixture.[23] Fiske replied on 15 August that he had anticipated nearly all of the recommendations made by the board: the bow and stern range finder on the *Baltimore* now had direct-reading instruments; telephones had been provided between the telescope observers; and the whole system was "very strong, simple and durable. . . ."[24] Because the improved model would not fit the *Yorktown*, Folger directed that it remain aboard the *Baltimore* and the older model be moved to the *Yorktown*.[25]

Late in 1890 when the *Baltimore* went to Europe, a U.S. naval officer stationed there wrote the *New York Times* that nothing aboard the ship excited more favorable comment from foreign visitors than Fiske's range finder; it was good, he wrote, to learn of something an American naval officer had invented at a time when most of the American navy was simply a copy of foreign navies.[26] In firing at a floating target, the *Baltimore* had achieved ranges which could not have been reached without her range finder; Fiske wrote in his memoirs *"I am quite sure that this was the first time that a range finder was ever successfully used in naval gunnery."*[27]

The French minister of marine, who learned of Fiske's invention when the *Baltimore* visited Toulon, asked for a copy of the report on it, as did the commander of the U.S. War Department's artillery branch. Other inventors were working on range finders, of course, and Fiske's work by no means monopolized the field. For example, Sicard corresponded during 1891 and early 1892 with Prof. Albert A. Michelson, who offered the navy a "telemeter" for only $350. Tests of it, however, proved it worthless for obtaining ranges on moving objects.[28] Nothing came of Wickes's suggestion to hold a competition between the Fiske and Michelson range finders; and Michelson, unable to perfect his equipment, gave up the struggle until invited to renew it ten years later by a new chief of the Bureau of Ordnance.

Meanwhile a nine-page report dated 10 November 1890 was made on the Fiske range finder aboard the *Chicago*. It read in part: "[The board] . . . finds the apparatus correct in principle and in its general application, but notes many defects . . . which render the individual apparatus in question inconvenient, incomplete, and impracticable for use in action on board a vessel at sea." As had the second *Baltimore* report, the *Chicago* report asserted that the gear was "susceptible to correction." Improvements were suggested to make the wiring permanent, furnish electrical lighting for the telescopes and reading instruments, cover the instruments with light metal turrets, place the galvonometer in the conning tower or in some other protected position, and provide telephone connections between the observers. The report also noted that distances up to 800 yards had been double-checked with a sextant and that the difference between the two calculations varied from zero to 40 yards for distances of between 550 and 880 yards. "In many cases," however, "the observations agreed exactly." After noting the great difficulty in measuring distances at sea precisely, the board concluded, "we are of the opinion that the instruments, poorly made and installed, would be of great value for the purpose of navigation when near land."[29]

The report, forwarded to Rear Adm. John G. Walker, who was commanding the squadron, eventually reached Folger. On 20 December, Folger told Walker that "after an examination of this report, the Bureau has concluded that the defects existing in this, the first range finder of its type, render it unadvisable to permanently install it on the *Chicago*. . . . Should the later pattern of range finder installed in the *San Francisco* prove entirely satisfactory, [however,] one will be supplied to the *Chicago*."[30] Meanwhile, Folger said, experiments with the gear should continue. Hence, there would be another testing board.

"The range finder of Lieutenant Fiske as installed in this ship," began the latest report, "is a most valuable addition to her efficiency." If "two ships [were] engaged, the one provided with the range finder would possess incalculable advantage over the other. With it, combats would end quickly." While acknowledging that the wires, strewn above the deck, should be placed below, the report concluded that the accuracy of data acquired "shows that the electric part of the device is very satisfactory. . . ." The inaccuracies in sighting a target "are due to two principal causes": human errors, introduced by the telescope observers, and "imperfect adjustment of the lines of sight of the telescopes." The report ended by stating, "It is the opinion of the board that the experiments show that the instruments are in good order and the pointing accurate, that they will give reliable results within 3° in ranges less than 5,000 yards, or at greater ranges when adjusted skillfully." The board suggested placing two sets on board, one for each side of the ship.[31]

When Wickes asked Folger for a copy of the report as favorably endorsed by Captain Schley, Folger declined, calling it "a confidential communication."[32] Wickes appealed directly to the secretary of the navy, Benjamin F. Tracy, pointing out that Folger had stated that the price asked for Fiske's range finder was "excessive." The reverse was true, Wickes alleged, for thus far his company had furnished the gear at a loss. It could make a profit only if the navy ordered a large number of sets at one time. He renewed his challenge to have a test made between a Fiske and a Michelson apparatus. Convinced that Wickes was being exorbitant in his demands, Folger declined to purchase additional range finders from him.[33] As Fiske stated in his memoirs, the American Range Finder Company, which was to have given him 20 percent of its profits, never made any profit from his equipment.[34]

While the *Baltimore* underwent gunnery tests prior to leaving for Europe, there had flashed into Fiske's mind "the most important idea I ever had." When the starboard battery began firing, a large fleet of schooners got in the way. With firing suspended, Fiske looked at the schooners through the telescope of the forward range finder and noticed how definitely its crosshairs moved across the sails as the *Baltimore* gently rolled and pitched. It occurred to him "that anybody could fire all the guns in the broadside from that place, and hit the target every time, by setting the telescope at the angle of depression equal to the proper angle of elevation of the guns, leaving the guns parallel to the deck, and firing when the roll of the ship brought the crosshairs on the target." Although he realized the difficulty of mounting a number of guns at exactly the same angle of elevation, he believed that larger ships and better workmanship would one day make his scheme practical. He therefore applied for and obtained a patent, granted 9 September 1890, on "A Method of Pointing Guns at Sea." His method was to fire a gun when the telescope attached to it, and parallel with its bore, had a target in its line of sight.[35]

According to Fiske, this method underlay the whole practice of modern naval gunnery and distinctly described the director system usually credited to Adm. Sir Percy Scott of the Royal Navy.[36] Was Fiske correct? In 1881, Scott had provided an electrical range transmitter that connected the spotting officer and battery, but the Admiralty did not issue it to the fleet until twenty-five years later.[37] Moreover, Fiske's instrument was used to obtain the range of a target, Scott's merely to send a range from one place to another in a ship. Finally, Fiske combined his gun-pointing method with patents he had already secured on "range and position finders." With these, the distance and direction of a distant object could be ascertained and, by means of electrical arrangements on their elevating and training gears, all the guns of a fort could then be concentrated upon the object. Fiske thought it would be possible in the future to put similar electrical gear on the guns of a ship. By combining this system with a range finder that had two armored observing stations, the guns could be directed and fired accurately from the conning tower.[38] Realizing the difficulty, however, of having all guns fire together, Fiske sought to adapt the system to individual guns. The greatest immediate problem to be overcome was how to place a telescope on a gun without having it recoil and strike the gun captain in the eye. Telescopes had already been applied to British artillery pieces and to the curved sight bar of the trunnion of a naval gun. The solution he devised was to place the telescope on the gun shield, which moved with the gun but did not recoil. The pointer, free from recoil, could therefore keep his eye at the sight while firing. By a simple arrangement, the telescope could also be used on turret guns.[39] On 8 March 1891, Fiske applied for a patent for "A Telescopic Sight for Ships' Guns"; it was issued on 5 September 1893. The telescope used was two feet long; its object-glass, two inches in diameter; the field of view, eight degrees; the magnification, fourfold. Shortly thereafter he asked permission to show his sight to Folger, who

30

agreed, listened to Fiske's explanation of it, and asserted that Fiske had "changed naval gunnery from a game of chance into a science."[40] The best way to test it, Folger added, was to send it to the *Yorktown*.

At about the same time Fiske had applied for a patent on his first range finder, he also applied for one on a "range-and-position-finder." The latter, to be used by gunners in a fort, would aid them by indicating the direction being taken by a ship, for they otherwise would shoot "blind" from behind their fortifications. An apparatus of this kind was installed at Fort Hamilton, New York. For shipboard use, Fiske added telephones so that the range finder operators could talk with the range indicator readers. "This was the first installation of a telephone ever made on board any ship," he asserted. A few months later he and the chief engineer of the Bell Telephone Company devised two sets of phones and put them aboard the *Philadelphia* for service trials; thus, the second installation of telephones in any ship.[41]

In October 1890, Fiske obtained six months' leave to visit Europe and demonstrate his range finder to the British, French, and Italian navies on behalf of the American Range Finder Company. He was accompanied by Jo and their seven-year-old daughter, Caroline.

Elliot Brothers, a London firm that manufactured electrical and scientific instruments, arranged to test the range finder using an ordnance board which included the inventor of the well-known Watkin Position-Finder. Not surprisingly, he found fault with the Fiske apparatus. Fiske and his family then went to Paris, where he received an invitation from the French minister of marine to have his range finder tested aboard *Le Formidable*, the flagship of the Mediterranean fleet, at Toulon. The French liked him so well that they permitted him to see things off-limits to European officers, especially those from a potential enemy navy. He went out with the fleet for maneuvers and was also present at a number of conferences on his range finder at which the captain of *Le Formidable* presided.[42] Fiske's stay in Toulon necessitated a six months' extension of his leave.

In March 1891, after the French tests ended, Fiske was cordially received at La Spezia, the principal Italian naval station. For two weeks he saw tests of his range finder conducted by a special board headed by a rear admiral. Because the British Admiralty had agreed to try his range finder, Fiske then returned to London and went on to Portsmouth, where officers gave his range finder severe tests, which it passed well. He then learned about a competitive, "optical," single-position range finder. It was both simpler and cheaper than his even though his was at the moment quicker to operate and more accurate. The publication of the 24 April 1891 issue of the British *Engineer*, which contained an illustrated article entitled

"Fiske's Range Finder and Elevation Indicator," lifted Fiske's spirits. The article fully described the theory and construction of his equipment, quoted from the favorable official French and Italian reports on it, and indicated that tests (in which an error at 2,000 meters was only 2.6 percent, or 52 meters, and at 3,000 meters 3.9 percent, or 117 meters) had shown an accuracy of performance unequalled up to that time.

Upon Fiske's return to Toulon, the French declared his range finder successful but suggested larger range-reading indicators. These he provided. While he awaited the results of new tests, he arranged for a trial of his range finder by gunners in a French army fort, Cap Brun. There he covered the wires serving his equipment with lead and buried them in the ground in order to preclude changes in their resistances caused by day- and night-time temperature variations. The range finder worked very well indeed. Then, at Toulon, his telescopic sight also worked well, but Fiske still found no British, French, or Italian officer who really believed in it. Nevertheless he was determined to produce a complete gunnery system whereby he could measure the ranges with a range finder, telegraph these to the guns with a range indicator, and use the ranges for hitting the target by a gun fitted with an absolutely accurate telescope sight. Meanwhile the French government accepted both the range finder on *Le Formidable* and the one tested at Cap Brun.

Despite his feeling that he had invented instruments of value not only in gunnery but for other arts, Fiske was regrettably forced by circumstances to give up their further development. He knew that an invention not brought to perfection soon became discredited and failed to attract the attention of others. He received a vivid illustration of this when, upon his return to New York, he visited the *Yorktown* at the Brooklyn Navy Yard to learn the results of target practice using the telescopic sight attached to the starboard forward 6-inch gun.[43] Comdr. French E. Chadwick, who was in command when Fiske had installed the sight, had since been relieved by Comdr. Robley D. Evans. "Old Gimpy" offered him a cigar and regaled him with a favorite story but said nothing about the sight. When Fiske finally inquired about it, Evans said he had never heard of it but sent immediately for his ordnance officer, Lt. Charles A. Bradbury, who said the sight was on board somewhere—probably in the ordnance storeroom. Evans told him to find it; fifteen minutes later Bradbury returned with it. Evans then asked Fiske to visit some day and show how it should be attached. Fiske replied he could do it in two minutes. He did so and also explained how it worked, but he felt that neither Evans nor Bradbury thought much of it even though the sight promised to revolutionize naval warfare.[44] Nor did the sight fare much better with the chief of the Bureau of Ordnance:

Folger barely mentioned it in his annual report for 1890 and then damned it with faint praise in his report for 1891.[45]

Upon arriving at Mare Island in January 1892, Captain Schley reported to the secretary of the navy on the performance of the *Baltimore* during the past two and a half years. He spoke very favorably of Fiske's range finder, saying in part:

> I am convinced that it is an indispensable part of the ordnance outfit of all our new ships. . . . The experience of this ship with the instrument shows further that the ships, in contests of the future, supplied with the Fiske Range-finder would possess an enormous advantage over those in which the distance had to be determined in the old way by gun-captains whose judgment would be affected by the excitements and tumult of battle. Indeed, I think I do not overstate its value when I express the opinion that in the naval conflicts hereafter, where ships are equal or nearly so, combats will be decided in all probability in favor of the ships with range-finders, or in case both contestants possess these instruments, actions can last but a few minutes at most, and during this short interval the destruction would be terrific.[46]

Despite Schley's favorable comments, not a word about range finders appeared in Secretary Tracy's report for 1892, for not even Michelson had been able to perfect his telemeter.[47] And even as late as 1897, when Fiske's range finders were surveyed, no range finder was deemed really suitable to the American naval service.

Upon returning from Europe in 1891, Fiske again considered forsaking a rather uninteresting but secure naval career and devoting himself to his inventions. His professional responsibilities had been few: to stand watch, go through various drills (including repelling boarders), and inspect, inspect, inspect. He was thirty-seven years old and still a lieutenant. From 1888 to 1892, the number of officers in the navy had remained quite static. As Fiske figured it, he would be a lieutenant until the age of about fifty, lieutenant commander from the age of fifty to fifty-nine, commander from the age of fifty-nine to sixty-one, and go through the grades of captain and rear admiral and retire at age sixty-two. It was not a very exciting prospect.[48]

Reductions of 115 line officers had been made by an act of Congress in August 1882, when the navy reached its post–Civil War nadir. Since then a revolution had occurred in the number and complexity of ships built, but the situation for personnel, especially those from the ranks of ensign to lieutenant, was, in Secretary Tracy's words, "so serious as to be little less than alarming," with future prospects even worse. Tracy suggested legislative remedies, but Congress did nothing. He renewed his suggestion in 1893. Again Congress did nothing. He tried again in 1894, 1895, and 1896; Congress still did nothing. In 1897, when John D. Long became secretary, he tried too. Still Congress did nothing and the glut of officers continued.[49]

Fiske's great hope was that the navy, in recognition of his accomplishments at home and in Europe, would give him duties so that he could use his knowledge of electricity and also perfect the ordnance and gunnery equipment of the "new navy." But the chief of the Bureau of Navigation was Commodore Francis J. Ramsay—tall, thin, erect, a man of stern countenance who seemed to be a narrow granite statue in uniform. Ramsay strictly enforced the principle that all naval officers were the same except in rank; he refused to consider their individual characteristics as they rotated every three years between sea and shore duty. Indeed, he once told Fiske that in the matter of inventions one officer could solve a mechanical design problem as well as another.[50] Like many, Ramsay's understanding of the line between inventor and design engineer was foggy. In any event, on 6 October 1891, two days after he visited the *Yorktown*, Fiske received orders to report to that ship; he had to make his decision. The American Range Finder Company wanted him to resign but could not promise an adequate guaranty for the future. His friends, however, counseled him to stay on, and the precarious state of his health convinced him to do so. Two days later the *Yorktown* went to sea for a fast run to Valparaiso, Chile.

The diplomatic impasse between the United States and Chile during the latter's civil war necessitated American naval preparation for a possible showdown. The ranking officers of the Chilean navy supported the congressional faction against their president and prevailed. The Harrison administration not only postponed granting the new government recognition pending further developments, but it so closely followed the laws on neutrality that some Chileans felt the U.S. supported the deposed president. This distrust grew when the United States recalled the Chilean ship *Itata* which had left California with arms for the congressionalist army. Congressionalists also suspected, incorrectly, that Patrick Egan, the American minister to Chile, was partisan to the presidential faction when he gave sanctuary in his legation to a number of Chileans the new government was hunting. Tensions mounted. On 16 October 1891, when Captain Schley of the *Baltimore* gave shore liberty to 115 petty officers and men, some of them were attacked with knives, stones, and clubs; the Chilean police and soldiers reportedly took little action to help. Eighteen Americans were stabbed or beaten, and two of them died, while only one Chilean was wounded.[51] But instead of using force against Chile, Secretary of State James G. Blaine asked for an apology and reparations. Meanwhile, Schley handled the local situation diplomatically.

In late November, Commander Evans took his little gunboat into Valparaiso Harbor without knowing whether war had been declared; but he was well aware that the Chilean warships there could easily destroy his ship. Two weeks later the *Baltimore* departed, leaving the *Yorktown* alone in the harbor to face the shore batteries and nine Chilean warships, including two battleships.

The U.S. minister plenipotentiary to Chile had obtained assurances from the Chilean government that American refugees could leave the country whenever they pleased, but the new government had then revoked its permission. Through his minister, Evans asked the Department of State what he should do with the refugees.[52] In keeping with his instructions, Evans acted as the protector of American interests and gave a home on the *Yorktown* to Egan and the various other refugees. On 19 January Evans left Valparaiso for Callao, Peru, which he reached six days later. That same day, 25 January, President Harrison sent Congress what amounted to a war message, but at the last moment Chile promised to make amends for the *Baltimore* affair and the danger of war faded.[53]

Before the *Baltimore* left Valparaiso, Fiske asked her officers how his range finder had behaved; he was glad to learn that at the conclusion of a year's test Schley had forwarded a favorable report on it.[54] During visits ashore in the afternoons, Fiske found the Chilean naval officers extremely polite to him: his range finder was to be installed aboard their new battleship, the *Capitan Prat*, being built in France. On the *Yorktown*, however, Fiske was nicknamed Algernon de Montmorenci, soon contracted to Algy; and the telescopic sight became "Algy's sight." Fiske took the bantering in stride but began to "doubt [his] own sanity" when he learned that every officer on board believed the sight useless. To confirm its value he visited the *Boston*, anchored nearby, and spoke with Lt. Albert Gleaves, who had some experience in ordnance. Gleaves told Fiske he was on the wrong track. Fiske made some drawings, took Gleaves to one of the guns while he offered explanations, and was finally rewarded with the exclamation, "By God! Jim, I believe you're right."[55]

On the way north from Callao, Fiske asked Evans's permission to try the sight. Evans agreed—as he had been ordered by the Bureau of Ordnance to do. When all of the four shots fired fell short of the target, Fiske realized that he had failed to adjust the sight properly and told Evans that it was very difficult to adjust on a ship that rolled as much as the *Yorktown*. Evans then asked the executive officer to look through the sight and give his opinion of it. To Fiske's dismay, the "exec" saluted Evans and reported, "I think it increases the difficulty of sighting, sir"; the officer had been cut over the eye when the gun recoiled.[56] Discouraged if not despondent, Fiske returned to his stateroom; and Commander Evans, in a letter dated 31 March 1892, sent an unfavorable report on the sight to the secretary of the navy.[57]

Instead of the rest he had expected when the *Yorktown* returned to San Francisco, Fiske had to help prepare her for operations in the Bering Sea. The ship was to be the flagship of the American force that cooperated with British ships in policing against pelagic seal hunters. (In the previous decade or so, they had reduced the Pribilof Islands herd by about half.) From May to October 1892, the *Yorktown* and her consorts—the *Mohican*, the *Adams*, and the *Rush*—spent alternate weeks poking into numerous bays and coves between Unalaska and Kodiak Island and at anchor in some harbor. The weather was generally foggy, and the seas were so rough that once everyone in the *Yorktown* got seasick. Few seal hunters were found; most had already been warned and had disappeared. Those ships boarded by the *Yorktown*, with Fiske sometimes commanding the boarding party, occasionally had some rather ingenious reasons for being in the Bering Sea: they were cruising for whales, or were otter hunters, or were fishing for cod; all had "no intention of sealing." Boats found violating the rules were sent to the collector of customs at Sitka, Alaska, who turned their captains over to a U.S. district attorney.

On 22 September, the *Yorktown* held her semiannual target practice near Unalaska. Knowing Evans's unfavorable report on the telescopic sight, Fiske obtained permission from the chief of the Bureau of Ordnance for another trial and an allowance of ten shots. During the morning, eighteen shots were fired, using the regular open sights, with the customary dismal results. As the time for his firing approached early in the afternoon, Evans went ashore and none of the other officers bothered to come on deck. The enlisted men, however, absorbed some of Fiske's enthusiasm. After four shots hit the target, wrecking it, the crew gave him three cheers that brought all the officers on deck. He then fired the fifth shot at the wreck. The last shot was the only one more than ten feet from the target. After Fiske went below to his stateroom, he concluded that he had developed an invention that would change not only the character of naval warfare but perhaps of the world. Several days later, a shot fired successfully at a moving target confirmed his conclusion. When he passed the shooting record along to Folger, chief of the Bureau of Ordnance, Folger asserted that further trials were justified and asked where the equipment could be purchased for testing in a ship in the Washington area.[58]

Fiske's telescopic sight provided an exactness with respect to the location of a target heretofore denied a gunner, particularly at night. Moreover, when used in combination with powerful and rapid gun-elevating mechanisms, it enabled the gun pointer to keep the crosshairs of the telescope constantly on the target. From one station, therefore, a whole battery might be laid in parallel and fired simultaneously by electricity when the roll of the ship brought the telescope sight on the target, thus accomplishing director firing. But director firing involved changes in ship handling, design, and communications. Because the commanding officer was very busy—conning his ship so as to keep her battery bearing constantly on a target, complying with signals if in company with a superior officer, worrying about using his torpedoes or avoiding those fired at him, and other duties—Fiske believed the commanding officer should delegate responsibility for firing to a fire-control officer. The latter, stationed high in the ship so that he could observe the fall of shot and determine the range to the target, would communicate the range to the gun captains who would merely fire on the vertical and lateral settings prescribed. The whole system depended on adequate communications and on construction of a fire-control station atop extant or new, tall, military masts.[59]

After a stormy ten-day trip which ended on 10 October, the *Yorktown* reached Mare Island and, to Fiske's joy, was directed to proceed to New York. In company with the *Baltimore*, the *San Francisco*, and the *Charleston*, she reached New York on 28 February 1893. Of Fiske, Evans wrote on his fitness report, he "seems much interested in electric contrivances at which he is constantly working." After having been aboard the *Yorktown* for sixteen months without ever spending a night on shore or ever taking a bath except out of a tin bucket when weather permitted, and having spent five months in some of the world's worst weather and seas, Fiske was especially happy to rejoin his family.

While the *Yorktown* underwent repairs at the Brooklyn Navy Yard, Fiske visited Washington and spoke at least three times between 8 March and 31 May 1893 with the new chief of the Bureau of Ordnance, William T. Sampson.[60] After reporting on the telescopic sight installed on the *Yorktown*, he was delighted to learn that Sampson was so interested in fitting other guns with the sights that he had put an officer in charge of the matter. Fiske also learned with joy that Charles Cramp and Sons, who were building the battleships *Indiana* and *Massachusetts*, wished to substitute electric for steam-driven training gear for their 8-inch turrets.[61] But he was crestfallen when Sampson objected on the grounds that electrical training gear had never been tested, thereby overlooking the electric turret-turning gear Fiske had placed on board the *Chicago* in 1888. Sampson, who took a great liking to Fiske (as well as having a great interest in his work), overcame the objections of Commodore Ramsay and on 10 July 1893 had Fiske ordered to the large cruiser *San Francisco*. At about the same time, the Franklin Institute of Pennsylvania awarded Fiske the Elliott Cresson medal for 1893 for his invention of the electrical range finder.[62]

In 1890, when the Bureau of Ordnance refused to buy additional range finders from the American Range Finder Company, Fiske asked Western Electric Manufacturing Company to produce his equipment. Enos M. Barton, the president and co-founder of the company, and his general manager, Harry B. Thayer, fully backed Fiske's work on the range finder, telescopes, engine-order telegraph, stadimeter, helm-angle indicator, speed and direction indicator, and, as will be seen, a torpedo-control device which the company modified and which was used as the basis of all early American work on guided missiles. For many years the company provided Fiske with a special private laboratory in New York City.[63]

In many ships, gunnery training occurred only during gunnery practice, perhaps four times a year, instead of being part of daily drill. Gun-sighting mechanisms were crude and inaccurate; up to five minutes were consumed in loading a single large gun on board a battleship; yet Fiske's equipment was resented by those who liked the old ways. Many commanding officers preferred to keep their decks spotless and the snowy paintwork unsoiled. Some resented the interference of target practice with their social activities ashore; others threw their ammunition overboard and lied about their scores.[64]

To Fiske's great pleasure, on 3 August 1893 a representative of the Western Electric Company assisted the "gunner's gang" in installing an electric range finder, an electric range transmitter, three range indicators, and a telescopic sight on the *San Francisco*, commanded by Capt. John C. Watson. Similar gear, Fiske learned, would be placed on the cruisers *Cincinnati* and *Minneapolis* and on the battleships *Maine, Texas, Indiana*, and *Massachusetts*.[65] On 17 August, with members of the naval militia from New York and Pennsylvania aboard for a week's cruise, Fiske saw his gear in use. The log for that day reads in part:

> Noon to 4 P.M. All the firing was done at ranges between 1900 and 1700 yards. . . . Ship going about 6 knots passing to and fro in target practice and at various speeds, stopping at times and backing. [The *San Francisco*] used the Fiske Range Finder and Transmitter and Indicators during target practice. . . . Eugene Beaumont of the Pennsylvania militia shot away the target at 1700 yards.[66]

Most of Fiske's fitness reports to date had been good, with his commanding officers noting that he worked hard to devise instruments for improving gunnery. Evans gave him "good to excellent" marks on his personal characteristics. On his "professional ability," however, Evans merely wrote "tolerable." Perhaps Fiske was thinking about his inventions instead of being alert while on watch on the *San Francisco*; the log for 27 August 1893 notes that "Lieut. B. A. Fiske, U.S.N., was placed under suspension for neglect of duty"—an incident he does not mention in his memoirs. Fiske remonstrated with Captain Watson, to no avail, and in the August report to the secretary of the navy of all officers under suspension, arrest, or confinement Watson reported Fiske's "neglect of duty," indicated that the punishment had been "suspension for one day," and added, "This officer feels this keenly as excessively severe." In the fitness report covering the period 13 July to 31 December 1893, Watson wrote: "Lt. Fiske is a conscientious officer of high character and of an active inventive mind but does not seem able to keep it on the details of daily duty as officer of the deck." Although offered the opportunity to rebut the poor reports on him by Commander Evans and Captain Watson, Fiske declined to do so. "Remarks" by Watson on the period 1 January–30 June 1894 read, "[Fiske] has improved in efficiency as a watch officer since last report"; and Watson's relief wrote for the period 3 June to 16 October 1894 "[Fiske] has given satisfaction in every respect."

From New York the *San Francisco* took a southerly course, with the navigator occasionally checking the range to such objects as lighthouses by Fiske's range finder. Near Port au Spain, scheduled target practice was held on 4 December 1893. Fiske urged Captain Watson to give his range finder a realistic test by not using the regulation anchored target. It was raining and the sea was very rough, but Fiske asserted that he wanted to fire under circumstances simulating battle. Watson agreed, and Fiske felt that the result was the most realistic target practice ever yet held in the navy.[67] In his memoirs, published in 1919, Fiske also argued that it was the greatest single step forward in naval gunnery up to that time. On 19 December 1893, moreover, Watson gave the secretary of the navy a glowing account of the performance of the range finder—both for gunnery and navigation—adding that the observing stations should be placed high in the ship rather than on deck in order to put them above such hindrances to sighting as powder and funnel smoke, boats, and various ship structures. As for accuracy, the average error per thousand yards was .55 percent. On 9 July 1894, a trial board reported that the telescopic sight was far superior to other sights but recommended an improvement (which Fiske promised to make) in the manner in which the telescope was mounted. When the

San Francisco went into the Brooklyn Navy Yard late in July, Watson sent in a favorable report of the year's trial of Fiske's apparatus.[68]

At Rio de Janeiro, the *San Francisco* had stood by with the *Charleston*, the *Detroit*, and the *Newark* to protect American lives and property during an insurrection against the government. Each day throughout January, February, and March 1894 as Fiske performed his duties, he could hear and see the firing around the harbor; at least vicariously he lived through a war. Finally, after Adm. Andrew E. K. Benham, a consummate diplomatist, had intervened in order to reopen trade, the Brazilian insurgents were defeated.[69]

Fiske was standing watch on 18 March when the *San Francisco* finally left Rio, to call at various Caribbean and Central American ports. Off Pearl Cay Lagoon, Nicaragua, on 5 May, the *San Francisco* engaged in gunnery practice. Using guns fitted with his telescopic sight, Fiske fired at targets set out at various ranges for most of three days. Practice ended on 9 May with a shot that carried the last target away.[70] Nothing Fiske did, however, ameliorated the situation in which a captain's promotion depended more upon the "housemaiding" of his ship than upon the efficiency of his crew.

When he was detached from the *San Francisco*, Fiske was given three months' leave and placed on waiting orders. From New York he went to Washington to talk with Sampson not only about his gunnery inventions but about certain other instruments he had invented that would augment the fighting capability of the navy and which he needed time to develop. Among these was the stadimeter, which he had invented while aboard the *Yorktown*; it was being manufactured by Western Electric. This handheld instrument contained two mirrors which, by means of a micrometer screw, could bring two images together and automatically read the distance to an object, if its height was known, or the height of an object, if the distance to it was known. As the manager of the Western Electric Company wrote Sampson,

> This instrument seems to us to have a field of usefulness in squadron sailing, in which we know its distance from the others in the squadron, but we have brought it out mainly as an adjunct to Lieutenant Fiske's range finder, to be used in case the range finder becomes deranged in action or in case the enemy takes up a position too far forward to admit of using [sic] the range finder. . . .[71]

On 3 January 1895, Sampson directed Western Electric to send one stadimeter to the *New York*, another to the bureau, and still another to the *Cincinnati*.⁷² By the middle of May, reports from the *New York* and the *Cincinnati* agreed that, as Henry Glass, commander of the *Cincinnati*, put it, the stadimeter "has proved of the greatest value. It is accurate in determining distances within its range. It is valuable in determining distances in squadron formations. It is almost indispensable in keeping proper distances in 'changing formation' in squadron movements. It has been found of great use in fixing the ship's position in port." Because of its weight (three-and-a-quarter pounds), Glass had found its constant use "somewhat tiresome" and, therefore, recommended that all its metal parts be made of aluminum.⁷³ On 18 May the commanding officer of the *New York* told Sampson that his navigator had reported that a stadimeter "should be furnished to every ship in the service."⁷⁴ Sampson took the advice to heart.

During one of his visits to Sampson while he was still on leave, Fiske ran into Commodore Ramsay, who disapproved of doing anything not in accordance with precedent. After a friend told Fiske that Ramsay had directed that he be put on duty immediately, anywhere, Fiske called on Sampson and told him of the impending danger. Sampson leaned back in his chair, gazed at Fiske for a long time, and then asked, "Would you like to take up the application of electricity to turning turrets?" Fiske replied that he already had been granted a patent on the idea. Moreover, Fiske told Sampson, he believed that hydraulic power was better than electricity and doubted that, in the light of his having a patent, it would be proper for him to take up the work. Sampson said that he did not care whether Fiske had a patent or not. Although he had declined to have electrical training gear placed on several ships under construction, Sampson wanted to know if electricity would be better than any other means for turning turrets. Seeing an opportunity for doing valuable work, Fiske agreed. Could he live in New York, closer to the centers of electrical experimentation, instead of in Washington? Sampson replied that he could live anywhere as long as he did the required work.⁷⁵

Between 1888 and 1895, Bureau of Ordnance records show that patents were granted for breech-loading ordnance, pneumatic guns, shells, revolving firearms, projectiles, percussion fuses, quick-firing guns, gun carriages, and appliances for sighting guns and rifles. Various civilians, including Michelson, worked to adapt range finders to naval use, but as far as I have been able to ascertain, Fiske was the only American naval officer to use electricity to create not simply elements useful in gunnery but a system of fire control.

Fiske had been very productive during the years from 1888 to 1895. In addition to his work with the *Vesuvius*, experiences during the civil wars in Chile and Brazil, and hunting sealers in the Bering Sea, he had to his credit the electrical ammunition hoist, range finder, range transmitter, range indicator, position indicator, turret-turning gear, the telescopic sight, the stadimeter, and the first installation of telephones on a warship. It was true that in both the British and American navies conservatives preferred not to spoil their ships' paintwork by firing their guns and that some target ammunition was dropped over the side. It was also true that, given the state of the art of electrical engineering, some components of Fiske's systems were poorly made and badly installed. Whereas the French, Italian, and Chilean navies adopted his range finder, the American bureau of ordnance chiefs—Sicard, Folger, and Sampson—had been very careful rather than just conservative. They had severely tested and retested Fiske's inventions, with the result that, as with the range finder and stadimeter, defects had been noted and passed on to Fiske for correction. But most helpful to Fiske in continuing his improvements would be the happy connection he had made with the Western Electric Company, which soon helped him provide "the nerves of a warship."

5

THE NERVES OF A WARSHIP, 1895–1896

Turrets could be turned by steam power, electricity, compressed air, or hydraulic power; each method had advantages and disadvantages. In 1894, following tests of an electrical turret-turning system in a monitor, battleship, and new cruiser, the chief of the Bureau of Ordnance, William T. Sampson, concluded that "all things considered, the Bureau is of the opinion that with good control electricity is preferable to any other method of turning turrets. . . ."[1] Bradley A. Fiske would soon be called upon to implement this decision.

After discussing the turret-turning problem with various electrical companies, Fiske decided that General Electric had the most promising solution. After G.E. had built the equipment, Sampson met Fiske in New York and traveled with him to Schenectady. Upon seeing the equipment in operation, Sampson was delighted, for he had won a battle against the Bureau of Construction and Repair, which lately had been given responsibility for turrets.[2]

On 13 November 1895, Fiske wrote Sampson outlining his reasons why the electrical turret-turning system was superior to any other and suggesting that it be used for the turrets of the cruiser *Brooklyn* then being built.[3] Sampson replied that naval constructor John H. Lennard, billeted at the Cramp Shipbuilding Company, was proceeding to Schenectady to report on the apparatus and that Fiske should explain the gear to him. Fiske did so and on 11 December Lennard wrote his report. Lennard agreed that Fiske's system moved a turret with the desired speed and degree of control. But, he reported, it did not permit pointing with the required accuracy; Fiske's system was about as reliable and accurate as a steam system. Simplicity, space, and particularly weight favored steam; in addition, a steam system would cost $6,200, Fiske's, $27,900. Finally, the adoption of the electrical system, Lennard concluded, would delay completion of the vessel.[4]

On 19 December, Philip Hichborn, the chief constructor, wrote to the secretary of the navy (via the bureaus of Ordnance and of Steam Engineering) that he did not favor the electrical system and recommended that steam be used in the *Brooklyn*.[5] Two days later, Sampson sent Fiske a copy of Lennard's report for comment; Fiske did so on Christmas Eve. He believed the electrical system to be the best and was despondent because the secretary of the navy, who would make the final decision although he lacked knowledge of the technical requirements of warships, might decide adversely and thus deny the navy a valuable device. In the end Fiske suggested that two of the *Brooklyn*'s turrets be turned by steam and two by electricity, thereby enabling both systems to be tested at the same time under similar conditions.[6] Pleased with the compromise, Sampson forwarded Fiske's idea to Secretary Hilary A. Herbert and supported Fiske against the bureaus of Construction and of Steam Engineering. Sampson agreed that Lennard had made a very able report; he had received several reports, however, from Lieutenant Fiske, "an acknowledged authority in such matters," and he recommended using both steam and electricity in the *Brooklyn*.[7] Despite objections from the Bureau of Steam Engineering, the acting secretary of the navy, William McAdoo, approved Sampson's recommendation on 25 January 1896.[8] When the *Brooklyn* was completed, a trial board conducted tests and on 3 March 1896 concluded that the electrical system was better than steam, thus sustaining Fiske.[9] In a fitness report for the period January 1–December 8, 1896, Sampson rated Fiske "good to excellent" in every category, adding under "Remarks" that "Lt. Fiske is an electrical expert of wide reputation."

Fiske's work had convinced Secretary Herbert of the value of electricity for auxiliary purposes. As a result, his successor, John D. Long, who became secretary of the navy in March 1897, directed that central electrical power plants be installed on the two battleships then under construction, the *Kearsarge* and the *Kentucky,* and in the even newer battleships *Illinois* and *Alabama*.[10]

Secretary Long also directed that telescopic sights be provided for all 4-, 5-, and 6-inch guns installed thereafter on ships. When the president of the American Range Finder Company, Edward Wickes, learned that the Bureau of Ordnance was manufacturing and issuing the sights, he wrote Sampson reminding him that the company had borne the expense of Fiske's developmental work and that Sampson was infringing on four patents Fiske held on the sight. On 26 May 1897, Wickes's patent attorney, Park Benjamin, formally notified Sampson of the infringement. In the spring of 1899, Sampson sued George Saegmuller, who manufactured the sights for the bureau, in the Supreme Court of the District of Columbia. Saegmuller said he had not "intentionally" infringed on Fiske's patents. Benjamin said he would drop the suit if the government paid Wickes $10,000 in damages plus a royalty of $25 for each sight the bureau manufactured. The new chief of the bureau, Charles O'Neil, sought the advice of Secretary Long, who in turn sought advice from the attorney general, John Griggs. When O'Neil suggested paying $25 for each sight manufactured, thus avoiding heavy court costs, Long demanded to know why the navy should pay anything. On the attorney general's advice, however, Long directed the navy to settle the matter, which it did to the satisfaction of the American Range Finder Company.[11]

During the two years Fiske worked for Sampson he developed certain philosophical ideas as well as the practical equipment that provided the "nerves" of a warship. From a conversation with Henry Morgenthau, later to be the U.S. minister to Turkey, Fiske treasured the remark, "One good idea is worth a year of hard work."[12] Somewhat later, he told Harry B. Thayer, manager of the Western Electric Company's New York branch, that Thayer never seemed to have anything to do. Thayer replied that other men did the required work. Fiske asked if Thayer's methods might be useful to him as a professional naval officer. Thayer replied that by avoiding the details of the work of others he could concentrate on his own job. He had divided his establishment into departments and expected their heads to come to him only when they got into trouble. He was thus free to plan how to do his work. Putting the earlier remarks of Harry Taylor together with those of Morgenthau and of Thayer, Fiske concluded, "Now the first thing to do is to look ahead; the second is to try to get good ideas; and the third thing is to arrange your work in such a way that when you have to do anything, you will not have to do it in a hurry."

At that time he thought it must be about as difficult to become a good lawyer, doctor, legislator, or administrator as a good naval officer. He believed, however, that the mental, moral, and physical requirements for a naval career were greater than those demanded by civil life.[13] He acknowledged that abuses could exist in autocracies as well as in democracies and that the fault was not with "the form of government, but with the politicians or other incompetents who misdirected it."[14] Yet he continued in an outspoken way to judge civilian leadership in the navy by impossibly high standards.

During the two years Fiske worked on turret turning he also constructed a number of new appliances he had invented while aboard the *Yorktown* and the *San Francisco*. In addition to the stadimeter, which has already been mentioned, these were the engine-order telegraph (or annunciator), the helm-angle indicator, the speed and direction indicator, and the steering telegraph.

With the same principle of resistance wires and voltmeter (or galvanometer) he had used in the range finder, Fiske made a helm-angle indicator. Whenever the helmsman turned his wheel, a contact moved over a resistance wire near the rudder and, by means of voltmeters placed in the pilot house or elsewhere, indicated the position of the rudder. The more complicated engine-order telegraph, which was built by Western Electric, permitted men in the pilot house to order the engines ahead or astern by stated amounts (one-third or full speed, for example) and to receive a reply from the engine room that the order had been carried out.

Each of Fiske's instruments was tested by trial boards and then given service trials lasting from six months to a year before being accepted.[15] By 1896, the *New York*, the *Indiana*, and the *Massachusetts* had engine-order telegraphs, helm indicators, and steering telegraphs installed; in addition the *New York* had a speed and direction indicator on board.[16]

Most of these inventions were radically new. The engine-order telegraph and helm-angle indicator represented the first successful attempts to overcome the handicaps to interior communication posed by the complicated structures of new steel warships. In an article in *Harper's* magazine for March 1896 entitled "The Nerves of a War-ship," Park Benjamin aptly compared Fiske's internal communications system with the nerves of the human body, carrying information to the brain and orders to the muscles. Fiske's range finder enabled a commander to determine the distance to a target. If the range finder were shot away, Fiske's stadimeter could be used. While gunners sighted through Fiske's telescopic sights and fired their guns with Fiske's electrical primers, the engines and helm were controlled by his engine-order telegraph and helm-angle indicator; speed was indicated by an improved version of his speed-indicator log. Fifty thousand ingenious Americans asked for patents every year, none of them for equipment useful to the navy; what had been done, Benjamin wrote, to improve the fighting qualities of warships had been done by Fiske. Conditions between two ships being otherwise equal, the ship containing Fiske's inventions would be controlled efficiently and should win the battle.[17]

Despite a worsening of his heart condition, Fiske continued his work, inventing things and writing articles. In October 1895, he noticed a disturbing intermittency in his heart beat and believed that it portended death. An experienced navy doctor failed to diagnose his problem and suggested he visit a nerve specialist. (Fiske later learned that the doctor had given him two years to live.) The nerve doctor prescribed a sedative, which helped somewhat, and greatly eased Fiske's mind by saying that his trouble was functional rather than organic. The following winter, when threatened with a cold, Fiske took ten grains of quinine before going to bed. When he awoke the following morning, his heartbeat was regular. Whenever his heart began to skip a beat thereafter, quinine would steady it. The trouble persisted, however, until he approached sixty years of age; after that he rarely noticed it.[18]

During 1896 Fiske decided to improve the flag hoist because flags often hung limply or were blown by the wind so that they could not be seen. He tried shapes of many kinds and colors before concluding that the semaphore, or revolving arms, could be seen farther than anything else of the same size. The arms could be made to move quickly with little electrical power and precluded the exposure of men aloft. On a mast he placed four arms, one under the other about ten feet apart. Each arm, about six feet long and a foot wide, worked simultaneously with a similar arm that moved at right angles to it. It was so wired that the touch of a letter upon a keyboard would move two or four arms to a predetermined position for a code letter. The Western Electric Company built the device just as Fiske left New York for the regular summer course at the Naval War College.

Fiske also tried to develop a sounding machine. By timing the drop of a weight of a certain shape attached to a wire until it hit bottom he would ascertain the depth of the water. Western Electric also built this device, which included a lead ball weighing twenty-five pounds. While at the War College he tried to experiment with it but could not find nearby water that was both deep enough and accurately measured.[19]

In June 1896 Fiske reported to Capt. Henry C. Taylor, president of the Naval War College. The college provided for the systematic study of war and its place in national policy instead of enhancing professional technical skills.[20] The course was made as easy and as pleasant as possible, with attendance at many lectures optional. There was a good library; the lectures were excellent; and the war games were interesting; yet most students refused to take the course seriously.

Fiske heard lectures ranging from the effect a Nicaraguan canal would have upon American naval strategy to war gaming and also a series on naval tactics given by Taylor. Among others, he read the works of Jomini, Soday, Mahan, Sir Philip Colomb, Bainbridge-Hoff, and Foxhall A. Parker. In addition to studying international law, the class tackled a naval problem assigned by the college staff or the Navy Department, with groups of six officers assigned parts of the problem. In 1896 they prepared tactical plans for the defense of various harbors but concentrated on Narragansett Bay, about which they traveled to get personal observations. War games were played too—one between two men each with a ship, one with teams of opposing fleets, and one dealing with an entire theater of war in which two nations were involved. And, for the second time in its history, the college attempted the solution of war problems: students were expected to write up the various aspects of a problem (say, a war in the Gulf of Mexico), draft war charts and defense plans, and write the necessary operation orders. Both staff and students were thus performing some of the functions of a general staff, which the navy lacked; during the winter the college staff completed the students' work.[21]

Of his studies Fiske found international law the most interesting—even if it was merely a collection of precedents and agreements, rather than of principles, and lacked the force to compel compliance. Hence, any nation that had sufficient power could act as it wished. Fiske also objected to an attitude held by many of the college staff, including Captain Taylor.

Taylor taught his officers that the materials of warfare were merely tools used by strategists. Furthermore, the study of history could prove useful—at least in avoiding the repetition of mistakes if not in providing satisfactory solutions to current problems. Fiske, however, believed that strategy was independent of mechanisms and argued that new materials affected strategy. Taylor courteously but forcefully told him he was wrong, that strategy concerned only unchanging principles. At any rate, Fiske's outlook was broadened by his studies, particularly by reading Jomini and Mahan. He was also provided with an excellent background for the high offices he would later hold. And in time Fiske praised men like Luce and Taylor for teaching their students to think about the navy as a whole and for leaving them alone to do their studying on the principle that one took away from the college whatever he learned while there.

Fiske joined the U.S. Naval Institute in 1886. The September 1896 issue of its *Proceedings* carried the first comment from Fiske and his article entitled "Electricity in Naval Life." The comment concerned a controversy started by Lt. William F. Fullam, who in an earlier issue had demanded that marines should be withdrawn from naval ships. Fiske agreed completely, saying that the naval line officer was amply able to handle the "military part" of the navy afloat or ashore.[22]

Fiske's lavishly illustrated article on electricity covered the subject extensively and attracted much attention both at home and abroad. By way of introduction, Fiske argued that electricity made ships brighter, cleaner and healthier; it lightened the task of enforcing discipline; it increased the accuracy of gunnery; it assisted the surgeon in diagnosing wounds and relieving pain; it gave the captain better control of his ship, and the admiral better control of his fleet. Electricity, Fiske wrote, added an element of intelligent interest and expectation to each new addition to the navy. Furthermore, it brought into active sympathy with the sea-going class a large and influential body of progressive men on shore.[23]

Use of electricity in the navy depended upon the provision of specially designed electrical apparatus and its care by knowledgeable men. Because the navy provided little incentive to study electricity, Fiske argued, those proficient in it went into colleges, laboratories, or electrical manufacturing companies, with a consequent loss of their skills to the navy. What better laboratory could be found than a ship? Among shipboard uses for electricity, Fiske discussed lighting, motors, telephones, helm-angle indicators, steering telegraphs, engine-order telegraphs, speed and direction indicators, range indicating systems, range finders, electric telescopic sights, and position finders. After discussing the care of electrical instruments (especially against their natural enemies—air and moisture), he predicted that electrical appliances would gain rapidly on hydraulic and pneumatic appliances and on auxiliary steam apparatus. Electricity had come out of the realm of illusion, Fiske wrote, and the electrician should be recognized as a professional scientist. In his memoirs Fiske wrote that the following paragraph from his article must have displeased elderly and highly placed officers like Commodore Francis Ramsay:

> Let us hope that we soon shall be a civilized modern ship, in which there shall be a fine large dynamo room like those under the great New York hotels, where power will be generated for lighting the ship, making the signals, hoisting the ammunition, turning the turrets, operating the telephones, hoisting the boats, ringing the bells, weighing the anchors, sounding the alarms, running the launches, firing the guns, steering the ship, etc. And why should we not have a neat electric galley, such as are frequent in New York, where the meals of all can be prepared in cleanliness and quiet, with only a fraction of the fuss and confusion now attending the getting of the food and the heating of the water? And why should not both officers and men, when they go on night-watch frequently in the wet and rain, be given a light repast, cooked on an electric stove, the size of a quart pot. Would the lookouts, or the quartermasters, or the officers, do their duty any less vigilantly if each had half a pint of hot coffee and a piece of nicely browned toast in his stomach?[24]

Most important, Fiske saw that electricity could be used to provide a ship captain with instant information on everything that was happening and enable him to give instructions quickly on what should be done. Instead of being helplessly directed by events, he would direct affairs. As for signaling at distances, Fiske argued, things were hardly better than in Nelson's day. It was possible to telegraph under the oceans and across the country but not to signal half a mile between ships. He concluded with two predictions: first, that wireless telegraphy would come to pass; and second, that a "central station" below the waterline would be provided for each ship.[25] He predicted correctly. By 1900, radio telegraphy was well along. Not only were the *Kentucky* and the *Kearsarge* being furnished more electrical power than any other vessels, ships of the *Alabama* class and three battleships and four monitors being contracted for would be provided similarly powerful systems. It must have pleased Fiske very much to have Secretary Long state, "The ease of manipulation, perfection of control, absence of heat, and facility of running cables as compared with steam, pneumatic, or hydraulic pipes, make electricity an ideal power on shipboard, and the trend of opinion is in favor of further extending its use."[26]

During the years from 1897 to 1900 when Fiske served in the Far East, few were interested enough to keep his equipment on naval ships in working order or to invent anything new in gunnery or in interior communications. Therefore, except for the telescopic sight and stadimeter, which found favor and extended use, his equipment was improved upon by others and gradually replaced: for example, his position finder, adapted to forts, was discarded once the telephone was made reliable. Nevertheless, at the age of forty-two, Fiske had enough inventions in his name to secure himself a favorable niche in the history of naval inventors.

6

THE SPANISH-AMERICAN WAR AND THE FILIPINO INSURRECTION, 1898–1900

The chief of the Bureau of Ordnance, William T. Sampson, wanted Fiske sent to the *Brooklyn* to test the electric turret-turning machinery and several other inventions he had had installed. Instead, on 10 December 1896 Fiske was ordered to report to the little gunboat *Petrel* being fitted out at Mare Island for duty with the Asiatic Squadron. She was 181 feet long, had a 31-foot beam, and displaced a mere 892 tons. She had a square sail on her foremast and fore and aft sails on her main and mizzen masts; for want of steam, the steering gear was operated by hand. Her armament consisted of four 6-inch breechloading rifles in open mounts and numerous guns in her secondary battery. With her new coat of white paint she looked like a millionaire's yacht; nonetheless she was not only overgunned but such a wet ship that she deserved the nickname "Stormy Pete." One may well wonder why Fiske, the navy's most prominent electrical engineer, with twenty-two years of service, should have been sent to such a minor ship.

The *Petrel*, with a crew of 130 officers and men including 10 marines, was commanded by Lt. Comdr. Edward P. Wood, who would be promoted to commander in June 1897. Her executive officer was Edward M. Hughes. There were two other lieutenants in addition to Fiske and Hughes, Charles P. Plunkett and Arthur M. Wood; two ensigns, George L. Fermier and William S. Montgomery; and three staff corps members. Fiske was the navigator. On 31 March 1897, with forty-six tons of coal on her deck, the *Petrel* began making passage to Hawaii; her crew was looking forward to the customary three-year cruise in the Far East. Fiske intended to make it a pleasure cruise, for he had arranged for his wife and daughter to meet him in the various ports of Japan, China, and Korea at which the *Petrel* would call. Jo, an accomplished pianist, and young Caroline, who played the violin, would occasionally perform before the musical circles of these cities.[1]

Captain Wood ran a taut ship and conscientiously carried out required drills. Fiske, nevertheless, had some time to spend with his family, take an occasional swim, and read American periodicals; he also found time to devise a method to control torpedoes by wireless telegraphy.

In an article Fiske read entitled "A Twentieth Century Outlook," the naval historian Alfred T. Mahan characterized the nineteenth century as one of peace. Towards the end of the century, however, national armaments had been rebuilt in Europe and a resurgence of imperialism had occurred. At a time of European encroachment upon the Orient Mahan argued that the United States should sluff off its isolationism and join the West in resisting "the sweep of the yellow race."[2] On 19 October 1897 Fiske wrote Mahan from Shanghai, suggesting that he develop the ideas expressed in his article into a book. Fiske's letter may not have been the deciding factor, but in 1900 Mahan published the book Fiske suggested.[3]

As noted above, while on the *Petrel* Fiske experimented with radio waves. He knew about Hertzian waves and about an appliance called "Bramly's Coherer" and deduced that it was possible to send out Hertzian waves of different frequencies and collect them with various apparatus set up at a distance. As he thought it would, the Western Electric Company declined to produce his invention, with its president, Enos Barton, saying that it was ahead of its time. Several months later Barton called his New York manager, Harry Thayer, from Chicago and told him "to take out a patent for Lieutenant Fiske and to do anything else that Lieutenant Fiske wanted him to do." Fiske prepared the necessary papers and patent applications, only to learn in February 1900 that a patent had been granted to another inventor, Nikola Tesla. The Patent Office had erred in granting the patent to Tesla while one on the same subject was pending, and Western Electric's lawyers were able to obtain for Fiske a patent that took precedence over Tesla's even though it bore a later date. Fiske's patent covered wireless control of distant objects, such as torpedoes, but he never found the opportunity to develop a practical application for it; and John Hays Hammond, Jr., who later used the patent in torpedo-control devices, never mentioned Fiske's work.[4]

While at Inchon, Korea, Fiske was amazed one morning to see three German warships larger than the *Petrel* at anchor. The *Petrel* had come up the channel during daylight because of the extremely high tides and treacherous currents, but the Germans had entered at night. Until then Fiske had rarely thought about the German navy. *"Since that morning in Chemulpo, when those three ships met my astonished gaze, I have kept my eye on the German Navy,"* he recorded. (The emphasis is his.) Moreover, when two German naval lieutenants dined aboard the *Petrel* in Hong Kong, Fiske realized that they knew more about the scientific side of the naval profession than any American naval officer he knew. Furthermore, the Germans excited him by telling him that their navy tried to utilize whatever special gifts a man had as long as they related to naval service—a practice not followed by the United States.[5]

Fiske learned of the sinking of the *Maine*—on 15 February 1898 in Havana Harbor—while the *Petrel* was in Hong Kong. The pleasure cruise was over. On 24 April, Secretary of the Navy John D. Long cabled Commodore George Dewey, commanding the Asiatic Squadron: "War has commenced between the United States and Spain. Proceed at once to Philippine Islands. Commence operations at once particularly against the Spanish fleet. You must capture vessels or destroy. Use utmost endeavors."[6] Dewey accordingly came down from northern China with the *Olympia* to join his cruisers—the *Baltimore*, the *Boston*, the *Concord*, and the *Raleigh*— and the gunboat *Petrel* in Hong Kong; there the revenue cutter *McCullough* joined up. Dewey then directed that his ships be repainted in war colors.

Because the American consul in Manila, Oscar F. Williams, did not reach the *Olympia* until the morning of 27 April, the squadron did not leave until after noon. As the ships headed for the Philippines, a three-day journey, their crews threw overboard all ship woodwork in order to reduce hazards from fire and injuries from flying splinters. The chaplain of the *Baltimore* was aghast when he saw his pulpit go over too.[7] The *Petrel*'s log for 26 through 29 April notes that Dewey ordered his ships be darkened and that although gunners slept by their batteries at night they practiced at them much of the day.

On the afternoon of 30 April, Dewey sent the cruisers *Boston* and *Concord* ahead to look for Spanish ships in Subic Bay, on the west coast of Luzon. When they found none, he had held a captains' conference and then led his squadron toward Manila Bay, sixty miles away. Steaming at eight knots through the south side of the channel, all lights were masked and only the stern lights showed. The dark silence in his ships remained unbroken until about midnight when the *McCullough* shot a flame from her smokestack. A rocket fired from Corregidor Island acknowledged that the flame had been seen, and a Spanish shot passed between the *Raleigh* and the *Petrel*. With Manila no doubt alerted, action was imminent. The first American firing, by the *Boston* and the *Concord*, silenced batteries on a little island called El Fraile, off which the *Petrel* lay at about midnight. As the squadron entered Manila Bay at about 3:00 A.M., men on the *Petrel* could see the lights of Manila. Wishing to approach Manila and the

Spanish fleet he thought would be there in daylight, Dewey slowed to four knots.

Fiske was on the bridge of the *Petrel* with her captain during the night. Soon after the firing at El Fraile, Wood, who refused to leave the bridge, told him to go below and get some sleep. Fiske walked by men resting, sleeping, or pretending to sleep near their guns. When he got into his bunk, he wondered whether a torpedo exploding under him might not squash him against the deck two feet above him. A few hours later, Wood called him to the bridge. "The Spanish ships are over there," he said, pointing to starboard, and Fiske realized that he was about to go into battle for the first time.[8]

Before leaving Hong Kong Fiske had obtained Wood's permission to rig a platform about forty-five feet up the foremast; it would serve as an observation station for the *Petrel*, which lacked a conning tower. From this perch above the funnel and gun smoke, Fiske would inform Wood of the distance to the enemy as calculated with his stadimeter. But the evening before, Wood had dampened Fiske's hope, and some men had suggested that when shells came close he would come down from aloft as though chased by the devil.[9] Now, however, he and a man named John Howard made for the platform.

In the early light of 1 May, Fiske could see to the south the ships of the Spanish fleet, toward which the *Olympia* now turned, her consorts in column astern. Batteries at Manila and Cavite and the guns of the fleet opened fire at 5:15 A.M. As Fiske lifted his stadimeter to his eye, a shell hit the water close by, sending up a geyser that drenched him and Howard. Howard merely wiped the water from his face and said "That was pretty close, sir."[10] At 5:40, Fiske saw the *Olympia* open up, then saw the ships astern of her as they came into range. From the earthquake below him he knew that the *Petrel* had engaged also. Dewey had his ships follow an elliptical pattern three times at eight knots and fire at ranges between five thousand and two thousand yards. Because the only electrical range finder in the squadron, on board the *Baltimore*, failed after the first round was fired and because the topmasts of the Spanish ships were housed, it was very difficult to obtain masthead heights with either a sextant or stadimeter. Firing ranges therefore were set at the distance to the beach, with corrections made by spotting. The American ships ceased firing only when smoke obscured the sightings. Fiske saw shells smash into the *Christina* and *Castilla*, and because projectiles were falling all about the American ships, he wondered how many Americans had been killed or wounded.

Spanish gunners concentrated on the larger American ships and paid little attention to the *Petrel*. The gunnery was terrible on both sides but worse on the Spaniards', with Fiske ascribing the poor showing of the Americans to the uncertainty about range and the top speed at which the gun captains fired.[11] Setting his stadimeter at an assumed enemy-mast height, he shouted the range to Wood, who transmitted it to the guns. After a few shots he got the range and thereafter the *Petrel*'s projectiles grouped themselves nicely about the target.

At 7:30, Dewey took the squadron out into the bay and called all captains to the *Olympia* because he had received a report of ammunition shortage. Every ship counted her stores, with the *Petrel* having two-thirds of her supply left; the report proved erroneous. When he entered the wardroom, Fiske asked how many men on the *Petrel* had been killed. To his great joy, the answer was none. Indeed, not a soul in the entire squadron had been killed, and only seven men on the *Baltimore* had been wounded slightly, even though some Spanish shells had struck and penetrated several American ships.[12]

When Wood returned at about 11:30, Fiske learned that the squadron would engage the shore batteries near Sangley Point as well as the Spanish ships. The *Petrel* was to enter the shallow waters about Cavite and destroy any ships that had taken refuge there.

Back up on his perch, Fiske saw the *Baltimore* destroy the batteries at Sangley Point. The *Petrel*, ordered to follow the *Baltimore*, fired at the *Don Juan D'Ulloa* for a long time without receiving a reply, for she had been abandoned. A shell meant for the Spanish ship, however, went over into the Cavite arsenal and through the dining room of the commandant's house where a number of people had gathered. The Spanish flag on the house was quickly replaced by a white one. As soon as word of the surrender was passed to the *Olympia*, Dewey ordered the *Petrel* to burn the smaller Spanish ships located beyond Cavite Point. Fiske presumed that trains of powder had been laid to their magazines, making the burning dangerous; nevertheless, when Wood directed Hughes, the executive officer, to burn them and called for volunteers, he was swamped with offers. As Hughes and his party—seven men in a whaleboat—set out, Fiske positioned the *Petrel* so that Hughes could communicate with her. When Wood said that he wanted as many of the tugs and launches as he could get from those near the arsenal, Fiske volunteered to get them. Impressing several Spanish sailors, he soon returned with two large tugs, the *Rapido* and the *Hercules*, three steam launches, and several smaller boats. With Hughes and his party now returned, the *Petrel* towed her prizes toward the American squadron, which lay within two miles of Manila.[13] The squadron had expended 132 tons of ammunition and 5,839 projectiles. The fact that only about 3 percent of the shells found their mark gave eloquent testimony to Fiske's long crusade to improve fleet gunnery.

On the morning of 2 May, with the *Petrel* in the lead, Dewey took his squadron to Cavite, obtained the surrender of the arsenal, and placed a force of American marines in charge of it. It was thereafter used for docking and repairing American ships.

On 3 May, Fiske was directed to board the *Manila*, a Spanish armed transport that had run aground unharmed ahead of the *Petrel* in the mud of Bacoor Bay, and try to free her. Gathering the men he needed, Fiske headed for what he called his first command. While he and his men searched the ship for concealed Spaniards or fuses laid to the magazines, the engineers started fires under the boilers. Fiske's men then put the guns in working order. Early next morning Fiske loosed the *Manila* from her muddy bed, turned her over to Capt. Frank Wildes of the *Boston*, and returned to the *Petrel*. His first command had lasted less than two days.[14] In his report to Dewey on the battle, Wood commended most of his officers but particularly Hughes and Fiske.

On 7 May, Dewey cabled Secretary Long, "I control bay completely and can take city at any time, but I have not sufficient men to hold."[15] During the following week, he sent various armed parties, some of them covered by the *Petrel*, to destroy the Spanish batteries located at various points about Manila Bay. Meanwhile such Spanish captures as the *Hercules* (renamed *Petrelita*) patrolled the many marine facilities located about the harbor. On 15 May, Dewey again told Long that he could take Manila "at any moment" but that "to retain possession and thus control [the] Philippine Islands would require . . . [a] well equipped force of 5,000 men. . . ."[16]

For the men on Dewey's ships, first weeks then months went by in enforced idleness, dull monotony, and enervating heat and dampness pending the investiture of Manila by troops that seemed slow to arrive. From what little mail came in, Fiske learned that the United States was having trouble not only with the Spaniards but with the Filipinos as well. Fiske met the Filipino leader Emilio Aguinaldo and noted how natives addressed him as "general." When Fiske visited the beach, the Filipinos asked to have the American ships fire on Manila and kill the Spanish soldiers and especially the priests there. When Aguinaldo attacked the Spaniards, Fiske wished him well,[17] but a fear that he might also attack the Americans caused the crews of Dewey's ships to remain ready at their guns and at night to sweep nearby shores with searchlights.

The prime diplomatic aggressor at Manila Bay was Germany; Adm. Otto von Deiderichs objected to Dewey's harbor regulations and insinuated that Dewey meant to recognize the Filipino flag. Aboard the *Petrel*, opinion about the Germans varied. Some thought that they were not trying to make things difficult for the Americans; others thought that like most Europeans the Germans tended to patronize a people who had a weak navy; still others believed that they resented the U.S. attempt to acquire the Philippines and sought a base from which to expand their own trade and political power in the Far East. Fiske's conclusion that Germany did not have bellicose intentions was correct; once they perceived that the Americans were in the Philippines to stay, they gave Dewey no further trouble.[18]

Late in June, when asked to write an article on the Battle of Manila Bay for *Century Magazine*, Fiske went to the *Olympia*. Dewey promised to give the article security clearance as soon as he could. Soon thereafter, Dewey visited the *Petrel*: even though a Spanish fleet including a battleship was heading eastward from Spain toward Suez, Dewey appeared unworried whereas, Fiske noted, Wood suffered from "nerves."[19]

Fighting between Spaniards and Filipino insurgents, which began at the end of May, continued through June while the *Petrel* searched for arms about Manila Bay's fortification, helped enforce the blockade, and exercised at gun practice almost every day. The first American troops arrived on 30 June, just as the rainy season began, and were taken ashore in boats towed by tugs manned by the *Petrel*'s crew. A second detachment arrived on 17 July, and a third on 30 July. Soon ten thousand Americans were to the south of Manila and countless Filipinos to the north. Since the two forces did not cooperate, it seemed to Fiske that they were "manufacturing glory."[20] Moreover, proclaiming that the Americans were fighting simply to liberate the Filipinos from the Spaniards, Aguinaldo established an independent government. Would he resist if the United States decided to take the Philippines?

On 7 August, after Dewey talked with the American army leaders and with Fermin Jaudenes, the governor-general and captain-general of the Philippines, foreign ships left their anchorages near the city, and the *Petrel* was alerted for action on 9 August. Just as she was poised to fire, the attack was postponed. On 9 August, Dewey and Gen. Wesley Merritt formally demanded the surrender of Manila. Dewey's aide visited the *Petrel* soon thereafter to state that the army was not ready and that ships would be given twenty-four hours' notice prior to taking action. Having keyed up to shoot and to be shot, Fiske and his fellows had to unwind.[21] When the bombardment of Manila was finally ordered to begin at 9:00 A.M. on 13 July, Fiske wondered why the *Concord* and the *Petrel* were just off Manila while the rest of the American ships were near Cavite. He calmed himself with the thought that junior officers should not concern themselves with matters their seniors were paid to worry about.[22]

That morning the *Petrel* cleared for action. The German and British ships were to the northwest; the bulk of the American ships and a Japanese squadron were to the south, off Cavite. When he came on deck at 8:30, Fiske saw that the thirty-nine heavy guns (ranging from 4.7 to 9.4 inches) in the batteries fronting Manila were manned. When Wood came on deck, Fiske offered him a telescope, saying, "I bet one of the officers last night a dollar that we would not be hit to-day even with a brick, and I expect to win the bet." Wood retorted that he would win his bet and that if the Spaniards had wanted to sink the *Petrel* they could have done so in five minutes. On orders from Dewey the *Petrel* took up a position some twenty-five hundred yards off Fort San Antonio and the other American ships left Cavite for Manila. Later, Fiske heard that Capt. Sir Edward Chichester had moved his *Immortalité* between the American and German fleets, but he did not see the movement, never learned of anyone who had, and was sure it never happened.[23]

Admiral Dewey, who had refused to let the Spaniards fire a few shots at the American fleet "to save their honor," was ready to support the army as it closed in on the city. Although his ships opened fire on Fort San Antonio, at the extreme southern end of Manila's defenses, Fiske suspected that something was amiss. He remarked to Wood, "I shouldn't be surprised if this whole performance was a sham."[24] Fiske then saw Spanish troops leave Fort Antonio and American soldiers take it. At about 5:00 P.M., the Spanish flag came down and the American flag went up. Dewey thereupon cabled Secretary Long that Manila had surrendered and that his squadron had suffered no casualties. Only the day before, however, on 12 August, the Navy Department had cabled Dewey: "The protocol, signed by the President to-day, provides that the United States will occupy and hold the city, bay, and harbor of Manila pending the conclusion of a treaty of peace, which shall determine the control, disposition, and government of the Philippines."[25] Since a new sun, that of 13 August, had already risen in the Philippines, the United States could not claim the islands on the basis of the military conquest achieved by American naval and military forces on 12 August.[26]

On 15 September, the *Petrel* was sent to Hong Kong for overhaul. Shortly after her return to Manila Bay, however, she was ordered to Taku, the port of Tientsin in the far north of China, where some Chinese were causing trouble.[27]

As the acting executive officer of the *Petrel* after Hughes was transferred, Fiske was particularly anxious that all go well with her. She made it to Taku by 17 October, but after remaining off Taku for three weeks she was ordered to Shanghai for boiler repairs. While in Shanghai, Wood forwarded to the Navy Department the names of officers who had displayed eminent and conspicuous conduct in battle: he listed Hughes first and Fiske second.[28] Moreover, in the five fitness reports he wrote between 16 December 1896 and 1 December 1898, Wood rated Fiske "excellent" in all categories, adding, "I consider him fit for any duty."

Fiske spent a month with his wife and daughter in Shanghai before the *Petrel* returned to the heat of Manila Bay a few days before Christmas. On 31 December, Fiske was sent to the *Monadnock*, a monitor, as her navigator.

Although the old *Monadnock* arrived too late to participate in the investiture of Manila, she was one of the many American ships to engage in the suppression of Filipino insurgency. Soon after Jo and Caroline Fiske had visited Manila, the *Monadnock* cooperated with American troops: by day, she practiced communications with the army; by night she played her searchlight on insurgents' trenches so that the army could observe any movements of manpower. During visits ashore, Fiske sensed great tension. At 9:00 P.M. on 4 February, the army informed the *Monadnock* that a general engagement was under way.[29] Thus began the attempt of American forces to subdue the Filipino rebels, a process not to be completed until 1901, following the capture of Aguinaldo.

Fearing that the *Monadnock* might hit American troops, Fiske went ashore to coordinate her firing with the army. For about a month she provided fire and call-fire support for troops; Fiske was very pleased with the accuracy of his telescopic sight with which her guns were fitted. On 23 February Dewey came on board. After watching the firing for several hours, he said to Fiske, "Look how that turret jumps, Fiske; we can turn turrets much better by electricity, can't we?" Dewey smiled, for he knew that the *Monadnock* had hydraulic turrets and that Fiske had succeeded in turning turrets by electricity on the newly commissioned *Brooklyn*.[30]

On 1 March Fiske went to the *Olympia* to take a physical examination for promotion. To his astonishment, for he believed his heart trouble was progressive, doctors said little about abnormal sounds from his heart and passed him.[31] Actually, to the conclusion of "no trace of ailment or disability now existing," the senior of the three doctors who examined him added "except a heart murmur." Because Fiske had had fourteen fitness reports written on him and good letters about him from five commanding officers, he was spared a written examination.

On 9 March, the *Monadnock* headed for a dry dock at Hong Kong. Upon her return to Manila Bay, just as Fiske was writing his mother that he did not think he would see any more action, the ship was directed to support American soldiers fighting Filipino insurgents to the south of Manila. The *Monadnock*'s duty lasted from 26 March to 9 June. During this period her crew had the choice of staying on deck in the burning rays of the sun and providing targets for Filipinos or remaining inside in almost one hundred degree heat. The five months he had spent in the Bering Sea were "stupid enough," wrote Fiske in his memoirs, but the Philippine experience was "oppressive."[32]

In January 1899, Fiske submitted designs for a turret range finder to Charles O'Neil, chief of the Bureau of Ordnance. Protected from the weather, such a range finder would last almost indefinitely and provide errors of less than 1 percent per thousand yards. Had there been a range finder aboard the *Petrel*, Fiske argued, he could have quickly obtained the range to the Spanish ships in Manila Bay and saved much ammunition.[33]

The *Monadnock*'s captain favorably endorsed Fiske's idea, and Dewey also approved. Fiske then requested authorization to test an experimental model built by the Western Electric Company. O'Neil believed that the gear would add to the efficiency of gunnery but, he told Fiske, he "did not consider it advisable to take it in hand at present. The Bureau will be glad, however, to discuss the matter with you personally when you return to the United States." Before Fiske returned home, the American Gun Sight Company (the name of the reorganized American Range Finder Company) and Harry B. Thayer, of Western Electric, won O'Neil's approval to build an experimental model for $2,200. When O'Neil said the price was too high, the Gun Sight Company waived its royalty and Thayer went to work.[34]

Late in January 1899 Fiske applied for voluntary retirement so that he could devote himself to his inventions. He feared that he would almost perfect an invention and spend a good deal of money on it, only to have it die in infancy when he was ordered to some distant duty. While awaiting a reply, he was transferred to his old gunboat, the *Yorktown* (under Comdr. Charles S. Sperry) as first lieutenant, or executive officer. He signed his last log for the *Monadnock* on 29 May and two days later left the ship.[35] Her captain had rated him "good" as a navigator and "excellent" in his professional qualifications.

As executive officer, Fiske was responsible for the entire routine of the ship: cleanliness, discipline, drills, minor punishments, maintenance, instruction, liberty, and leave. Moreover, he was on call twenty-four hours a day, seven days a week, at the mercy of the commanding officer and department heads who brought him all kinds of problems to solve. It was in mid July during a call at Hong Kong for dry docking the *Yorktown* that he received a reply to his request for voluntary retirement—simply "No."[36]

From Hong Kong the *Yorktown* proceeded via Manila Bay (where Fiske learned that he had been promoted to lieutenant commander), to Lingayen Gulf, where with three other gunboats she fired at insurgents who had taken over the town of San Fernando. For long months thereafter, either independently or carrying army officers, the *Yorktown* operated as one of the various ships that visited the islands of the Philippines to obtain from their governors pledges of loyalty to the United States.[37] Sperry rated Fiske "very good to excellent" as an executive officer.

On 24 December, Rear Adm. John C. Watson, who succeeded Dewey, ordered Fiske detached, when relieved, to take passage on the *Iris* to Manila, and then to transfer to the "ambulance ship" *Solace* for passage to San Francisco, where he was to report to the commandant of the navy yard at Mare Island for reassignment. On 31 December, Fiske saw a small boat from the *Iris* come alongside and his classmate, Lt. Comdr. John M. Bowyer, come over the side. "How are you, Jim?" asked Bowyer. "I'm your relief."[38]

Before he went to sleep that night, Fiske reviewed his tour in the Far East: the trip of the little *Petrel* across the great Pacific and calls at ports in Korea and northern China, visiting with Jo and little Caroline in Chinese cities and in Manila, then war preparations and the interesting events of the war with Spain and with the Filipino insurgents. He also recalled that the captain of the *Petrel* had reported him for "eminent and conspicuous conduct in battle" and that Dewey had included his name on a short list of men mentioned for "heroic conduct." On his chest Fiske wore a bronze medal awarded by Congress to those who had participated in the Battle of Manila Bay.

Upon arriving in Manila, Fiske obtained permission to return home at his own expense rather than on a U.S. transport. He proceeded via Hong Kong, Nagasaki, Kobe, and Yokohama, visiting scenes reminiscent of earlier experiences and adventures. He truly enjoyed the trans-Pacific journey during which he had all the pleasures of being at sea and none of the responsibilities. In San Francisco he returned to "real civilization" and took a train eastward, joining his family five days later at the Plaza Hotel in New York.

7

THE GENESIS OF MODERN FIRE CONTROL, 1900–1907

When Fiske returned home from the Philippines he learned that Jo had purchased a house just nearing completion in New York City and had furnished it with extensive purchases she had made in Europe, Africa, and the Orient. The Fiskes moved into their new house on 1 May 1900.

One item Fiske conveniently did not mention in his memoirs was his efforts to have Adm. George Dewey intercede for him in obtaining recognition for his wartime actions. Dewey had indeed recommended him highly, but the chief of the Bureau of Navigation felt that Dewey had not distinguished Fiske's conduct "from many similar cases in which a commander in chief had recommended recognition or reward and in which the Department . . . declined to take action. . . ."[1] And that was that.

Fiske kept busy in his new billet as inspector of ordnance at the E. W. Bliss Company, in Brooklyn; he wrote the Bureau of Ordnance 153 letters during the last nine months of 1900 and 266 in 1901.[2] He also corresponded with Western Electric about an improved range finder and obtained a patent on an apparatus for a ship's conning tower. When his request to personally explain his inventions to the secretary of the navy was declined, Fiske offered the bureau suggestions on how his range finder should be tested. He also worked on equipment to be used on the *Adder* and the *Plunger*, early models of John Holland's submarine.[3]

Fiske knew that the automotive torpedo, invented a generation earlier but bereft of wartime accomplishment, was not highly regarded in any navy and was being kept alive only by the exertions of an "obstinate minority."[4] At the Bliss works, however, chief engineer Frank M. Leavitt was developing a superheater to increase the energy in the compressed air in the torpedo's flask. Fiske helped him and before the end of his tour

62

conducted the first successful test of the superheated torpedo; the result was that this type of torpedo was adopted the world over.[5] To increase a torpedo's range still further, Fiske suggested that a turbine drive be adapted to it; to improve its accuracy, he suggested a more powerful gyroscope. With bureau approval, he and Leavitt carried out experiments with a turbine-driven torpedo which soon replaced the reciprocating engine types used by the American navy. By the time he was detached in February 1902, Fiske was predicting torpedo ranges of twenty thousand yards—a prophecy that caused officials at the Bliss works and at the bureau to wonder if Fiske had lost his mind.[6]

Among other things Fiske did while engaged in "work of a routine character" at the Bliss Company was to make a whistle by which a deck officer could alert the crew when the water-tight doors were to be closed, as in an impending collision, so that no men would be caught in closed compartments. Experiments he conducted on the *Brooklyn* showed promise, and soon Western Electric produced the system for numerous ships. Later the whistle was replaced by an electrical device similar to that sounded when a submarine prepares to dive.[7]

While Fiske was stationed in the Far East, his semaphore system was installed on a mast of the *New York* and a competing system on another ship. Fiske's system was declared superior, but water seeping into the electric solenoids that moved its arms prevented them from working. In trying to improve it, Fiske involved the Western Electric Company, numerous ships, several agencies of the Navy Department, and various testing boards. But so much time passed before it was perfected—fifteen years—that wireless radio made the semaphore obsolete.[8]

On 25 November 1900 a board directed to evaluate the wireless radio reported favorably. In 1901, the Bureau of Equipment bought duplicate wireless radio sets from French, German, and British inventors and a fourth from an American, Lee de Forest. It established wireless stations at the Washington Navy Yard and at Annapolis, thirty miles away. If the results warranted, tests would be conducted by sets placed on various ships. After a board reported on the performance of the various systems, on 27 March 1903, the bureau purchased twenty sets of the German Slaby-Orco system; in September it bought twenty-five more. Thirteen radio sets were placed at naval stations along the Atlantic and Gulf coasts, the rest on various ships. In 1905, a Wireless Telegraph Board was formed consisting of Capt. John A. Rogers, Fiske, and his classmate George Henry Peters. Using the *Topeka* and the lighthouse station at Navesink Highlands, New Jersey, as sending and receiving stations, the members of the board took turns at the two stations. Static provided a good deal of interference most of the time, but in one instance, when it was minimal, a record for long distance was established with a 158-mile transmission. By the end of 1905, forty-four ships had been equipped with wireless sets; four more were being given the equipment; twenty-three shore stations had been so equipped; and thirteen additional shore stations were being built.[9]

While aboard the *Petrel*, Fiske had sent the Navy Department a sketch and description of a large telescope pivoted at eye level and supported on a frame by a counterweight. Although he never received a reply, Fiske toyed with the idea while in the Far East and upon his return built the apparatus and submitted it. The department gave permission to test it on the battleship *Massachusetts* for six months. Fiske put it on board in November 1901. When he joined the ship as her executive officer, he saw it in continual use. In May 1902, the captain wrote a favorable report on the device; and Fiske described it in a brief article in the *Naval Institute Proceedings*.[10] The department, however, directed that it be removed from the ship. Lt. William S. Sims, director of target practice, then borrowed it for spotting in connection with a target-practice system he was developing. In 1905, when Adm. Albert S. Barker, commander in chief of the Atlantic Fleet, asked Fiske where he could obtain a similar telescope, Fiske offered to loan him his, the only one in existence. Barker thought the Navy Department should buy it, and Fiske sold it to the department for $500 although he had invested $1,500 in it. In 1907, various officers at the Naval Observatory who wanted the navy to adopt a telescope asked Fiske to submit his instrument in a competition among instrument-makers. Fiske turned to Western Electric, which produced an instrument much like Fiske's original and won the competition. Production bidding, however, was won by another firm which had no previous expenses to recoup and no royalty to pay. As far as Fiske was concerned, although he had lost $1,000, the navy now had his telescope on all major ships.[11]

When his tour as inspector of ordnance ended, Fiske called on Commodore Charles O'Neil, who told him that he had faith in his telescopic sight but that reports about it from the fleet were so bad that it must be withdrawn from service. O'Neil thought highly of Fiske; on his fitness report the commodore wrote that Fiske "is well known to the Bureau as an accomplished and effective officer having an unusual knowledge of electricity." But he greatly upset Fiske by threatening to remove what Fiske considered the best improvement made in naval gunnery in several centuries. Was not

O'Neil aware of the miserable gunnery success of American ships while the British forged ahead under Capt. Percy Scott?

It was in 1896 that Scott had replaced old sights with an ordinary telescope and trained his pointers until they accomplished continuous-aim firing. Six years earlier, however, on 15 May 1890, Fiske had applied for a patent for "A Method of Pointing Guns at Sea"—continuous-aim firing. On 9 March 1891, he applied for a patent on "A Telescopic Sight for Ship's Guns," for which a revised patent was issued on 5 September 1893—about five years before Scott attached his telescope to a gun. In any event, in the annual prize firing conducted on 26 May 1899, the 4.7-inch guns on the HMS *Scylla* attained the phenomenal score of 80 percent on target shooting at a distance of some fifteen-hundred yards. Scott took the cruiser *Terrible* to the Far East in 1899. In the annual contest of September 1900, his main battery scored 60 percent and his 6-inch guns scored 76.8 percent. It was Scott's gunnery devices, teaching methods, and evident success that would impress Lt. William S. Sims.

As Scott forged ahead, reports from American ships around the world were uniformly bad.[12] As yet, the Bureau of Ordnance had undertaken none of the corrective steps in material and training Fiske had suggested. On his part, he had dropped ideas for a telescopic sight and tried to develop a range finder. He told Commodore O'Neil angrily that the trouble was not with his sight but with the poor material the bureau furnished the fleet, adding that the sight he had placed in the *Yorktown* ten years earlier was better than any made by the bureau since. Reluctantly, on the advice of an aide, Lt. Joseph Strauss, O'Neil agreed to leave the Fiske sights on board for a while.[13]

In 1895 Congress funded two 11,000-ton battleships designed by the Board on Construction, the *Kearsarge* and the *Kentucky*. Lieutenant Sims picked up the *Kentucky* as she left Gibraltar late in 1899 for the China Station and found grave faults with her. On the way to his ship, which was at Canton, he stopped at Hong Kong and from Scott learned things about his gunnery improvements Scott would not tell most officers of other navies. In March 1901, Sims reported on Scott's gunnery achievements aboard the *Terrible*. In July, the Bureau of Navigation ordered some of Scott's devices for training gun pointers. Reports from Sims dated August and September 1901 were also seriously considered by the Board on Construction.[14]

Sims's reports coupled with abominable American gunnery scores prompted the Bureau of Navigation in October 1900 to create the billet of inspector of target practice, first filled by Lt. Comdr. Albert P. Niblack and then by Sims. Like Fiske, Sims, and various others, Niblack believed that poor ships and poor guns were traceable to poor naval administration. He urged that not only machinery but naval administration be shifted to officers who actually fought ships.[15]

Knowing that Theodore Roosevelt, who had just been elected president, was keenly interested in improving the navy, Sims risked a court martial on 16 November by writing directly to him.[16] Without betraying his insubordination, Roosevelt invited further correspondence and directed that Sims's reports be distributed to all officers, a chore Niblack performed.[17] Niblack wrote Sims on 15 January 1902: "You have quite won out on this business, but I don't mind saying that your language has unnecessarily hurt people. I have been able to smooth things over here by being on the spot."[18]

In Sims, Fiske found a colleague who spoke forcefully if not disrespectfully to his superiors, airing criticisms Fiske himself had modestly voiced about the Bureau of Ordnance and about naval administration for almost two decades. Sims loudly proclaimed that the navy's technical bureaus gave insufficient attention to available civilian talent and to naval inventors. Moreover, Sims argued, the government should cooperate with private industry in providing equipment. Failure to produce good ships, he concluded, stemmed primarily from the lack of a board of "well-informed, high-ranking officers of experience" to set forth the characteristics of fighting ships.[19] Sims's first victory came on 7 January 1902, when O'Neil agreed to fit ships with loading and firing-practice machines and said he would gladly receive suggestions for improving the dexterity of gunners and the quality of ordnance equipment.[20]

On 15 February 1902, Sims submitted a comparison of British and American gunnery in a devastatingly critical report detailing failures in American marksmanship and equipment—gun-pointing, telescopic sights, gun mounts, and the like. While endorsing the report, O'Neil said that Sims was too pessimistic, had overrated the Royal Navy, and was too sanguine about continuous-aim fire. O'Neil apparently was unaware of Fiske's electrical gun-elevating gear, even though his annual report mentioned it: O'Neil provided mathematical "proof" that it would take five men at the elevating gear of a 6-inch gun ten seconds to follow a ship roll of five degrees.[21] It did Sims no more good than it had Fiske to reply that continuous-aim firing was already being accomplished successfully by the British. But Sims sent a copy of his rebuttal to Henry C. Taylor, chief of the Bureau of Navigation, who not only agreed with it but, like Sims and Fiske, proposed the adoption of a naval general staff.[22]

In 1902, as inspector of target practice for the Asiatic Fleet, Sims introduced his gunnery system in the Southern Squadron. His theories were soon proven correct in practice, although the caveat that only shots which hit a target should count led some ships to fire one gun at a time in clear weather and on a smooth sea. Sims was then peremptorily ordered home, where he loudly praised the unprecedented target practice scores made with the help of Scott's telescopic sights. (One improvement had been the addition of a rubber cushion to protect the gunner's eye from the eyepiece.)[23]

When Sims succeeded Niblack as inspector of target practice, he told Taylor that defects in telescopic sights and their mounts were "so fundamental as to preclude the possibility of success under battle conditions." With the support of President Roosevelt, Sims forced the Bureau of Ordnance to improve gun sights, turret gear, and fire-control systems so that they could stand the rigors of rapid firing.[24] He also caused a rift between older and more conservative captains, to whom target practice was a nuisance, and the young bloods (along with an occasional older officer like Fiske) who demanded utility rather than beauty in a warship. By raising a "hell of a hornet's nest," as Lt. Homer Poundstone put it, Sims focused attention on what Fiske had been preaching for years—and not only the attention of the Navy Department but also of the president of the United States.

Fiske had the same contempt for bureaucratic inertia as Sims but knew more about the problems faced by the Bureau of Ordnance. In explaining why Sims rather than Fiske became the engineer of the gunnery revolution, Elting E. Morison noted that "Fiske, as an inventor, took his pleasure in great part from the design of the device. He lacked not so much the energy as the overriding sense of social necessity that would have enabled him to *force* revolutionary ideas on the service. Sims possessed this sense." In Fiske, Morison found "the familiar plight of the engineer who often enough must watch the products of his ingenuity organized and promoted by other men."[25] At any rate, Fiske no doubt found Sims at his best when Sims complained that the Navy Department paid little attention to naval inventors and that no improvement in ship construction and gunnery could come without the adoption of a naval general staff. These points will be discussed later.

The *Massachusetts*, to which Fiske was detailed as executive officer, was one of three "seagoing coast-line battleships" of the *Oregon* class authorized in 1890. Fiske felt right at home with respect to her electrical machinery. Each of her three steam-driven G.E. dynamos produced 24 kilowatts and 300 amperes at 80 volts; her voltmeters and ampere meters were made by Western Electric; her lighting system was provided by Thomson-Houston. In addition to eleven telephones, she carried Fiske's engine-order telegraph, revolution indicator, and steering telegraph. The range finder, "of the

Fiske pattern," however, "had been removed on 7 December 1897 and turned into store."[26]

In 1902, the North Atlantic Station was expanded into a fleet consisting of the Battleship, Caribbean, and Coast squadrons, each under a rear admiral, and the whole was commanded by the commander in chief of the North Atlantic Fleet. When fleet exercises were called for, the squadrons concentrated. Thus, they joined in the Caribbean during August 1902. High on the agenda was the testing of Sims's target-practice system. The *Indiana*, whose men had rarely fired her guns, beat the China Station's record with an average of 40.6 percent with her 6-inch guns; the *Alabama* took the prize with an average of 60 percent hits; and perfect scores were made by thirty-three gunners. During the target practice, which was held in good weather and smooth seas, gunners fired at short ranges and slow speeds, and the rapidity of firing was not counted. Nevertheless, Sims had proved that properly trained gunners could shoot well.[27]

Much taken with the idea of fleet drills, Fiske suggested that the navy adopt that system instead of wasting "its time and energies on long, aimless, tiresome, and exasperating 'cruises' in enervating climates, far from home." He urged the establishment of "home bases" from which the fleet could go out to drill but often return at night, thereby giving its officers and men opportunity for at least some family life.[28]

As executive officer, Fiske performed the daily, weekly, and fortnightly inspections required of him. About a month before scheduled target practice he stressed gun practice and selected his best pointers for the regulation firing runs. On the day before the firing, he cleared his ship for action; on the day of the shoot, he would have every man take a bath and don clean clothes as a precaution against infection from wounds. The men tense, the guns bore-sighted and ready, he would report "ready" to go on the range. There four minutes of shooting provided the culmination of a year's worth of training.[29]

Although busy with tactical drills and exercises, Fiske nonetheless also had to supervise the Luce plan recently adopted by the department for educating enlisted men. To Fiske, the amount of education required was out of proportion with the duties of the navy as a whole. How could division officers teach their men, many of them illiterate, the theory and practice of wireless communications, steam engineering, naval construction, ordnance, torpedoes, and the like? The attempt was soon abandoned.[30]

On 16 January 1903, while the *Massachusetts* conducted stationary target practice off Culebra, Fiske saw a great cloud of white smoke issue from the rear of its starboard 8-inch turret. Nine dead men fell out of the turret; one man, on fire, jumped overboard. Fiske immediately sounded the fire-quarters alarm. After the man in the water had been rescued, the *Massachusetts* took him to a hospital at San Juan, Puerto Rico. A court of inquiry and general court-martial established that death and injury in the turret had been caused by accident. This last in a series of similar accidents, however, caused a thorough revision of the navy's drill book for gunnery practice.[31]

Sims's gunnery system, adapted from Scott's, was merely the spotting system Fiske has used when, stadimeter in hand, aloft on the mast of the *Petrel*, he had spotted shot in the Battle of Manila Bay and performed an act that was, in his own words, "really epochal, in that it initiated a new era in naval gunnery."[32] Moreover, before he left the *Massachusetts*, Fiske had designed a standardized dotter machine for general issue. A suitably marked paper would record hits made, thereby enabling a gunner to know where room for improvement existed and to compare his record with that of others. After showing Sims plans for the machine, Fiske had Western Electric build one; he had it patented and offered it to the Bureau of Ordnance, which gave him no encouragement, issuing instead, to a number of ships on a trial basis, what he considered poorer machines made by others. His judgment was upheld when the Bureau of Ordnance found Scott's aiming devices "entirely unsatisfactory."[33]

Because he believed that the navy was placing too much emphasis on spotting and not enough on range finding, Fiske tested two range finders and an optical Barr and Stroud model aboard the *Cincinnati*. The last was simpler than his system and needed only one observer; Fiske agreed with Sims and others that it was much superior. He believed, however, that under conditions of poor visibility the optical would perform less satisfactorily than his electrical arrangement. He decided to keep quiet until the navy realized this fact and then bring his system again to its attention.[34] But his argument that the range finder should be the basis of gunnery training and that spotting should be secondary met with disagreement from O'Neil, particularly because Sims's spotting system appeared to be working very well.[35] Moreover, as Fiske was keenly aware, his range finders were vulnerable to damage and depended on good communications between the range-finder operator and the men in the turrets. As has already been mentioned, early in 1899 he had placed an optical range finder inside a turret, with only its glasses exposed. His application for a patent on a "combined range-finder and turret," entered 28 June 1900, was granted on 20 November.

So interested was Fiske in the fleet target practice of 1902 that he requested a postponement of his promotion to commander. He realized that the promotion meant the greatest change that took place in an officer's career, even greater than that from captain to rear admiral, because it moved an officer from the class of subordinates, with little personal responsibility, into "command rank." But it would have also meant his transfer from the *Massachusetts*. Fiske's request was granted, and he was able to take part in what he called the "first modern target practice our fleet had ever held." When detached from the *Massachusetts* in May 1903, at the age of forty-nine, he stepped ashore knowing that the life of a subordinate officer was behind him forever.[36]

Fiske proceeded to Washington to seek approval from O'Neil for the development of his turret range finder, pointing out that any good optical range finder could be used and that he would gladly make the bureau a gift of his invention. O'Neil, however, believed the project utterly impractical. Saying that concussions from the guns would disarrange or disable the delicate optical glasses, he would not even put Fiske on waiting orders to let him work on it. Determined to develop the system, Fiske won a postponement of two weeks in his orders sending him to a second summer course at the Naval War College. With the help of Western Electric, his instrument was ready in the fall, when O'Neil granted permission to test it on the second-class battleship *Maine*.

As in 1896, Fiske broadened his intellectual horizons at the Naval War College. A lecture Admiral Luce delivered on 2 June led him to see that fighting was merely a means of deciding a contest between nations harboring different ideas. The nation with the more clearly defined purpose, that had selected the best methods to accomplish that purpose, and that had the best machines ready when war broke out *"must win."* As Fiske put it, he now saw war *"as a matter of brains"* in which military force was used to carry out plans made in support of the national purpose.[37] At the conclusion of the course he bridled a bit because he had a house in New York but was ordered to duty as inspector of ordnance at Cramp's shipyard in Philadelphia. He nevertheless followed what he admitted were perfectly proper orders. Capt. French E. Chadwick, president of the War College, gave him 4.0 (the top grade) for his academic performance.

Stationed at Cramp's for two years, Fiske found his duty "routine" because he was well versed in ordnance and mechanical appliances and had excellent assistants. He was, therefore, able to go to New York frequently to work on the optical turret range finder which Western Electric was building at his expense. When he tested it from atop the company's building, it showed an error of 98 yards to the Statute of Liberty—a distance of 6,580 yards.[38]

Late in 1903, Fiske went to Pensacola, where his range finder would be tested aboard the *Maine*. Climbing to the turret top, he found to his joy that instead of being blown overboard, range finder and all, the shock of firing was not too great and did not harm the mechanism. Noting that the range finder was not sufficiently accurate, however, Fiske made a stronger one and also completely redesigned its optical parts. In April 1905, he asked the chief of the Bureau of Ordnance, Newton E. Mason, to give the range finder his personal attention. Fiske requested that Mason use his influence with Adm. George Converse, chief of the Bureau of Navigation, to have him, Fiske, detailed for his next duty as the commanding officer of the new monitor *Florida* and to have his turret range finder mounted on her.[39] Despite his cantankerousness, just before retiring from the service O'Neil had given Fiske a grade of 4.0. To the question "Would you have any objection to said officer being under your command?" O'Neil had answered, "No objection whatever."

In the fall of 1905, reports on Fiske's turret range finder aboard the *Maine* stated that although the instrument was not injured by gunfire, concussion had jarred its optical parts out of adjustment. In forwarding the reports to Fiske, Robley D. Evans, commander in chief of the Atlantic Fleet, wrote that the range finder had been found wanting and would be removed from the *Maine*.[40] Fiske immediately took the range finder to the Western Electric Company, where it was strengthened as he indicated, and then asked the Bureau of Ordnance for another trial, pointing out that in a series of ten observations made on a target 6,580 yards distant, the instrument had erred by only 51.5 yards—astounding accuracy for the day. The bureau referred the matter to Evans, who demurred; as a result the bureau refused Fiske's request. Fiske argued that the instrument he wished to test was not the original one but another on which he had expended an additional $500; the answer was again no. Not one to give up easily, Fiske tried again on 3 May 1906, when in command of the *Minneapolis*, but the results were similar. He then unofficially explained the situation to Evans, who authorized the placing of his instrument on the *Maine* for tests to be conducted early in 1907. But again the bureau said no, and Fiske bided his time.[41] Meanwhile Mason marked his fitness report 4.0.

In 1903, Sims directed that the speed of firing as well as accuracy would now count in record target practices. But improved accuracy and greater speed depended on better equipment, including an improved telescopic sight. Having found the service sight inadequate, Sims and Ridley McLean had furnished the Bureau of Ordnance with designs for an improved model, only to have O'Neil retort that it was easier to teach men to shoot than for his bureau to provide quickly the high quality gunnery material demanded by the ships.[42]

Throughout 1904 reports from the fleet suggested improvements as well as registering complaints. Mark L. Bristol, Sims, John Hood, and Evans all submitted numerous ideas, including suggestions that fire-control stations be located above the funnel gases and that simple but adequate communications be provided between the fire-control stations and the guns. Fiske asked for tests of his eye-level telescope, of his combined turret and range finder, and of a new speed indicator and also suggested the use of periscopes in all turrets and torpedo-firing stations.[43]

Irritated by complaints from the fleet, O'Neil directed ship captains to try to improve the poor sights they had until new ones could be issued.[44] Irritated in turn, Sims wrote a report intended to reach the president. As he hoped, it galvanized Roosevelt to action. When O'Neil said it would take seven years to replace the old sights, Roosevelt called in the "young insurgents" to state their side of the matter. Sims said that telescopic sights could be produced by private industry within about a year. Roosevelt thereupon told the bureaus that they "must find the money to resight the Navy with the best possible design of instruments or I shall take the matter up with Congress and tell them that the Navy's sighting devices are obsolete and inefficient."[45] The fleet was resighted within two years, and Fiske credited Sims with having saved the telescopic sight.

Sims was not, however, to have everything his own way. Several flarebacks that caused loss of life brought criticism that the emphasis on speed in gunnery was not only unnecessary but dangerous. Sims replied sarcastically that the quality of equipment was poor and the fire-control communications systems were "useless." Moreover, he told President Roosevelt that staff officers alone could not provide good ship designs. Sims also told the General Board that new ships should be equipped with only homogeneous, heavy, primary batteries, preferably of the 12-inch size.[46]

Fiske, who was older than Sims, had been held in some disregard by the department for some time, and little attention was paid to his demands for introducing director firing. He had no better luck with his suggestion, made 11 June 1904 to O'Neil, that periscopes be provided so that turret officers could observe the fire of their guns from a central position and at the same time direct operations within the turrets. The periscopes were small, Fiske said, and should not cost more than fifty dollars each; he even sent O'Neil a sketch.[47] O'Neil replied that experiments were being made along this line, but that "certain defects have been reported in the periscopes used on submarine boats, and unless obviated, [these] would apply to the use of periscopes in turrets."[48] Fiske's suggestion that two masts be provided for battleships, however, was referred to the Navy Department with the recommendation that it be referred to the Board on Construction for discussion.[49]

Criticism of the fire-control system was reaching home: on 18 February

1905 a revised method of gunnery training and target practice was issued. In addition Secretary of the Navy William Moody ordered the fire-control communications systems be improved.[50] In his annual report for 1904, O'Neil said that no range finder tested had proved "as good as that now generally provided the services."[51] Believing that "a proper system of interior communications on board a man-of-war in order to control the firing of the guns is absolutely necessary to obtain the maximum efficiency of gun fire," O'Neil's successor, Mason, ordered telephone and visual systems tested. More important, he established a board on fire control to outline a system of adequate communications to tie range findings, spotting, and fire control together. Pending a report, Mason asked the building bureaus and the bureaus of Navigation, Ordnance, and Equipment to agree to the removal of all fire-control equipment from ships under construction and to replace it with essentially the Fiske system: "(a) a range finder station in the lower fore and one in the lower main top and (b) each station to be able to signal ranges and deflections direct to any group or groups [of guns], at will, or to the Central Station"—the latter being a plotting room located below deck. With the bureaus of Equipment and of Construction in agreement, Mason asked Evans to submit his suggestions and also ordered the manufacture of fire-control equipment stopped until a new system could be decided upon.[52]

The members of the fire-control board authorized on 21 November 1905 included a retired commander, George W. Denfeld, as the senior member and Sims, Bristol, George B. Bradshaw, and Lloyd H. Chandler—all lieutenant commanders. Sims brought the board confidential information about British fire-control and battle-practice methods he had obtained during a visit to England in June 1905. He also furnished the information to Fiske, who complimented him highly not only for having written "the best paper on naval gunnery I have ever seen" but also for writing in such a way "that every officer must be impressed with the moderation and concise logic of your language."[53]

Sims's report, submitted on 21 December, described the current state of the art and illustrated the principles Fiske had been trying for nearly fifteen years to have adopted. The conclusions read:

> The fire of each separate caliber of main-battery guns, when firing at the same target, should be controlled by a separate fire control officer.
>
> The fire control officers of main battery guns should occupy as elevated a post as possible, especially when controlling long-range gun-fire.
>
> All guns of 3″ or less belong to torpedo defense and should be grouped into four groups, one for each quadrant and each under a separate fire control officer. . . .

Secondary battery fire controllers need not be so high because the ranges are shorter.

The commanding officer should communicate his general battle orders to each fire control officer and leave to such officers the details of obtaining and transmitting the ranges and the necessary battle orders.[54]

In reply to questions from Sims, Fiske furnished a disquisition on range finding using the stadimeter and other methods. He added that the navy needed an "experimental ship"—which he, of course, would command.[55] With respect to his report on fire control, Fiske wrote Sims:

Many objections occurred to me on first reading: but these disappeared, one by one, as I re-read. I can find no fault at all—only virtue all through; and I am sure this report will bring about as great an improvement in battle gunnery as your own special work has already done in target practice. I think the Board right on every point,—and yet it hits my turret range finder an *awful* whack. Nevertheless, I think a battle ship ought to have turret range finders, *if* they can be made good,—for use as a last resort. . . .

Many of your principal recommendations I have advocated for . . . years, as you know: —viz., gunnery central station below, salvo-firing for broadside guns; increased use of telephones—etc., etc., etc., in fact, I was *the first man* to install—or even propose—electric range indicators & battle order indicators;—I *think* I was the first man ever *to go aloft* in battle, as I *did* at Manila, to *direct* the *gun fire*. I was the first what you call *fire control officer*. . . . Sounds like bragging:—I guess it really is! . . .[56]

In accordance with the conclusions of the fire-control board, on 19 March 1906 Mason decided to place an experimental fire-control system aboard the battleship *Virginia*, to be commissioned on 7 May. In seeking transmitting instruments "which fit existing conditions," Mason won approval from the other bureaus to buy equipment manufactured in London by Vickers.[57]

On 26 October, after witnessing target practice, Sims stated in a special report to President Roosevelt that the results had been good even if poor communications between fire-control officers and their guns had slowed the pace of firing; he recommended that construction begin on the equipment suggested by the fire control board in 1905.[58] Fiske's ideas, percolated to Mason and the president through Sims, were finally beginning to bear fruit.

Fiske had been extremely productive between his forty-sixth and fifty-second birthdays. He had served for four of those six years as inspector of ordnance, yet even while doing so he had improved his original range finder and in several ways had bettered the torpedo. He had invented a warning whistle for shipboard use, worked long and hard on his four-arm semaphore system, served as a member of a wireless telegraph board, invented a powerful eye-level telescope, and continued demanding that the navy pay more attention to naval inventors and cooperate with private industry to obtain improved naval equipment. He had improved upon one of Percy Scott's gunnery training devices and had invented the turret range finder. He had served as the executive officer of a battleship, suggested a plan for fleet training that would heighten the morale of ships' crews, and further broadened his horizons during a tour at the Naval War College. It had not been his voice, long calling in the darkness, but that of Sims—backed by the president's—which had shaken the navy out of the doldrums and into achieving praiseworthy gunnery standards. Yet with the adoption of his concept of providing equipment and communications by which a fire-control officer could transmit corrected ranges and firing orders to all guns, the navy verged upon creating a modern fire-control system.

8

NAVAL POLICY
AND THE NAVAL PROFESSION, 1898–1908

While performing his duties and also inventing naval mechanisms, Bradley A. Fiske worried about the character of the navy: it seemed to be concerned only with material and men, giving insufficient attention to the strategic principles that governed their employment and lacking a professional leader who could provide strategic direction. "These ideas got such hold on me that they had to come out,"[1] he said; his essay entitled "American Naval Policy" was published in the *U.S. Naval Institute Proceedings* in March 1905. In it he argued that the preparedness necessary to successful military action could be provided only by a naval general staff whose chief, if opposed by the secretary, would have recourse to Congress. Because of the essay Fiske leapt to the forefront of those who had been demanding since the Spanish-American War a progressive reorientation both of naval principles and of naval organization.

Although older "insurgents" like Fiske, Stephen B. Luce, and Henry C. Taylor, and a younger group including Homer Poundstone and William S. Sims, demanded a naval general staff, Secretary John D. Long objected to one. On 13 March 1900, however, by administrative directive Long established a General Board of the Navy that would provide the secretary with advice on war plans, shipbuilding programs, characteristics of new construction, personnel requirements, and the like. In time of war, he said, it would be "a strategic board." But a secretary could reject the board's advice, even dismiss it summarily. After resigning in May 1902, Long warned against instituting a general staff for the navy even if the army should establish one.[2]

Long's successor, William H. Moody, saw improvement of naval administration as "an object of solicitude," for only in his own office could the conflicting interests of the bureau chiefs be reconciled. While he believed in civilian supremacy, he also wanted the inexperienced secretary to be given the best military advice obtainable. Proposals for reform included

76

the reorganization of the navy yards, consolidation of the bureaus, and the creation of a general staff. Although Moody accepted the idea of a general staff, he favored granting it "no authority except such as may be conferred upon it from time to time by the Secretary." In the end, Congress would determine how the department could best be organized.[3]

In his essay, Fiske charged that American ships had not been correctly designed, that naval science and tactics remained undeveloped, and that naval administration slighted military considerations. Like large business enterprises, which had boards of directors, the navy should have a policy board, or general staff. And one should be created now, Fiske reasoned, for during wartime it would be too late. Fiske also favored coordinating the military, diplomatic, political, and economic policies of the nation into a coherent whole. Once national policy was devised, the navy could request the men and materials needed for its support.[4]

While the essay won Fiske much favorable attention in the public and military press and the Naval Institute's prize for the year—$200 and a gold medal—it did not provoke Congress and the Navy Department to adopt his progressive reforms, least of all a naval general staff.

Fiske asked Sims to comment upon an advance copy of his essay. Although Sims congratulated him "on having presented more radical and more original thinking than is contained in any other similar articles that I have read," he declined public comment because his own criticisms of the navy had already caused great bitterness among the "principal dignitaries." Moreover, he disagreed with several of Fiske's points and said the essay was too long and poorly written.[5]

Rather than being angry at a junior who had picked his essay apart, Fiske asked Sims to reply to a long letter he had written on 25 February 1905 in which he noted that deficiencies in ships had been perpetrated by staff officers. These officers, Fiske contended, built ships merely on mathematical and engineering principles, ignoring military principles; he suggested that important military principles would be followed in construction if there were a general staff armed with executive powers.[6] Sims replied in at least two letters which he requested Fiske to burn. A paragraph of Fiske's letter to Sims, dated 18 March, beautifully illustrates Fiske's conception of the different approaches he and Sims took:

> I appreciate your moderation in resisting the temptation to swat our enemies or opponents in discussing my essay, through the unselfish fear that—as things are now—you might injure its influence thereby. But I do think you mistake for enemies men who are only opponents. I think it right to tell you that you are *very highly regarded* in the Service, and that

more than nine tenths [sic] of the officers believe you have done useful work of the highest order: but I have heard some of your cordial admirers deplore the fact that you often offend people, especially your seniors, by language and a manner that are unnecessarily harsh. They say you are your own worst enemy.

I accept your decision, not to discuss my essay, with unabated good nature and regard. . . .[7]

After Sims had replied in another letter which Fiske probably did burn, Fiske revealed to him how rocky the road to reform had been:

Yes, I know I have often been called "visionary," "impracticable," a "crank," a "bookworm," a "laboratory officer," etc. But Admiral Taylor comforted me a good deal, when advising me to keep on pushing the semaphore, by saying—"Remember—the visionary of today is sometimes the genius of tomorrow."[8]

Neither Fiske's essay nor another entitled "The Civil and Military Authority"[9] made any discernible impression upon congressmen. They alone could create a general staff, but they were thoroughly committed to civilian supremacy over the military and could not see how the secretary could delegate responsibility to subordinates without reducing his own authority.

In 1904 Secretary Paul Morton skirted the need for a general staff, but his successor, Charles J. Bonaparte, stated in 1905 that the poor system of naval administration worked only because of the good qualities of the men who administered it. Bonaparte promised to reduce the number of bureaus and redistribute their work. But because the work of the department was being done "well, even remarkably well," he initially did not propose a radical reorganization.[10]

In response to questions from President Roosevelt, however, Sims suggested that the naval organization be so remodeled that there would be no divided responsibility in the preparation for war and that the secretary be given a general staff.[11]

After a year in office, Bonaparte came to see the need of "a very radical and thorough-going change . . . in the organization of the Department." He suggested that Congress abolish the Board on Construction and provide four sections for the department: one under the secretary, one under the assistant secretary, and two under officers of flag rank who would handle operations and material, respectively.[12] Adm. George Dewey, president of the General Board, was appalled by Bonaparte's suggestions and convinced that under Bonaparte "the Navy is going to hell"; he told Roosevelt so, and threatened to resign unless Bonaparte was replaced. Roosevelt complied.[13]

Fiske expanded upon his reasons for advocating a general staff in the March 1906 issue of *Naval Institute Proceedings*. A general staff, he said, implied no surrender by civilian authorities of their "perfect control" over a military service; rather it implied abstention from interference in purely technical details best left in the hands of professional officers. Moreover, he asked what had prompted Congress in 1904 to authorize 13,000-ton battleships when it had authorized 17,000-ton ships in 1903.[14] Bonaparte had asked nine line officers including Sims, for their opinions on shipbuilding rather than seeking the collective advice of experts on ship construction. Sims objected to the procedure, as did Poundstone, Fiske, and others.[15] Fiske argued that "we should make our battle-ships as large as the state of the engineering arts permits" and that while decisions on shipbuilding should be made by the secretary, they should be made only on the advice of a naval general staff. Fiske and fellow progressives felt happier in 1906 when Congress, for the first time, did not stipulate the tonnage of new construction and authorized construction of the *Delaware*, which displaced 20,000 tons.

Fiske supported the building of large, all-big-gun ships because a fire-control system for guns of one caliber would be much simpler than one for mixed batteries. One system could fire more quickly in salvos producing only one "splash," and the firing of the big guns would not be disturbed by the noise, smoke, shock, and splashes of other guns.[16]

Over the years Fiske had been unable to get the Bureau of Ordnance to adopt several of his inventions or to manufacture adequate equipment. Gunnery training and target practice had also been weak until Sims came along. Fiske believed he deserved credit that was denied him. Sims, for example, lauded Percy Scott for improving naval marksmanship. Fiske told Sims that while he appreciated what Scott and Sims had done, his invention and the introduction of the naval telescopic sight was as great a factor in improving marksmanship as was Scott's system of training. Therefore, Fiske continued, "If you see your way clear to giving me any credit, along with Admiral Scott . . . —why—I should not be displeased. . . ." He also indicated that Sims was in the same boat, "in a way." If a promotion board looked only at Sims's official record, Fiske asked, "What have you got to show for all your work?"[17] Fiske either knew more than he let on or made a brilliant guess, for as described below, Sims's official record was brought up to date only on direct order of the president.

Early in 1907, most likely, Sims wrote a "Memorandum on Fiske's Work, 1904–1907." It reads in part:

> If the story of my naval activities is written up, I hope particular pains

will be taken to give Fiske credit for the original and disinterested work he did in our progress from inefficiency to relative efficiency.

He is one of the few thinkers in the navy. Also a natural inventor. He devised the first telescope sight, greatly improved the range finder, invented the stadimeter and many other "machines." His writings are well known. His vision as to the fundamental necessities of gunnery was always sound, and if attention had been given to his criticism and suggestions, our reforms would have been started earlier and would have progressed more rapidly. That they did not do so was due chiefly to the character of the man—to an innate kindliness that largely disqualified him as a fighter. He could not bring himself to condemn those who opposed him, even when he was perfectly aware that they were dishonestly defending personal reputations endangered by his criticism of their mistakes. . . .

The chiefs of bureaus were the official judges of their own work. They almost always resisted criticism, and as the civilian secretary accepts their decisions because they are legally his military advisers, it was impossible even to get a hearing. . . . Fiske's criticism and recommendations were successfully resisted, and the only hope of progress was through a "demonstration of this condition of affairs," and a consequent discrediting of the resisting P.D.s. Even this would probably not have succeeded without the influence of President Roosevelt and the publication of the mistakes in the press. . . .[18]

As Sims said, Fiske—one of a handful of officers who made constructive suggestions for improving both naval material and administration—lacked Sims's aggressiveness (if not vindictive manner) and the important contact with President Roosevelt. Fiske, therefore, used his pen to reach the professional naval community. His persistent and continuing demand for a naval general staff, a subject discussed in part in the next chapter, would get him in trouble in 1913, when he became the aide for operations, because he challenged civilian control over the military.

In 1906, almost fifty-two years old and having served in the navy for thirty-two years, Fiske was understandably unhappy: he was still a commander and would be retired by age before being considered for flag rank. Moreover, he might well find it extremely difficult to handle a ship 410 feet long, with but a 21-foot beam, and as fast as the 7,375-ton *Minneapolis*. When he assumed command of this protected cruiser, therefore, on 4 June 1906, he felt that his crew was looking upon the last days of a condemned man.[19] In spite of his fears, however, he soon excelled in ship handling.

After the *Minneapolis* served as the flagship for the Naval Academy practice squadron during the summer of 1906, Fiske assumed command of a temporary fifth cruiser division participating in a fleet review by President Roosevelt on 3 September in Oyster Bay. Since he made no errors and the review went well, Fiske felt relieved.[20] He then transported some marines to Cuba, where they were to preserve order during the presidential election. En route, he was involved in such an interesting rescue of a shipwrecked mariner that he wrote a description of it for the *Naval Institute Proceedings*.[21]

Although American troops remained in Cuba for three years, most American ships were withdrawn quickly. The *Minneapolis* was ordered to Philadelphia to be decommissioned, and Fiske was sent to command the 3,500-ton monitor *Arkansas* at the Naval Academy. He approved the last log entries of the *Minneapolis* on 17 November. For his service on her he received a fitness report grade of 4.0.

Because he expected to be promoted to captain in about eight months, Fiske looked forward merely to training midshipmen during the winter and then serving with their training squadron the next summer before being transferred.

Unlike many commanding officers, Fiske frequently gave up the conn so that his officers could learn shiphandling. His executive officer, Yates Stirling, for example, had commanded nothing larger than a 250-ton gunboat, yet Fiske let him "drive" the *Arkansas* for extended periods even though in one instance he almost stranded her.[22]

During his pleasant but professionally dull duty, Fiske wrote an article in which he suggested that ships could sail safely in fog if they were connected by telephones.[23] Meanwhile, he was authorized by the Bureau of Ordnance to secure his turret range finder on the *Arkansas* and to expend five 12-inch shells. Lt. Comdr. G. W. Williams, sent to compare the accuracy of his apparatus with a Barr and Stroud range finder, found the two substantially comparable. He reported that Fiske's apparatus could stand the concussion but that its placement atop a turret violated "the adopted principle of central ship fire control." He therefore disapproved Fiske's system. Fiske remonstrated with the bureau, stating that he was merely trying to provide an accurate range finder for a turret. If a ship's fire director was destroyed in battle, the fight could still continue from single turrets. He never received a reply—yet in later years his turret range finders were fitted to all new battleships.[24]

Fiske also tried to learn how to ascertain the location of a ship when the horizon could not be seen by measuring the altitude of a heavenly body and the distance to another ship whose angle to the horizon was known.

For his efforts he received a commendatory letter from the superintendent of the Naval Observatory and high praise in the *Army and Navy Journal.*[25]

While the *Arkansas* was anchored at Bath, Maine, Fiske received orders to proceed to Washington for a physical examination for promotion to captain. Though they found him greatly underweight, doctors reported that he was in excellent health for a man of fifty-three. Of the thirty men with whom Fiske had graduated from the Naval Academy in 1874, only four—all captains—remained on duty. On 29 August 1907, Fiske was placed on waiting orders. For his duty in command of the Naval Academy Practice Squadron, Thomas B. Howard graded him 4.0—"excellent."

Early in October Jo Fiske became ill. Although she began to improve slowly, Fiske realized that he must soon leave her for new duty. He called at the Bureau of Navigation and learned that he was to command the *Illinois,* one of the battleships to start on a round-the-world cruise in December. In late October Jo became so gravely ill that her doctors said she might not live despite an operation. Fiske was in a personal and professional predicament: he would not leave Jo, yet to decline his new command could spell professional suicide. In a personal letter, he asked Rear Adm. Willard H. Brownson, chief of the Bureau of Navigation, to give him command of a ship near his home. If this could not be done, Fiske said he would accept command of the *Illinois.* The sympathetic Brownson detailed him to temporary recruiting duty in New York City,[26] for which service he was given a grade of 4.0.

During the winter of 1907, while Jo improved slowly, Fiske found time to work with his turret range finder and horizometer at the Western Electric Company—work he did entirely at his own expense. Once the range finder gave accurate readings, he asked the Bureau of Ordnance to test it for the shocks attendant the firing of guns. A board compared it, therefore, with two Barr and Stroud range finders. The report, dated 13 November, stated that Fiske's apparatus was as good as the Barr and Stroud equipment at short ranges and better at long ranges but condemned the mechanical arrangement by which Fiske had secured it inside a turret. Fiske's expostulation to the bureau proved unavailing, and the report stood.[27]

On 1 April 1908 Fiske was detailed as captain of the Philadelphia Navy Yard. With Jo still quite ill, he set up bachelor quarters; as one might guess, he took his turret range finder with him. On 12 May 1908, he protested to the Bureau of Ordnance the report of the last testing board. The bureau then established still another board which, on 19 June, not only upheld the previous report but recommended against further shipboard tests. Although

Fiske had improved his horizometer, it too was given an adverse report by the board. Not until 1910 would major new ships be fitted with Fiske's turret range finder, the basic patent for which he had taken out in 1900.[28]

As has already been noted, the chief of the Bureau of Ordnance, Newton E. Mason, obtained approval to install on the battleship *Virginia* experimental fire-control equipment purchased from Vickers. On 25 April 1907, Mason asked Robley D. Evans, commander in chief of the Atlantic Fleet, to report on her fire-control system. Evans appointed a board to observe the ship during battle practice held on 20 September.[29] The board's unanimous approval of the equipment and its recommendation that the equipment be installed on other ships fully endorsed contentions Fiske had been making for some time: the importance of centrally located fire-control stations below deck, a reliance on range finders instead of on spotting, and the necessity of improved communications. Consequently, late in 1907 fire-control systems were installed on the other ships that would make the world cruise. Subsequently, similar equipment was installed on all other major combatant ships.

Despite evident improvement in fleet gunnery, Fiske tenaciously persisted in arguing that spotting should be used merely as a refinement to range finder's ranges. Believing that "adoration of spotting was like the adoration of the British Navy"—because of Sir Percy Scott's claims—he wrote an article entitled "Courage and Prudence." He would place a ship's captain in an armored conning tower (from which he could look out via a periscope instead of through slits in its sides) and a man below the waterline of a ship at a table containing a plotting board. With information supplied by range finders, this man could calmly plot successive marks and quickly determine the relative course and speed of the enemy ship and pass the information to the gunners.[30] The idea smouldered until 1910, when a Fire Control Board adopted it and, by adding new equipment to that provided all big ships in 1908, made it the basis for modern fire control. It had taken twenty years of technical improvements in ordnance and communications equipment to bring to reality the idea for director-controlled, continuous-aim salvo firing which Fiske had first conceived in 1888.

Meanwhile, in March 1908, Fiske was directed to testify before the Senate Naval Affairs Committee. The committee was investigating aspects of ship construction with which he was unfamiliar, and he could not enlighten them. His first appearance before a congressional committee, some of whom surely must have wondered how he ever reached the grade of captain, lasted just ten minutes.[31]

Had Fiske so concentrated on his duties, inventions, and sick wife that he was unaware of what was going on in the navy, even of the battles in which he had great interest—battles for a naval general staff and for improved gunnery? This description would be inaccurate. While he tried to improve the material side of the navy through his inventions, Fiske had also used his pen to win converts, in both professional and popular circles, to the notion of a Navy Department organized and managed in a "scientific" way, in accordance with the best business practices of the day. That was the burden of his essay entitled "The Naval Profession," published in June 1907.[32]

Fiske began his long, discursive essay by noting that the United States had never prepared for war and that it was high time it did so. He held civilian leaders responsible for determining the nation's war plans, providing the logistics to support them in times both of peace and of war, and thus for the outcome of a war as well. Moreover, despite the works of Mahan, Philip H. Colomb (of the Royal Navy), and others, Fiske felt that no adequate book existed on naval strategy or tactics. While Mahan and Colomb pointed out mistakes to avoid in the future, what was needed, Fiske argued, was a study that applied naval principles to contemporary conditions. Germany led in the field, and if we fought her, he predicted, we would be "whipped."[33]

Fiske then discussed the duality in the naval profession, for an officer was "a scientific person as well as a sailor." Fiske claimed that the navy did not have the best equipment or highly trained men because of three factors: first, failure on the part of high ranking officers to realize the duality of their profession; second, failure of officers in general to correlate the military and the engineering arts; and third, the conservatism of the most senior officers. The remedy lay with the system used by large industrial concerns: that is, establish an experimental department to improve old appliances, invent new ones, and examine all schemes submitted by outside inventors and test those deemed worthy.[34]

Fiske confessed that he should have divided the essay into two parts, one on the naval profession, the other on naval strategy. Nevertheless, the work shows that at fifty-four years of age, he had reached an intellectual peak. He knew the naval history of the world and the international relations of nations. He used illustrations from mathematics, physics, and optics and mentioned a number of recently published works on engineering, ship construction, tactics, and strategy. And his reading in history convinced him that unprepared nations lost wars.

As an engineer—one half of the "dual profession"—Fiske would have to wait until 1915 before the navy created the "experimental department" he demanded. As a line officer—the other half of the "dual profession"—he would wait in vain for a general staff that would correlate the national and military interest. Reaction to Fiske's essay as voiced in the *Proceedings* ran the gamut from its being called "disturbing and useless," to paens of praise. It was given "Second Honorable Mention" (third prize) in the Naval Institute's annual essay contest.

Defects in naval material and organization revealed during and since the Spanish-American War engaged the attention of many both within and outside the navy; Fiske, Sims, and Luce were prominent among the former group. No real reforms, however, had been accomplished. Then, in an article entitled "The Needs of the Navy," Henry Reuterdahl, the American editor of *Jane's Fighting Ships* and a close friend of Sims's, so savagely condemned the newest American battleships that he aroused popular distrust of them. Ship armor was poorly placed, Reuterdahl said; the ships themselves were slow compared with those of the best foreign navies. Guns were often crowded into poorly protected spaces; ammunition hoists were too small and too slow to furnish all the shells needed in battle; and open shafts leading from the magazines to the turrets of the big guns and large ports on the turrets, he charged, eagerly invited disaster. Serious explosions on certain ships had already occurred, but Reuterdahl said it was the conservatism of the building bureaus that blocked the remedial actions demanded by a number of younger officers. Moreover, he wrote, American ships had no guns to protect them from torpedo attacks forward or astern. Battleships had too few torpedo tubes; the navy had only half the number of destroyers it needed; and the promotion system caused stagnation in the ranks. Reuterdahl placed the blame for these and other defects squarely on the chiefs of the building bureaus. Reuterdahl's (and by implication, Sims's) views reached a large audience. They were widely commented upon in the press and the subject of many editorials; they had a great impact on President Roosevelt and led to a Senate investigation.[35]

The chairman of the investigating committee was an antinavy man, Eugene Hale. Hale listened as various weaknesses were noted by reformers but did not inquire into their causes, which the insurgents attributed to poor naval administration. He suppressed some testimony unfavorable to the construction bureau chiefs and did not let Sims speak on the matter of naval reorganization. Thus the battle developed into one of line versus staff officers.[36]

What Fiske did not tell Hale, he had spelled out in his essay "The Naval Profession." Moreover, anything he did not say was part of the testimony of other line officers unassociated with the building bureaus. These views countered the testimony of the bureau chiefs and found much support in newspaper editorials and magazine articles.[37] Irked by the unexpected testimony and critical public comment, Hale dismissed the committee and failed to issue a report.[38]

On 9 June, in a letter to the secretary of the navy, Lt. Albert L. Key questioned the military requirements of battleships—both under construction and projected. A copy of the letter went to Sims. Sims alerted Roosevelt, who called a conference of approximately sixty officers at Newport on 21 July.[39] By calling the conference, Roosevelt appeared to support the insurgents. But thirty-eight of the fifty-seven members had helped design the ships in question, and, after two weeks of discussion, the conference voted to authorize only minor changes. The question of whether ships should be built to military specifications or for structural convenience was settled in favor of the conservative majority which would not admit error or reform the bureau system. The insurgents felt that Roosevelt had let them down. At Sims's prompting, however, Roosevelt intervened, and certain defects Key revealed were corrected in future construction.[40]

On 1 December, upon becoming secretary, Truman H. Newberry offered his own reform plan: enlarge the General Board to include representatives from all the bureaus, amalgamate the Bureau of Construction and Repair with the Bureau of Steam Engineering, and add several line officers to the new organization.[41] If conservatives could live with Newberry's plan, insurgents could not.[42] On Sims's advice, Roosevelt asked Congress to create a naval general staff. The president wanted authorization for two battleships, however, and had to avoid a fight over naval reorganization. In his customary way he pitted the contending forces against each other. After Congress okayed the battleships, Newberry appointed a Commission on Naval Reorganization in early January 1909. Although the members favored a general staff, Newberry had them sign a report to the contrary. The subsequent reports of Moody's board (appointed by Roosevelt on 22 January) and of Adm. William Swift's board (appointed by Secretary of the Navy George Meyer) will be discussed later, in connection with Fiske's 1913 appointment as aide for operations, one of the posts created by these reports.

Although he was unhappy with almost every aspect of the naval service, Fiske nevertheless had worked hard at being a naval officer. He had commanded the cruiser *Minneapolis* to his own satisfaction and that of his superiors. He had performed well as commander of a temporary cruiser division and had uncomplainingly used the squat *Arkansas* as a floating school. Meanwhile he had continued experiments with his turret range finder and won commendation for his development of the horizometer.

Because he would not leave Jo while she was ill, he had declined command of the *Illinois,* which was to sail with the Great White Fleet, and instead served ashore—first in recruiting duty, then as captain of the Philadelphia Navy Yard. When Jo's health improved, Fiske was determined to return to sea, even if on a cruiser instead of a battleship.

Fiske was extremely critical of the navy in his article on "The Naval Profession." Although reformers had gotten the material bureaus to provide better gunnery equipment, fire-control gear, and fire-control organization, conservatism was too strongly entrenched in the bureaus, the department, and in Congress to be overthrown at the time; and President Roosevelt placed the acquisition of additional battleships before naval reform. Nevertheless, in late 1908, the navy was on the verge of an administrative reorganization that would greatly affect Fiske.

9

THE CAPTAIN'S CRUISE
AND THE STARS OF AN ADMIRAL, 1910–1912

In December 1908, as the Great White Fleet neared San Francisco, Fiske's stadimeter was providing better ranges at short distances than did the fleet's range finders. A range finder "corrector" he provided was also tested and found to be satisfactory.[1] In his report to Rear Adm. Robley D. Evans, who was commanding the fleet, Ridley McLean, the fleet ordnance officer, supported Fiske by recommending that range finders be placed high on a mast, above funnel smoke yet free from vibration. Eagerly awaited, therefore, were tests of a new type of military mast (or fire-control tower), such as Fiske had suggested, on the new small battleships, the *Mississippi* and the *Idaho*.[2]

Early in June 1908, when his wife had recovered, Fiske asked for command of a battleship, even one cruising with the Great White Fleet. But the battleship commands were all filled. Would he take a new armored cruiser, the *Tennessee?* Fiske took the ship (on which, by coincidence, his experimental turret range finder had been installed), moved Jo and Caroline to Atlantic City, and left for San Francisco and an expected absence of two years.[3]

Fiske first took the *Tennessee*, flagship of the Second Division of the Pacific Fleet (under Rear Adm. Uriel Sebree), to Bremerton for alterations and repairs, particularly to the fire-control system, and then returned to San Francisco. The plan for the fleet was to go to Honolulu and Samoa, return to Honolulu, then go on to Magdalena Bay; its eight cruisers were to tow eight destroyers as an experiment and for practice. Fiske discounted the tactical value of the towing exercises and suspected that the reason for the voyage was to put a considerable fighting force near Japan while President Roosevelt handled the extremely sensitive problem of Japanese immigration.[4]

In preparation for target practice in Magdalena Bay, Fiske adjusted his range finder and corrector. The *Tennessee* finished eighth of the thirty ships, a ranking Fiske considered "most honorable."[5] Even though his officers considered him eccentric on the subject of range finders, Fiske concluded that the practice showed that full reliance should be placed on range finder ranges.[6]

While the First Division went to Valparaiso, Admiral Sebree took the Second to Coquimbo. On 20 January 1909, a fire was seen ashore. Having conducted fire drills when captain of the Philadelphia Navy Yard, Fiske obtained permission to command a fire brigade. The hotel was not saved, but perhaps the town was, and Sebree wrote Fiske and certain others letters of commendation.[7]

Irritated by an article in *Brassey's Naval Annual* for 1908 that attributed improvements in naval gunnery to Adm. Sir Percy Scott alone, Fiske wrote "The Invention and Development of the Naval Telescope Sight." Although he would not deny Scott any credit, he concluded that "credit for the accurate naval gunnery of the present day does not primarily belong to the *British* Navy, but to the *American* Navy; and . . . the naval gunnery of today did not have its birth on board the H.M.S. *Scylla*, on the Mediterranean Station, at some time *after 1898*, but on board the U.S.S. *Yorktown*, at Unalaska, on *September 22, 1892*."[8] The American navy was first to adopt the naval telescopic sight and the electrical range indicator. Tests with the electrical range indicator were carried on in 1893 and 1894; the gear was installed on various cruisers and battleships in June 1896; Fiske had even explained his methods in the *Naval Institute Proceedings* of June 1896. Moreover, the first ship to use fire control from aloft in battle was the *Petrel*, at the Battle of Manila Bay on 1 May 1898. Picked up by the public press, scientific magazines, and army and navy publications, Fiske's article offered a clear challenge to Scott and the British, yet it failed to elicit a single word from them.[9]

As the Second Division called at various ports on the west coast of Central America, Fiske requested another test of his turret range finder. The request picked up nine endorsements from the bureaus before it reached the General Board. Although the board noted that "the matter has been very thoroughly gone into by Boards appointed for that purpose and by the Bureau of Ordnance," it concluded that the turret range finder seemed "worthy of further consideration." It had taken the board ten years to finally see Fiske's point that a turret range finder was not a replacement for fire-control systems but merely a back-up device in case they were disabled or destroyed.[10]

On 19 April, after four hectic days of firing on the range at night and during the day (and after his customary Sunday inspection of ship and crew), Fiske pointed the *Tennessee* toward San Francisco. On 2 May, he took her to Bremerton for repairs and alterations that took until 20 August to complete. His pleasure at having done well during the first half of his "captain's cruise" increased when Jo and Carrie came to visit.[11]

When they learned that Sebree, now commander in chief of the Pacific Fleet, would cruise in the western Pacific, Jo and Caroline decided to visit Shanghai again and join Fiske there. While sailing westward, Fiske held frequent battle practice drills because he knew that good target scores best showed a ship's efficiency. When the fleet arrived in Manila Bay on 26 October, Sebree directed two of the squadrons to anchor and the third to go on the range. In turn, the ships of the Third Squadron—the *Tennessee, Washington, California, West Virginia,* and *Colorado*—held subcaliber practice, fired on the subcaliber range by day and night, and then engaged in both day and night main battery firing. Fiske always conned his ship while it was on the range. On 10 December, when firing had ended, the squadrons began making passage for China. After the Navy Department had studied the scores, it listed the *Vermont,* the *Tennessee,* and the *Maryland* as the best gunnery ships. The practice paid off. Secretary George Meyer sent commendatory letters to the various captains, executive officers, navigators, and gunnery officers. Fiske was exceedingly pleased to have received four such letters during his "captain's cruise."[12]

From Manila Bay the fleet proceeded to Shanghai, where Fiske was able to be with his family from 13 to 31 December. Jo and Caroline then went on to Yokohama, Fiske's next port of call, and together they visited Tokyo. On 6 January 1910, Fiske and Austin M. Knight, captain of the *Washington,* called officially on the Japanese minister of marine. Then Sebree and his captains were received by the Mikado himself. The fleet left Yokohama on 21 January. When it stopped at Honolulu, on 1 February, Jo and Caroline again joined "Captain Tennessee," as Fiske was called by the Japanese.[13] On 9 February, the *Tennessee,* the *Washington,* and the *California* left for Bremerton; Fiske was placed in charge of the *Tennessee* and the *Washington.* In his memoirs Fiske noted to himself:

> I am monarch of all I survey
> My right there is none to dispute.[14]

In addition to handling the *Tennessee* for eighteen months, Fiske built an automatic device that showed a ship astern the exact position of her rudder; he also began working on another device that showed the speed and direction of the engines. Although the first invention won endorsement by the Pacific Fleet chain of command, the department ordered him to remove it from the *Tennessee* "immediately." Fiske gave up trying to perfect the second instrument. The simple electric steering gear he devised, however, found some favor and was installed in a number of ships.[15] Moreover, on 6 January 1909, the department authorized battleship tests of his conning tower containing a periscope.

Fiske also wanted to have emergency orders for steering a ship and directions to the engines emanate from two stations below deck—one at the base of the conning tower, the other in after-steering. To this end he requested permission to alter the voice tubes from the *Tennessee's* conning tower to the engine room. He experimented with steering the *Minneapolis* and the *Tennessee* from after-steering and found places in these compartments in which magnetic compasses—the gyrocompass had not yet been invented—worked well. On 13 May 1909, the General Board told Secretary Meyer that Fiske's system should be installed on all ships.[16]

On 30 December 1908, successful tests were made of the new fire-control towers on board the *Idaho* and the *Mississippi*. Upon their return from the round-the-world cruise, all battleships were fitted with after-steering, new basket-mast fire-control towers, and improved fire-control communications systems.[17]

Just before he ended his tour in Washington, Sims gave Roosevelt a directive for appointing a board, including Alfred T. Mahan, Stephen B. Luce, and Richard Wainwright, that would recommend a plan to reorganize the Navy Department. Roosevelt asked Sims to sound out Mahan. Mahan recommended the establishment of a general staff in which a chief of staff, although always subordinate to the secretary, would personally advise the secretary.[18] Roosevelt appointed the Mahan board, but (as Fiske predicted) Sims had been made to pay for severely criticizing those responsible for ship construction and gunnery equipment. Most of his reports and recommendations were destroyed by those who received them, and his fitness reports did not give him credit for much of the work he had done since 1897. Roosevelt immediately directed Secretary Newberry to correct Sims's record; Newberry complied.[19] On the back of the completed record Sims wrote: "This gives the best general account of the trials and tribulations a reformer must face—bureaucratic conceit, resistance to criticisms, threats of punishment, etc."[20] Two days later, on 25 February, he left the Office of Target Practice, which he had occupied for six years, to take command of the battleship *Minnesota*. Although Sims was the youngest man ever to be given such a command, his departure from Washington meant that insurgents were no longer welcome in the Office of Target Practice.

While Fiske, Sims, and other reformers tried to get rid of conservative bureau chiefs, the chiefs, in turn, tried to remove or at least diminish the insurgents' influence. Their continuing battle showed that the reform effort could move from matters of principle to attacks on those in authority, and that in the process some heads would be cracked—Sims's almost was and Fiske's would be after his appointment as aide for operations.

Having had command for a year and a half, the average length of a captain's cruise, Fiske fully expected to be detached from the *Tennessee*, meet his family in San Francisco, and return to New York. Instead he was given command of the *South Dakota* and the *Tennessee* and was directed to take them via the Straits of Magellan to Maldonado, Uruguay, and report to Rear Adm. Sidney H. Staunton, commander of the Special Service Squadron of the Atlantic Fleet. So while his family proceeded to New York, Fiske headed south. With the *South Dakota* maintaining proper course and speed, he now found time occasionally to think on various subjects.

In his 1907 essay entitled "The Naval Profession" he had compared the power of a ship with that of an army. The power was, of course, mechanical. The thought then came to him that what Mahan called "sea power" was really naval power—a conclusion to which Mahan most certainly would object. As time provided, Fiske worked on an article analyzing sea power; he would show that it was naval power and then prove that naval power was essentially mechanical power.

The cruise provided time for other observations as well. In the Straits of Magellan, albatross followed his ship until it was far into the Atlantic. Amazed at the ease with which they kept up, Fiske vowed to learn about "aeroplanes" at his earliest opportunity because he saw their tremendous value in time of war.[21]

When Admiral Staunton shifted his flag to the *Tennessee*, Fiske readily agreed to serve as his chief of staff and quickly undertook, as his first task, to arrange for the visit of the Special Service Squadron at the Argentine government's centennial celebration.[22] Meanwhile he received a letter from the (prospective) first aide for operations, Richard Wainwright, who spoke for Adm. George Dewey as well. Wainwright asked whether Fiske would serve on the General Board. Fiske was overjoyed, for serving on the board was the best shore duty a captain could have if he cherished aspirations of flying a flag at sea. Moreover his selection meant a stamp of official approval: Fiske knew how carefully Dewey chose his coworkers.[23] After being relieved on 13 August, Fiske had himself taken ashore; he had finished his captain's cruise.

On 25 August 1910, Fiske reported for duty with the General Board, which was meeting at the Naval War College from 1 July to 1 October. Its eight members formed the executive committee and, with a number of ex-officio members, served on various standing and ad hoc committees. In

October, when the board returned to Washington, the Fiskes moved into a pleasant downtown apartment.

While on duty with the board, Fiske would decide many technical questions and also help write war plans and personnel legislation. Of particular interest to him were naval aviation, fire-control matters, and Elmer A. Sperry's work on gyroscopes. When the Bureau of Steam Engineering requested authority to requisition an aircraft for the cruiser *Chester,* he agreed with the board that "the value of aeroplanes for use in naval warfare should be investigated without delay and recommend[ed] that the Department approve the request."[24] He was delighted too that the board had approved plans for placing revolving fire-control towers atop the large conning towers on the newest battleships, the *Utah* and the *Florida,* and had approved four periscopes for the conning tower of the battleship *Pennsylvania,* which would be laid down on 27 October 1913.[25] Twenty-three years after Fiske had first made the suggestion, it had finally been adopted.

Assigned originally to material—ships, guns, and the like—Fiske learned about the work of men like Elmer A. Sperry. While working on a telemeter system for fire control that would include gyrocompasses, Sperry had hit upon the gyro-repeater system that, once perfected, would revolutionize fire control. The gyro itself would greatly facilitate the steering of ships and had possibilities for improving ship stability. The system had not yet been perfected, but both the chief of the Bureau of Ordnance and the General Board encouraged Sperry to improve his work.[26]

In December 1910, Fiske was put in charge of the Second Committee, the war plans section. To his amazement, he could find no war plans, no means of drafting them, or anyone who knew how to do so. The sole exception was Capt. Templin Potts, who had spent three years as naval attaché in Germany before becoming the director of the Office of Naval Intelligence. After hearing Potts describe the German naval staff system, Fiske began to regard naval officers as cases of "arrested development." Since the American navy had tactical drills but no fleet tactics, something had to be done.[27]

American war plans were made by a cooperative effort. The Office of Naval Intelligence provided an information section; the war plans committee of the General Board added administrative, operating, logistical, and other advice; and then the whole scheme was tried out on the game board at the Naval War College. The two major extant plans were the Atlantic War Plan and the Asiatic War Plan. On 1 October 1910, Meyer directed that the plans be made current, adding that they should not only get a fleet to an operating area but should "include the strategic plan recommended after arrival of the fleet near the scene of hostilities."[28] With the war plans brought up to date, in March 1911, Dewey told Meyer that "the General Board designates Germany as the next country against which a naval war plan should be formulated."[29]

Fiske found these "war portfolios," as Meyer called them, very disappointing. They were too general in character and left too many options to a fleet commander. Their writing was divided between two agencies in Washington and one in Newport. Fiske disagreed with Meyer's contention that "it is not considered that political discussions or economic dissertations on the probable causes or effects of the war [in the war plan] are desirable." Fiske also supported the War College view that every strategic plan should include an administrative war plan, that is, a plan by which a commander in chief could carry out the strategic plan. Last, he strenuously supported the creation of a Council of National Defense that would coordinate the foreign policy, military, and logistical requirements for war. Only after the nation's statesmen had determined national policy, Fiske asserted, could the military agencies make proper strategic plans.[30] Rep. Richmond Pearson Hobson, a Democrat from Alabama, introduced the necessary legislation in 1911. The bill died but, as will be seen, the idea finally bore fruit in 1915.

Fiske quickly realized that the General Board had little influence in guiding national naval strategy. It lacked a statutory basis. Its advice must please the secretary of the navy without provoking the bureau of chiefs. To avoid a conflict between the board and the chiefs, Meyer instituted an aide system in October 1909: four high-ranking officers would advise him on personnel, operations, material, and inspections; two of them—the aides for operations and for material—were to be members of the board.

Fiske kept the promise he had made to himself soon after reaching Washington to take up the study of aeronautics, saying "There was not much to learn for a man who had the knowledge of mechanics that I had gradually acquired in my experience as inventor and navy officer; in fact, I was surprised to find how little there was to learn, and how little had been done, especially by armies and navies, and especially by our army and navy."[31] The lack of adequate war plans and the possibilities of aviation prompted him to suggest, with respect to what passed for a war plan against Japan, barring the landing of Japanese amphibious forces in the Philippines by destroying them with aircraft. Taking off from four stations he would establish on Luzon, each squadron would include one hundred or more aircraft and associated equipment and personnel. After gaining approval from Dewey and several board members, Fiske proposed the idea to the full board. There Wainwright protested so emphatically against taking up the time of the board with "wild-cat schemes" that he demurred. Four years later, at the beginning of the Great War, Fiske thought it unfortunate that the board had not adopted his recommendations for developing naval aviation. Had it done so, and had Meyer approved, the United States might have entered the war with a naval air armada that could have greatly hastened the end of the war.

After reading Fiske's memoirs, published in 1919, Wainwright noted that Fiske had advocated the use of aircraft in 1911, "at a time when the efficiency of the airplane, even as a scout, was all to be developed in the future. . . . To prophesy for the future the head may be in the clouds but to provide for the present the feet must be firm on the ground."[32] Fiske retorted: "The mere fact that a certain apparatus is [presently] unreliable is no reason for refusing to try to develop it and make it reliable."[33]

One of many ideas Fiske had postponed perfecting while commanding the *Tennessee* was a "combined range finder and turret." Upon joining the General Board, he learned that a Fire Control Board had recommended in 1910 that a turret range finder be placed in a battleship then under construction and that later battleships be furnished with the devices if they proved successful. The innovation was successful, and all new battleships after 1911 were provided with turret range finders. In addition, the Fire Control Board recommended adoption of the plotting system Fiske had suggested in his essay entitled "Courage and Prudence," written three years earlier. Although his pioneering experiments with the turret range finder had cost him $6,000, he felt that the work had not been in vain. Two of his important inventions had been adopted, and he was content. Nevertheless he was so disturbed that the last fire-control board had not mentioned him as the inventor of the telescopic sight that he wrote an article, entitled "The Relative Importance of Turret and Telescope Sight," to set the record straight.[34]

As already noted, on the *Tennessee* Fiske had given considerable thought to the theory that navies and armies were mere improvements over primitive weapons used by savages. Toward the end of his cruise he wrote up his ideas and submitted them under the title "Naval Power" in the prize contest held by the Naval Institute.[35] He stated that Mahan had confused sea power and naval power: a merchant marine in time of war, for example, was a liability. Moreover, sea power should be thought of in terms of mechanical power which could be managed in two ways, by "controllability" and "directability." Cain's club and a modern navy, Fiske argued, were thus analogous.

A navy must possess more mechanical power than an army, Fiske continued, because of the power needed to move the naval element. Thus a battleship like the *Arkansas* was more powerful than an army of six hundred thousand men. Then, in marked contrast to his pugnacious spirit, he asserted that the primary use of a navy was defensive. The American navy, Fiske wrote, must defend the nation not only against invasion but against blockade as well. We were now an industrial, not an agrarian nation; and because the various elements that made industrial production possible were interdependent, the nation's productivity would be vastly disrupted even if some small part were damaged or destroyed. Only actual invasion could produce greater damage than a blockade, Fiske said. It was less the Union army that won the Civil War, he added, than the Union navy, which made it impossible for the Confederacy to arm, provision, and equip its army.[36]

He warned against letting the American navy fall behind that of potential enemies because a powerful navy was not only a defense in time of war but a deterrent to war. We must look ahead, Fiske wrote, at least ten years. While ships and guns could be built in perhaps a quarter of that time, it would take ten years "at least" to produce men who could handle the navy skillfully and who possessed the mental and spiritual qualities needed to direct a war. Cain had only his club to handle; modern navies were large aggregates of complicated machines that must be operated with a much greater skill.[37]

With some prescience, if not as a devotee of economic determinism, Fiske predicted that the United States would increase her trade, grow more prosperous with time, and engage in a worldwide contest for wealth that would bring about friction and possibly war. Instead of building a strong navy to take unjust advantage of weaker nations, the United States must use her navy to prevent other nations from forcibly despoiling her wealth and glory. With respect to other naval powers, he advocated parity with the richest and strongest of them, particularly with Great Britain.[38]

The section of the essay most often reprinted or made the subject of editorials was its eloquent plea for more liberal treatment by the navy of inventors. As yet, the navy wanted inventors to demonstrate working models and did not sponsor inventions through navy-funded development. Fiske believed it was the duty of the navy to encourage not merely engineering skills and mechanical ingenuity but real invention. "We must hold as high an ideal in this matter as we do in the matters of strategy, tactics, and engineering."[39] The navy, Fiske concluded, should treat inventors as sane and reputable men who sought to be useful to the service.

Fiske's essay won "honorable mention," but few Americans paid much attention to it, and most officers did not take him seriously. This didn't bother Fiske. He was pleased that the General Board did not reprimand him for asserting that the primary purpose of a navy was to prevent blockade

and was happy when the essay was translated for some foreign service maga-
zines. Furthermore, five years later Waldemar Kaempffert, editor of *Popular
Science Monthly*, asked him to rewrite the section of the essay that com-
pared the power of navies and armies. He did so, and in October 1915
Kaempffert ran the article under the title "If Battleships Ran on Land."
It attracted attention in the United States and also in English and European
service journals.[40] It was probably coincidence that about a year later the
British produced tanks, or what Fiske called "land battleships."

While at Newport with the General Board during the spring of 1911,
Fiske passed his physical examination for promotion to rear admiral (even
though he weighed only 132 pounds, the vision in his right eye was only
14/20, and the hearing in his left ear was badly impaired). Thus, the physically slightest of the thirty men in his academy class, and the one whose
last year had been most untraditional, was the only one to become a rear
admiral. He had spent 53 percent of his nearly four years as a captain on
sea duty; and on his fitness reports for the year he spent on the General
Board Dewey marked him 4.0—excellent in all respects.

Wainwright, president of the Naval Institute, was to retire from the
service in December 1911; his successor as aide for operations would be
Rear Adm. Charles E. Vreeland. Fiske voted for Vreeland as president at
the board's annual meeting held in October, only to learn on 14 October
that he was the new choice. Of course he was delighted to serve—and
eventually held the post longer than any other man.

In the meantime, on 1 October, Fiske received coveted orders to command a division of the fleet. On 21 October, aboard the cruiser *Washington*
anchored at Norfolk, he assumed command of the Fifth Division. As his
two-star flag fluttered in a slight breeze and he received a thirteen-gun
salute, he recalled a sentence he had once read: "To most naval officers the
stars of an Admiral are as unattainable as the stars of the sky."[41]

Until Wainwright had become aide for operations, a fleet commander
was also burdened with the tactical and administrative duties of a division
although the other division commanders had little to do. To qualify the
junior flag officers for higher command, Wainwright held division commanders responsible for the efficiency of their ships. Thus, Fiske was one
of the earliest division commanders to serve while fleet administration was
being decentralized and the opportunity to exercise command was increased.

With his division, consisting of the *Washington*, the *Tennessee*, the
North Carolina, and the *Montana*, Fiske joined Rear Adm. Hugo Osterhaus,
commander in chief of the North Atlantic Fleet, for a naval review in

October on the Hudson River. No sooner had the fleet reached the Southern Drill Grounds than Fiske was ordered to take the American minister to San Domingo, William W. Russell (who was in Washington on leave), to that island republic, where there was considerable confusion following the assassination of its president. Russell, a Naval Academy graduate several years younger than Fiske, had left the navy to enter the diplomatic service. Fiske found him a delightful shipmate. Soon after Russell had restored tranquility, with "the assistance of Admiral Fiske," Secretary of State Philander C. Knox thanked Meyer for forwarding a report Fiske made and also thanked Fiske for his excellent work.[42]

After two gunboats had been sent to relieve his cruisers, Fiske returned to Norfolk and learned that the aide for operations wished to see him. In Washington he was told that his division would participate in a strategic fleet game. As Fiske's ships stood out of Hampton Roads on 3 January 1912, portents of a forthcoming gale abounded. Two days later, with the "enemy" found, Fiske used the superior speed of the *Washington* to cut off the battleship *Rhode Island* from the rest of the enemy force. Violent winds and rough seas soon made it impracticable to carry out the planned operations, yet Fiske proceeded at thirteen knots all one night in an attempt to find Adm. Thomas Howard, who soon called off the exercises because of the bad weather.

Once again Fiske was directed to proceed to Washington for new orders. These merely involved taking the *Washington* and the *North Carolina* to Key West to help celebrate the completion of the railroad laid on bridges linking the Florida Keys. No large ship had dared transit the narrow and shallow channel to Key West. At great risk, Fiske inched his way through, and after that time large ships used the harbor. Having proved his point, and the celebration finished, Fiske took the *Washington* to the Norfolk Navy Yard for alterations in cabin arrangements to accommodate Secretary of State Knox, who would visit Central America.

Having rapidly learned about aircraft, Fiske wondered whether the "flying boat" being developed by Glenn Curtiss could launch torpedoes against transports and even against battleships. Could it be, he asked his old friend Park Benjamin, that such a simple idea as dropping torpedoes from aircraft had not been patented? Benjamin, who kept track of aeronautical patents, was sure it had not. Fiske therefore told Benjamin that he had "invented not only a new weapon, but a *New Method of Warfare*" and asked for patents covering practically everything that could be dropped from a plane. When the Patent Office objected, Fiske narrowed his definition but still received a strong basic patent, dated 16 July 1912; it covered attaching a torpedo to an aircraft and included the mechanical means for dropping, starting, and directing it at a surface target.[43] *2/03/2*

In April 1912, when Admiral Howard left the Third Division of battleships to go on shore duty, Fiske replaced him as commander. The North Atlantic Fleet contained two squadrons, with the senior division commander in charge of the second. While his first squadron was at Newport in the early part of May, Fiske took the eight battleships from Provincetown to Salem Harbor. There, late in the afternoon of 10 May, a hydroplane approached his flagship, the *Georgia*. As it landed gracefully astern, Fiske sent a messenger by boat to invite its two occupants aboard. His invitation was accepted by W. Starling Burgess and Phillips Ward Page. Arrangements were soon made to have Page drop alongside the *Georgia* the following morning and take Fiske up. Although he kept the matter secret, the morning papers were full of stories about the "flying admiral"; Fiske was the first American admiral, in official uniform, to fly. At any rate, less than two minutes after getting aboard, he was skimming over the water at a tremendous speed and enjoying a sensation now familiar to most Americans —the sharp rise, the increasing speed, and finally the enlarged perspective provided by high altitude. Fiske went up, of course, to learn whether airplanes could carry and drop bombs and to test the practicability of dropping torpedoes from them given the noise, movement, and confusion that surrounded the pilot. The only distraction he noted was the noise of the motor, to which he adjusted rapidly; he found the plane's motions less jerky than those of a destroyer. As he passed over a string of boats carrying men back from the beach to their ships, Fiske told himself that a few bombs could prevent any boat from reaching the ships. What impressed him most was the quickness of the whole flight, for he was gone from his ship for only fifteen minutes, during five of which he had actually been airborne. Yet in that five minutes he had been flown around and over the entire harbor and town of Salem. Very greatly impressed by his experience, he immediately wrote an official report to the Navy Department and asserted that the airplane could be made a very important naval weapon.[44]

While the fleet did exercises, Fiske experimented with his horizometer, only to conclude that "though I continually improved the instrument, the requirements of naval gunnery increased more rapidly than my improvements advanced."[45] But he persisted with his work on range finding and in October 1912 published an article entitled "The Mean Point of Impact" that stressed the need for accuracy. According to Fiske, the article aroused both officers and men to increased diligence in range finding and affected the army as well, for the chief of artillery ordered every officer in the Coast Artillery to study the article.[46]

When the senior division commander was sent to shore duty, Fiske became second in command of the fleet. In this exalted billet he conducted both the first squadron and the first division during night fleet drills with conspicuous success. With the exception of the flagship of the fleet commander, he had directed the operations of twelve battleships and sixteen destroyers. In another instance, he was the victor in a war game involving a "friendly" and an "enemy" force. In still another instance, he directed half of the fleet in "capping the 'T'" of the "enemy." At the end of the four war games held that summer, Fiske was declared the winner of them all.

For a number of years Fiske had experimented with making optical instruments, among them one that would do way with towed targets for target practice. Early in 1912, during a shoot, it occurred to him that a small glass prism placed before a telescope sight would refract light rays a number of degrees to the right or left. Looking through the telescope one would not see the ship being used as a target because one's vision would be directed to the right or left of it. He had invented "check fire," as navy hands call it after the admonition that if an observer sees the ship being used as a target he will call out "check fire." The Bureau of Ordnance approved his request to conduct tests, and in succession he fired 6-inch shots "at" a cruiser and 12-inch shots "at" the dreadnought *Delaware*. A problem of which he was aware—that the prism must be perfectly horizontal lest the light rays entering it be tilted up or down—was tackled at his request by Elmer Sperry, who said he could construct a gyroscope that would keep the prisms truly horizontal.[47]

In October 1912, Fiske participated in the naval review of the fleet held on the Hudson River. While he was in New York City, Edward Marshall, a *New York Times* reporter, asked to interview him on the status of the navy. Fiske gladly obliged, and the Sunday *Times* (13 October) devoted an entire page to the interview. He could have been critical about the navy on many, many scores, yet he had the good judgment to merely extol the navy for what it had done and was doing. One exception was the field of aeronautics, in which he believed it could be doing better.[48]

Following the review, the fleet visited Charleston before returning to Norfolk, where speculation brewed about Osterhaus's relief. Although he was second in command, Fiske did not apply for the post because he knew that Rear Adm. Charles J. Badger, senior to him, wanted to command the fleet. After Badger was selected, Fiske was detailed to relieve him as aide for inspections.

In his fitness reports, Osterhaus rated Fiske between 3.8 and 4.0. Among the comments were that Fiske had "made [a] considerable study of naval strategy . . . [and that he was an] inventor . . . calm—even tempered—forceful—bold and painstaking."

Fiske's last duty at sea was to witness his two star flag slowly hauled down the mast of the *Florida*. It was given to him by the captain of the ship. Tucking it under his arm, he was taken ashore in what had been his barge, and he grew somewhat philosophical, saying,

> Life has great changes for all of us. But few changes are as great as when an admiral leaves his flagship behind him forever, and leaves behind him, also forever, the life of the sea, and the charm of the sea, and the danger and the splendor, and that wonderful thing—command.[49]

Pleading the illness of Mrs. Fiske as a reason for declining command of a battleship that was to make a world cruise, Fiske sailed the *Tennessee* practically around the world without incident and compiled a creditable performance at target practice. He revealed great personal courage in fighting a hotel fire; performed well as chief of staff to Admiral Staunton; defended himself against claims that Sir Percy Scott had been the first to obtain the idea and provide the equipment needed for director-controlled, continuous-aim fire; sided with those who urged creation of a central station below deck from which to evaluate information received from range finders and other equipment and send firing directions to the guns; conceived of the possibility of after-steering; and suggested an armored conning tower with a periscope through its top. No greater compliment could be paid him than Admiral Dewey's request to serve on the General Board.

Fiske's tour with the board permitted him to seek solutions to the most challenging problems facing the navy. Most important, he had seen how war plans were drafted and had realized the dire need to provide an administrative section for them—one under which the bureaus, and through them the productive capacity of the nation, could be geared to provide the logistic support for plans actually implemented. Quick to see the value of aircraft for war purposes, Fiske was among the first to suggest its use in time of war. He had also patented a torpedo plane. His turret range finder and many of his ideas concerning fire control and the structure and equipment of fire-control and conning towers were adopted by the fleet. He had loudly proclaimed the need for a naval research-and-development program. He had been elected president of the U.S. Naval Institute. Promoted to rear admiral, he had successfully handled cruiser and battleship divisions. At the age of fifty-eight, there were few other billets Fiske could fill, either afloat or ashore. For the foreseeable future, he would serve in Washington as one of the aides to the secretary of the navy.

10

IN THE LION'S DEN, 1912–1914

On 13 July 1909, Secretary of the Navy George Meyer appointed a board composed entirely of naval officers, under the direction of Rear Adm. William Swift, to report on naval reorganization. The board, which sat from 2 August to 11 October, in essence followed the recommendations of the Moody board. Some of the changes could be implemented by administrative action, others required legislation.[1] Feeling that he would be unable to obtain new legislation, Meyer instituted by administrative directive a system of four aides—for operations, material, inspections, and personnel. Each aide would coordinate the work of those bureaus in his area of responsibility, and together would serve the secretary as a cabinet. Meyer left the General Board unchanged but transferred to it the functions of the Board on Construction, which he disbanded. His reforms greatly pleased insurgents old and new because line, rather than staff, officers would serve as the aides and because each aide chosen was a die-hard insurgent.[2]

Because the aide system was instituted while Congress was not in session, it lacked legal sanction; and, of course, it was opposed by the bureau chiefs and their longtime congressional allies. Meyer, supported by Adm. George Dewey, asked for a year's trial. If Congress changed the system, then Congress—rather than he—would be responsible to the country. When Congress failed to act, the reorganization remained in operation, but friends of the bureaus in Congress blocked all attempts to legalize it.[3] Moreover, because the aides were denied executive and administrative duties, they could seek only to "coordinate" the bureaus. Yet for the first time since the adoption of the bureau system in 1842, the fleet was placed under the control of a military man. The aide for operations, Richard Wainwright, was soon so overworked that Bradley A. Fiske and the other insurgents recognized that he needed several assistants.[4]

The aide system had been in effect for three years when Fiske became the aide for inspections on 6 January 1913. With evident surprise he told his diary on 8 February, just one month later, "Secretary Meyer sent for me about 3 p.m. and gave me the astonishing information that he wished me to assume the duties of Aid for Operations on Monday! Today is Saturday!" And on 11 February: "I foresee a strenuous time, especially when the new Sec[retary] comes. Captain [William F.] Fullam has been told to report as Aid for Inspections in my place."[5]

Fiske had been in his new office for less than a week when William S. Sims wrote Fullam that he must lead the insurgents' fight in the department because "the new Aide for Operations [Fiske], admirable though he be intellectually, professionally, and personally, is constitutionally opposed to conflict of any kind."[6] Sims would eventually eat those words. Moreover, Fiske would be challenged less by Fullam than by Albert Gustavus Winterhalter, the hard-driving aide for material, as the adviser in whom Josephus Daniels, the new secretary of the navy, would place his utmost trust and confidence.[7]

Fiske was responsible for war plans and the efficient operation of the entire fleet. In addition, he and Winterhalter acted as the liaison between Daniels's aides and the General Board.. In Fiske's division were the Office of Naval Intelligence, Office of Target Practice and Steaming Competitions, the Naval War College, and a section of Movements of the Fleet. Along with the other aides, he was a member of the secretary's Advisory Council, which considered all questions affecting departmental policies and methods of coordinating the work of the divisions. But questions of other kinds were also discussed—strategic, logistical, administrative, legislative. In addition to holding meetings almost daily, the aides met twice a week with the executive committee of the General Board, weekly with the secretary of the navy, and monthly with all the bureau chiefs and the secretary. As Meyer directed, all communications between bureau chiefs and the secretary and assistant secretary must pass through the appropriate aide; all conclusions and recommendations reached by the aides in their individual or collective capacities would be forwarded to the secretary and assistant secretary.[8]

As the senior liaison man between the secretary and the General Board, Fiske submitted matters to the board for study; as a member of the board, he rendered judgment on a bewildering variety of subjects. He reported to the secretary whether a particular board recommendation was unanimous or provided a tally of the votes. Both he and the secretary thus knew the degree of unanimity existing between the aides and the board.[9]

Fiske thought that although improved by Meyer, the organization of the department could be improved still further. Additional technical knowledge was needed to build and operate new ships such as the *Arkansas* and the *Wyoming* (which displaced 26,000 tons and fired so fast and so far that spotters could not control their firing).[10] Despite his many duties, Fiske continued to try to invent equipment to permit director-controlled continuous-aim fire at long ranges. He also tried to persuade Sims to serve again as director of target practice, but Sims declined.[11] Although Meyer was served by Fiske for only two months—too short a time for Meyer to make "a decided comment"—he wrote that Fiske "shows excellent comprehension of his duties."

On 4 March 1913, following the presidential inauguration ceremonies, the new secretary, Daniels, made a courtesy call on Meyer. Meyer suggested that he "keep the power to direct the Navy here" and for emphasis slapped his desk. He called the aide system "the best organization that possibly could be effected" and warned Daniels to permit no change that would take control of the navy out of his hands.[12]

Fiske believed Meyer to be a modest man, in no sense "stuck up."[13] He did not have to be a physicist or engineer to be an administrator; nevertheless, knowledge of these fields would enable him to understand clearly the recommendations made to him by engineers, ordnance officers, and the like and be able to talk with them in their own language.[14] How about Daniels, a newspaper man? At a reception Daniels held for the aides, Fiske "found Mr. Daniels to be an extremely attractive man, with a geniality of manner and an evident companionableness that were in marked contrast to the cold manner and New England reserve of Mr. Meyer." Until the end of 1914, Fiske's diary abounds with such remarks: Daniels "was a man of refinement, sympathy, and good nature, whose serenity was rarely ruffled and whose politeness was unfailing."[15] Nevertheless, as early as 10 April 1913 Fiske was ready to resign.

Daniels—a Jeffersonian Democrat, a devout Methodist, a prohibitionist, and a white supremacist—knew that his political radicalism and fundamentalist morality sat badly with the admirals, whom he assumed were conservative. He saw the navy as a hidebound institution that persisted in keeping its outmoded traditions and customs; he therefore questioned everything his admirals told him. He chose Victor Blue to be the chief of the Bureau of Navigation merely because he was a fellow North Carolinian and a personal friend.[16] Above all Daniels underscored civilian supremacy.

Lacking knowledge of the navy, Daniels violated naval etiquette and made changes that irked many officers—and particularly Fiske. Daniels directed that staff as well as line officers use line titles and enforced his policy, announced 24 March 1913, that no officer would be promoted unless he had performed the sea duty required of his rank—no exceptions. The most celebrated case was that of Capt. Templin Morris Potts, aide for personnel. Potts was commanding the battleship *Georgia* when, at Wainwright's request, Meyer made him the chief intelligence officer. Potts had served so well in that post and then as aide for personnel that Meyer refused his request in early 1912 to go to sea. When time came for his promotion, Potts passed the required examination, but Daniels said that because he had not served sufficiently in his grade at sea, he was not ready to command a division of battleships and would not be promoted. Most probably Daniels wished to leave the position vacant and rely on Victor Blue to fill the navy's billets.[17] At any rate, Daniels ordered Potts to sea, overlooking Fiske's expostulation. On 10 April, Fiske told his diary that all the aides, or at least he, should resign. The other aides convinced him instead to stay on, and Fiske agreed that "we will not resign under any circumstances; but withstand as much as possible any actions contrary to the good of the Service and the safety of the country, until we are actually dismissed from our present positions." On 11 April, Admiral Dewey wrote Pres. Woodrow Wilson via Daniels to urge Potts's promotion. On 16 April, Wilson wrote Dewey noting Dewey's loyalty to his friends but reminding him that it was the president who made the rules.[18]

On the way to Secretary Daniels's home on 13 April, Fiske told Adms. Hugo Osterhaus and Seaton Schroeder that his term as aide for operations might terminate that very afternoon. After forcefully arguing with Daniels about Potts for an hour and a half, Fiske's conclusion was reinforced. But Daniels shook hands with him when he left, and Fiske departed with the feeling that he had spoken with a sincere man who nevertheless had been given bad advice.[19]

Fiske felt that as secretary Daniels did some good things. He sought congressional approval for promotion based upon selection instead of having the "Plucking Board" retire the more senior men; he prohibited Naval Academy graduates from resigning at will; and he intended to restrict the chiefs of bureaus and the commandant of the Marine Corps to single four-year terms. He had laundries installed on the ships and in various ways made shipboard life more bearable for the men. Yet he would not admit that there was discrimination in the navy, although all the Negroes were messmen.[20] Daniels also felt there was no need to follow the chain of command; anyone in the fleet who had a complaint could write him directly.

Until the summer of 1913 Fiske could tolerate most of Daniels's administration. One exception was his failure to see the navy as a whole; by concentrating on its economic, moral, and social aspects and neglecting the military aspect, Fiske felt that Daniels was blowing various parts of the navy out of proportion. Perhaps his upcoming visit to the Naval War College would widen Daniels's horizons.[21]

In 1911 a "long course" of eighteen months had been instituted at the college. Among its four students were Sims and Yates Stirling, who, like Fiske and Ridley McLean, avidly supported a reorganization of the Navy Department. Sims went to Newport because Fiske suggested he could "help out" with Daniels.[22] Daniels noted that the local newspapers and the few books in the library were "enough for an excuse to drop in for a bit of news and a chaser" at the resplendent bar. Why were only ten officers present when the college plant could handle a hundred? The college president stated that the Bureau of Navigation would not send officers, who were needed at sea; Daniels believed that too many officers enjoyed desk duty at shore stations. At dinner, Daniels invited suggestions on how the administration of the college and of the navy could be improved and on how the value of the college to the department and to the fleet could be increased. Fiske sensed that Daniels would have more officers sent to the college but that "the difficulty lies too deep to be reached so easily."[23] Daniels then said, "What I wish you would tell me is the first and most important single act, which I can perform to most help the Navy." Sims began to say that he should appoint a board. He got no farther because Josiah McKean rudely interrupted to say that he should immediately make the aide for operations his sole military adviser.[24] Although all the officers present agreed, Daniels replied that he could not give up too much of his authority and shirk what should be his responsibilities. He would hear nothing of what Stirling called "the most vital fault in our naval administration," that is, "the absence in the organization of the Navy of a legalized Naval General Staff, such as the Army has, and practically all the great navies of the world."[25] But Daniels did take a great stride forward in directing that two classes of twenty students each be sent to the college and requiring that no officer be promoted until he had taken its courses in residence or by correspondence.

Daniels's cure for "the most serious defect in the Navy . . . the lack of democracy," was to dignify the enlisted men and augment their education. "Every ship must be a school," he said, adding, "It must be true in the American Navy that every sailor carries an admiral's flag in his ditty box."[26] Fiske thereupon concluded that Daniels was ignoring "important things," concentrating upon "unimportant" things, and that he must be educated in naval ways. In July 1913, Fiske told Daniels that he believed that the War College was too divorced from the practical navy. He would "study up [on] the system" if Daniels approved his spending the month of August at

College, Fiske realized that Daniels wanted him out of operations. Various cellent."[27]

From Newport, Fiske invited Daniels to spend a week at the college so that he would "get a viewpoint of *the Navy as a fighting machine,* rather than as simply a *Department of the Government,* which you could not get in any other way, and which no Secretary of the Navy has ever got."[28] Daniels begged off, saying that he had already visited the college, but he did appear there on 15 August.[29] While he agreed that graduates should be given preference for duty on the General Board, in naval intelligence, as naval attachés, as the staffs of flag officers at sea, and on the college staff, members of the General Board got nowhere when they urged him to accept their recommendations for the building program for fiscal year 1915. The board wanted Daniels to ask for a continuous, instead of an annual, building program and for a council of national defense, rather than only for what he thought Congress would provide.[30]

When Daniels recommended Fiske as president of the Naval War friends told Fiske to hang on, which he did for about two weeks; then he the college instead of taking annual leave. Daniels called the idea "extold Daniels that he would not set a bad example to the service: he would go to the college if Daniels insisted. The next day, he told Dewey of his impending move. Dewey disapproved wholeheartedly, adding that Fiske was the only "logical" man to relieve Charles J. Badger as commander in chief of the fleet. "I'll see the Secretary about this," he told Fiske. Not for five weeks, however, did Daniels agree to keep Fiske on as aide for operations.[31]

In his continuing effort to educate Daniels in naval ways, Fiske sent him a British study of naval administration on 22 August; four days later, Fiske sent a paper he had written on the administration of the Navy Department. The latter covered twenty-two topics in five pages and was accompanied by a four-page memorandum on naval administration prepared by the Naval War College. Fiske pointed out that naval power was relative, that the U.S. Navy was inferior to the other great navies, and that getting the navy ready for war "is the paramount duty of the Secretary of the Navy." Daniels should meet with his aides daily, Fiske suggested, and give them instructions.[32] Daniels promised to read the material Fiske sent him.[33] But feeling that he was making no headway with Daniels on important matters and wishing to keep himself covered in case of trouble, Fiske sent copies of his letters of 6, 22, and 23 August to Col. William C. Church, editor of the *Army and Navy Journal.* The chief aim of the department, Fiske told Church in confidence, was not to "educate" but to teach particular skills, adding that "Josephus Daniels has failed to comprehend *the genius of the Navy*."[34]

Feeling that he had failed to have Daniels understand "the genius of the Navy," Fiske blurted out his feelings in person to the secretary on 19 January 1914. As he recorded in his diary:

> The Secretary became very angry with me this afternoon, because I said that we wished he would take up some of the more important things and give them his careful attention. I did not intend to be quite so blunt, and I was sorry afterward, and told him so: for he became very red and got up from his chair excitedly, and said he was paying attention to important things, and working very hard. He is such a kindly man, and tries so hard to do his duty, that I feel that I was betrayed into language that seemed like a criticism of him. Of course, we do think that he gives his attention too much to details, and not enough to important matters, and it would be well if he would and could change. But I suppose it will be some time before he can really come to the military point of view. The real trouble is not at all with him personally, but with the system whereby a civilian without any experience in naval matters, or even large affairs, is suddenly called to decide questions that it is simply impossible for him, or for any human being similarly placed, to understand.

Fiske sympathized with any move to improve the enlisted men, yet he saw education merely as a means to an end, that is, making a man expert in his job. He believed, therefore, that Daniels was going too far when, effective 1 January 1914, he ordered that both academic and practical instruction be given on off-duty time at all ships and stations during the first two years of a man's enlistment and then on a voluntary basis.[35] When Fiske spoke for the other aides against the plan, Blue replied for Daniels by saying that "our officers do not object to orders."[36]

Daniels also changed procedures at the Naval Academy. He detailed a civilian professor as head of the English Department, replaced academy alumni with presidents of technical schools and of liberal arts colleges on the Board of Visitors, and ordered that hazing cease. Daniels had sent Fullam to be the superintendent of the academy; when Daniels "interfered" with his handling of hazing cases, Fullam resigned, whereupon Daniels sent him to command the decrepit cruisers on Puget Sound that passed as the U.S. Pacific Reserve Fleet.[37]

Although Fiske patiently explained the advantages of legalizing the aide system, reorganizing the department, and creating a Council of National Defense, Daniels remained obdurately opposed on all counts. To his chagrin and disappointment, Fiske found that on many points Winterhalter and

Fullam's successor as aide for inspections, Augustus Fechteler, supported Daniels rather than him. As he wrote in his diary on 23 November 1913, "I was practically arguing the navy's case against the Sec[retary] and two of his Aids!"

Fiske was among the first to urge the rapid development of U.S. naval aviation. While a member of the General Board, no one had offered more recommendations than he on building up both air and lighter-than-air power.

In June 1910, when he flew from Albany to New York City, Glenn Curtiss ushered in a new era in American aeronautics. In October, Dewey told Secretary Meyer to consider providing space in new scouting vessels for airplanes and dirigibles. By the end of 1911, a civilian pilot had flown from a special platform built on the scout cruiser *Birmingham*, and Curtiss had shown that hydroplanes could be used by ships lacking special landing platforms. When Fiske became aide for operations in 1913, however, all the major naval powers greatly outshone the United States in naval aviation.[38] On 16 July 1913 Fiske asked Daniels to obtain the opinion of the General Board on the utility of aviation for the fleet.[39] The board recommended soliciting the ideas of Capt. Washington I. Chambers, who was the assistant to the aide for material in charge of aviation matters. Chambers described a tangled administrative arrangement: one bureau provided motors, another all other materials, still another handled personnel, and nothing was being done about the scientific study of aeronautics. Fiske thereupon recommended that an Office of Aeronautics be established under one of the aides, arguing that the work of the three bureaus involved could not be coordinated from an office in one of them.[40] The General Board not only adopted the recommendation unanimously, but it suggested that a director of naval aviation be detailed to work under Fiske.[41] The approval of these recommendations on 30 August marks the beginning of American naval aviation administration.

Believing incorrectly that Chambers was more interested in solving the aerodynamic and hydrodynamic problems of flight than in quickly developing a naval air service, Fiske sought a director for naval air and even considered asking Daniels to shift him from being aide for operations to aeronautics as his sole duty. In January 1914, however, he bulldozed Comdr. Mark L. Bristol into serving as his naval aviation assistant, had him moved from the Bureau of Navigation into his own Division of Operations, and won approval from the president to change *Navy Regulations* so that on the following 1 July there would be established an Office of Aeronautics. Fiske had thus won recognition for a new departmental activity. When he could not find office space for Bristol, he let him share his own desk for a year and a half—an admittedly awkward situation.[42]

Fiske had aircraft placed on Sims's flagship, the *Birmingham*. The scouting and spotting performed by her planes and others on the *Mississippi* in April 1914 off Veracruz, Mexico, not only helped the army and navy to coordinate their activities in the investiture of Veracruz, but helped convince Daniels of the worth of naval aviation. As we shall see, however, with the outbreak of war in Europe, Fiske parted company with Daniels on the subject of naval aviation because the administration would not give it the support he demanded.

Fiske wrestled with Daniels on the problems of manpower shortages on the ships and the slow flow of the officers' promotion list. In mid January 1914, he told Daniels that the fleet was short about 1,300 men and asked that 7,000 men be added by the spring of 1916. Daniels refused to ask Congress for them. In mid May, Daniels declined Fiske's compromise recommendation to add 4,000 men to the fleet. As we shall see, although Fiske renewed his importunities after war broke out in Europe, Daniels would still not be moved.[43]

Fiske saw all around him that admirals were serving but a few years before retiring. The government, therefore, lost the services of men skilled in the art of command and was burdened by a swollen, costly retired list. With 60 percent of the line officers now ensigns or junior lieutenants, Fiske calculated, the current junior ensign would be promoted to lieutenant commander upon reaching sixty-two, retirement age. Moreover, the number of officers provided for by law would be insufficient by 1923 to man the growing number of fighting ships, let alone the auxiliaries. When Daniels and Congress rejected Fiske's advice and left the promotion problem unsolved, a number of officers applied for voluntary retirement.[44]

Fiske supported Daniels in seeking legislation to create a number of admirals and vice admirals, for American naval officers in foreign waters usually were outranked. Bills providing for from two to six vice admirals were introduced in both houses of Congress early in 1914. Primed with a letter Fiske had written and Daniels forwarded,[45] the chairman of the House Naval Affairs Committee, Lemuel P. Padgett, introduced a bill that would make the commanders in chief of the Atlantic, Pacific, and Asiatic fleets admirals and their seconds in command, vice admirals. "I think we ought not to oppose this plan," said Fiske, "but get what we can, lest we get nothing."[46] When the bill passed, Daniels promoted the three fleet commanders in chief to admirals and gave the rank of vice admiral to the second in command of the Atlantic Fleet, but he did not believe that either the Pacific or Asiatic fleet rated vice admirals at the time. Now American fleet commanders had ranks commensurate with those of foreign navies; Fiske may have rued his decision to support Frank F. Fletcher as commander in chief of the Atlantic Fleet instead of opting for the position himself, thereby obtaining a higher rank.

In his first statement to the press, in March 1913, Secretary Daniels advocated a two-battleship program and other ships that would move the navy into a position "second to none." As Fiske admitted, Daniels established a unique record: Congress approved every building recommendation he made throughout his eight years except for completing a large program after 1918. But Daniels's recommendations were not those offered him by Fiske and the General Board. Rather than accepting the board's policy, adopted in 1903, of building forty-eight battleships by 1920, Daniels spoke of finding the "golden mean" between what the navy needed and the nation could afford. For fiscal years 1914 and 1915 he recommended about half the number of ships the board had advised. When he stated that the navy would soon be stronger than at any time in history, Fiske countered by pointing out that it would be seriously short of personnel; he also questioned the habitability of fleet submarines and noted that destroyers lacked antiaircraft defenses. Fiske was also the only member of the board to vote against the numbers and types of ships it recommended for the 1916 building program. In the end, however, saying that he would decide how many of what types of ships to recommend to Congress, Daniels left the board with power merely to prescribe ships' characteristics.[47]

Even more important to Fiske than the numbers of ships were fleet tactics, in which Americans were far behind. Upon reading about plans for German fleet maneuvers of 1914, in which twenty-one battleships, three battle cruisers, five small cruisers, sixty-six destroyers, eleven submarines, an airship, airplanes, a train, and twenty-two minesweepers would be controlled by one admiral, Fiske suffered "that kind of shock which . . . an amateur is apt to feel when he sees a professional at work."[48] In mid March, therefore, he asked the General Board to approve an administrative plan by which the department could get the bureaus to take steps to prepare for war. When Fiske handed him the plan, on 29 April, Daniels refused to sign it. Three days later Fiske wrote in his diary: "I argued for half an hour. I might as well have tried to scratch a diamond with an iron file! I could not make him see that [the] Dept. is not really ready *now*!" No wonder Fiske waited until Daniels went out of town to ask the assistant secretary, Franklin D. Roosevelt, to sign any papers he knew Daniels would not. Fiske stopped this technique, however, when it became obvious that Roosevelt could not match Daniels's clout on Capital Hill.[49]

Another matter on which Fiske and Daniels violently disagreed was the abolition of the officers' wine mess. As Fiske recorded in his diary on 6 April 1914: "Feeling as to stopping of wine mess by Sec. is not one of surprise. Officers think it unwise, and that effect will be to influence officers to smuggle whiskey and cocaine on board, and to take meals on shore, where they can drink whiskey—instead of wine and beer aboard." Liquor had been prohibited to enlisted men since 1899. By a general order effective 1 July 1914, Daniels wiped out officers' messes throughout the service.

As far as Fiske was concerned, Daniels was using military discipline to cloak his prohibitionist feelings. Fiske expostulated orally. Then on 27 May, backed unofficially by the General Board, he began to write a letter stating that Daniels's order was an insult to the navy and to every officer in it. The order, Fiske said, created two erroneous impressions: it merely abolished the use of wine and beer because distilled liquors had been abolished fifty years earlier; and it implied that enlisted men were sober because they were denied liquor, whereas officers were not sober because they were allowed it. Fiske closed the letter saying, "Another effect [of the order] would be an increased temptation to use cocaine and other drugs"—a sentence thereafter misquoted.[50] Despite his protests, Daniels told Fiske to enforce the order. Although he was greatly tempted to resign, Fiske was dissuaded from doing so by Mark Bristol. The deed done, he gave Daniels the unfinished six-page letter on the wine mess and asked him to read it. Daniels said he would.[51] Fiske felt somewhat better after Franklin Roosevelt told him on 4 June that Daniels was annoyed with Fiske's attitude on the wine-mess order, but that when he, Roosevelt, had told Daniels that he was highly impressed with Fiske, Daniels had said "Yes. Fiske's all right."[52]

Still another confrontaton between Fiske and Daniels resulted from misunderstandings with respect to Fiske's desire to become commander in chief of the fleet. Badger was commander and Frank F. Fletcher was second in command. Fiske wished to succeed Badger on 1 July 1914, with the hope of teaching young officers to consider sea duty more important than shore duty, but he did not officially apply for the position. Fiske also told Daniels that Fletcher wanted to relieve him as aide for operations in June 1915 and that he had talked the arrangement over with Fletcher several times.[53] Officers like Sims supported Fiske, and Daniels certainly thought highly of him—as his comments on Fiske's fitness report for the period 30 September 1913 to 31 March 1914 indicate: "Admiral [Fiske] is an able and conscientious, as well as resourceful officer, and as Aid for Operations displays ability of high order. . . . [He is] a learned and able adviser, a wise member of the Aids, and a faithful and distinguished officer."

On 30 April, Fiske asked to be sent back to his old battleship division when Fletcher was made commander in chief. Dewey, Wainwright, and several other high-ranking officers agreed that this should be done, but Fletcher told Fiske "positively" that he was willing to be the aide for operations and let Fiske command the fleet until he retired. One can only imagine Fiske's feelings when, at his suggestion, Daniels telegraphed Fletcher (who was in Mexican waters) to see if the arrangement suited him and Fletcher said it did not. Fiske told Daniels of his amazement and said that he expected Fletcher to write him a letter of explanation. When the letter came, Fletcher asserted that an officer recently arrived from Washington had told him that Daniels had decided to make Cameron Winslow, one of the most senior officers, commander in chief and that he—Fletcher—had, therefore, chosen the position of aide. When Fiske told Daniels about Fletcher's letter, Daniels said that he had decided on Fletcher rather than Winslow. Fiske, of course, raised no objections, for he had repeatedly said that Fletcher would be both a good admiral and a fine commander and that he was happy where he was.[54] Fiske wrote Fletcher a sincere letter of congratulations even though he wrote in his diary that Fletcher owed much of his reputation to him.[55]

Soon after Fiske had been reappointed as aide for operations, war clouds appeared in Europe. On 26 July, he wrote in his diary: "Servia has defied Austria's ultimatum. Russia must help Servia and Germany must help Austria! Wonder how war can be avoided." Again, as in 1913, he asked Daniels's permission to spend the month of August with the General Board at Newport instead of taking annual leave. Daniels agreed, and on 31 July Fiske arrived at Newport amid news from Europe that led him to believe war was imminent. He must, therefore, do all he could to get his navy prepared for any eventuality. He asked Adm. Austin M. Knight, the senior officer of the General Board present, to call a board meeting as early as possible the following morning. At that meeting, Fiske urged that a letter be written to Daniels, pointing out the danger of the United States being brought into the war and the need to start taking immediate steps to put the navy on a war footing. Following the meeting, Fiske wrote in his diary:

> Aug. 1. Gen. Board—or rather the members present here—Knight, Fiske, Knapp, Hood and Shoemaker—sent [a] letter to [the Navy] Dep't, pointing out possible causes of danger in regard to European nations, especially in matters connected with our neutrality—and concluded [the] letter by recommending that all battleships (except such as are needed in Mex[ican] and Caribbean waters) be sent to their home yards, to be docked and gotten ready. I also sent a letter recommending this, as Aide for Operations and referring to G. B.'s letter.

In his memoirs, published in 1919, Fiske cited this entry and added "I think this was the first step toward preparedness that was taken in the United States."[56]

In 1908, stimulated in part by the Senate investigation into naval affairs, Theodore Roosevelt had appointed the Moody commission to study naval reorganization. Fiske took to heart the commission's "General Principles Governing Naval Organization." He also applauded the report by the Swift board which Secretary Meyer followed in creating posts for four aides who would individually administer naval operations, material, inspections, and personnel and collectively serve as an advisory council to the secretary. After only thirty-four days as aide for inspections, Fiske had become the aide for operations, a position equivalent—for all practical purposes—to chief of naval operations. Fiske was thus the chief military adviser to the secretary of the navy and the chief liaison man between the secretary and the General Board and also between the secretary and the bureaus. Fiske was acutely aware that much remained to be done in matters of war plans, material, personnel, and the officers' promotion system, but it seemed that wherever he turned he was blocked by Daniels. One exception was improving the Naval War College and obtaining legislation to create several admirals and vice admirals.

Daniels cut the building program recommended by the General Board in half; he would not accept the naval policies devised by the board or Fiske's administrative plan by which these policies would be supported by the bureaus; he refused to increase the number of naval personnel; and he was not concerned with the growing might of other navies or with their naval administrative procedures. By immersing himself in minutiae, Daniels revealed his lack of capacity to delegate responsibility. Not only was he a poor administrator, he was suspicious of naval officers, except for certain favorites.

Fiske was very upset when Daniels, who firmly objected to a naval general staff, let the aide system lapse but added an aide for education to supervise the education of enlisted personnel. By mid 1914, had Dewey not intervened, Daniels would have shunted Fiske off to be the president of the Naval War College. Daniels declined to support Fiske's demands for a Council of National Defense or for an administrative plan by which the bureaus could support the fleet; he also declined to give naval aviation the support Fiske believed it should have. In fairness to Daniels, however, it must be added that he was following administration policy not to augment the national defenses while the United States was a neutral power.

Daniels's abolition of the officers' wine mess was a particularly sore point with Fiske, as was the secretary's deliberateness in reaching decisions on matters Fiske thought important; as a result the navy was not being prepared for the war Fiske was as sure the United States would eventually enter as Daniels was sure it would not. In the next chapter we will see that these eighteen months had not been sufficient to enable Fiske to convert Daniels to his professional point of view.

11

JAPAN AND MISSIONARY DIPLOMACY, 1913–1915

The worst mistake Bradley A. Fiske made in evaluating Josephus Daniels was to underestimate the secretary's abilities. In keeping with the principle of civilian supremacy, Daniels, like Pres. Woodrow Wilson, was determined that military men should not decide national policy. Fiske learned this lesson well during the 1913 war scare with Japan and in Wilson's moralistic posture towards the Mexican Revolution.

Angered by a California law forbidding "aliens ineligible for citizenship" to own land, Japan protested to the Wilson administration, which sought appeasement through diplomacy.[1] On 25 April 1913—the very day, ironically, that the General Board completed a revision of the strategic section of the Asian ("Orange") war plan, Fiske noted that "the President and Secretary of State are exceedingly anxious not to do anything to anger Japan."[2] He was even more upset when he learned five days later that the president had ordered a freeze on all military and naval movements.[3]

Thinking in military terms, as they should, Fiske, the General Board, the secretary of war, the army chief of staff, and the Joint Board of the army and navy wanted to direct military commanders in the United States, Hawaii, and the Philippines to prepare to meet all eventualities. On 2 May, Fiske won unanimous approval from the General Board for his resolution asking Daniels to furnish information to the secretary of war concerning steps being taken to prepare for a possible war; in turn, the secretary of war was to tell Daniels what the army was doing. Working quickly, the General Board furnished Daniels a mobilization and movement plan on 8 May that would prepare the navy for war. When President Wilson directed that no action be taken to implement its recommendations,[4] Fiske wrote in his diary on 10 May, "Certainly we are losing the very best and most valuable time to make those preparations for war that all History shows to be priceless."

On 13 May Fiske wrote Daniels a confidential memorandum and the next day forwarded a detailed estimate of the likelihood of war with Japan.[5] At a cabinet meeting held on 13 May, Daniels read Fiske's memorandum and asked whether ships in the Yangtze River should be sent to the Philippines; Fiske had suggested this, but Daniels was opposed.[6] On 14 May, the Joint Board unanimously approved sending the ships in the Yangtze to Manila and strengthening naval forces in Hawaii and on the Pacific side of the Panama Canal Zone. Also on 14 May, Fiske submitted to Daniels an extensive plan for preparing the navy for possible war with Japan,[7] adding that the War Department favored such preparations. Daniels bridled, saying that army men should not initiate naval activities and that ships would move only when the president so directed.[8] At the cabinet meeting of 16 May, Wilson directed that no war preparations would be made and no ships would move while he sought peace with Japan through diplomatic negotiations; and Daniels so informed Fiske. Moreover, when the Joint Board suggested moving ships, Wilson suspended its meetings.

On 18 May, an agreement was reached by which the dignity of Japan would be maintained without infringing on California's right to legislate. Not until 18 July, however, did Wilson agree that ships could be moved from Shanghai, with the proviso that Fiske insure that there would be no movement toward the Philippines or Japan.[9] Although the General Board had completed the strategic and administrative sections of the Asian war plan on 25 November 1913, its members decided that it would be futile to present Daniels with a paper on the subject at the time.[10] Nevertheless Fiske "expressed the opinion that a strong aerial force, in the Philippines, equipped with machine guns would be the best protection against an army force attempting to make a landing in the Philippines."[11]

If any danger of war with Japan had ever existed, it began to vanish late in May after the diplomatic agreement had been reached. Despite this, "the General Board continues to issue war-like letters," Needham L. Jones, Daniels's naval aide, told Albert Gleaves, commandant of the Philadelphia Naval Yard, adding, "but they are promptly locking up the files."[12] It was Daniels's position that the navy must not initiate policy but must remain merely an agency for carrying out national policy as defined by the administration. To Fiske, however it was incomprehensible that American military forces should not be permitted to prepare for a possible war with Japan, especially since the United States stood at what Fiske considered a grievous disadvantage. This lesson in civilian control would be reinforced when the administration kept the major portion of the Atlantic Fleet doing gunboat duty off Mexico while Fiske demanded that it be prepared for possible operations in the European war.

In 1910, the overthrow of the Mexican president, Porfirio Díaz, by Francisco I. Madero initiated a period of civil insurrection. Although President Taft was determined to let the Mexicans settle their own problems, a General Board study dated 21 September 1910 is entitled "Mexican War Plan"; another, dated 22 October 1910, is entitled "Seizure of Tampico in Case of War."

Early in February 1913, when the full-scale revolution against Madero began, it seemed probable that an American relief expedition would have to be sent. At 1:00 A.M. on 12 February, Fiske was called to the White House to confer with President Taft, Secretary of State Philander C. Knox, Secretary of the Navy George L. von Meyer, Secretary of War Henry L. Stimson, and the army chief of staff, Leonard Wood. Taft asked Stimson how long it would take to organize a relief expedition. Having recently undertaken a tactical reorganization of the army, Stimson replied that he would have to send only one telegram, to the general commanding the division chosen to sail. The authorization to send that telegram was given, and on the morning of 13 February three infantry divisions were placed under waiting orders to board transports at Newport News, Virginia. This was the kind of efficiency Fiske found commendable. Meyer then directed Fiske to send Rear Adm. Frank F. Fletcher and three battleships to Veracruz and one battleship, under Rear Adm. Henry T. Mayo, to Tampico "because of the insurrection." Knox indicated, however, that ships were being sent only to protect foreigners and their interests and indicated no change in Taft's "hands-off" policy toward Mexico's contending factions. Soon thereafter Gen. Victoriano Huerta had Madero murdered and established a provisional government that quickly provoked a new civil war under the leadership of such men as Venustiano Carranza. Unwilling to bind President Wilson by quick and unseemly action, Taft left him with the question of how to react.[13]

Opinions on how to deal with Mexico varied greatly: the United States could use "overwhelming strength" against her; seize Mexican ports and border cities; appoint an investigatory commission; or use commercial instead of military intervention.[14] Fiske supported the realistic policy of recognizing Huerta, saying, "This seems good policy, since *some* government is needed and it must be supported."[15] President Wilson disagreed, however, and as aide for operations, Fiske had to support four battleships off the Mexican coast even though he, along with the Council of Aides and the General Board, wanted the ships concentrated in home waters.[16]

Admiral Fletcher remained off Veracruz, and Admiral Mayo off Tampico, to guard valuable American oil properties. While Fletcher drafted plans to blockade Mexico and capture and occupy Veracruz, Wilson specifically directed that he not land forces unless it was Fletcher's judgment that there was absolutely no other way to save foreign lives in Mexico—and then only after receiving permission.[17]

John Lind, sent by Wilson to present an offer of mediation to Huerta, prophetically concluded that the United States would soon be compelled to land troops; and Fiske asserted that the "Mexican situation is getting worse and worse."[18] Believing military action imminent, General Wood asked Daniels what the administration's policy toward Mexico was. Daniels did not know. Wood called upon the secretary of state, William Jennings Bryan; Bryan answered, "Search me."[19] In a similar vein, Fiske told Col. William C. Church, editor of the *Army and Navy Journal,* that the navy under Daniels was like "a big powerful automobile pushing along a crowded street, in charge of a chauffer who does not understand his machine, and does not know the Rules of the Road."[20]

On 27 October, with the intention of forcing Huerta out, Wilson ordered four additional battleships to Mexico. Fiske told Daniels that he and Wood agreed that a naval blockade of Mexico would be futile unless American soldiers closed its land frontiers also. Furthermore, he said, "The continuous idle life of our ships in Mex[ican] waters and the[ir] present dispersion from [the] fleet was . . . *exactly* what Japan and Germany must desire us to do. The Kaiser must be dancing jigs of joy!"[21] Daniels, like Wilson, thought that the more ships in Mexican waters, the sooner Huerta would resign. Fiske told him that "Huerta would never be bluffed to resign, or that he would resign, unless forced to do so by the Mexicans themselves."[22] In Wilson's annual message to Congress, delivered 2 December, he established the policy of "watchful waiting"—an approach not reassuring to his military leaders. These leaders, in addition, resented what they considered administration interference with military operations. Fletcher, for one, objected to Lind's meddling and alerted Fiske. Fiske also believed that Lind, "almost an ass," was not needed to mediate with Huerta, when a man of such diplomacy, tact, and firmness as Fletcher was on the scene.[23]

For about six months Fletcher's forces stood an extremely monotonous and uncomfortable watch off the Sierra Orientale, with many of his ships in the mouth of the broad Pánuco River. Tampico lies several miles up this river. Fiske had no quarrel with Fletcher; he simply believed that the battleships should not be anchored off Mexico. On Sunday, 5 January 1914, Fiske suggested to the assistant secretary of the navy, Franklin Roosevelt, that merchant ships or transports be substituted for Fletcher's battleships. On Monday morning, 6 January, Roosevelt proposed the plan to Daniels as his own idea because Fiske had told him that the secretary would listen more carefully to his civilian assistant than to an admiral. Instead of offering the plan at a cabinet meeting, however, Daniels suggested sending marines to take Mexico City "in case of outbreak there," a plan Wilson approved. Daniels asked Fiske how many marines were available and how long it would take them to get to Veracruz. Fiske told him the number but said that there was already a sufficient force off Veracruz to take the city; all that remained was to coordinate the plan with the army. Could the marines reach Mexico City? Daniels asked. Fiske smiled and replied that they certainly could not. Daniels then talked with the secretary of war, Lindley M. Garrison. On 8 January, at a conference with Daniels, Wood, and Fiske, Garrison said that if Huerta were to leave Mexico or to die, anarchy would ensue, requiring a "relief expedition." Fiske disagreed, and Wood supported him. Fiske dispatched the marines Daniels wanted off Veracruz to await orders at Guantánamo instead.[24]

Fiske gleefully wrote in his diary on 14 January that Daniels had told him that "he thought it might be possible to get [the] battleships away from east coast Mexico, and replace them with a special service squadron comprised of cruisers and two transports of Marines. Good." On 15 January, Fiske spoke several times with Daniels, Roosevelt, and Wood. "Things look," he said, "as if we might carry out the special service squadron plan, and also the attack on our east coast from a supposed German Fleet next summer."[25] As we shall see, however, Fiske was whistling in the dark with respect to the return of the battleships.

On 8 February, upon returning from a cruise on the *Louisiana* to test his prism firing system, Fiske noted that there was "little change in Mexico, but a vast change in the situation since [Wilson] has lifted the embargo on arms, and rebels can now get them from U.S."[26] Although Fletcher thought the ensuing week had been pretty quiet, Fiske said that "matters will get worse at Tampico pretty soon. Too bad, as this will operate against my plan of reducing the force in Mexico."[27] Although his hunch was correct, the incident that provoked the invasion at Veracruz started not with him but with Admiral Mayo.

On 9 April, Mayo learned that the day before Mexican Federalist forces had arrested a marine courier from the American consulate in Tampico and had briefly detained the crew of a whaleboat from the *Dolphin* sent to purchase supplies ashore. Mayo responded aggressively to what he took to be flagrant disrespect for his service. On his own responsibility Mayo sent Comdr. William A. Moffett to demand an apology for the "insult" within twenty-four hours from the commander of the Federal garrison in Tampico, Gen. Ignazio Morelos Zaragoza. Mayo also wanted an assurance that the officer responsible would receive severe punishment and "that you hoist the

American flag in a prominent position on shore and salute it with 21 guns, which salute will be duly returned by this ship."[28] By his "quarterdeck diplomacy" Mayo had raised a local incident to an international one—a fait accompli—in which he, not the administration, was dealing with Mexico.

Because Wilson was absent visiting his fatally ill wife, Bryan and Daniels concluded that "Mayo could not have done otherwise," but Fiske realized that such a salute returned by Mayo signified recognition of Huerta's government. Wilson, however, wanted to use the "Tampico incident" to force a showdown with Huerta.[29] Because General Zaragoza apologized, Huerta said that Mayo should withdraw his ultimatum. Moreover, Huerta asked how the United States could demand a salute from a government it refused to recognize. With Wilson out of town, Bryan extended the deadline for meeting Mayo's ultimatum to 13 April because it was Holy Week and public life had halted in Mexico City.

On 13 April, Daniels told Fiske that Mexico had asked Bryan whether a salute to a flag hoisted on the *Dolphin* would suffice and whether such a salute would be returned. Fiske answered affirmatively to both questions, but added that Daniels should check with counselor Robert Lansing at the State Department. At 10:45 P.M., Bryan directed Fiske to cable Mexico that the United States insisted upon the salute. An angry Fiske called Daniels to tell him that Bryan had no right to give orders to him or to Daniels. Moments after Fiske had gotten Daniels to agree to direct Fletcher to tell Mexico that a salute by it would be returned, Huerta announced he would not fire the salute. Daniels thereupon asked Fiske to learn exactly what it was that Mayo had said in his "ultimatum" to Mexico.[30]

Early on 14 April, Fiske spoke with Bryan and Daniels about Mayo's ultimatum. After speaking with Bryan, President Wilson told Daniels that the United States would not return a salute. Fiske said that the navy took a different view—that it saluted nations with which the United States was at peace and that the United States should be gracious enough to return a salute. Bryan then sent him five questions on international law to answer. Fiske's answers pleased both Daniels and Bryan and were passed on to the president. But Fiske's joy evaporated when Wilson, ignoring Fletcher's offer to go to Mexico City and seek a solution to the problem, directed that "the salute [by Mexico] will be fired," demanded that Mexico fully comply with the demands of the United States, and ordered the strengthening of American naval forces off Mexico, based on the peculiar logic that it was "possible to deal with a dictator by the Navy without precipitating war."[31]

On 14 April, General Huerta suggested submitting the Tampico incident to the Hague Tribunal. Wilson refused, insisted upon "prompt acceptance" of his terms, and ordered the Atlantic Fleet to gather off the east coast of Mexico and the Pacific Fleet off its west coast. Daniels then told Fiske that its commander in chief, Charles J. Badger, would lead the Atlantic Fleet to Tampico "as [a] big naval demonstration." Fiske immediately headed for Norfolk to make sure that Badger understood his orders. As explicitly as he could, he told Badger that the administration was prepared to enforce Mayo's demand for a salute. If Huerta refused, "force would probably be resorted to" even though Wilson sincerely wished to avoid war. From notes he made while Fiske talked, Badger wrote a letter to Daniels as proof that he had been informed by Fiske of the administration's policy; pleased, Daniels showed the letter to Wilson. Fiske must now supply the needs of no less than eighty-three U.S. vessels off Mexico.[32]

While Badger headed south and Fiske north, Huerta telegraphed Washington that he would raise and salute the American flag if assured in writing that the salute would be returned, gun for gun, just as Mayo had suggested. At 1:00 P.M. on 18 April, Wilson replied with his own ultimatum: Huerta must comply with his demand to fire the salute by 6:00 P.M. Sunday, 19 April, or on Monday he would "lay matters before Congress with a view to taking such action as may be necessary to enforce the respect due the nation's flag."[33]

The time had finally come for Wilson to seek military advice. Fiske was to ask the General Board what Wilson should do if Huerta refused to meet Mayo's demand and what courses of action the president could take without a congressional declaration of war. The board advised asking Congress for authority to use the military services. If Huerta did not comply within a specified time, the board recommended that the president should declare a belligerent, not a pacific, blockade of Mexico by land and sea, pointing out that a pacific blockade could not be enforced against third powers supplying Mexico with munitions. Fiske asked what the United States would do if Huerta complied with its demands; the board said it had not been asked that question. Moreover, it declined to mix military and political policy matters. It offered him, however, an "informal guideline": Huerta must comply with Wilson's demands or the navy would remain off Mexico until the revolutionary disturbances were settled and Mexico made reparations for injuries and insults to Americans perpetrated not only by Huerta but by Carranza and Villa as well.[34]

On Sunday, 19 April, at a meeting of the board held at his request, Fiske supported a belligerent blockade of Mexico; Victor Blue supported a broader intervention, being demanded by the administration. The board "stood pat" on Fiske's proposal. "Things were very lively during evening," Fiske recorded in his diary. "Huerta's time was up at 6 p.m. and it was not until midnight that news came that Huerta had refused. Got home at 1 a.m. Blue, [Daniels], and I sent [a] telegram to Fletcher." On that Sunday,

Fiske also directed William S. Sims to take aboard his flagship, the cruiser *Birmingham*, several aircraft and their crews; then the *Birmingham* was to join the *Mississippi*, which also carried aircraft, off Tampico.[35]

On Monday, 20 April, while Wilson was telling his cabinet that he would use force against Mexico but that there would be no war, Mayo was preparing to seize Tampico. Meanwhile, the American consul, William Canada, reported from Veracruz that the German Hamburg-American liner *Ypiranga* would dock at 10:30 A.M. on 21 April and discharge two hundred machine guns and fifteen million rounds of ammunition for Huerta. With those supplies Huerta could hold out not only against his domestic opponents but resist American forces as well; 20 April was the day of decision in which military advice was crucial.

The Joint Board and the cabinet met separately at 10:30 A.M. The board discussed plans for Mexico, with Fiske noting that cooperation between the army and the navy was not provided for, that holding Tampico would do little good, and that the United States should instead seize Veracruz as a gateway to Mexico City.[36] Meanwhile the cabinet discussed methods of preventing the *Ypiranga* from reaching Veracruz. Because ships of third powers could not be seized at sea, the cargoes must be immobilized after they were landed but before they were transshipped. Therefore Mayo was ordered to Veracruz, which he could reach overnight, and Badger was diverted from Tampico to Veracruz, which he could reach in two nights. Untroubled by how to fight Huerta but not declare war on Mexico or by how to stop the *Ypiranga* without issuing a war blockade, Wilson addressed Congress at 3:00 P.M. By a vote of 323 to 29, the House supported a policy that disclaimed any intent to make war upon the Mexican people but which would use force against Huerta. Debate in the Senate, however, promised to be prolonged. At 8:00 P.M., Fiske joined the president, Bryan, Garrison, Daniels, Wood, Blue, and Lind at the White House. It was decided that operations would be conducted at Veracruz and that the landing of military supplies for Huerta would be prevented by stopping all ships, foreign as well as American.[37] At 8:30, Fiske telegraphed Fletcher "to be ready on short notice to land [at] Vera Cruz, seize custom house and vicinity." He also directed Mayo to Veracruz, leaving only the cruiser *Des Moines* in Tampico's outer harbor.[38] At 2:00 A.M. on 21 April, Canada telegraphed that three trains awaited the *Ypiranga*'s cargo, and Mayo stated that the ship would dock at 10:00 A.M.[39]

Disregarding the recommendations of the General Board, Wilson and Daniels decided that Fletcher would take the custom house and thus prevent the *Ypiranga*'s cargo from being landed. At 4:00 A.M. Daniels telephoned Fiske to send Fletcher his orders. A few hours later Fiske received word that the *Ypiranga* had been stopped and that "Fletcher had landed at 2 p.m. and taken custom house, 4 Americans killed, 21 wounded."[40]

When Germany complained about the stopping of the *Ypiranga*, Bryan apologized and thanked Germany for diverting the ship from Veracruz. Meanwhile, Daniels tried to tell Badger how to use his ships; Fiske objected to such interference.[41] On Wednesday, 22 April, Badger reported his arrival at Veracruz in support of Fletcher. Chafing under what he regarded as political meddling in military action, Fiske again "pointed out to [Daniels] . . . the unwisdom of interfering with Badger, except for clear reasons of policy for reasons known here and not known to Badger, etc." He also tried to convince Daniels and the State Department counselor, Robert Lansing, of the need to establish a belligerent blockade of Mexico. Fiske was shocked when Daniels refused to do so because the administration wished not only to hurt Huerta but also to help his liberal opponents. "Gosh—" was Fiske's exclamation.[42]

As Fiske predicted, Wilson's moralistic course led to military intervention. Shaken first by the loss of American and Mexican lives, Wilson was then jolted by the news that the *Ypiranga* would deliver her cargo to Huerta at another port. Wilson thereupon reimposed the embargo. As Fiske noted, "Carranza resents violation of Mex[ican] territory by U.S.! This is what Army and Navy have expected."[43] Indeed, at Veracruz Badger asked for help from the army and for permission to sink or capture Huerta's four small gunboats carrying troops that might attack the American forces. Fiske advised Daniels to let Badger sink the gunboats and to get President Wilson to establish a land and sea blockade of Mexico. But Wilson vetoed Fiske's ideas even though they also represented the thinking of the army. "I have heard a suggestion today that there may be a question as to [Wilson's] sanity! Certainly, he seems to have 'the big head,' " Fiske wrote in his diary.[44]

As Fiske's diary attests, he fought an ongoing battle with Daniels and the administration over several succeeding days. On 24 April, he noted with pleasure that the army had finally left Galveston for Veracruz and that he had asked Daniels to let him, rather than Cameron Winslow, command the special service squadron off Mexico. Daniels demurred, saying there was no one to take Fiske's place. He did agree, however, that when the Mexican situation was straightened out, Fiske and Fletcher could exchange billets. Two days later, Fiske noted that he had remained at the Navy Department until 3:00 A.M. on 25 April: he had received a report from Fletcher stating that civil government could not be restored in Veracruz and that martial law would be imposed on the city. Although only President Wilson could decide whether Fletcher or Gen. Frederick Funston should be in command of Veracruz, Fiske favored Fletcher because of his familiarity with the situation and his good judgment. Daniels too favored Fletcher, fearing that for the sake of notoriety, Funston would "do something to bring on war."

On 25 April, Argentina, Brazil, and Chile offered their good offices to solve the Mexican imbroglio. Wilson quickly accepted. "Nothing will come of it," said Fiske;[45] events showed the remark was too hasty. Fighting between Huertista and American forces ceased, but the civil war in Mexico continued. The meeting at Niagara Falls, Canada, from 20 May until July, was a farcical performance, for Wilson would not let the mediators discuss the Tampico affair. Wilson meant to keep American troops in Mexico until he was "finally and fully satisfied that the [reform] program contemplated will be carried out in all respects." This presupposed Huerta's ouster and perhaps the reaching of Mexico City by Constitutionalist forces.[46]

On Sunday, 26 April, Fiske joined Garrison, the assistant secretary of war; Wood's successor as army chief of staff, William W. Wotherspoon; Daniels; and Blue in preparing recommendations for the president on how the army and navy should operate at Veracruz. Wilson agreed that Fletcher would keep his three thousand men ashore until they were relieved by army troops which were due to arrive in three days. After that, marines serving ashore would serve under Funston, but sailors and marines needed on board would return to their ships.[47] The navy had performed a unique accomplishment not only in taking a foreign city but in administering it for a week before command shifted to the army on 30 April.

Fiske worked to secure the return of American refugees from Mexico, to get Federalists and Constitutionalists to neutralize foreign oil properties near Tampico, and to win Daniels's approval of his exchanging positions with Fletcher. Fiske also suggested that the United States regularize its proceedings against Mexico by announcing a blockade and urged that a naval general staff be created. Daniels spoke with Wilson and reported, as Fiske noted, "in effect that [Wilson] did not wish to make blockade, as it was an act of war! Oh Lord!" When Daniels disapproved a naval staff, Fiske vowed to tackle him on the subject again.[48]

On the evening of 8 May, Fiske attended memorial services held in New York to honor the Americans killed at Veracruz. On the return trip, in company with Franklin Roosevelt, Fiske found Secretary Daniels "most companionable and pleasant." Little "business" was discussed, and when Fiske referred to the need for a chief of staff, Daniels changed the subject. Nor would Daniels approve Fiske's suggestion of adding four thousand enlisted men to the service. Fiske had also recommended that the United States do nothing about the navigation lights extinguished along Mexico's east coast. Mexicans owned the lights, Fiske held, and they had the right to put them out if they wished. Supported by the State Department, he won his point.⁴⁹ Irked because the *Ypiranga* had delivered its arms to Huerta at Puerto Mexico after Fletcher stopped her from landing at Veracruz, Fiske shocked Daniels by telling him that "it was [in] Germany's great interest to block U.S. in every possible way, and keep our Navy deteriorating in tropical climate as long as possible, because she knows she is to fight U.S. some day."⁵⁰ Fiske was shocked in turn when, on 2 June, Bryan visited Roosevelt's office —Daniels was off politicking in North Carolina—and asked him to report the location of the four Mexican Federalist gunboats. American ships were prohibited from carrying war materials to Mexican ports. According to Fiske, Bryan "was anxious lest they [the gunboats] prevent these arms getting to the Constitutionalists. Yet the adm[inistration] *pretends* to be neutral between them." The administration, Fiske felt, was acting in bad faith, for while it mediated at Niagara Falls, it also sought to prevent Federalists from blockading Mexican ports so that munitions could be delivered to the Constitutionalists.⁵¹

On 8 June Huerta lifted the blockade of Tampico. As Fiske explained to Daniels, Huerta could still seize ships seeking to deliver contraband to Carranza; Daniels agreed that Fiske should tell Badger to keep the Federalist gunboats under surveillance lest they seize ships under the pretext of finding contraband. However, on 13 June—Fiske's sixtieth birthday—the American ship *Antilla* landed a cargo of munitions for the Constitutionalists at Tampico without molestation from Badger. "This administration is posing as very much better and holier than other people!" exclaimed Fiske. "How perfectly hypocritical."⁵²

Bankrupted by the United States' hold on the custom house at Veracruz, Huerta resigned on 15 July and fled into exile five days later. Styling himself the "first chief," Carranza began to eliminate Huertistas; he demanded that the United States evacuate Veracruz and insisted that he could handle Mexico's internal problems by himself. On 8 September, Wilson lifted the arms embargo. Soon the number of American warships on the west coast of Mexico was reduced, and on 15 September Wilson ordered the transfer of authority at Veracruz from American to Carranzista hands. The American exodus began on 23 November; two days later, when a Mexican gunboat entered the inner harbor and saluted the flag of the senior American admiral, the salute was returned gun for gun. Instead of the prelude to extended operations, Wilson's seizing of Veracruz had been a military finale. Now, perhaps, Fiske would get his ships back.⁵³

Fiske opposed the administration's neo-imperialistic policy in the Caribbean as well as its moral imperialism in Mexico. Bryan would protect the Panama Canal and, by supporting the Monroe Doctrine, forestall European intervention in Latin American countries; in return these countries must, therefore, behave. By exercising economic controls, prohibiting revolutions, agreeing to protectorates, and resorting to force, Bryan made the Caribbean ever more an American lake.

In 1913, to bolster the strategic security of the Panama Canal, Bryan wrote a new treaty with Cuba giving the United States an enlarged area for its naval base at Guantánamo. He also wrote a treaty to end the dispute between Panama and Colombia. It was blocked in the Senate, however, by a fear that Theodore Roosevelt would be impugned, among other reasons. Not until 1921, with Roosevelt dead, was the treaty approved. To ease the shaky financial and political conditions in Nicaragua, Bryan drafted a treaty in which the United States would give Nicaragua $3 million for an option on an alternate canal route and the right to build a naval base in Fonseca Bay. Thus Bryan revealed himself to be more of a nationalist and a realist than many of his critics realized. Had Fiske commented upon Bryan's dealings with Cuba, Panama and Colombia, and Nicaragua, it seems certain that he would have approved them. He held Bryan in extremely low esteem, however, because of his handling of Mexico; possibly this estimate was carried over particularly to the questions of San Domingo (now the Dominican Republic) and of Haiti, to which Bryan turned his attention in 1914 and 1915.

A 1905 treaty authorized the United States to adjust San Domingo's financial obligations. In March 1913, a revolt began against its president. "For moral effect," Bryan asked that American naval vessels be sent to San Domingo during the revolutionary disturbances.

On 6 May 1914, after conferring with Roosevelt and Lansing, Fiske directed the commanding officer of an American warship in Puerta Plata to support the government of Bordas José Valdez and to tell Bordas that the "U.S. would recognize [a] blockade of Puerta Plata, if Bordas would declare and make it effective."[54] During the afternoon of 23 May, Daniels had Fiske, acting for the State Department, direct the U.S. minister, William W. Russell, to proceed to San Domingo.[55] Bryan, meanwhile, said he would hold the rebel leader responsible for his actions. Indeed, should he succeed, the United States would withhold recognition from him and also deny him San Domingo's share of the customs collections. On 2 June Bryan sent for Fiske at 10:40 P.M. because he wished to send a dispatch to Puerta Plata. "Administration is getting into a fine mess in S. Domingo," Fiske noted in his diary, "by firing out W. Russell a man with 14 years diplomatic experience in Spanish-American countries, and substituting a green man 'fresh from the people,' as [Bryan] says, named [James M.] Sullivan."[56]

Under threat of bombardment by American warships if fighting continued, Bordas and his opponents rested their arms temporarily and received from Wilson and Bryan a pledge to support a new president if "revolutionary movements cease and all subsequent changes in the Government of the Republic be effected by the peaceful processes provided in the Dominican Constitution." Thus San Domingo was on the verge of becoming a quasi-protectorate of the United States.

On 1 July, Daniels confided to Fiske that conditions both in Haiti and in San Domingo were worsening, adding, "Will have to put the Platt Amendment over all the countries between us and Panama." Startled, Fiske wrote in his diary, "Golly. . . . So that is the game of this administration—while it is protesting its superiority to all schemes of national aggrandizement and aggression."[57]

In the case of San Domingo, at least, Bryan's plan worked. The revolutionaries were directed to pledge their allegiance to a new provisional president or be arrested by American marines. When a full-fledged president was elected in October, he was recognized by the United States. He was told by Bryan, however, that no further insurrections would be tolerated and was given a list of reform bills his congress must pass.

Haiti, served by six presidents between 1911 and July 1915, was similarly distraught with financial problems, economic stagnation, and endemic revolutions. But in addition, the United States was worried that Germany was negotiating a $2 million loan to Haiti involving certain port rights, the control of customs, and the right to establish a coaling station at Mole St. Nicholas. Acutely conscious of the need to protect the Panama Canal, Bryan wanted either to buy the mole or to try to prevent its sale to a European power, especially Germany. Haiti's newest president, pro-American Michel Oreste, demurred but promised that his government would never transfer the mole to a foreign power.

To protect American lives and property, Bryan talked with Daniels, who had Fiske send the *Nashville* and the *Montana* to Haitian waters. Bryan then demanded of Oreste the same constitutional guarantees he had required of the new government in San Domingo.

On 12 July 1914, Fiske received a dispatch from the commander of American ships off Hispaniola that "seems to show that [the] State Dep't is embarking on a much more ambitious scheme in Haiti than the *official* letters to [the] Navy Dept from [the] State Dept indicate." Fiske declined to send ships and marines to Haiti merely on a verbal request from the State Department. When the department provided the necessary letter, he had to find both ships and men. As Fiske put it, "We have not the men

(1000 at least needed) unless we withdraw them from Vera Cruz. Of course, we must not take them from the battleships. I sent Russell's despatch to [Wilson] for his information. Russell wants *more* small ships. Certainly I do not wish to use destroyers for such purposes as running despatches around coast of Haiti!"[58]

Pending acceptance by Haiti of the governmental structure he outlined for it, Bryan acceded to a Haitian request that American troops be landed whenever disorder occurred. The secretary went to see Roosevelt. As Roosevelt told it, Bryan rushed into his office shouting, "I must have a battleship at Guantánamo by tomorrow morning." Roosevelt replied that this was impossible because the nearest battleship was four days' travel time away from Cuba. Bryan insisted: "But I must, I must have it. American lives are endangered at Haiti." Roosevelt repeated the impossibility of granting such a request but added, "We have a gunboat in the vicinity that could be in Guantánamo Bay within twenty-four hours." Whereupon Bryan exclaimed, "Oh, that's all right; when I say 'battleship' I mean anything that goes and has some guns on it."[59] Roosevelt soon had a warship with marines sent to Guantánamo Bay for use when needed, and Bryan continued to negotiate treaties banning guns and preserving universal peace.[60] Soon thereafter Fiske spoke with Roosevelt, who agreed with him "that [Bryan] has completely reversed his declared anti-imperialistic policy and that he has been led into it!"[61]

Bryan offered his familiar plan for constitutional and financial reforms to the newest president of Haiti, Davilmar Theodore, when he was inaugurated on 10 November 1914. Theodore refused, however, and Bryan would not recognize him, thus numbering Theodore's days. Early in 1915, when Vilbrun Guillaume Sam challenged Theodore, Sam's way was eased by Rear Adm. William B. Caperton of the *Des Moines*; Bryan told Wilson that he was ready to intervene "whenever the time is ripe."[62] Was not the time at hand? Wilson asked. Bryan stalled and then resigned in mid June.[63]

Bryan was trying to protect American lives and property and to stabilize the political and economic life of both San Domingo and Haiti. He opposed having the Mole St. Nicholas fall into German hands on both nationalistic and strategic grounds, fearing the danger to the Panama Canal and the possibility of French control of Haitian finances if France were to contest American hegemony in the Caribbean. Averse to the use of force, he rejected military intervention. In August 1915, however, Wilson directed the occupation of Haiti by American troops. Once pacified, Haiti was forced to become a quasi-protectorate of the United States.[64]

Admiral Bradley A. Fiske

Events in Japan, Mexico, San Domingo, and Haiti beautifully illustrate how Fiske, the ranking naval officer, was prevented by President Wilson and Secretary Daniels from managing naval affairs. As Fiske saw it, the administration should set national policies; and if these called for military support, the military men, the experts, should not be interfered with when they provided it. Although he did not want war with Japan, Fiske thought it wise to prepare the fleet nevertheless. In this objective he was preemptorily blocked. He well knew that it would take time to get the fleet—short of enlisted personnel, guns, and mines—ready for war; and he wanted the fleet concentrated instead of scattered around the world. Moreover, Fiske felt that the organization of the Navy Department ought to be reformed. He also believed that the advice furnished by the General Board and the Joint Army and Navy Board—the best advice American military men could produce—should be accorded respectful consideration by administration leaders.

Fiske was terribly upset by President Wilson's and Bryan's leadership in foreign affairs. He believed, as Leonard Wood did, that a naval blockade of Mexico would be ineffective unless communications with Mexico were cut by both land and sea. By contravening international law, the administration had acted immorally, Fiske felt, in trying to force Huerta out; furthermore, the diplomats used by the administration were much less well versed in international law and diplomacy than were the leading American naval officers. In Fiske's opinion, logic—the way naval officers learned to make estimates of a situation—was evidently unknown in either the White House or the State Department. Had adequately trained and experienced diplomats been used, Fiske would not have had to fracture the fleet throughout the Caribbean and Gulf of Mexico. But most repulsive of all to him was the fact that moralists like Wilson and Bryan could prate about spreading American democracy to "benighted" nations and, in the end, forcibly seize the objects of their best intentions. Although they would deny it, the antimilitarists were really more militaristic than military men themselves.

12

PREPARING THE NAVY FOR WAR, 1914

On 28 July 1914, a month after a Serb patriot assassinated Archduke Franz Ferdinand, heir to the Austrian throne, Austria-Hungary invaded Serbia. On 1 August, Germany declared war on Russia; the next day Germans began marching through Luxembourg en route to France; and on 4 August Britain declared war on Germany, and Japan sided with her. The Great War had begun.

As in 1913, Bradley A. Fiske spent his annual leave during the summer of 1914 at the Naval War College. On 1 August he told the General Board that he had been blocked by the president from assembling the fleet and preparing it for service in light of the critical situation developing in Europe. Fiske asked the board to help draft a letter to Josephus Daniels, the secretary of the navy, to this effect.[1] The board wrote the letter, with Fiske thinking that the president would not send the battleships back from Mexico because "he does not wish to give the impression that [the] U.S. is considering the use of force."[2]

On 5 August President Wilson took his first step to insure American neutrality by forbidding the transmission of non-neutral radio messages. Fiske directed his service to give no information to belligerent ships and established a new Office of Communications in his Operations Division to censor radio traffic.[3] But he believed the president wrong in adopting neutrality. "Why not [have the] U.S. declare war on Germany—I say! This would lighten our neutral obligations and lessen the injury to our commerce. There would be no real risk, because British fleet can control the seas," he wrote in his diary.[4]

On 6 August, Fiske recommended, and the General Board unanimously agreed, that the board should return to Washington "at once" in order to be readily accessible to Daniels. In his diary, meanwhile, Fiske confided, "The only answer to the sword is the sword. . . . Now this war was brought on by civilians: peace will be brought on by the Army and Navy."[5] His discomfort at being under civilian control was evident: it was, he wrote, "utter folly to put civilians at [the] head of [the] Army and Navy in any country. Not only useless, but dangerous. [The] Navy can never be gotten away from politics, so long as its head is a politician, who is there because he is a politician!"⁶ As if in response, Daniels told the General Board to remain at Newport; and Wilson directed that all military men, both active and retired, not publish anything about the war. Fiske thereupon noted that "all this is consistent with the general plan of the present—Jeffersonian— administration to minimize the value of the A[rmy] and N[avy], and to keep them down—to make them appear on the same plane as policemen and firemen! Simply used, as instruments, by a superior and supremely able and efficient—civilian body!"⁷

Although he "burned" to command the fleet, Fiske thought it better for the time being to "observe, consult and decide as to new lines of study, work and progress," adding, "Perhaps I can gradually evolve some scheme whereby a more intimate connection with, and control of, [the] fleet can be had in Navy Dept."⁸ On 17 August Fiske proposed concentrating the Atlantic Fleet, holding target practice and conducting tactical drills, and devising "a more comprehensive and rational battle practice for the Fleet than has yet appeared." "Progress?" he asked himself, answering, "I think it will turn out so." But Daniels's veto of the plans arrived on 26 August. Augustus F. Fechteler, the aide for inspections, wrote Fiske that the plan "is put off by Cabinet 'for the present.' Gosh: the Fleet is deteriorating, like an eagle in a cage."⁹

Fiske held Germany responsible for the war even though he himself was "somewhat pro-German." Germany would not have gone to war, he reasoned, had she not thought she could win; and Fiske feared that the German staff methods would not be learned quickly enough either by her European enemies or by the Americans. He concluded, therefore, that the chances of success greatly favored Germany and that the United States was in "a situation of the greatest possible peril" because of Germany's "hatred for the United States." But he failed to spell out either the "peril" or the reasons for "hatred." Nor did he suggest outright American intervention in the war against Germany.¹⁰

Rather than confer with Fiske, Daniels recalled his civilian assistant, Franklin D. Roosevelt, to the capital. When Roosevelt arrived from his speechmaking on 30 July, he found that "nobody seemed the least excited about the European crisis." Twelve battleships were off Veracruz; the rest of the fleet was scattered about the globe. "A complete smash up [in Europe] is inevitable, and there are a great many problems for us to consider," he wrote Mrs. Roosevelt on 1 August. "Mr. D.[aniels] totally fails to grasp the situation and I am to see the President Monday a.m., to go over our own situation."[11] As for Daniels, Roosevelt found him "feeling chiefly very sad that his faith in human nature and civilization and similar idealist nonsense was receiving such a rude shock. So I started in alone to get things ready and prepare plans for what *ought* to be done by the Navy end of things."[12] Roosevelt greatly exaggerated his own importance and the burden of his work, for on 14 August he began a campaign for nomination as U.S. senator from New York—at full pay, Fiske noted. When Roosevelt returned to duty, on 8 September, twelve battleships were still in Mexican waters. Their material condition was poor, the morale of their crews even worse. While Daniels spoke of sending the fleet to Europe to bring American refugees home, Roosevelt asked Fiske to have the General Board write a letter, which he would take to the president, suggesting that the battleships be brought north. Fiske obtained the letter, with the net result that Daniels ordered exactly one ship home.[13] Furthermore, the secretary failed to keep Fiske and other professional naval advisers fully informed of administration policy.

Upon arriving at the Navy Department on 1 September, Fiske found an atmosphere of perfect calm rather than one of excitement; the exception, perhaps, was Franklin D. Roosevelt. Fiske reported to Daniels, had a "good talk" with him, and "tried to impress him with [the] seriousness of [the] Fleet's unpreparedness." But he failed to do so.[14] Fiske then attended a meeting of the General Board which recommended that the ships in Mexican waters be returned home. Roosevelt had made a similar recommendation to Daniels on 2 August, and Alfred T. Mahan had done so on 3 August. Nevertheless Daniels remained unmoved. With the officer corps muzzled, Fiske hoped against hope that Roosevelt would plead his case for preparedness.

As the early days of September passed, Fiske felt that his position as aide for operations was becoming "excessively disagreeable." As he put it, President Wilson "carries to extreme the idea of dealing only with the heads of Army and Navy, the Sec[retary] and Ass[istant] Sec[retary]." Daniels, Fiske complained, "does reverse, and deals with my subordinates and takes advice of *everybody*. I lose both ways!"[15] On 9 September Fiske got the General Board to write a letter asking the president why the battleships should not come north and detailing the unsatisfactory status of the fleet. No fleet operations had been held since target practice during the fall of 1912, after which ships had gone to Mexico and elsewhere. With the battleships doing gunboat duty, the fleet commander could not organize and train his fleet as a whole and impress his views upon it. Target practice was being horribly neglected, as was the training of personnel. In consequence, morale was low, and the material condition of the ships off Mexico was poor because of their long detention in tropical waters.[16] Although Wilson made an uneasy peace with Mexico and recalled American troops from Veracruz late in November, he directed that the battleships remain in central America, with any returning north to be relieved by others going south. Fiske was thus denied the opportunity to rectify the serious discrepancies afflicting the fleet. Meanwhile Fiske detailed two captains to serve on the Joint State, War, and Navy Neutrality Board established in mid August and arranged with Robert Lansing, counselor of the State Department, for the coordination of naval and foreign affairs.

It made no sense to Fiske to have Daniels tell him that his, Fiske's, work was superior to that done under the Taft administration, that criticism of the status of the navy must stem from political motives, or to write on his fitness report (for the period 31 March to 30 September 1914) that Fiske was "a learned and able officer." What was important to Fiske was that the navy be strong enough to defend the nation's interests and that its strength be compared not with what it was under Taft but with that of our potential enemies. Nor did the secretary of state, William Jennings Bryan, help by crusading for his "cooling off" treaties even while the war was being fought. On 12 September, Fiske heard Bryan make an "out and out peace speech! Gosh. This foreshadows his attitude and that of [Daniels] in coming contentions as to [the] lessons of this War towards U.S. Army and Navy!"[17]

On 14 September, Fiske tried to arrange the semi-annual target practice and maneuvering-exercise program for the fleet. He felt that the "trouble is not with Mr. Daniels, as an individual, but with the fact that he is given absolute and uncontrolled power over a great machine he does not understand."[18] Daniels denied Fiske permission to publish a short article on "The Mathematical Certainty of War," saying that naval officers were interdicted by presidential order from speaking or publishing articles about the war.[19]

On 17 September Fiske represented Daniels at ceremonies held in New York City in which Fletcher relieved Charles J. Badger as commander in chief. Badger reported for duty with the General Board just in time to help the board advise Daniels on what changes should be made in the building program and personnel legislation because of the war in Europe. The board unanimously recommended that "the United States policy should be to have a Navy second to none." Meanwhile Fiske asked Capt. John Hood to write a paper to be sent to Daniels and also "tried to get [Daniels] to see the wisdom of putting more Army at Vera Cruz and taking away the navy."[20] After conferring with Maj. Gen. William Wallace Wotherspoon, the army chief of staff, Fiske noted that Wotherspoon agreed with him that "there seems to be almost a determination to deny the fact that the military in-gredient exists in our national and international life."[21] As proof of the last remark, on 18 September Daniels disapproved the General Board's recom-mendations on the building program and personnel needs for fiscal year 1916. He "rather insists," Fiske recorded, "on G.B. simply sticking to pre-vious recommendations and saying GB had no reason to change. . . . [Dan-iels] will publish [the] report—if it is on lines he likes."[22] Actually, Daniels postponed asking the board for its recommendations until the last possible moment before submitting his annual report, so that the board could con-sider lessons drawn from the European war. The board thereupon withdrew Hood's paper, which supported Fiske's demands to improve the navy, and took no action on construction or personnel matters until 1 October.

On 28 September, while witnessing the aerial acrobatics of a naval pilot with Daniels and Roosevelt, Fiske spoke in support of Capt. Mark Bristol's request of $2 million for naval aviation for fiscal 1915. He also "tried very hard to impress [Daniels] with [the] gravity of . . . unpreparedness of [the] fleet."[23] The next day, in addition to objecting when the secretary wished to send three additional ships to Mexico, Fiske told Daniels quite bluntly that "if public attention were called anxiously and critically to the navy, because of antagonistic relations with Germany or other country—that the navy could not stand inspection, because it has been kept so divided up for a year and a half."[24] With great perceptiveness, he also told Daniels that the United States would have trouble with Great Britain in two ways: first, if Britain made foodstuffs contraband; and second, if the United States built a large merchant marine.[25]

On 1 October, Daniels asked Fiske, "Why don't you take the chairman-ship of the Board to test the [Willard] Isham shell?" Although somewhat taken aback, Fiske said he would if Daniels so wished.[26] Clearly Daniels wanted him out of the way, but he did not press the point. He then accom-panied Fiske to discuss with the General Board the building program and personnel legislation for 1916. Daniels asked if the success thus far achieved in the war by smaller ships, from cruisers to submarines, had changed the mind of the board with respect to building battleships; the board's opinion was that dreadnought building should continue. Daniels then asked how aircraft should be developed and how he should spend $300,000 available for the purchase of planes. The board suggested that American manu-facturers would be stimulated by the money to buy the best foreign designs and that they would build aircraft for the navy in a comparatively short time.[27]

On 6 October, and again on 7 October, Fiske told Daniels that Japan's taking of the Marshall Islands from Germany increased the difficulty the

U.S. Navy would have operating in the Pacific. On 8 October, Fiske told him that the navy needed five thousand additional men more than it needed another battleship. Fiske thought he had made an impression, but he got nowhere when he tried to convince Fletcher and Albert G. Winterhalter, the aide for material, who "feared abatement of the building program."[28] By this time, however, he had some official as well as unofficial support for his demands for preparedness from those Americans who believed that no lasting peace could be obtained until Germany was crushed.

Fiske and both Roosevelts saw the navy as too weak to support national policies, but Wilson echoed Bryan in saying that even the European victor in the Great War would be too exhausted to challenge the United States. The president relied on a "citizenry trained and accustomed to arms," rather than on a standing or reserve army, and a "powerful navy" for purposes of defense. Therefore, Wilson said, he would keep the army and navy estimates for fiscal year 1916 close to those for 1915.[29] Daniels turned down Fiske's suggestions that the aides receive legislative sanction, that their title be changed from "aide" to "chief of division" (which would more accurately describe their duties and also parallel the designation used in other government departments), and that no bureau chief ever serve as acting secretary, saying, "Absolute control of the Navy by a military head or by a general staff composed solely of naval officers is contrary to the spirit of our institutions." He then cryptically noted in his diary: "Fiske & [Capt. Harry S.] Knapp. Want German staff."[30] Daniels's comment was wide of the mark. A great deal of attention was being given to departmental reorganization and administration, and Fiske was supported by many similarly sincere and devoted officers who believed that reorganization would help prepare the navy for effective service.

Fiske persisted in his attempt to persuade Daniels to prepare the navy for war. On 15 October, Rep. Augustus P. Gardner, a Republican from Massachusetts and Daniels's most vehement critic in the House, introduced, at Franklin D. Roosevelt's suggestion, a resolution asking for a national security commission to investigate "the question of the preparedness of the United States for war, defensive or offensive."[31] On 21 October, Roosevelt told the press that ninety-eight ships would have to be withdrawn from service if some eighteen thousand additional men were not provided. Despite being taken to task by Daniels, Roosevelt continued to demand more preparedness.

Although Congress was not greatly impressed with Gardner's resolution, many individuals and a large number of newspaper and magazine editors favored additional defense. A group of private citizens in New York City formed the National Security League in support of Gardner's demand, and

Lemuel P. Padgett, a Democrat from North Carolina and the chairman of the House Naval Affairs Committee, agreed to hold hearings beginning 3 November on the subject of naval preparedness. On 18 October, unable to make headway with Daniels, Fiske wrote Col. William C. Church, editor of the *Army and Navy Journal*, telling him that the "Navy Department has no means for getting from [a] peace condition to [a] war condition . . . due to [the] lack of [a] General Staff, etc. I am sure the weak point in the armor of the present administration is the silly handling of the Navy Department by Sec[retary] D[aniels]. . . ."[32]

"Wearied" by Fiske, who perennially demanded the creation of a naval general staff, Daniels resolved to keep naval authority in civilian hands.[33] On 20 October, Fiske asked himself how Daniels could explain the excellent work of the General Staff in the War Department: "I think a fight will start on this subject pretty soon." Capt. Roy C. Smith had joined Fiske's office on 15 October as director of target practice. Fiske made Smith one of his assistants and directed him to get well posted on American war plans. With his "war staff," composed of Smith, Lt. Comdrs. William P. Cronan and Zachariah H. Madison, and Lt. Leigh Noyes, Fiske discussed such questions as "the preparation of a real and practical War Plan, by which we can mobilize if war comes and then handle our forces."[34] During the afternoon of 21 October, he met Representative Gardner, who was visiting Roosevelt at the department. Gardner asked Fiske for a tabulation showing how far behind the navy was from the General Board's shipbuilding program. On 21 October Fiske asked George Clement Perkins of California, a member of the Senate Naval Affairs Committee, for an interview. Instead Perkins called on Fiske at his apartment at Stoneleigh Court, where Fiske explained his ideas on naval administration and his inability to have Daniels adopt them. Senator Perkins said he would talk with Congressman Gardner but felt that nothing could be done without the support of the administration.[35]

That evening at ten o'clock, Fiske and the secretary of the General Board, Edward H. Campbell, met Gardner and Roosevelt at the Metropolitan Club. They gave Gardner the information he had asked for and Fiske "explained the whole navy situation." Roosevelt felt that Fiske had "burned his bridges behind him" by revealing the shortages in manpower, but Fiske assured him that he had not made public anything that could not be found in naval registers and directories.[36] On 22 October, when the congressman called at his office, Fiske pumped Gardner full of facts in a two-hour meeting. That night, Senator Perkins again called at Fiske's apartment, this time to state that neither Fiske nor other officers could accomplish a thing except through the secretary and, in Fiske's words, "that

I might be misunderstood and misrepresented." Disdaining such advice, Fiske told Roosevelt on 24 October that they must not accept any "palliative" for the current situation but must insist upon having a general staff. Roosevelt replied that he would agree if there was any chance of getting one. Fiske told him that he thought there was an excellent chance "if we held firm." Roosevelt thereupon promised support.[37] On the same day a *New York Herald* editorial called for a general naval staff and the *Army and Navy Journal* published a column entitled "Proper Control of the Navy." Only Fiske knew that the first had resulted from his contacts with a former naval officer now with the *Herald*, J. D. J. Kelley, and that the column in the other had resulted from a letter he had written to its editor.[38] But the message was not getting through to Daniels; that very day he stated publicly that a general staff was not consonant with the principles of a republic.[39]

On the morning of 26 October, Daniels came to the office for only a moment. Fiske had "lot to talk about with him," but Daniels went out "speechifying." After he had gone, Fiske held another meeting of his war staff, this time with Adm. Austin M. Knight as a temporary member. It was decided that Fiske should "try to develop a real and practical War Plan, by which we can mobilize if war comes and then handle our forces." He added, *"Only real obstacle is the Sec."*[40] The next day Fiske handed Daniels a four-page paper he had written, entitled "Meditations Concerning Organization." The gist of it was that no one was responsible for drafting war plans and having them implemented. As insurance, he sent a copy to William C. Church, editor of the *Army and Navy Journal.*[41]

A major item in Fiske's administrative war plan was additional personnel. He thought he had Daniels convinced when Victor Blue, chief of the Bureau of Navigation, said (in a letter dated 28 October) that, as Fiske noted, "we could cut down the crews of certain vessels and stations and have more men in the navy than are needed!" Fiske added: "Before this, I realized that he [Blue] and the Aid[e] for Material [Winterhalter] were siding with the Secretary against me. This was hard to bear."[42] He nevertheless called another meeting of his war staff and discussed army and navy reorganization plans, both British and American, dating back to the turn of the century. On 31 October, when he offered to bet, giving two-to-one odds, that the nation would be at war within two years, none of his staff took him up.[43]

It was Lieutenant Commander Cronan, of his war staff, who suggested that Fiske summarize his recommendations to Daniels on preparedness and file the paper in the navy's official records. Cronan reasoned that the United States would get into the war. If it did so with the navy unprepared, disaster would follow and Fiske would be held responsible. It would be wise, therefore, to state the facts and record them in advance.[44] Fiske wrote the paper and awaited a favorable moment to give it to Daniels. On 5 November, spending half an hour together, Daniels tried to win Fiske's support for the administration and get him not to demand increased naval appropriations. Fiske declined and handed Daniels his paper.[45] Without sending a copy to Fiske, however, Daniels wrote the General Board that "no emergency" existed and that it could only "confidentially" discuss "our naval policy in connection with the present situation in Europe," thereby undercutting Fiske's efforts to perfect various war plans. In addition, Blue made Fiske's demand for more men seem unnecessary by saying that he could so reassign personnel as to have 843 superfluous men available on 1 October 1916. The board postponed the personnel matter until its next meeting and took up Fiske's paper on preparedness.[46]

The paper, which Fiske asserted was the most important he ever wrote, deserves our attention. The navy, Fiske argued, was unprepared for war. No one should get unduly excited about preparing for a war that might not come, he contended, but preparation was nevertheless wise, in the same way that people accept a smallpox innoculation. In his position as senior adviser to the secretary of the navy, Fiske had informed himself as best he could about the comparative strengths of the major navies of the world and of the probability of America's going to war. The current war, he felt, would be a long one, would involve additional nations, and at its end would provoke serious readjustments of boundaries, insular possessions, treaties, and agreements. Peace could not be expected for five years, Fiske wrote, during which some incident like the blowing up of the *Maine* would draw the United States into war. The best naval opinion, he said, was that the United States would be drawn into the war, that that danger should be faced, and that reasonable steps should be taken to avert it. The U.S. Navy was unprepared, Fiske claimed, in three ways. First, the navy was short both of officers and men. It took four years to create officers through the Naval Academy; nevertheless our defense should depend on regulars instead of reserves. To man the ships needed for war, Fiske calculated, the navy needed 19,600 more men. Second, Fiske argued that the navy department was deficient in organization and in its present status could not meet the dangers threatening it. A general staff was needed to prepare for war and, perhaps, to conduct a war as well. This general staff would supply the secretary with information needed for reaching and carrying out strategic decisions. The purely advisory General Board performed only 1 percent of the duties which would be undertaken by a general staff. The past three months of the European war had proven that a navy lacking a general staff was not being provided with the most modern improvements. Third, Fiske argued, the navy was deficient in training because of insufficient personnel, departmental organization, and the lack of sufficient numbers of small ships. Among others, the Moody board and the Swift board had recommended the establishment of a general staff, but their recommendations were not carried out. "In my opinion," Fiske wrote, "the failure to adopt those recommendations was serious, and will invite disaster if a great war comes."[47]

Daniels read the paper carefully, said nothing, remained unruffled, and returned it to Fiske, who retired to his office and reported his failure to Smith and Cronan. He put the paper in his desk, saying that he would speak to Daniels about it at a later time.[48] Then, although believing that it would not do any good, and without informing Daniels, he filed it, under date of 9 November 1914, but he sent a copy of it to Church.

On 7 November, Fiske told the General Board that a fight over preparedness and naval reorganization would soon erupt in Congress and that "the more firm the administration is the more strenuous will be the fight and the more determined the attack of the big navy men. . . ."[49] Daniels had asked Fiske how many ships of each class would be needed if the nation went to war. Although Fiske thought this was Daniels's way of finding out whether eighteen thousand more men actually were needed, he asked the General Board to prepare a list of ships for the secretary when he met with the board on 10 November to discuss the personnel problem. Fiske also asked the board to show into which port every ship would go if the European mobilization plan was put into effect.[50] Daniels, meanwhile, asked the board for its recommendations on the 1916 building and personnel programs and for a separate letter on "emergency steps which should be taken from conditions arising from the present European war," adding that he would meet with the board on 11 November. The board unanimously agreed to incorporate into the letter to Daniels a recommendation for the appropriation of $5 million for the development of a naval air service and also an amendment stating the number of trained personnel needed "at the present time, to assure the national defense."[51]

Fiske was talking with Daniels on 10 November about the number of ships and men required when the paper from the board arrived. Daniels told Winterhalter and Blue, who were present, to remain, and asked Fiske to return in two hours. When Fiske returned the three men were united against him. As Fiske recalled, Secretary Daniels

> was very insistent that [the] GB should not submit papers calling for more men than the Pres[ident] and Admin[istration] wanted, and [he] said [the] GB should study plans and have answers ready, to be given *when asked for.* Winterhalter and Blue agreed. Blue said [the] GB should not decide on

whether war should be declared or not or if [such a] probability existed. I replied that [the] GB averaged 59 years of age and it was our business to make up our opinion as to [the] probability of war and advise [Daniels] (Confidentially) about it. We reached no agreement.[52]

Following the meeting, Fiske showed Roosevelt a copy of his letter to Daniels on the "unpreparedness of the Navy." Roosevelt liked the letter, calling it "bully," and said that he would keep it to use in preparing an article for publication.[53]

When Daniels appeared before the board on 11 November, Admiral Dewey said that he wanted the board's recommendations published; if the last paragraph, on personnel, would prevent its publication, it should be deleted. The members voted to eliminate it. Dewey then said that the board had prepared a supplementary confidential letter stating that 19,600 extra men were needed to meet an immediate emergency and that Daniels should seek at least 15,000 of that number.[54]

When the *Washington Post* and the *New York Herald* mentioned the need for 19,600 men, Fiske realized that there was a leak somewhere in the General Board. Daniels called Fiske to investigate. Fiske found that Winterhalter and Blue had been at the 11 November meeting and assumed that the two had talked: both men smiled when Daniels said that despite his wish, the General Board's letter had retained a demand for 19,600 additional men. Fiske then argued against the three men and their position that the board should merely make plans and keep quiet. The "interview ended with my agreeing to return their letter to [the] GB, suggesting [it] omit any mention of 19,600."[55] After revising the letter, Dewey had it filed with the war plans. Upon receiving a letter from Blue on the personnel situation, Dewey said it would be discussed the next day.[56]

The day of decision was 13 November. Winterhalter objected to the recommendation of $5 million for the acquisition of aircraft and also to the board's recommendations on personnel. Dewey ordered a vote on each paragraph. Over Winterhalter's objections, each paragraph was accepted for inclusion in the letter. Then the letter as a whole was voted upon, the result being seven in favor and one—Winterhalter—opposed. A letter from Daniels to Fiske was then read in which Daniels stated that if the minutes for 11 and 12 November recorded his statements before the board, he wanted to go over them and revise them. The members then voted to delete any mention of what Daniels had said; the vote was six to one in favor of doing so, with one abstention.[57] On 16 November, Fiske told the board that Daniels objected to the board's conclusions about the difficulties of mobilization and its demand for more men; he said that Daniels "would prefer not to print those paragraphs." All seven men present except Hood voted in favor of excising the paragraphs in question.[58] The next day, Admiral Dewey revealed that Daniels had personally asked him to have the paragraphs omitted.[59] Thus Daniels had succeeded in getting all the members except Hood to agree to leave out of their report (which would be published as part of the secretary's annual report) any reference to the need for additional men. Fiske felt that it was more important that Daniels see the need for the men than to have the information published. In the end, he said, "I was the last to give in; Hood never did."[60]

On 17 November, Daniels received the General Board's pruned recommendations on the building program and personnel for 1916. The board pointed out that the navy was "deficient ten battleships built, building, and authorized, from that contemplated in the 1903 ship program"; noted the "dangerous situation" because the navy had only twelve aircraft, "no more than two of which are of the same type, and all reported to have too little speed and carrying capacity for service work"; called for the expenditure of $5 million for naval aviation; and spoke of the need for more personnel, more trained personnel, a naval reserve, and a naval militia, but it included no numbers of men.[61]

Fiske left Washington for a week in order to witness target practice. Upon his return on 23 November, he found no change in Daniels's attitude. He confided in his diary on 26 November, "I wonder how long the Bryan-Daniels duo is going to last. Sometimes, when my thoughts have gotten away for awhile from official matters, and I suddenly realize that more than 90 million intelligent people have committed their destinies to the people now controlling them, I am startled by the feeling of incredibility that comes over me." The previous day, he had written Daniels saying that the General Board's recommendations made it necessary to take various ships out of commission. His conclusion was debated by the board on 27 November;[62] and for the next week argument followed argument, with Fiske noting on 3 December:

> Blue and I had an argument this a.m. [in] which developed the fact that Blue and Winterhalter are allied against me. As they back up [Daniel's] ideas (at least ostensibly, and I think Blue does sincerely) I am liable to be bounced any day. This issue as to whether or not we have enough men to man the fleet we would use in war is a most serious issue.

Strong support for Fiske's stand came from testimony given before the House Naval Affairs Committee in December. Yates Stirling bravely told about inadequacies in his submarine flotilla and recommended the creation of a naval general staff, despite a letter handed him by Winterhalter in which

Daniels reprimanded him for criticizing the department. Stirling realized that he would contradict much of Daniels's testimony and become a political football between the Democrats who supported Daniels in saying that all was well with the navy and the Republicans who said otherwise. Stirling later explained how Fiske came to be in such poor graces with Daniels and how Fiske's staff had supported him:

> The opposition, the Republicans, found out that I had received a reprimand from the Secretary just before coming before the Committee. It was this way. Admiral Bradley Fiske was Aide for Operations. He and Winterhalter were in competition for the favor of the Secretary. Operations should have held precedence over material, but at that time and even yet, it is a case of who is the stronger character or has more stubbornness in his makeup. Winterhalter had won. Bill Cronan, Fiske's aide, knew of my letter and naturally saw that the Republicans on the Committee learned of it. Anything to embarrass the Aide for Material.[63]

Fiske characterized 17 December, the day he testified before the House committee, as "the unhappiest time in my life." Dewey told him several times, "I wouldn't have your job for anything in the world; but you're the best man for the job, and you've got to hold on to it."[64] Unfortunately, the aging admiral was too ill to testify in support of Fiske.

As the German war machine smashed French and British resistance, Fiske concluded that although Germany was "threatening the very existence of the United States," Americans were "watching the spectacle as a child watches a fire spreading."[65] He had tried persistently to get Daniels to agree to establish a general staff, ask for more enlisted men, train the men better, and establish a naval reserve. Moreover, he was irked because Daniels secretly used Blue to do some things for which Fiske, as aide for operations, was responsible, such as making out the schedule for the employment of the fleet. Fiske's visits to the fleet showed that the few ships maneuvered and fired poorly and that officers were keenly aware of their inadequacies.

The navy needed more men, said Fiske; Daniels disapproved. Fiske objected to dividing the fleet; Daniels would not concentrate it.[66] The secretary published the report of the General Board but, Fiske noted, it "does not say [that] he told [the board] he would not print it unless [the board] left out the part asking for more men. [Daniels's] report is absolutely the reverse, in its character, of my report to him, made only three weeks before; and yet I am his military adviser! One headline [in Daniels's report] is proof of the Preparedness of the Navy."[67] Fiske interpreted the report as the parting of the ways. During his eighteen months as Daniels's major military adviser, Fiske had been unable to convince the secretary of his ideas. He must appeal over Daniels's head to Congress and to the people.[68]

On 3 November, Blue told Padgett's committee that the navy needed only 161 additional officers and 338 additional enlisted men to bring it to full peacetime strength and needed only 4,565 for war purposes.[69] On 8 December, Badger said the fleet was short of battleships, destroyers, auxiliaries, and ammunition and that the number of men needed to bring the fleet to wartime strength was 18,556—a far cry from Blue's estimate.[70] Fletcher thought 5,000 men were needed to bring the fleet personnel up to wartime strength and that it would take from four months to a year to train them. On the number of men, then, Fletcher basically agreed with Blue. But in a letter to the committee, he later corrected himself and said the shortage amounted to some 10,000 men.[71]

In beginning his testimony, given on 10 December, Daniels supported the regular construction program because, he said, no emergency existed. The navy had enough men, but a naval reserve might prove useful. He objected to the council of national defense demanded by Fiske because, he argued, it would violate the principle of the separation of the powers and lead to autocracy and militarism. Daniels had all the expert advice he needed, and he held that "the Navy is in good shape" and that "any suggestion . . . that there is not perfect coordination between the fleet and the War College is incorrect." Furthermore, the value of the educational system he had established for the men was "of incalculable value—incalculable."[72] The secretary supported the development of naval aviation, but by private industry rather than a departmental research and development program.[73] But Daniels was somewhat unsure of himself: on 15 December he asked Fletcher to provide a statement "for insertion in[to the minutes of the] hearing as to whether or not there is lack of coordination in the administration of the fleet and what the War College says it should accomplish."[74]

Franklin Roosevelt, who had spent two hours in Fiske's office on 15 December obtaining information, testified on 16 December to the need for a naval reserve and a scientific way of assessing the relative strength of the navy. Roosevelt believed that the fleet was unbalanced. Eighteen thousand men were needed if all ships were commissioned for war purposes, he said, and from thirty to fifty thousand additional men would be required to put into effect confidential war plans.[75]

Fiske was disturbed by the character of much of the testimony. Fletcher, for example, had "brought out many naval needs, but I think he made the Personnel situation too rosy. I am disappointed at [the] neutralness and colorlessness of testimony of Badger."[76] Fiske wanted somehow to get to testify and thus "get the real truth before the nation." On the morning of 16 December he telephoned Rep. Richmond Pearson Hobson, an Alabama Democrat, and suggested that "if he wanted to get straight news about the Army," he would get the committee to call for testimony from the chief of the army general staff. Hobson replied "A word to the wise is sufficient." That evening Hobson invited Fiske to appear before the committee the next day.[77] Fiske then planted various questions to be asked with Rep. Ernest W. Roberts, a Republican from Massachusetts.

When Hobson asked Fiske to discuss "the line of policy . . . the line of grand strategy, and the . . . strength of the fleet today," Fiske said he would defend the country by obtaining control of the sea wherever the enemy was, in enemy waters or in those of the United States. Battle cruisers, which the navy lacked, would be useful, Fiske said, and he would use mines defensively along our coasts and offensively off enemy shores. Questioned by Roberts, Fiske stated that the navy should have many more than the two mine layers it had, and 20,000—instead of the 336—mines at hand. Hobson then asked if "aerial navigation is coming to be a serious part of the operation of defense." After describing the various scouting functions aircraft could perform, Fiske noted that it was also possible for aircraft carried in warships to bomb enemy cities from between four to six hundred miles out at sea. The scout airplanes carried to Mexico in 1914 could have bombed Tampico and Veracruz as easily as not. There was no defense against aircraft accompanying a fleet except other aircraft. The U.S. Navy, Fiske said, did not have a proportionate number of aircraft compared to other major nations.

Fiske was asked if the navy had any ships that could be sent to scout for a European or Asiatic fleet known to be sailing for the United States or one of its possessions. His answer was no. In response to a follow-up question, Fiske explained that the General Board merely made recommendations and the secretary made the decisions. Then as he had been primed to do, Roberts asked how long it would take to get the navy ready to fight.

> ADMIRAL FISKE: I would say five years.
> MR. ROBERTS: Five years?
> ADMIRAL FISKE: Yes.
> MR. ROBERTS: I am surprised.

Having shocked the committee, Fiske offered an extended explanation of how he had reached his conclusion, ending with his description of how a naval general staff could better prepare the navy for war than the aide system.[78]

When Rep. Augustus Gardner appeared before the committee on 18

December, he said he wished more of "the truth" could be obtained from witnesses like Fiske and Stirling, who had the courage to speak out. He asked the committee to support the recommendations of the General Board rather than those of the secretary, and specifically—with respect to personnel —those of Roosevelt and Fiske rather than those of Blue. As for aircraft, all Daniels did, Gardner claimed, was "dawdle, dawdle, dawdle." Gardner also supported Hobson and Fiske on the need for a permanent council of national defense and a naval general staff. Unfortunately, he became so obstreperous that the chairman had to intervene in what was clearly a political battle between the Democratic majority of the committee and Gardner, a Republican. So the hearings proper ended.[79]

Newspapers printed most of Roosevelt's and Fiske's testimony. The *New York Times*, for instance, noted that Fiske had illuminated "amazing deficiencies" in naval material and "dealt impressively with the improbability of a coherent course of action with the present organization of the navy."[80] Various naval officers called on Fiske at home to offer congratulations. On the morning of 18 December, many navy and army officers at the department shook Fiske's hand and a group waiting in his office enthusiastically praised him for what they deemed a personal favor. But the glory was short-lived: at about 8:30 the next morning a messenger summoned Fiske to appear before Daniels. The happy group suddenly became solemn; several men told Fiske, "Daniels is going to fire you." Fiske agreed. If he were not fired, Daniels would at least send him far away—say, to Olongapo in the Philippines. He found Daniels seated, palms down on his desk, looking very pale. After exchanging greetings, Daniels looked at Fiske fixedly for a few seconds, asked him for a copy of his testimony, spoke briefly about some unimportant matter, and dismissed him. Fiske told the group in his office that nothing had happened, whereupon they expressed their gratification and dispersed to their own offices. But Daniels would not forget.

Fiske had taken Daniels's annual report as the basis for appealing over the secretary's head to Congress. Daniels took Fiske's testimony as a justification for overlooking him henceforth. Up until 17 December, although the two men had strongly disagreed on the need to prepare the navy for war, their personal relationship had been friendly and pleasant. Although Daniels had little empathy or understanding of the professional attitude and aspirations of the career naval officer, Fiske liked him as a man; he appreciated his kindness of heart and steadfast adherence to the Christian principles he professed, and he was frequently tempted to cease pressing his ideas upon him. "But," Fiske reasoned, "I often told him that I was the only man in ninety million people to hold before him the military side of the navy, and

I felt it my duty to persist." Daniels, Fiske added, "always told me that I was right in so doing, and for a long while I thought that I was gradually impressing him with our dangers." Fiske's testimony, however, caused Daniels's attitude toward him to change entirely; now a cold formality replaced cordiality. Said Fiske later, "My period of misery had passed. I knew that I had done right, and that my testimony as the official expert of the Navy Department, had roused a powerful minority to a realization of the peril of the nation."[81]

The response of the Wilson administration to the Great War was to remain neutral and to muzzle its military men. It feared that the return of the battleships from Mexican waters and the shifting of the General Board from Newport to Washington would be judged as war preparations. In late July 1914, avidly supporting administration policy, Daniels recalled Roosevelt (a civilian)—not Fiske, his chief military adviser—to Washington. Believing it necessary to prepare for any eventuality, Fiske, supported by Roosevelt, the General Board, and many naval officers, wanted to concentrate the fleet and bring it up to wartime standards in all respects—material, personnel, organization, administration. He was keenly aware that "politicians" made national policy without reference to military leaders, that the president sought Daniels's counsel rather than his, and that Daniels, in turn, favored naval subordinates whose ideas pleased him more than those of his chief adviser. If Fiske had had his way, a council of national defense would advise the president on the coordination of political, foreign policy, and military matters and professional career officers, rather than civilians, would give the president military advice. Were he, as aide for operations, given control of the fleet, Fiske felt certain he could bring it into the intimate relationship it must have with the Navy Department. Denied such control, he saw that fleet as "deteriorating, like an eagle in a cage." When he turned to Roosevelt for help, Fiske found that it was Daniels, not Roosevelt, who carried weight on Capitol Hill. But what did these "politicians" in Congress know about professional naval matters? Daniels was a good man, but he lacked the scientific training needed to understand the operations of his forces.

Try as he might, Fiske failed to win Daniels over to his point of view. Fiske wanted to build up naval aviation and increase the number of men in the fleet. Fiske demanded a navy capable of upholding the national interests. But Daniels agreed with Wilson: no nation emerging from the Great War could challenge the security of the United States; there was, therefore, no need to strengthen the army or navy. Fiske wanted the aide system to be granted legislative sanction; he wanted to change "aide" to "chief of division" and let only aides, not bureau chiefs, serve in the absence of the secretary and assistant secretary. For his pains, Daniels said that Fiske wanted a "German" staff.

Fiske and Daniels were poles apart on the meaning of a naval general staff. Fiske saw an American staff as a planning center that would draft plans for every conceivable eventuality and draw up training programs and war games. Regular alternation of service would occur between the field and staff, as was done on the General Board, with the distinction that the chief of staff would have direct access to the president after consulting with the secretary of the navy. Since all major foreign nations used a general staff, Fiske saw nothing sinister in it, and he wished that it could be given a precise place in the constitutional edifice of the government. To Daniels, however, a general staff smacked of "Prussianism." By this, of course, he meant the apparent abdication in Germany of civilian authority to that of the military, the substitution of the military for the state itself, and the victory of the idea, held since Bismarck's time, that the only answer to democracy was troops. A general staff was simply not compatible, Daniels felt, with the principles of a republic.

After studying the naval organizations in Great Britain, the major European powers, and Japan, Fiske concluded that they were better than America's. When Daniels declined to accept his recommendations on reorganization, at the suggestion of one of his war staff, Fiske filed his paper on the unpreparedness of the navy in the official records. Shortly thereafter he took Daniels's refusal to accept the General Board's recommendation for increasing the number of enlisted personnel as the parting of the ways. The deep division of thought between Fiske and Daniels was increased by their differences on the questions of the naval aviation program, the efficiency of the fleet, and the relative strength of the navy. During the hearings held by the House Naval Affairs Committee late in 1914, Fiske had "played politics"—arranging for Hobson to have him testify and furnishing committee members with leading questions, including the one that elicited his response that it would take at least five years to make the navy ready for war. Fiske had voiced the attitude of the great majority of his fellow officers and, by going over Daniels's head, had alerted the American people to the inadequacies of their military establishments. He, of course, realized that in doing so, his days as aide for operations were numbered.

13

THE PARTING OF THE WAYS, 1914–1915

Public and private endorsement of his oft-reprinted testimony of 17 December 1914 reached Bradley A. Fiske for several weeks. The *New York Tribune* saw him as "Daniels's severest critic"; the *New York World* held that he alone showed a way to have a good navy—by adopting a general staff; and the *New York Sun* thanked him for having "turned a searchlight upon the deficiencies of the navy." The *Army and Navy Journal* added that he was supported by many other naval officers.[1]

Fiske believed that opposition to a general staff by the secretary of the navy, the bureau chiefs, and staff officers as a whole was "political." In Congress, Democrats supported Daniels against the Republican minority who favored additional naval preparedness. Given that situation, Fiske felt that he must engage in "politics" in order to achieve his objective of a general staff. He would, however, tackle Daniels once more. He had a "very emphatic talk" with the secretary, "in which I said my duty required me—as his only military adviser to keep military deficiencies before him *all the time*—a most ungrateful task!"[2] Daniels replied that Sen. Henry Cabot Lodge and Rep. Augustus P. Gardner were trying to "down the navy and *some naval officers* [were] *helping them*. I supposed," Fiske wrote, "he includes me—and I am confident he will get rid of me if he can." Fiske continued: "[Lt. Comdr. Zachariah H.] Madison tells me he heard [Rear Adm. Frank F.] Fletcher and [Rear Adm. Albert G.] Winterhalter saying to each other in [Daniels's] presence that [the] Aide system affords all the Gen[eral] Staff necessary. Et tu Brute, Fletcher! Fletcher told me later he meant 'if the Sec[retary] was sympathetic and behind it.' I told him that no one else would understand him to mean this, unless he *clearly* said it."[3]

At a meeting of the General Board, attended by Rear Adm. Austin M. Knight, president of the Naval War College, Fiske asked all those present to demand a general staff and hinted that he would renew his demand to the board for departmental reorganization after Congress adjourned.[4] Impatient with delay, however, and distrusting Daniels, Fiske explained to Rep.

Richmond P. Hobson the need for a general naval staff. Hobson, the hero of the *Merrimac* episode during the Spanish-American War, had resigned from the navy in 1903. Elected to Congress in 1908, he won a seat on the House Naval Affairs Committee. He supported a large navy, a naval science program, naval aviation, and a council of national defense.[5] Fiske thought he would also support creation of a naval general staff.

On 2 January 1915 when Hobson called, Fiske gave him a pamphlet on the army general staff system and the text of the legislation that had established it.[6] On Sunday, 3 January, Fiske took a number of documents to Hobson's home, noting that the congressman "became thoroughly interested." The question was how best to proceed. To seek legislation modifying the aide system would not do because Daniels would contend that the system was adequate. Why not propose real reform? This decision reached—and without telling Daniels—Fiske asked Capts. Harry S. Knapp, John Hood, and William B. Oliver and Lt. Comdrs. William P. Cronan, Madison, and Dudley W. Knox to meet with him at Hobson's home at 10:30 P.M. In about two hours these men drafted legislation to create an Office of Naval Operations whose head would be "responsible for the readiness of the Navy for war and be charged with its general direction." Fifteen assistants would draft war plans.[7] When one of the conspirators noted the power Fiske would have if the bill passed, Fiske retorted that he would not be the chief of naval operations. Quite the contrary, passage of the bill would likely cost him the most prestigious professional position in the navy and end his career.[8]

The conspiracy continued on the morning of 4 January, when the six officers met in Fiske's office and agreed on the typewritten draft of their bill. At 10:15 A.M., Hobson arrived and then went to see Daniels. Hobson later told Fiske that Daniels had said he would "go home" if the bill passed. "How foolish! Now he has the chance to back it up and get back into good opinion of the country," commented Fiske. Hobson took the bill to Congress, where a subcommittee of the House Naval Affairs Committee approved it quickly and unanimously. Hobson then asked Fiske to prepare a brief so that the congressman could argue the matter before the full committee the next day. Fiske, Cronan, Madison, and Knox met in Fiske's office that evening and drew up the brief, which Knox delivered.

On 5 January, newspapers headlined the approval of Hobson's bill by the subcommittee, and Adm. George Dewey asked Fiske to tell Hobson he was "delighted." That afternoon, the chairman of the House Naval Affairs Committee, Lemuel P. Padgett, called on Daniels; Fiske did not know what was discussed. The next day, Hobson told Fiske that Padgett's full committee had agreed unanimously to incorporate the provision for a chief of naval operations in the naval appropriations bill.[9] Except for Dewey, Hobson, and the six officers Fiske had called upon, no one else knew how Hobson's bill was written.

The evening papers of 6 January and morning papers the next day spoke about a "bureau of operations"; not only the Republican *New York Tribune* but the Democratic *New York World* applauded the idea. Fiske believed it must have hurt Daniels very much "to see the *World* taking a stand so antagonistic to him."[10] On 7 January, Hutch I. Cone, chief of the Bureau of Steam Engineering, wrote William S. Sims, predicting, "If our own people handle it right they can make a General Staff out of it under the name of 'Bureau of Operations'."[11] Sims replied on 9 January: "According to this morning's New York papers, the Secretary has given his approval to the proposed Bureau of Operations. This looks like a change of heart (under pressure). This is probably the beginning of a rational [re]organization."[12]

Despite much public and private support for his plan, Fiske knew that Daniels would oppose it. Clearly, the testimony Fiske had given Congress the previous December still stuck in Daniels's craw: on 23 January Daniels asked Admiral Dewey for his personal view on Fiske's statement that it would take at least five years to "get the Navy up to a state of efficiency." The secretary asked to have Dewey's comments no later than the afternoon of 26 January—in duplicate and marked *"Personal and Confidential."*[13] When he posed the same questions to fleet commanders, Fletcher, among others, upheld Fiske's position.[14]

Fiske had worked hard to win over various officers who, in turn, would put pressure on Daniels to approve a naval general staff. For example, he talked with the judge advocate general of the navy, Ridley McLean, who in turn tried to win over Victor Blue, chief of the Bureau of Navigation, as Knox also had.[15] At a General Board meeting on 19 January, however, Charles J. Badger and Winterhalter argued, as Fiske noted, that the "proposed legislation would virtually abolish [the board]. . . . I think I silenced criticism," Fiske wrote, "and convinced even Badger and Winterhalter! Quite a victory!" On 24 January, after he and Knapp spoke with Daniels for some two hours, Daniels agreed to "help to get Hobson's amendment through the House."

Fiske was overjoyed to hear Daniels say he would work for passage of Hobson's amendment, but events of the next two days showed Daniels in his true colors. On 26 January, the secretary called Knight out of a General Board meeting and reprimanded him for a speech delivered the previous day in which Knight had criticized departmental organization and had espoused the kind of naval general staff Fiske supported.[16] Fiske believed that "all Knight did was to tell the truth." According to Daniels, however, an "aroused and indignant" President Wilson had him order Knight to confine his remarks to questions asked him by congressional committees.[17]

On 28 January, Fiske learned that Daniels had asked Dewey to comment on Fiske's remarks that the navy lacked war plans. Dewey replied that work on war plans was proceeding well, whereupon Fiske told the admiral he had fallen into Daniels's trap. Since Daniels bitterly opposed having a chief of naval operations, he "would use Dewey's letter to convey [a] false impression."[18] As Fiske predicted, Daniels wrote Representative Padgett forwarding Dewey's comments that all went well with the war plans and that the General Board, with the aides for operations and material, comprised an adequate staff organization. Fiske thereupon telephoned Hobson, who called on Dewey and, together with Fiske, assured the admiral that creation of an Office of the Chief of Naval Operations did not mean that the General Board would be "wiped out."[19]

Fiske then learned that the provision for a chief of naval operations had been stricken out of the House naval appropriations bill on the technicality—a point of order—that new business could not be added to it. Moreover, Hobson warned Fiske that Daniels would try to have the Senate modify any legislation the House passed creating a chief of naval operations. At Fiske's suggestion, Hobson got the Senate Naval Affairs Committee to add a provision to its naval appropriations bill creating a chief of naval operations.

Prodded by Fiske, on 3 February the General Board sent preliminary administrative sections for both the European and Asian war plans to Daniels and to the bureaus. Fiske also emphasized the need for truly realistic war games that would show the nation what was needed in the way of an "adequate Navy."[20] He thus countered the administration's policy of not preparing for war.

On 19 February Daniels requested Victor Blue, Ridley McLean, and David W. Taylor to help draft a letter asking the Senate Naval Affairs Committee to reject the Fiske-Hobson plan for an Office of the Chief of Naval Operations. The letter (a copy of which went to Representative Padgett) asked that the words in the Hobson bill, "A Chief of Naval Operations . . . who shall . . . be responsible for the readiness of the navy for war and be charged with its general direction" be changed to read "A Chief of Naval Operations . . . who shall . . . be charged . . . with the operations of the fleet, and with the preparations and readiness of plans for its use in time of war." Daniels added, "You will first notice that the principle of civilian control of the Navy Department is not violated. It will be the duty of this officer who, by the nature of his post, will be thoroughly conversant with existing conditions in the fleet, to recommend to the Secretary such changes as may, in his opinion, be necessary to develop the maximum efficiency of the Navy."[21]

Instead of celebrating George Washington's birthday, Fiske and Daniels had a "very heated and disagreeable talk . . . lasting an hour and a quarter. . . ." The conversation roamed from Knight's speech to Fiske's testimony of the previous December; Daniels "showed great heat in denouncing both." During that afternoon, Dewey invited Fiske to go driving and Fiske poured out a sad tale to the sympathetic admiral. On 24 February, the *New York World* advanced the sensational suggestion that the entire Atlantic Fleet, 125 ships, make a sham attack on New York City. Knowing that such an operation would expose the navy's unpreparedness, especially in personnel, Fiske asked Roosevelt what could be done to get the department ready for war, for the "Sec[retary] seems *very* sure nothing is needed and that everything is ready!!!"[22]

On 25 February, the full Senate agreed to creation of an Office of the Chief of Naval Operations in the emasculated form passed by the Senate Naval Affairs Committee. On 27 February, five members from each house met in conference on the naval appropriations bill. Hoping against hope that they would agree to something better than the Senate proposed, Fiske dictated for Rep. Ernest W. Roberts, one of the House conferees, who came to visit him, a compromise "suggestion . . . about half way between [the] Senate and House provisions." Roberts said he would try to get Padgett to propose Fiske's plan to the conferees "as a basis of agreement and action." Fiske telephoned the same suggestion to Hobson, also a conferee, who promised support.[23] But it was all in vain, for on 1 March the committee upheld the Senate's version. On 3 March, just one day before it adjourned, Congress passed the naval appropriations bill, with Fiske noting that its provisions (discussed below) were "all due of course to [the] probability of war, and possibly just a little to my testimony as to our unpreparedness and the favorable comments on it by the public press."[24]

As passed by both houses, the bill established an Office of the Chief of Naval Operations but omitted the fifteen assistants who were to write war plans, as suggested by Fiske and Hobson. Fiske thought the bill "accomplished nevertheless a greater advance than any other naval legislation had accomplished in many years"; some officers said that it was as great a boon as the act of Congress of 1880 authorizing the steel ships of the "new navy."[25] Fiske's conclusion, however, was too sanguine. The Fiske-Hobson plan made the chief of naval operations responsible for preparing the navy for war and for directing its management, including the power to coordinate the work of the bureaus. The Daniels plan made the chief responsible only for operating the fleet and providing war plans, thereby retaining the management function in civilian hands and leaving the bureaus uncoordinated. Fiske was left with merely the shell of a good idea.

Although Daniels cut to twenty the forty-eight new ships recommended by the General Board for 1916, in the long run other provisions of the Naval Act of 1915 were even more important. In addition to creating the Office of the Chief of Naval Operations, it authorized engineers to concentrate solely on their profession without the interruption of other duties; provided that officers and men of the navy and Marine Corps be detailed to aviation duty; established an advisory committee on aeronautics and a naval reserve; authorized a number of admirals and vice admirals; provided for a 32 percent increase in the number of naval constructors; and provided for promotion by selection of the upper officer grades.

For two weeks following the passage of the act, Fiske met with the General Board to plan war games scheduled to be held between 10 May and 15 June.[26] Some members were unenthusiastic about the games; Badger asserted they were in the province of the fleet's commander. Fiske retorted that foreign navies had their general staffs make war plans in order to establish a consistent policy instead of letting each commander draft hasty plans according to his fancy. When Daniels approved the games, he did so only on the condition that the defending U.S. fleet not be defeated.[27] Meanwhile, on 20 March, Fletcher hit Daniels even harder than Fiske by saying that "the fleet has outgrown our present organization." "I am convinced," Fletcher continued, "that the present administration work of the Commander-in-Chief would go to pieces under war conditions."[28]

There was considerable speculation as to who would be the first chief of naval operations. Some said Daniels wanted Winterhalter. Both Admiral and Mrs. Dewey spoke very highly of Fiske, but Dewey told him that he thought Daniels wanted Fletcher. Sims, suggested by the *Army and Navy Journal*, had some support in the fleet, but he too thought Daniels wanted Fletcher.[29] Dudley W. Knox, who thought Fiske should be named,[30] wrote Sims most perceptively saying

> Few people realize what a h——— of a time Admiral Fiske has [had] trying to keep the wheels moving in a way even remotely simulating business. He deserves great credit for sticking to his job in the face of many major discouragements, and for running the show in the most disinterested way possible. He is one of the very few men we have ever had in high office who have not worked for "Self first."[31]

Fiske wanted a war game to show "what would really happen" if a hostile fleet attacked the East Coast. He meant, of course, the German fleet. He agreed to have a "hostile" force much smaller than the German fleet make the simulated attack because of the condition Daniels imposed upon him and because it was the feeling of the General Board that "if the hostile force supposed in the war game should be so large, it would not be a game at all, but a one-sided slaughter."[32] Fiske pushed for completion of the game plans because he felt that he must leave the department after Daniels named a chief of naval operations. Moreover, were all its details not settled before he left, Fiske feared the whole scheme might fail.

On 16 March, when Fiske, Roosevelt, and the General Board agreed on a war game "which would represent facts as they would probably be in case of an attack on our coast," Daniels publicly announced that the navy had never been more efficient. On 19 March Fiske reported to the General Board that Daniels would take up the matter of the war games with the president. Approval was finally granted on 6 April.

Fiske also pushed for his administrative war plan and sought to update fire-control materials and procedures. Daniels approved of Fiske's writing the administrative plan but declined repeatedly to sign it and thus make it effective.[33] On 18 March, Fiske carefully explained the plan to Daniels and stated that Admiral Dewey approved it; Daniels disapproved "for the present." Fiske then presented papers he had written dealing with two additional sections of the war plan, one entitled "Meditations on Organization," the second "Meditations on Mobilization." Daniels said little and simply returned them.[34] "At the end," Fiske wrote in his diary, "he [Daniels] said, 'The only trouble with our organization is that Operations has not enough power and authority.' I answered, 'That is all I have ever said.' This last remark . . . shows he has at last come to some comprehension of the military needs of the Navy." Daniels still retained a high regard for Fiske; on his fitness report for the period from 1 October 1914 to 31 March 1915 the secretary called him "an able officer, inventor, and student."

During mid March, Fiske pondered his predicament. Although most officers supported him, Winterhalter and Blue had Daniels's ear. Only Dewey and Cameron Winslow were Fiske's superiors as strategists, but neither could become the chief of naval operations. It was with grim humor that he realized that Daniels would not name him, the third best strategist in the navy, as chief of naval operations.[35] Nevertheless, he was not through fighting.

When relieved as aide for operations, Fiske thought he would either head the naval aviation section or an experimental department he had suggested as early as 1907. When he spoke about heading a naval development board, on 24 March, Daniels "seemed much impressed."[36] The next day,

Fiske told the secretary frankly that he did not wish to remain as aide for operations. Daniels replied that perhaps Fiske should head a naval inventors board that was to visit Europe for several months.[37] Fiske's distrust of Daniels, however, was evident. He told Col. William C. Church, editor, and Charles Allen Munn, publisher of the *Army and Navy Journal*, that "Daniels is taking credit for the idea [of a naval inventors board], as he will take credit for creating the Office of Chief of Naval Operations."[38]

On 24 and 26 March, Fiske asked a subcommittee of the House Naval Affairs Committee to restore the fifteen assistants who were to draft plans for the Office of the Chief of Naval Operations—a provision deleted in January. The subcommittee agreed, as did the full House, and Fiske evaluated the assistants who would constitute a general staff. As he had predicted, Daniels took credit for the legislation in his 1915 annual report.[39]

Speculation about the new chief of naval operations abounded. What would his duties be? What limits would be placed on his authority? Sims wrote to Mrs. Sims on 7 March:

> Fiske should be selected, even if he is replaced before long. [The new chief of naval operations] should be the highest ranking man who is available, and if possible one who has had command as an admiral afloat. The position will be difficult on account of the opposition of the bureaus, and therefore the new Chief should "draw as much water" as possible.[40]

Although Daniels never seriously considered Fiske for the job, the final straw was Fiske's effort to reinstate the assistants for the chief of naval operations. For Fiske, it was a trivial matter—Daniels was dealing directly with Fiske's subordinates in the Office of Operations. In addition, Fiske thought Daniels had been "discourteous" in asking the advice of other officers without telling him. During the afternoon of 1 April Fiske accused Daniels of treating him unjustly ever since he had testified before Congress in December 1914, and he offered to resign. Daniels merely asked when his resignation would take effect. At the secretary's convenience, replied Fiske. He would arrange it, said Daniels, thus ending the conversation.[41] The next day, Fiske handed Daniels his letter of resignation. Across the bottom of it Daniels wrote: "Accepted to take effect upon date to be fixed later."

Fiske's closest friends told him that they were amazed he had hung on as long as he had and that his resignation was a sacrifice performed for the good of the navy. Fiske received "lots of letters and messages." He had a "fine letter from Senator [James Edgar] Martine [of New Jersey], deploring my resig[nation]" and a letter from Fletcher, too, saying the officers of the Fleet want me to be CNO and saying he will tell [Daniels] it is the only thing for him to do. . . . F. D. Roosevelt deplores my resignation."[42]

Representative Gardner was quoted as saying, "Admiral Fiske has paid the penalty for his courageous outspokenness, and now, mark the others as they follow him down the plank. Yates Stirling is likely to be next. He is the man who called attention to the rotten condition of the submarine flotilla."[43]

Fiske at first brushed off newspaper reporters who sought details and then realized his error, for through them he could have explained the reasons for his resignation. In any event, for the next week his resignation provoked articles, editorials, and cartoons in the leading newspapers. The press supported him, yet treated his resignation as a piece of sensational news comparable to a divorce scandal or railroad accident. He had resigned, said the *New York Times*, because he did not like Daniels's policies, because he knew he would not be named chief of naval operations, and because he was "piqued" when Daniels bypassed him and asked men who were his juniors to perform certain tasks.[44] On the other hand, Fiske was praised for having the courage to follow his convictions. A man of wide experience, one whose writings were studied as "classics" in the fleet, perhaps he was too pessimistic about the status of the navy. Although Fiske was pleased by the professional qualities of the navy's officers, he lacked confidence in the good judgment of its civilian head. "It seems," said the *Times*, "that in these perilous times it is not to be doubted that he has the good of the Navy and the country at heart"; hence his "withdrawal . . . is not of trifling importance." Moreover, the *Times* said that the fact that he did not seek to become chief of naval operations was "somewhat disturbing."[45] Were a foreign military leader to resign under similar circumstances, mused Fiske, the country would demand an investigation and either the officer or his chief would be punished, for differences between the leading civilian and leading military man threatened national security. Fiske had testified in December 1914 that it would take five years to prepare the navy for war, thereby contradicting Daniels's testimony that the navy was already well prepared. The press made it seem that he had resigned merely because Daniels would not institute the measures he urged. In the end Fiske appeared as a seven-days' wonder to the public and then was forgotten.[46]

Fiske's resignation baffled men in the fleet. On 4 April, Sims said, "We are wondering what it means, whether he will be the new Chief of Operations, and if not, what duty he will have, if any. Perhaps he will have the Pacific or China fleet with the rank of Admiral, as the officers now in command will soon be relieved."[47] According to Cone, "My guess is that . . . Winslow will come here as Chief of Operations. He is here now and I think will take the job if the Secretary will allow him to write the regulations under which he works. . . ."[48] McLean sent Sims a confidential copy of his proposed duties for the chief of naval operations, saying that only Sims and Winslow were being considered for the position and that Sims should take it. Sims, however, believed that Daniels had merely bowed to public criticism and would use Fiske not to benefit the service but merely "to gain the confidence of the service which he now wholly lacks." Moreover, Sims said:

> If the Secretary were a big enough man, he could make the best showing by appointing Fiske. If the Secretary now acknowledges that a coordinating military head is necessary, it necessarily follows that Fiske's criticisms . . . were correct. Fiske criticized the *Organization* we have had for the past 50 years, for which the Secretary was not responsible. Fiske never criticized the Secretary. The Secretary made his own trouble by trying to refute the testimony in the effort to support Congress in its desire to maintain the same old bureau system. He thought he could get away with it. . . . An uneducated man from a small town in the South tries to turn the Navy into a university. Cheer-up![49]

On 17 April, at Daniels's request, Fiske listed those changes which had to be made in *Navy Regulations* to establish the Office of Naval Operations. That same day Fletcher talked for an hour with Daniels; he then reported to Fiske that he had told the secretary that the fleet wanted Fiske to be the chief of naval operations. On 19 April, Fletcher and Winslow called on Daniels. Fiske did not learn what Winslow said, but Fletcher confided that he had urged Daniels "in most emphatic language" to appoint Fiske to the post both for professional and political reasons. Franklin Roosevelt also agreed; as Fiske recorded, the "opinion of all is that Fiske ought to be Ch[ief of] Nav[al] Op[erations] with [Thomas] Howard next choice."[50]

On 24 April, Fiske spoke with Dewey, who revealed that he had told Fletcher to urge Daniels to choose Fiske as the chief of naval operations.[51] Cronan, however, who was wise beyond his years, had written Sims two days earlier, "Coming events cast their shadows before, . . . all of which means that we of Operations are going to get the hook."[52] After canvassing the roster of flag officers, Daniels offered the position of chief of naval operations to Cameron Winslow, who declined on the ground that the office lacked the necessary powers and that he preferred a general staff, an attitude shared by the twelve other rear admirals. In discussing with the president the search for the proper man, Wilson "enlightened" Daniels by asking why he did not select a captain if no admiral suited him.[53] To the amazement of Fiske, the navy, and the nation, on 28 April Daniels announced that he had chosen Capt. William Sheperd Benson, commandant of the

Philadelphia Navy Yard; Fiske decided to leave the department as soon as he could.

The only praise for Benson's appointment this writer has been able to find among Fiske's peers came from McLean. McLean's judgment is suspect, however, because he thought Daniels had done more to prepare the navy for war than any other secretary with the possible exception of William C. Whitney.[54] Yet McLean took time to write Fiske a truly fine letter crediting him with creating the Office of the Chief of Naval Operations and expressing great sorrow that Fiske had not been selected to fill the post.[55] In contrast, Admiral Knight, Capt. Roy C. Smith, and Ernest J. King all disapproved of Benson's appointment, with King saying that Benson "was the kind of person who felt compelled to run everything himself, and in his concern over detail would lose control of the general situation."[56] Albert Gleaves sneered to his diary that on 18 May he had dined with *"Rear Admiral* Benson!"[57] And Fiske was completely taken aback by the selection of one who had never "shown the slightest interest in strategy or been on the General Board, *or even taken the summer course at the war college."*[58] As Benson's superior when they both had served in the first division of the fleet, Fiske had noted on every fitness report that Benson would make a good superintendent of the Naval Academy. But he never "reckoned [him] one of the 'bright men' of the Navy"; it was incomprehensible to Fiske that Benson should have been chosen over such men as Howard, Knight, Knapp, Hood, and Oliver.[59] Ironically, Benson would be governed in his new office by regulations Fiske had written and Daniels approved.

One of Fiske's last acts as aide for operations was to appoint Capt. Roy C. Smith as the senior member of a board on fire control. The first board of this kind was ordered on 21 November 1905, the second major one in 1910. With reports of the Battle of the Falkland Islands at hand, Rear Adm. Joseph Strauss, chief of the Bureau of Ordnance, requested that Fletcher use director firing during the next fleet target practice "in order that the Bureau may determine definitely its value."[60] Smith's report, dated 11 August 1915, was never made public; together with comments made on it by the fleet, the report was considered by still another board, convened under Charles P. Plunkett on 27 December 1915. Plunkett's was the first report to comment on "director-firing systems" and to recommend that such systems be provided in all new construction. Consequently, all turret ships that operated during World War I carried the fire-control systems on which Fiske had worked for long years.[61]

On 29 April, Daniels told Fiske to go to the Naval War College after he was relieved by Benson on 11 May. No sooner had Benson relieved Fiske than Capt. Volney O. Chase reported as his assistant; Fiske noted,

"I never had an asst!" He bade Daniels good bye, saying "I wish to say that I have never been treated with more courtesy by anybody than by you, and that, from my point of view, our differences have been wholly professional." Evidently he took Daniels by surprise, for Daniels "seemed considerably flabbergasted, and stammered out that he entertained a high regard for me."[62] Fiske then departed.

For two years as aide for operations, Fiske had been annoyed by the need to insist that Daniels recognize what Fiske saw as elementary principles. Although most line officers supported him, Fiske had to carry on his fight alone against Daniels's attempt to mismanage the navy and render it ineffective in defending the country.

During his first two years, Daniels stressed democracy, education, prohibition, parsimony, and humanitarianism. He might better have concentrated upon the material and personnel readiness of the fleet and the preparation of war plans. To advocates of a strong navy like Fiske—and there were many in the navy and outside of it—Daniels appeared moralistic, pedantic, and provincial. The journalist and historian Burton J. Hendrick, for example, said Daniels regarded his office "as an experimental laboratory for trying out Mr. Bryan's ideas."[63] Franklin Roosevelt said bluntly, "I have any amount of work to do and J. D[aniels] is too damned slow for words— his failure to decide the few big things holds me up all down the line."[64]

Fiske believed that deviations from the discipline which held the navy together and upon which its efficiency depended impaired the service from seeking its objective—victory in battle. Daniels's diversions, particularly into social and moral matters, deflected the navy from this objective. Where to draw the line between advice and policy was even more important. The secretary must rely on naval officers for technical advice in carrying out national policy. Had Fiske been trying to advise or to direct Daniels? If the latter, his efforts stood no chance because President Wilson supported Daniels's insistence that military men have nothing to do with shaping national policies.[65]

In his autobiography Fiske confessed that perhaps he had overrated the importance of his position and was tactless in telling Daniels that his attitude toward the navy "threatened the very foundations of national defense." By sponsoring legislation, he had also risked a court martial. Fiske, in addition, was naïve in overlooking the fact that Daniels was not a free agent: the secretary of the navy had to support the administration or lose his post. Daniels did not learn that Fiske had gone behind his back in the matter of creating the Office of the Chief of Naval Operations until years later. Above all, Daniels opposed creating the naval general staff Fiske wanted.

As he left the department, Fiske concluded that he had prevented a lowering of the efficiency of the navy and had contributed to it five items of permanent benefit. These were: first, establishing the Division of Aeronautics; second, instituting strategic war problems for the fleet; third, "proving that the country trusts army and navy officers more than it trusts any one else"; fourth, "making Congress realize the needs of the navy more clearly than it had ever done before"; and fifth, establishing the Office of the Chief of Naval Operations.[66]

Two other ideas of Fiske's became established facts in time—an agency within the Navy Department for recognizing and developing new inventions, and the administrative section of the general war plan. Daniels's refusal to sign the administrative plan provided the greatest single difference of opinion he had with Fiske. Soon after Benson was installed, however, Daniels signed the plan. Fiske could justifiably crow later that *"that plan and the office of chief of naval operations are the means by which the Navy Department got ready for war, and by means of which it operated during the war and has operated since."*[67]

Daniels prevaricated in taking credit for Fiske's ideas in his 1915 annual report. Fiske, not Daniels, had formulated both the Office of the Chief of Naval Operations and the administrative plan. Perhaps the kindest thing that can be said for Daniels is that he grasped the prerogative that was his as secretary of the navy to assume credit for work done by those who served him.

On 21 May 1915, Fiske took Franklin Roosevelt to lunch at the Shoreham Hotel and suggested he prepare to take over "if JD gets canned."[68] Roosevelt hoped that Daniels, who thought much as Bryan did, would resign if Bryan resigned over Wilson's neutrality policy; and Roosevelt implied his disgust when Daniels did not.[69] On 9 June, the day Bryan resigned, Sims wrote to Cone: "We are all much interested in the split in the cabinet, and are wondering what the result will be, politically and otherwise. Are we to lose Joppiflous [Daniels]? If so, there will be many a dry eye!"[70] After lunching with Daniels and the secretary of commerce, William C. Redfield, on 23 June, Franklin Roosevelt made an extremely interesting observation: "I know for a fact that the President has not had the advice of a single officer of the Army or of the Navy on the question of what we could do to carry out our declared policy."[71]

Until the United States entered the war on 6 April 1917, Fiske tried to educate the nation to prepare for the inevitable. He had been out of the office for just ten weeks when, on 21 July 1915, President Wilson asked Secretary Daniels and Secretary Garrison to put the best minds of their services to work on a draft of an "adequate national defense" program to present to Congress in November. It was Fiske's great misfortune and miscalculation that he had pressed Daniels too early and too hard.

14

A QUESTION OF VERACITY, 1915–1916

On 12 May 1915, the day after he was relieved as aide for operations, Bradley A. Fiske became chairman of a board that was testing the Willard Isham shell. On 1 June he asked Secretary of the Navy Daniels whether he should report to the Naval War College on 5 June, as ordered, or continue the shell experiments; Daniels permitted the delay.[1]

Meanwhile, in mid May, the Atlantic Fleet conducted Fiske's war games. William S. Sims, who witnessed them, declared that "the enemy fleet could easily avoid the U.S. fleet and get to the coast" and that the fleet commander violated "every military and common sense principle."[2] When he reported this to the new chief of naval operations, Benson said that the commander deserved to be replaced. It was ironic, but Daniels confessed to Sims what he would not admit to Fiske: he found the condition of the fleet "very painful."[3]

Fiske conducted tests of the Isham shell until the end of June. On 3 June, he spoke on naval preparedness at the annual dinner of the Naval Academy Graduates Association, at which Daniels appeared as an uninvited guest. Fiske noted that the navy was unprepared to guard the nation against the formidable navies of other nations. Moreover, he said we had not tested our war plans, mobilization plans, or wartime organization; nor did we have a proper system of communications. It was up to naval officers who knew the situation to inform the public. If they did not, Fiske said, "they were unworthy of the uniform they wore and [had] failed their country in its hour of need just as effectively as if they deserted in time of war."[4]

After his speech, Fiske received many letters of congratulations and a great deal of favorable editorial comment.[5] So impressed was William C. Church, editor of the *Army and Navy Journal*, that he asked Fiske to spell out exactly what the navy needed. Fiske, extremely angry with Secretary Daniels, replied that the first thing needed was "men—20,000 more for peacetime, 100,000 more for war, and a Naval Reserve." To help balance the fleet, Fiske said, at least four battle cruisers should be provided. But most urgently,

> *We need a good* Secretary. We need a good Secretary *now.* . . . We need a Secretary who will *help* the navy—not *hinder* it. We need a Secretary who will not sell out the interests of the Navy for political advantage and newspaper advertising. We need a very able man, a wise man—a *highly educated man.*
> *We need preparedness in the Secretary as well as in the Navy itself.* No matter how much money Congress may give the navy, the navy cannot get into an efficient state so long as the present Secretary remains in office. He is a millstone around the neck of the Navy. He has done the navy a great deal of positive injury, and his mental makeup is such that he will not be able to help *continuing* to do injury.[6]

Four days later he sent Church and Richard Wainwright copies of six letters he had written Daniels during the past two years on the lack of preparedness, thus fortifying these friends with ammunition if Daniels tried to charge him with shortcomings in the navy.[7]

On 13 June Fiske celebrated his sixty-first birthday, noting that he must retire in one year. On 28 June Daniels ordered him into "cold storage" at the Naval War College. Fiske disliked being rusticated and was also upset because Jo's health was beginning to fail. Nevertheless on 29 June, when he reported to Daniels on the Isham shell and bade him good bye, he was tactful "and said I had no grouch or enmity; also that no advice which I had ever given him and he had followed had ever turned out wrong or got him criticized."[8] Fiske reported at the War College on 1 July. Since Austin M. Knight, the college president, did not dare put Fiske on his staff, he gave him a desk in the library and left him alone. Fiske attended some lectures but also experimented with an antiship, aerial "depth bomb" or "depth charge." A direct hit would cause it to explode; were it to miss, the bomb would explode by hydrostatic pressure. But Fiske never fully developed the bomb and later refused credit for having invented it.[9] While he was at the college, Fiske asked Elmer A. Sperry about patenting and developing the gyroscopic gun-director system and the prism system of target practice, became extremely interested in developing a torpedo plane, and did a good deal of writing.

And, of course, he had time to think. Was it possible he asked himself, that he had been wrong in demanding preparedness? Was he really a "militarist"? Would nations soon abandon war or restrict armaments by mutual agreement? With "as open a mind as I could command," he read works on history, government, and war. History told him that war always characterized human civilization. But was it possible, as many contemporaries believed, to establish a league of nations that would enforce peace? A month-long study of psychology convinced him that men would never change and that future wars were inevitable unless some "monster of efficiency" like the Roman Empire enforced peace on the world. Daniels approved publication of an article by Fiske on this idea entitled "The Mastery of the World." Although Daniels cautioned him about "the undesirability of making comparisons between or referring to nations by name, particularly those engaged in the present war,"[10] Fiske soon followed it with a number of other articles in the *North American Review*: in November, "Naval Principles"; in December, "Naval Preparedness"; in January 1916, "Naval Policy"; in February, "Naval Defense"; and in March, "Naval Strategy." When Finley Peter ("Mr. Dooley") Dunne asked him to write for *Collier's*, Fiske retorted that he preferred to write for the *North American Review*. But when Dunne offered ten cents a word for six articles totaling thirty thousand words, he had second thoughts.[11]

Fiske wrote the first three *North American Review* articles while he was convinced that the United States would soon enter the war and was doing nothing to prepare. He overlooked the administration's miraculous change in attitude: President Wilson had directed Daniels, on 21 July 1915, to "get the best minds of his department to work on the subject of a wise and adequate naval program"[12] and, early in October, to prepare plans for a five-year naval building program including $500 million for new construction. On 12 October, Wilson approved the plan; three days later, he submitted it to Congress. In addition, Daniels asked Congress for a 20 percent increase in personnel, for $5 million for an experimental laboratory to be used by the Naval Consulting Board, and for funds to augment naval aviation and ammunition stockpiles.[13] A beginning had been made, and Fiske applauded. His diary entry for 14 November, for example, records that "press feeling about JD is improving" and, as if addressing Daniels, "Your [1915 annual] report shows you are beginning to understand the requirements of your job!" Although Wilson claimed that his interest in national defense was rooted in his passion for peace, men like William Jennings Bryan and Rep. Claude Kitchin—men of his own party—opposed preparedness;[14] and the Sixty-fourth Congress failed to act upon it despite Wilson's efforts to take the issue to the people in a tour during late January and early February 1916.[15]

Fiske's major theme in the articles he wrote during the winter of 1915 was that preparation for modern war demanded careful planning, as demonstrated by the history of the Civil War and the Spanish-American War. He argued that "strategy"—the definition of policy by civilian leaders—was better than "war strategy"—operations conducted by military men—and that bad strategy could no more carry out good policy than good strategy could execute badly conceived policy. Hence policy and strategy must be coordinated.

Fiske credited Germany's efficient navy to its use of war games. He wished, therefore, that American naval officers would learn the German way of making estimates of a situation and that the administration would then accept these assessments as coming from trained and responsible professionals.[16]

Although Fiske's articles won much popular approval,[17] on 24 December 1915 he had "a most unpleasant interview" with Daniels. Fiske reminded the secretary that he had taken no leave in ten years, that he had no duties at present, and that he was due to retire in six months; he requested leave so that he could take his ailing wife "farther South." Daniels approved ninety days leave on the understanding that he would take Mrs. Fiske south. Fiske explained that he wanted to go no farther south than Washington. Daniels then gave him thirty days. As Fiske turned to leave, Daniels remarked that his attention had been called to Fiske's article on "Naval Preparedness." Were he not an admiral, Daniels said, he would have Fiske court martialed. Fiske retorted that the secretary had approved not only that article but two others. Daniels snapped that he thought the articles were to be written for the *U.S. Naval Institute Proceedings*. Fiske said that when approval was sought, no publisher was mentioned and that nothing he wrote was news to military men. He was merely trying to make things clear to the general public. Where had he gone wrong? Fiske asked. Daniels cut short the interview by saying, "You cannot write or talk any more; you can't even say that two and two make four"[18]—a remark that soon appeared in the *New York Times* and other newspapers.

Daniels's muzzle embarrassed Fiske because he had agreed to write articles for *Collier's*, the *North American Review*, and the *New York Sun* and to speak to the Commercial Club of Chicago and the Marine League of the United States.[19] Both organizations made a "fuss"; John W. Scott, president of the Commercial Club, even telegraphed the president directly. Wilson was away, however, and his secretary referred the telegram to Daniels. On 4 January Daniels told Scott that it was better for civilians to lead the fight for preparedness, while naval officers follow the unbroken policy of not attempting to influence legislation.[20]

Three days later Fred A. Britten, a Republican member of the House Naval Affairs Committee, condemned Daniels's "muzzling" of Fiske and transferring him from Washington because Fiske had testified honestly before the committee.[21] On 11 January, chairman Lemuel P. Padgett supported

Secretary Daniels in a verbal clash with Britten. Britten invited Fiske to lunch to discuss naval affairs, but Fiske declined because he had been forbidden by Daniels to speak. Britten withdrew the lunch invitation so as not to embarrass "the greatest strategical officer of the Navy" and then angrily demanded a committee inquiry into Daniels's muzzling order. Thereupon Daniels denied to Padgett that he had forced Fiske to break his contract with *Collier's*, demanded that naval officers support the administration's naval policy, and referred to directives issued during the administrations of Roosevelt and Taft that ordered officers not to try to influence legislation. Only after Rep. Thomas S. Butler, a Republican from Pennsylvania, interceded did Britten withdraw his demand for a congressional inquiry.[22] On 12 January, Daniels denied that he had known Fiske meant to write for *Collier's*. On 13 and 14 January, Peter Dunne (of *Collier's*) called on Fiske at his home; Dunne said he would try to win permission for Fiske to publish in the magazine. During this time, Fiske received two highly prized letters: in one, former President Roosevelt praised his articles in the *North American Review*; the other was a handwritten invitation to lunch at Sagamore Hill.[23] The sweetest news came on 18 January: he learned that on 18 May last, seven days after he ceased being aide for operations, Daniels had finally signed the administrative plan Fiske had been pushing for two years.[24]

Fiske received numerous invitations to speak and write. Finally, on 13 March, Daniels gave permission to publish "Naval Strategy" in the *U.S. Naval Institute Proceedings*, but by striking out the last five pages he deleted the conclusions to which Fiske's reasoning led.[25]

During January 1916, Fiske closely followed the testimony Daniels gave the House Naval Affairs Committee, which was considering estimates the secretary had submitted the previous October. Daniels stated that the United States ranked fourth in the world as a big-gun navy, that it needed the five-year building program and more men, and urged many other things he had initially rejected when Fiske had suggested them. Britten then shocked Daniels by asking if he recalled refusing to publish the General Board's 1914 report to him unless the board deleted its recommendation to add 19,600 men to the fleet. Daniels said he did not recall the event but admitted to Padgett that Victor Blue, chief of the Bureau of Navigation, had erred badly in reporting that he had a surplus of men.[26]

Britten then asked Blue if anyone was ready to contradict Fiske's December 1914 statement that it would take five years to prepare the navy for war. Blue snapped that it might take Fiske five years to do it. Britten asked how the other officers regarded Fiske; Blue replied, "Admiral Fiske is very highly thought of as an inventor."[27]

Rear Adm. Charles J. Badger so flattered Daniels during the hearings that Fiske labeled him an "ultra-conservative." In contrast, Rear Adm. Cameron McRae Winslow, commander in chief of the Pacific Fleet, voiced Fiske's position on the need for a naval general staff. Moreover, Winslow testified that the Navy Department should be controlled by naval officers because "it is impossible for an outsider to understand a profession of the nature such as we have."[28] Fiske fully agreed. As he wrote in his diary on 20 February: "I am propagating the idea that [this] country must demand that hereafter no Pres[ident] shall appoint a Sec[retary] of Navy except for fitness for that particular task, fitness including qualifications in naval strategy and engineering. . . ." Furthermore, Fiske felt, the creation of the Office of the Chief of Naval Operations was only a initial step in the right direction. The chief of naval operations should be authorized to prepare the fleet for war. "I cannot help feeling," he added, "that the military side of naval administration should be in military hands; and that would seem to be a general staff."[29]

Rear Adm. Frank F. Fletcher, like Knight, echoed Fiske by saying that the fleet was too small to protect our national interests. He favored giving the chief of naval operations the same broad authority Fiske did in the Fiske-Hobson bill. Because the secretary had too wide a span of administrative duties, Fletcher urged the use of some system (such as that of aides) so that the secretary would deal with only five or six officers instead of with fifteen or sixteen. Fletcher also thought, like Fiske, that the fleet needed thirty thousand more men, that it would take three to four years to train these men properly, and that the chief of naval operations should have at least fifteen officers to help him draft war plans.[30]

Sims testified that the chief of naval operations lacked the legal right to issue a single order; but he could be given that authority without diminishing in the least the absolute authority of the Secretary. Defects in various ships were traceable to poor organization—to the bureau system, for the bureaus failed to cooperate and refused to reform in the face of constructive criticism. Reform could come only through reorganization, the adoption of a general staff, and Sims recommended giving the chief of naval operations thirty-six officers to help him, rather than the fifteen often mentioned. Thus, like Knight, Sims supported Fiske.[31]

Benson, the chief of naval operations, thought that the fleet needed fifteen thousand more men and that he should be given a number of officers to work on war plans. He regarded his office as being "identical with that exercised by the body known as a general staff in other services." Asked about the value of naval aircraft, he replied that they could be used only to scout for the fleet and to defend bases. With aircraft as with ships, Benson recommended building only prototypes and delaying construction of large numbers of them until Congress had declared war and provided funds. The navy at that moment had sixteen effective aircraft; forty-one more were on order.[32]

When Rep. Ernest W. Roberts pursued the subject of a naval general staff, Benson confessed that he knew nothing about the naval staffs of other countries, but he asserted that he was very happy in his office because Daniels signed whatever papers he gave him and he himself gave orders whenever the secretary and assistant secretary were absent. In contrast, Daniels had questioned the papers Fiske brought him. The secretary's perfect confidence in Benson is revealed in Benson's comment, "I know that any order I sign is accepted without question."[33]

On Sunday, 19 March, Fiske talked with Britten and another member about his testimony.[34] On 24 March, Padgett asked if he had any "additional or different" suggestions from those he made to the committee fifteen months earlier. Fiske stood by what he had said earlier, but he had more to say. Other navies, Fiske argued, particularly Germany's, had prepared for war; the United States Navy had not; the major naval powers had general staffs, the U.S. Navy did not. Fiske testified that he had repeatedly advised Daniels to seek legislative sanction for a general staff, without which the United States would lose at war. The committee provided for a chief of naval operations and for fifteen assistants to prepare war plans rather than for a naval general staff. Moreover, if the U.S. should get into war, Fiske contended, "the only men the navy could count on for . . . effective service would be the men already wearing the uniform." No one, he concluded, had contradicted his earlier statement that it would take five years to prepare the navy for war.[35]

In answer to questions, Fiske asserted that the chief of naval operations should have many more than fifteen assistants, that all strictly naval matters should be directed by naval men, and that the secretary should administer and exercise a veto over recommendations offered by professionals. Lacking control over the bureaus, naval industrial plants, powder factories, ship yards, and stations, Fiske said, the chief of naval operations could not possibly coordinate their work. In case of trouble, no one man was responsible. Fiske was asked whether his recommendations would make the chief of naval operations into the secretary of the navy. Fiske thought not. What he really wanted, he admitted, was "to make it impossible for a Secretary, coming in, to change everything without the consent of Congress." Pressed on this point, he said that incoming secretaries sometimes radically changed the navy's policies. Now, however, a secretary could not abolish the Office of the Chief of Naval Operations nor deny him whatever number of assistants was fixed in law. Representative Roberts added that Daniels, opposed to such a chief until Congress forced one upon him, now took credit for having established the position—credit that properly belonged to Fiske.[36]

Fiske was asked whether he still thought it would take five years to bring the navy up to wartime efficiency. He replied that it would take even longer if the present naval organization was retained, even discounting the presence of a chief of naval operations, and that in the name of efficiency he would urge that the secretary of the navy be a naval officer.[37]

Fiske was also asked if he knew how Daniels had gotten the General Board to delete its recommendation for 19,600 additional men late in 1914? Fiske described what had happened. He was asked if it was true that Daniels had granted him only thirty of the ninety-days' leave he had accumulated and gagged him when he wished to speak or publish. Fiske replied affirmatively. Further questions revealed the work Fiske had done to develop naval aviation and his feeling that in a year much more could be done in aviation than in shipbuilding. He was then asked, "What legislation would make our present fleet effective at an early date?" Fiske thought four things were needed: a general staff, twenty thousand additional men, the building of battle cruisers, and the development of naval aviation—this last item should be the first priority. In response to a question on why Fiske had resigned as aide for operations, the following exchange occurred:

> ADMIRAL FISKE: There was only one reason a man could resign from a position like that—that he was not in accord with his chief . . . in the matter of preparedness. . . . I am quite sure that the German Navy must be at least . . . twice as good as ours. . . .
>
> MR. STEPHENS: Are we to understand that you believe our Navy is inefficient more largely because of administration than because of personnel and material?
>
> ADMIRAL FISKE: Yes; but of course, incorrect administration produces bad results in personnel and material.[38]

Fiske's testimony highlighted how he had helped create the Office of the Chief of Naval Operations and how Daniels had induced the General Board in 1914 to strike out its recommendation for 19,600 additional men for the fleet. As he later wrote Church in confidence, Fiske had known for a year that he would be called to testify; to some degree, the hearing had been staged:

> During that year, I studied and reflected and discussed *during nearly all of my waking hours*, on just the subjects that I testified about.
>
> *Between you and me, nearly all the questions asked me relating to strategy, Gen. Staff, etc., I had arranged should be asked of me.*[39]

On the committee, Republicans approved and Democrats opposed Fiske's ideas. Fiske was happy, however, because the naval witnesses had supported his demands for a general staff and for a number of assistants to write war plans for the chief of naval operations.[40]

Franklin D. Roosevelt testified on 28 March that the navy needed twenty-five thousand additional men and that it was not ready for war against a strong naval power. In response to a question about whether the department was organized so that it could perform all the tasks of a general staff, Roosevelt said no, but admitted that ·the system was too new to permit a valid evaluation. He was asked if the original Fiske-Hobson bill would have given the chief of naval operations more power than the amended bill. Roosevelt thought it would because it granted control of both the military and civilian functions of the department. Moreover, the chief of naval operations could not now "order" the bureaus to support war plans until the secretary approved them. Roosevelt felt that the chief of naval operations ought to be free to determine policy by delegating minutiae to subordinates. Were he to have a small general staff, the navy would revert to the system of three navy commissioners it used from 1815 to 1842. Because he thought such a staff would become autocratic and stultify progress, Roosevelt opposed the kind of general staff Fiske wanted.[41]

Secretary Daniels began his testimony on 30 March by saying that experienced officers disputed his estimate of the need of ten thousand more men by figures all the way up to thirty thousand. He was pleased with the Office of the Chief of Naval Operations, which did away with the aide system, "a fifth wheel" in organization. Now, Daniels said, a military man was in charge of the "military business" of the department even if he lacked authority to direct the bureaus. This, however, was as it should be, Daniels contended, for "it is not believed that any system by which the Secretary of the Navy would be virtually a figurehead can operate satisfactorily under American institutions, which are based upon the ultimate subordination of the military to the civil."[42]

When asked if he would agree to specify the duties and status of the chief of naval operations in law (thus deleting them from naval regulations), Daniels said, "I think you then limit the executive power and limit the usefulness of the office." Roberts said the law gave the chief responsibilities but not power; Daniels retorted, "The fatal defect would be to give the Chief of Operations administrative powers."[43]

On the size of the navy and whether it was ready for war, Daniels hedged. Everything depended, he said, on who the enemy was. Representative Padgett then asked about his differences with Fiske and why Fiske was not appointed to the General Board following his resignation, as Adm.

George Dewey recommended. Daniels said the reason was that Dewey had changed his mind and preferred a "practical man" and that "Fiske was too theoretical." Did Fiske resign over differences with the secretary on preparedness? No, Daniels said, he resigned over a difference in administration: Fiske preferred "Old World" methods. He also persisted, Daniels claimed, in being named commander in chief of the fleet. Denied the appointment, Fiske thereafter "did not seem to be in harmony with the policy of the department." Had the Office of the Chief of Naval Operations not been created, Daniels said he would have asked Fiske to retire as aide for operations "because he was not in harmony with the department." When the new office was created, it was determined that Fiske should not be appointed, and Benson was selected instead.[44]

Representative Britten asked if Daniels had a copy of Fiske's letter of 9 November 1914 on preparedness. Daniels could not recall it. Did he remember, Britten asked, a letter from the General Board, dated 3 August 1914, "warning you of the necessity of getting the Navy into a state of preparedness." Daniels could not recall that letter either. When asked to furnish the committee with copies of these letters, Daniels refused, saying that they were confidential. Questioned about whether he had had the General Board delete from its report to him the recommendation for 19,600 additional men, Daniels swore he had not.[45]

While the hearings proceeded, a number of Fiske's friends corresponded with him on the subject of naval reorganization. Henry Reuterdahl, the marine writer and artist, who had spent parts of three days with Fiske during January, prepared an article he hoped would have effects similar to those that followed his criticisms of the navy in 1908. The navy's judge advocate general, Ridley McLean, saw a chance to use Reuterdahl's article as a vehicle for demanding a general staff.[46] Sims, who read the article when it appeared in the *Metropolitan* magazine, agreed that "it is impossible for any one civilian to administer the technical details of the Navy" and that such "technical details of the profession should be run by a General Staff."[47] He urged Reuterdahl to write an article on the need for a general staff. Sims then asked McLean, "How much real authority should a chief of staff be authorized to exercise?" adding, "Fiske helped us a lot by standing by his guns." Moreover, since Daniels was, in Sims's opinion, "the greatest obstacle to progress, . . . the essential first step is a new secretary who is a man of ability, of large affairs, and not a politician."[48]

Meanwhile McLean prepared a bill that made the chief of naval operations the executive officer of the Navy Department under the secretary.[49] In the end, Fiske told Sims, the House naval appropriations bill, passed on

10 April, wrote "into permanent law substantially the present regulations governing the office of naval operations."[50]

Fiske and his friends did not intend to take his personal "roasting" by Daniels lying down. On 4 April, Fiske conferred with Adms. Seaton Schroeder, Hugo Osterhaus, and Richard Wainwright at Schroeder's home. The three concluded that Fiske should ask the House Naval Affairs Committee for permission to refute Daniels's testimony.[51] Fiske wrote a letter and on the morning of 5 April read it to the three admirals and adopted a few suggested changes. At their suggestion he handed the letter to the secretary of the committee, then sent a copy of it to Church with the request that he publish it.[52] In it Fiske asked that he be allowed to explain his differences with Daniels over the wine-mess order, his desire to become the commander in chief of the fleet, his ideas on a naval general staff, on the need for additional preparedness, and on how Daniels had the number of 19,600 men deleted from a report to him by the General Board.[53]

Most of the leading papers of the country published accounts of Fiske's letter under a scarehead and told of the cheers given Fiske when he was before the committee and the jeers given Daniels.[54] Fiske was, of course, pleased to have "lots of letters from friends about it."[55] Padgett shut him out, however, saying that the hearings were closed, the committee had other business, and to reopen past differences between him and Daniels served no public interest.[56] On 12 April the controversy took a turn favoring Fiske when the Senate unanimously adopted a resolution, introduced by Henry Cabot Lodge, calling for the correspondence Daniels had declined to furnish the House Naval Affairs Committee. Moreover, during a personal call, Dewey told Fiske that he had requested to have Fiske serve on the General Board and that Daniels was wrong in saying he had changed his mind.

On 19 April, Daniels's aide called Fiske to say that Fiske's preparedness letter of 9 November 1914 could not be found. Fiske sent the secretary a copy. When Daniels could not find a copy of the General Board's letter of 3 August 1914, he asked Dewey to furnish one. But Dewey replied that there was no copy. There was a letter dated 1 August, resulting from Fiske's calling a special meeting of the board, but it dealt with his suggestion to withdraw American battleships from Mexican waters. Thus, it was not until 21 April that Daniels complied with the Senate request to furnish the other letters.[57]

In his communication, the secretary explained his unsuccessful search for the General Board's letter of 3 August and stated that he had never read Fiske's letter of 9 November. It will be recalled, however, that Daniels did read the letter on 5 November and then returned it, and that Fiske had filed it under the date of 9 November. Fiske's diary entry for 19 July 1916 reads: "[William P.] Cronan writes me that he *saw* the Sec[retary] and me conferring about my letter of Nov. 9, 1914." An entry dated 21 March 1917 reveals that a subordinate took the letter from the files as ordered by Albert G. Winterhalter. "So Winterhalter is the man: doubtless he got 4 stars for doing this treasonable act!" said Fiske.[58]

In concluding his testimony before the committee, Daniels responded to urgings by Padgett and struck Fiske hard, saying that their differences had been inspired by Fiske's failure to achieve his personal ambitions, not by a desire to increase naval preparedness. Daniels also had his own interpretation of their differences over the wine-mess order and of Dewey's desire for "a less theoretical man" to serve on the General Board.[59]

Unhappy with the turn of events, Fiske wrote the president of the Senate, Vice-president Thomas R. Marshall, on 29 April. Daniels's statement to the Senate, he said, "constituted an accusation against me of a grave breach of official propriety—in fact, of actual underhandedness—of an attempt to conceal an important letter from the Secretary; while as a matter of fact, I was always scrupulously careful never to permit him to receive, or to remain under, any mistaken impression, or to be in ignorance of any important matter, if I could prevent it [and the testimony has] injured my reputation for fair dealing." He then requested permission to appear before such persons as the vice-president might designate to prove—by reference to his diary and to statements by persons present at the time—that the letter was shown to Daniels, "that there has been a lapse of memory on the part of the Secretary." Fiske felt that if his request was declined, as much publicity should be given his letter as was given Daniels's.[60]

Marshall was not sure he should submit Fiske's letter to the Senate, saying, "I don't know how far the right of petition goes. I don't know whether or not a naval or military officer is allowed to criticize his superiors in memorials to Congress." Senators on the naval committee agreed that the letter could be submitted, with Lodge saying that Fiske should be allowed to answer Daniels and Benjamin R. Tillman, who supported the secretary, saying that Fiske was in a "mud hole" and that no harm would come to anyone else if the letter was read.[61] When Tillman read the letter to the Senate, on 4 May, he ascribed its authorship to Fiske's malice, wounded vanity, and disappointed ambition. Senator Lodge replied that Tillman was doing Fiske an injustice. Daniels had twice questioned Fiske's veracity, once before the House Naval Affairs Committee and again in his letter answering the Lodge resolution of inquiry. Lodge closed by saying that he did not wish injustice to be done to a distinguished and patriotic officer.[62]

Such newspapers as the *New York Sun*, the *New York Times*, and particularly the *New York World* demanded an investigation into the veracity of Daniels and Fiske. The *Times* asserted that "the advice Admiral Fiske tendered to Daniels in 1914 was timely and important, and it should have been heeded without delay."[63] Furthermore, the *Times* said such an "illustrious" officer should not be forced to endure the implications of being a fabricator without an opportunity for defense. The matter "concerns the whole country."[64] On 12 May C. S. Thompson, chairman of the Executive Committee of the American Defense Society, wrote directly to President Wilson in much the same vein.[65] On 22 May, Wilson's reply set the matter to rest, for it contained Daniels's acceptance of Fiske's word. Thus, said the *New York Times* on 24 May, "Fiske Is Vindicated."[66]

Late in April, with his retirement impending and Jo's health rapidly worsening, Fiske found a suitable apartment in New York City, settled Jo there, and returned to Newport to finish his active duty.

On 1 June, addressing the annual Naval Academy alumni banquet, the new chief of naval operations slashed at the man who had made his office possible. When Benson entered the office, he said, he found only "the fragments of organization"; he had reorganized the fleet, given special attention to naval aviation, won approval for mobilization and administrative plans, taken an inventory of merchant shipping available in time of emergency, reorganized the naval districts, and so on. His cooperation with the secretary and the bureaus was "most cordial and complete" because the secretary had created a council and also a Naval Consulting Board.[67] Since the new chief had done little except enjoy the fruits of ideas Fiske could not get Daniels to adopt, he characterized as "unprofessional" Benson's lauding of Daniels and gushing about the improvements he had made while in office.[68] The loquacious William F. Fullam wrote Sims after reading the speech: "I still think Fiske was right and that it will take us five years at this rate to get ready for war with a first class power. It would appear that the only way to get anything these days is to truckle and trim, and I am not prepared to do that by any means."[69]

On 11 June, Fiske wrote cryptically in his diary: "Leave Newport for N.Y. tonight and bid farewell to my naval life." On 12 June the *New York Times* said of him in part:

> None of our naval officers has a clearer comprehension of modern naval needs. . . . Admiral Fiske can still be of great service to his country. His services as a navigator and his purely military services have been noteworthy, and he is known all over the world as an inventor of many devices of great value. The number of his inventions now in use in our own navy and others

is 51, and of these the stadimeter, the naval electric semaphore, and the turret range finder are the best known.[70]

Upon returning to New York the next day, Fiske noted in his diary that he had retired on his sixty-second birthday. At a celebration for him held by the American Defense Society, Fiske received a "wonderful ovation" and was presented with a book engraved in gold with his name. "I made a speech in answer, and then several photographers and 'movie men' took pictures of us."[71] It was fitting that one who did so much to stimulate the preparedness of the country should be ushered back into civilian life by an organization devoted utterly to that cause.

Fiske had officially called Daniels's attention to the unpreparedness of the navy on 9 November 1914. Daniels ignored Fiske's warnings and did nothing. As soon as Fiske retired as aide for operations, on 11 May 1915, Daniels shunted him off to Newport even though, as Fiske told Dewey, he wished to serve on the General Board and remain in Washington with his wife, who was quite ill. While at the War College, he had designed an aerial depth charge; more important, his study of history and psychology had confirmed his belief that wars would be fought as long as men existed. Fiske published a series of articles during the winter of 1915, when the certainty that the United States would become involved in war increased his anxiety over its unpreparedness. Meanwhile, the administration modified its policy and called for improved defense, and Daniels finally signed Fiske's administrative plan for war. Fiske considered the proposed five-year naval building program insufficient because it was too late: it took four years to build a battleship, ten to train a junior officer, and twenty-five to produce admirals experienced enough to command fleets. Moreover, he knew from his own experience that the Navy Department was not properly organized to conduct a war and that a naval general staff would be essential in preparing the department for war.

On 24 December 1915, when Fiske asked permission to take the leave he had accumulated and stay with Mrs. Fiske in Washington, Daniels gave him thirty instead of ninety days. Daniels also muzzled the officer corps, in keeping with regulations that prohibited officers from influencing legislation. As a result, Fiske had to break numerous commitments for speaking engagements and promises to write articles.

In questioning Daniels before the House Naval Affairs Committee, Britten elicited the information that Daniels had suppressed the 1914 recommendation by the General Board that 19,600 men be added to the fleet;

that he had disagreed with Fiske and other admirals—including Knight, Winslow, and Sims—on the need for a naval general staff and additional preparedness in both ships and aircraft; and that he had complete confidence in Benson, who lacked both executive authority and sufficient officers to provide a war plans division. Above all, Daniels objected to Fiske's desire to have the civilian secretary handle the department's purely administrative matters and naval professionals the strictly military matters. He also opposed having the duties of the chief of naval operations spelled out in law so that they could be changed only by the Congress, not by the secretary.

Under questioning, Fiske admitted to the committee that he, along with several other officers and Representative Hobson, had prepared the bill creating a chief of naval operations and a corps of officers that would provide continuity at least in strategic matters while secretaries, politically appointed, came and went. Even with the creation of a chief of naval operations—for Daniels had succeeded in blocking the war plans division—Fiske felt that it would still take the navy five years to prepare for war, and on this matter he had the cordial support of most naval officers. Under questioning, Fiske detailed Daniels's record: the secretary had refused to concentrate the fleet in home waters, leaving it stationed off Mexico; he had refused to publish the General Board's request in 1914 for 19,600 additional men; he had refused to grant Fiske more than thirty of the ninety-days' leave he had accumulated; he had prevented Fiske from serving again on the General Board, directing him to proceed to Newport despite Mrs. Fiske's illness; he had ordered Fiske not to write or speak on defense matters; he had severely cut the General Board's recommendations for new ships and aircraft; he had declined to fund research and development programs for aviation; he had refused to give the chief of naval operations authority to coordinate the departmental bureaus so that they could support a strategic plan; he had countered the best professional advice offered him on the unpreparedness of the navy; he had affronted the entire officers corps by issuing the wine-mess order; and he had denied that Fiske had submitted to him the letter on preparedness of 9 November 1914.

After Daniels blasted Fiske for acting out of wounded vanity and an unfulfilled ambition to command the fleet, Fiske sought recourse from the House Naval Affairs Committee; the chairman, however, supported Daniels and declined to let Fiske appear. Lodge got the Senate to direct Daniels to submit the letters from the General Board and from Fiske which Daniels said he had never seen. Fiske then used the right of petition guaranteed civilians and in his letter to the vice-president asked that he be authorized to respond to Daniels's charge against his integrity and honesty. Although most of the press upheld Fiske, in the Senate, opinion divided along partisan lines, with Democrats like Tillman opposing him and Republicans like Lodge supporting him. The issue was set to rest only when the president himself vindicated Fiske by noting Daniels's comment that although he did not recall Fiske showing him the letter, he was willing to take the admiral's word for it.

15

RUMBLES OF WAR—AND WAR, 1916–1917

Bradley A. Fiske no sooner established himself and Jo at Jamestown, Rhode Island, for the summer, than Burton J. Hendrick, an editor of *The World's Work*, asked him to write several articles. Fiske agreed pending approval from the secretary of the navy.[1] Fiske declined highly paid employment with a shipbuilding company because he wished to conduct experiments that might be useful in the war he felt sure was coming. His first suggestion to the Navy Department was that placing strips of wood on masts and otherwise breaking up smooth lines on a ship would inhibit an enemy in obtaining the correct range.[2] Hs also spoke widely about getting the nation and the navy ready for war.

Typical of the addresses Fiske delivered during the summer of 1916 was that to the American Defense Society. It was, he alleged, not a foreign foe that was dangerous to American security, but "the politician who prevents our getting an adequate army and navy." Moreover, the public must be made aware that our national security depended upon our naval strength. Because trained staff officers were unavailable, Fiske urged that some officers be detailed immediately to the Office of the Chief of Naval Operations and gain some experience in drafting war plans.[3]

Not until 29 August 1916 did Congress adopt the "reasonable" defense program President Wilson had demanded in October 1915, but it did so with the understanding that the purpose of increased defense was peace, not war.[4] On that date Congress also authorized a Council of National Defense that fairly fulfilled demands Fiske had been making as early as 1911 and called for a three-year building program, costing $500 million, to include 156 ships of all classes, with work on 56 ships to begin within six months. Congress also called for a naval experiments laboratory, increased appropriations for naval aviation, augmented enlisted strength, a naval reserve, and staff aid for the chief of naval operations. After Wilson signed the bill, Fiske commented, *"Thus was the navy finally given a general staff against the opposition of the Navy Department and half of the House Committee. I feel that I have not lived in vain."*[5] William S. Sims credited Fiske's criticisms with the progress made in defense matters since he had left the Office of Aide for Operations in May.[6] "By retiring from his position as Aide for Operations in 1915 [Fiske] had ensured the maintenance of his principles," Sims's biographer has noted.[7] According to Lt. Comdr. William P. Cronan, a member of Fiske's "war staff," Fiske was the navy's Emory Upton because he had demanded a definite military policy and a naval general staff that would coordinate the work of the bureaus in preparing the navy to implement national policy.[8]

Fiske's happiness with the Navy Act of 1916 was considerably diminished by personal worries. Both he and Jo had been ill throughout much of 1915 and 1916. He attributed his headaches and aching eyes to stomach trouble. In mid October 1916 he was treated by a physician for a "very painful sciatica," but in June 1918 was pronounced quite fit following his routine, annual naval examination.[9] Jo's story, however, was altogether tragic. On 23 May 1916, when she learned that she had received a $37,000 check as a final payment on her father's estate, she told Fiske that "the calculations about banking it etc. gave her pains in back of [her] head and in [her] stomach."[10] Fiske arranged to have her examined by Dr. Graeme Hammond, who said she had had a nervous breakdown but showed no signs of dementia; he warned that it might take a year before she recovered completely. "She is much better," Fiske noted on 31 May, "but not quite well."[11] In mid July he noted that Jo was "better, but still nervous"; on 30 August, she was "not well, but [it is] probably only a little indigestion"; on 4 September, however, "Jo has been taken very ill." On 9 September Fiske took his wife to Roosevelt Hospital. When told that she needed a gall bladder operation, she took the news well. She recovered well from the operation, but her mind remained terribly disturbed for several months.[12]

On 17 October, after her doctors agreed that Jo should be declared incompetent and placed in a sanitorium, Fiske made the necessary arrangements. Two days later, however, when he made his afternoon call, Fiske recorded, "She was the same as in forenoon, but seemed to know me and to be affectionate to me. She said faintly but clearly 'You have been very good to me.' Also 'You have a kind heart.'" On 20 October he called at a law firm to learn what he must do to have Jo declared incompetent, saying as he did so that "I hate like fury to do this, but I fear I must." Fiske's diary entries record Jo's progress.

October 22: I don't think she recognized me.

November 2: Nurse told me she thought Jo would pass away during the night.

November 3: Dr. . . . told me that Jo is getting weaker, and that he thinks she will gradually fade away, but that she will have no pain. . . .

Then the miracle:

November 4: She was awake and seemed stronger than for two or three days; moved her arms a little and tried to talk, etc. I could not understand her or tell whether she recognized me.

November 5: Telephone from hospital says Jo is very much better. . . . I think she recognized me.

November 8: She was certainly brighter.

November 16: Brighter and clearer in mind.

November 30: She seemed to talk to me, to understand what I said, etc., but she did not quite "place" me. . . . I do not think her mental condition is improving, though her physical is.

December 13: In p.m. . . . seemingly brighter than usual. Called out loud [for their daughter] "Carrie, Carrie."

December 20: I think her mind is trying to clear up. She answers questions better, is more observant and her articulation is better.

December 21: Jo was sitting up in a big chair. . . . She . . . talked quite clearly though not quite rationally.

December 22: She got up on her feet twice this forenoon.

December 24: Jo more nearly rational than she has been for two months.

On 28 December, Fiske brought Jo home. On 14 February, he took preliminary steps to have guardians appointed for her; he was made the guardian of her person and the Farmers Loan and Trust Company, guardian of her estate.[13] The next day he noted in his diary, "This is our 35th anniversary. . . . *Jo* [was] *nearer rational in the afternoon than she has been since the middle of October.*" Early in March 1916, Jo was so much improved that she recognized everyone; and in mid March Dr. Hammond said she was fully competent mentally to sign a power of attorney. The day she did so, Fiske remarked "She was as clear in her head today as ever in her life."

During Jo's long stay in the hospital, Fiske rose at his usual early hour, read several newspapers and journals at breakfast, worked until he visited her between 11:00 and 12:00, then busied himself during the afternoon until he could visit from 5:00 to 6:00, and usually spent part of the evening at his desk. He was thus able to accomplish a multitude of tasks. In July 1917 Scribner's agreed to publish *The Navy as a Fighting Machine.* In the book, which appeared in October 1916, Fiske tried to bridge naval and civilian thought. He thoroughly examined and analyzed American naval problems, stressed the need for making logical "estimates of the situation," demanded a definite naval policy for which a scientific naval strategy could be prepared, and with words and statistics showed the intimate connection between policy and strategy. The Conference Committee on Preparedness furnished a copy to every congressman, and Fiske sent one of the first copies to Theodore Roosevelt. Perhaps the words about it he enjoyed most came from the former president, who wrote: "There is no one man to whom the United States Navy owes as much, during the last three and a half years, as to you. You have shown the very rarest type of courage in standing up for it."[14]

Early in October 1916, the U-53, the *Deutschland*, under the command of Lieutenant-captain Hans Rose, surfaced off Newport, Rhode Island. Rose visited ashore but sought no stores or provisions. He then lay off Nantucket Shoal Lightship; in one day the *Deutschland* sent six British and neutral ships—none of them American—to the bottom. It was Daniels's opinion that the U-53 had not violated American neutrality; he concluded that perhaps its sinkings were made "only to convince Americans of the dangers of war."[15] When Fiske was interviewed, however, he stated that the visit of the U-53 was most opportune because it showed people the dangers of being unprepared much better than any argument, history, or statistics. If the U-53 could get to Newport undetected, Fiske argued, she could go into New York Harbor or to Philadelphia or Baltimore or Boston. And if one submarine could, many could. If a U-boat could come over, Fiske asked, what prevented a German fleet from doing likewise? And he wondered how we could defend ourselves against such a fleet. Fiske felt we should thank the U-53 for pointing out that no warning would be given prior to an attack. Moreover, he pointed out, the U.S. had no scout cruisers or battle cruisers with which to locate an enemy fleet. Were an enemy fleet merely to blockade the United States, Fiske concluded, our ships would be stopped, our factories would close, unemployment would rise, and our great exports would cease; it certainly was time for the United States to prepare.[16]

Though the election of 1916 was close, President Wilson was returned to the White House. Fiske, thereupon, uttered one of his rare comments on politics: he thought that nine-tenths of the nation's military men—except for the southerners—preferred the Republican party because it took a broader outlook on international affairs, was less partisan and provincial, and was "more favorably inclined toward an adequate army and navy." He certainly was correct on the last point, for Republicans rather than Democrats lined up in support of Wilson's preparedness program in 1916. But Fiske still thought that military men rather than civilians should govern the war-making mechanisms of nations.[17] The war game Fiske had devised, played in the summer of 1916, revealed the navy's need for battle cruisers, swift scouts, and more efficient hydroplanes. The department gave him no credit for devising the game but did realize its worth, especially in showing the poor status of naval aviation.[18] Except for Glenn H. Curtiss, aircraft builders concentrated on "land machines" rather than on naval craft. The industry was new; production methods were not standardized. Perhaps the $3.5 million authorized for aviation for fiscal year 1916 would improve things. Even so, however, the missions of army and naval aviation still had to be worked out.[19]

Early on, Fiske had foreseen the usefulness of aircraft: attacking ships and submarines at sea with bombs, torpedoes, and guns; bombing enemy bases and stations; attacking enemy aircraft in the air; serving as the eyes of fleets at sea; defending and protecting naval bases and stations from naval and aerial attacks; escorting coastal shipping; patrolling coasts; locating mine fields and directing minesweepers to their destruction; spotting for gunfire; delivering important messages, thereby denying the enemy information through interception of radio messages; conducting diversionary operations; and obtaining photographs and motion pictures of enemy forces. But the chief of naval operations, William S. Benson, could see only two uses for naval planes—for scouting and for spotting shot in battle. No wonder Fiske commented that "Benson made awful testimony before [the] House Naval Committee against aeronautics!!! Practically busted all I had done. . . . B-r-r-r, B-r-r-r. And this from a commissioned officer in the navy of the country of Langley and the Wright brothers, in November 1916!!!"[20]

Fiske also thought that the lack of American naval bases, dry docks, and repair facilities put the navy in peril. The largest battleships could be docked only at New York, Norfolk, Bremerton, and Hawaii; there was no place south of Hatteras or in the Gulf of Mexico where battleships could be repaired. This situation prompted him to comment sharply, "The American people are as ignorant of their dangers as a baby sitting on a railroad track."[21]

Fiske realized that his demands for preparedness made him obnoxious to various influential people including Daniels. He was so convinced that the United States would soon enter the war, however, that he felt he had to cry out regardless of the consequences. Warned by Daniels that he must not speak of the United States at war, Fiske prepared with great care only two of the four articles Hendrick had asked him to write for *The World's Work*. In the first, he concluded that the naval appropriations bill of 1916 was passed too late, particularly with respect to naval aviation and the training of officers for general staff work.[22] In the second, "The War's Most Important Hint to Us," he pleaded that inventors be supported during peacetime in their attempts to provide novel instruments for war, for in time of war, it might be too late.[23]

Although he was tending to his sick wife, working on gunnery systems, writing copiously, creating sensors for detecting submarines, and trying to develop a torpedo plane, Fiske also delivered a large number of public addresses during 1916 and 1917 on the need of preparedness. In these he warned the public to "prepare or perish," chastized the nation for being "effeminized" and "given to luxury," stated that "if we got into war now, we would have a situation we could not master," and charged that the public did not know what an army and navy were for. He called for a new strategy, one in which air power would "bring a preponderating force to bear on a given point before the enemy can prevent it." Britain and Germany already were using torpedo planes, and he believed that "the torpedoplane under favorable conditions would make the $20,000 airplane a worthy match for a $20,000,000 battleship." Then Daniels again applied the muzzle.[24]

Fiske requested clearance for an address he was to deliver on 20 March to the American Defense Society, of which he had been elected a trustee. Daniels denied it. Fiske informed the society's secretary, who told the press, and newspapers like the *New York Herald* editorialized about the "War on Admiral Fiske." Fiske also submitted a speech he was to deliver to the Navy League on 27 March. Daniels not only disapproved it but demanded a written explanation of Fiske's conduct. At this point, the various organizations Fiske had promised to address lodged official protests, and the newspapers made the muzzling a *cause célèbre*.[25]

After Wilson's failure to bring the belligerents to the conference table in December 1916, the president addressed his terms for peace not to the heads of governments but to the peoples of the warring nations in his "peace without victory" speech delivered before the Senate on 22 January 1917. Germany rejected the terms and on 31 January announced that unrestricted submarine warfare would begin the very next day. She also placed such restrictions on neutral ships that Wilson concluded, "This means war." Fiske recorded his feelings in his diary: *"I am glad I took the measures I did as Aide for Operations on Aug. 1 and Nov. 9, 1914. I did all I could to get the Govt to act, but without success!"*[26]

On 3 February Wilson broke diplomatic relations with Germany. But he told Congress he could not believe that Germany was serious and that only "overt acts" could cause him to break his friendship with the German people and their government. He also asserted, however, that Congress might have to grant him authority to protect the rights of Americans to sail the high seas. On 5 February, Fiske noted in his diary:

I telephoned to Adm. Benson, CNO, saying I wanted to do all I could and suggesting I be put on Naval Consulting Board, or take charge of building aeronautic defense. He said he would keep my suggestion in mind. I do not think [Daniels] will give me any employment I want! I told Benson to tell [Daniels] I had no ill will against him, and never had. I also told him I did not want to go far away if I could help it as my wife was at death's door here and has been in bed five months. I talked with [Elmer A.] Sperry, who said I should be on Consulting Board. Called [Frank Julian] Sprague on Board, who took me to lunch with 6 members of his office. They all appealed to me for advice.[27]

On 7 February the Senate approved Wilson's course of action toward Germany. In the meantime, on 4 February, Daniels and the secretary of war, Newton D. Baker, set their departments to work on full mobilization plans. Moreover, the naval appropriations bill for fiscal year 1918, which Congress passed on 3 March, was the largest of its kind in history. "Too late, too late," Fiske commented. Ships could fight only if provided sufficent and efficient personnel, he said; moreover, battleships were useless against U-boats, and the navy lacked battle cruisers and particularly aircraft with which to fight Germans. To editorials that suggested that he should be made secretary of the navy if the United States entered the war, he retorted, "I don't want it. My work to be my best must be 'inventional'."[28] On 25 March, he officially notified the Navy Department that he was working on a torpedo plane and requested permission to continue with it. Daniels approved.[29]

While American cargo and passenger ships hugged their harbors because of the U-boat menace, a strong demand arose for arming and escorting them. On 26 February, Wilson asked Congress not for war but for authority to protect Americans at sea by force of arms. A reporter asked Fiske if arming of merchant ships would provide adequate defense against U-boats. Fiske replied that naval officers favored arming merchant ships but that these would stand no chance of surviving a conflict with a submarine. He was asked about Wilson's suggestion of having large ships drop submarine chasers as they approached the barred zones. Fiske replied that in addition to the difficulty of lifting the boats down and up, such small boats would be effective only under the most perfect sea and weather conditions.[30] The House of Representatives passed an armed-ship bill on 4 March, the day the congressional session ended. A dozen pacifist senators filibustered, however, and blocked its final passage. Because various appropriations bills had not been passed, Wilson had to call Congress into extraordinary session.

The American public had not quite gotten over being stunned by Wilson's release of the Zimmermann note on 1 March when Russia revolted and the czar abdicated. The Zimmermann telegram finally convinced Wilson that Germany was not sincere about wanting peace and all along had planned to "dominate the world by a crushing victory." After the czar abdicated on 15 March, Wilson could state that all of the Allies had democratic governments. Fiske saw it somewhat differently, noting, "I do not think this is a war of autocracy against democracy, but of an *efficient autocracy against several inefficient democracies.* . . . An autocracy is not necessarily more efficient than a democracy. Vide Persia vs. Athens, 490 and 408 B. C."[31] Meanwhile, on 9 March, Wilson had ordered merchant ships armed and their navy armed guard crews to shoot in defense on sight. Three U-boat sinkings of American ships on 18 and 19 March further inflamed the public's demand for war. Now determined that war was inevitable, Wilson ordered naval ships in the Caribbean to concentrate at Norfolk (a move Fiske had suggested when war broke out in Europe in August 1914), moved the special congressional session up from 16 to 2 April, and directed that naval personnel be brought to full strength. On the evening 2 April he read Congress his war message. The Senate approved a joint war resolution on 4 April, the House did so the next day. Wilson signed it at 1:18 P.M. on 6 April; five minutes later Daniels telegraphed the fleet to mobilize.

Were the nation and the navy prepared for war, as Daniels alleged? Or were they unprepared, as Fiske asserted? Fiske wrote in his diary:

> *April 6:* U.S. declared war today. *U.S. caught unprepared again.* Lord have mercy on us. . . . God punished the children of Israel sometimes for their sins. Perhaps he is going to punish us for making Bryan Sec[retary] of State.

When the United States went to war, the "war on Admiral Fiske" ended. As a naval officer, he said, he had no right to say whether or not the United States should have entered the war. He felt, however, that "if a nation does go to war, it ought to go to war prepared." In Fiske's metaphor, the United States was entering the war like an actor who had not learned his part and did not have his costume ready; George Washington would have been ashamed.[32]

16

FISKE'S TORPEDO PLANE, 1917–1931

While working to develop a torpedo plane, Bradley A. Fiske also tried to educate the American people on the strategic uses of air power. Both German and Allied planes were bombing cities, ports, even trenches. Then on Christmas Day 1914, an action Fiske deemed "an entirely new idea in warfare" was carried out: a British force off Heligoland sent seven hydro-planes to bomb Cuxhaven, at the mouth of the Elbe. Why could not the U.S. Navy adopt this idea?[1] Unable for years to get the Navy Department or Congress to adopt his views, Fiske asked the governor of the Aero Club of America on 16 April 1917 to urge the immediate dispatch of a large air-plane force to Europe. One thousand "battleplanes," he said, would have the destructive power of 100,000 soldiers.[2]

As early as November 1914, Park Benjamin had urged the Navy De-partment to provide an aircraft carrier to carry Fiske's "bold conception," a torpedo plane.[3] In January 1917, the Aero Club asked Fiske to chair a committee supervising torpedo plane development and provided $2,500 to defray his expenses. Rather than develop large seaplanes that could drop full-sized, 2,000-pound torpedoes, the committee decided to work on a small torpedo of 200 pounds that could be dropped by existing flying boats and hydroplanes.[4]

On 3 May, after learning that the British merchant ship *Gena* had been sunk by a German aerial torpedo, Fiske wrote an article in which he begged for production of a torpedo plane, arguing, that "Hindenburg never sleeps"; Park Benjamin spread the idea in the *Independent*. Fiske asked Benjamin, as his patent attorney, to apply for a patent on the idea that a dirigible would pull a boat towing a submerged microphone that would relay noises to operators in the dirigible. The patent was granted on 23 May. Fiske offered the government "the free and unrestricted use of the invention," but the Patent Office classified it and warned Fiske to keep his work secret during the war "under penalty of the invention being held abandoned." Fiske then offered the patent to the Navy Department, which submitted it to the

187

Special Board on Anti-submarine Devices, located at New London. On 11 February 1918, the board reported that its experiments showed "the impracticability of the towed detector as outlined on account of water disturbances at the speeds which were considered." Moreover, wireless radio communications between dirigibles, submarines, and antisubmarine craft were already available.[5]

On 17 May 1917, the E. W. Bliss Company told Fiske that it would provide at no cost to him a 175-pound torpedo but that it was too busy to build him an aeroplane. On 19 May, however, Inglis M. Uppercu, president of the Aeromarine Plane and Motor Company, offered Fiske a seaplane and test pilot. Thus, on 23 May, Fiske arranged for Bliss to deliver the dummy torpedo for testing on the promised plane; he bemoaned the government's slowness in developing the torpedo plane, thus letting the Germans "steal" his idea.[6] In addition, during the spring, Fiske wrote not only the introduction to a book entitled *Textbook of Naval Aeronautics*, edited by Henry Woodhouse, a member of the Aero Club, but also two of its chapters. In the introduction he listed six major ways in which naval aircraft were used for war purposes—among them, launching torpedoes; and in the chapters he pointed out that the airplane could deliver weapons faster than any other means.[7]

Fiske favored stopping U-boats from leaving their bases by sending small craft under aerial cover to countermine their defensive minefields, as well as destroying German surface ships in their harbors with torpedo planes. The latter idea was applauded by such newspapers as the *New York Herald* and *New York Times*, by Benjamin, Wilbur Wright, and various military journals. When the chief of naval operations, William Benson, told Congress that the "Navy needs only such small aeroplanes as can be carried on navy ships," Fiske exclaimed, "This seems *incredible*."[8]

On 15 June Fiske wrote president Alan R. Hawley of the Aero Club, repeating that the most immediate peril to the British and French food supply was the U-boat and that the most effective foe of the submarine was the torpedo plane. The British torpedo planes that sank four Turkish ships in the Sea of Marmora in August 1915 and the German torpedo plane that sank the *Gena* off the coast of England on 1 May 1917 were of considerable size and power. For its cost, Fiske argued, the torpedo plane was the most powerful and mobile weapon in the world. Used in sufficient numbers, these planes could gain control of the North Sea and the approaches to the German coast, prevent the sortie of U-boats, and thus "wipe out the German menace." Fiske contended that the Allies could send seaplane tenders close enough to Germany to enable the planes to attack German ships in Kiel and Wilhelmshaven—ninety and forty-five miles distant, respectively. He asked the Aero Club to bring his letter to the attention of the "proper persons." The club's Board of Governors endorsed the letter and sent copies of it to Congress and to the press.[9]

Several weeks later, impatient with procrastination in Washington, Fiske prodded Hawley with another letter and also told William S. Sims, commander of American naval forces in Europe, that he had been "getting red in the face" trying to prove the validity of attacking the German fleet with torpedo planes flying under fighter cover. He asked Sims to evaluate his idea. Sims replied, "I have not the slightest doubt that if the seaplane torpedo you advocate is practicable, and can be built for use in time, it will do the stunt you project. . . . Show the principal dignitaries that it is practical. Get it built and the people who are fighting the war will be more than glad to use it."[10]

Thus far the British admiralty had failed to conquer the U-boat; Fiske said, therefore, that it was up to the United States to contribute a plan. *"So far as I know, I am the only one on the Allies' side to contribute any plan whatever. The Allies have simply fought a war on lines laid down by Germany."* Moreover, he added, "If any lesson has been taught by history more clearly than any other lesson . . . it is that if one does not keep up with the procession he will be left behind."[11]

With Daniels chary of aviation funds, Fiske grasped an offer from the Italian government and the Caproni Company to furnish a huge triplane for modification into a torpedo plane; he also called on the editors of the *New York Times* and of *Life* "to get after JD on aeronautics."[12]

The 1 August dropping of Fiske's dummy torpedo marked a milestone because the test was ordered by Benson, who also directed the Bureau of Ordnance to produce an 800-pound torpedo.[13]

On 15 August, Fiske wrote Hawley a third letter, stressing the need to use bombing and torpedo planes against German ships and U-boat bases. A week later, Sims commented: "Everything you say concerning the torpedoing aeroplane is all right. There is only one thing that stands in the way of it, and that is enough planes and enough fighting planes to protect the torpedo dropping planes." He added, "We, being unprepared after 3 years of war, cannot supply any considerable number for about a *year*." Fiske replied, "All these things I have been sleeping with at night," adding, "These very difficulties are more than balanced, in my opinion, by the fact that the supreme resources of the United States can overcome them." Fiske felt sure that the nation had resources to build the needed aircraft. "We must," he wrote, "make the unexpected happen."[14]

On 25 August Lt. Godfrey L. Cabot of the U.S. Naval Flying Reserve and Fiske signed an "agreement" by which Cabot gave Fiske $30,000 to develop a "torpedo carrying seaplane." Although Fiske commented, "This is patriotism of the first order," privately he lamented that the amount would not attract manufacturers already swamped by government contracts amounting to $640 million to build regular aircraft.[15] That same day, Lord Northcliffe, head of the permanent British mission in the United States, telegraphed Fiske for an appointment. When they met on 12 September, Northcliffe said he believed in Fiske's torpedo plane and in his idea of bombing Kiel, adding, "I wish to God you could be in England now and stir them up."[16] On 17 September the Aeromarine Company, which was to build Fiske's torpedo plane, declined because, it said, of commitments to the navy and army. "I fear that the attitude of Secretary towards me will block my efforts at bringing out a powerful torpedoplane," Fiske wrote in his diary.[17] When Lieutenant Cabot also offered Benson funds to develop a torpedo plane, Benson asked for the opinion of Ralph Earle, chief of the Bureau of Ordnance.[18]

After inspecting a Caproni biplane (the triplane was not yet available) on 29 September, Fiske was convinced that it could not carry a heavy torpedo from England to Kiel and return. He asked, therefore, that launching gear be fitted to a Caproni triplane. Meanwhile Glenn Curtiss wrote Fiske that he was designing a 1,000-horsepower seaplane for carrying torpedoes. On 3 November the Bliss Company shipped the dummy torpedo and launching gear to Langley Field, and Fiske was confident of success. Both Capt. William V. Pratt, Benson's assistant, and Capt. Noble E. Irwin, head of the aviation section in Benson's office, wanted the torpedo plane developed "strenuously," and Pratt told Fiske he had asked Earle to test the 8-inch torpedo. On 28 November, two days after Fiske had asked the secretary of the navy to reconsider his rejection of the torpedo plane, Daniels sent him a letter endorsing the unfavorable reports by Benson and Earle. Unless other important work was sacrificed, said Earle, it would take at least a year to manufacture and test a large torpedo and a torpedo plane and to devise methods for their employment. "Thus," Daniels wrote, "the Bureau concludes that no matter what developments are now undertaken by us, they will have no serious effect on the result of the war."[19] Fiske was further depressed when he heard from Curtiss that the builder's other work precluded efforts on a torpedo plane. Fiske called the news "pretty near a knock out for me."[20] Not one to give up easily, however, he asked Daniels to reconsider Benson's and Earle's unfavorable recommendations; Daniels reconsidered but did not change his mind.

On 23 December, in a fourth letter to the president of the Aero Club, Fiske argued that since the German navy was the weakest part of the German military machine, the principle of concentration dictated a strong attack upon it. If aircraft capable of delivering heavy torpedoes from England or France to Kiel and returning did not as yet exist, Fiske said, they should be produced. The mere existence of the German fleet necessitated its destruction.[21] The letter, published repeatedly by the press, provoked Daniels's censors to ask if Fiske had authorized its publication. Fiske said he had, adding, "*Careful reading of my letter by the Secretary himself is earnestly requested*; for careful reading will show that this letter was not in any correct sense a discussion of suggested methods of operation against the enemy. It was a distinct suggestion *made by myself, and by myself only*; and was intended as an argument for the development of *my own* invention."[22]

On 31 January 1918 Fiske wrote to the bureaus of Ordnance and of Navigation: he contended that a plane large enough for bombing and torpedoing Kiel and Wilhelmshaven was at hand. Even as he wrote, however, he received such a severe reprimand from Daniels that he decided to drop his efforts. Aside from Daniels, Benson, and Earle, however, Fiske did receive much encouragement. Sims wished him godspeed in developing the torpedo plane; the superintendent of the new naval aircraft factory at the Philadelphia Navy Yard told him that the flying boats he needed could be built there;[23] and Theodore Roosevelt and other Defense Society leaders wished him well in augmenting naval air power.[24] Although Daniels still objected to his project, on 23 January Fiske went to Washington to see, among others, naval constructor Jerome C. Hunsaker, Benson, and Franklin D. Roosevelt about getting the navy to build torpedo planes. Fiske then asked Daniels to send representatives to witness a test of the capacity of a large Caproni to launch a heavy torpedo. His discouragement is evident in a diary entry for 24 January: "Benson does not see the issue clearly. . . . I do not think there is any use in pushing torpedo plane scheme any longer."[25]

Pending a reply from Daniels, Fiske wrote a preface for the second edition of *The Navy as a Fighting Machine*, which included lessons learned from the war since the first edition appeared in 1916. According to a review in the *Naval Institute Proceedings*, he had "carried on the life work of Mahan. For if there be any successor to the American philosopher of sea power it is Admiral Fiske."[26] Such praise was edifying, but Fiske still had to convince Daniels or Benson to let him prove the worth of his torpedo plane. The department, he was informed, believed such a plane was feasible but would not build one because there were no targets the plane could safely hit. When Fiske learned that the department had copies of designs of British torpedo planes, he asked to borrow them so that he could build a plane secretly at his own expense. He was turned down.[27]

Fiske admittedly "lost flesh that I could not spare in fruitless exasperation, and in imagining what would have happened" if his recommendations had been accepted. Had not Daniels and Benson abolished the Division of Aeronautics he had established while aide for operations, perhaps flotillas of bombing and torpedo planes could have started across the Atlantic on 7 April 1917. In any event, during a visit to Washington on 19 June he noted that "everybody [was] much more receptive towards [the] possibilities of aeronautics, including torpedoplane than ever before." He talked with Benson, Irwin, Earle and the navy's chief constructor, David W. Taylor. They agreed to send the dummy torpedo which was at Langley Field to the Philadelphia Navy Yard. On 20 June he wrote that at the Philadelphia aircraft factory he saw "an F-5 [that] could carry a 1,000-lb. torpedo on each side and attack Kiel and Wilhelmshaven etc. by flying to Azores, Portugal, England, and attack."[28] Hopeful of success, Fiske—age sixty-four—applied for active duty in connection with the plane. Daniels merely said he would put the application on file. On 25 June, Fiske continued his attack: he noted that while "in Washington yesterday, [he had] talked with [Leigh C.] Palmer, Benson, Earle, Irwin, and [John] Towers and F. D. Roosevelt. All agree as to practicability of carrying a torpedo on each side of F5L and launching both." On 19 July, after noting that the British admiralty had ordered 150 aircraft fitted with torpedoes, Sims told Hunsaker, the naval constructor, that he was distressed that the British were doing what Daniels refused to do. Hunsaker must then have talked with Taylor, for on 25 June Taylor asked Sims to "Please forward [to the Bureau of Construction] full details of Sopwith torpedo-carrying seaplane including photographs and characteristics." Sims did so, and his endorsement of Fiske's project carried weight; on 1 July, Irwin asked Taylor and Earle to advise him on whether experiments should be made with the F-5.[29]

Fiske, not satisfied, found it "disgraceful" that the U.S. Navy did nothing about a torpedo plane "except reject it." When Benson told him he wanted the F-5 tested, Fiske commented, "What a late concession, after all his bucking against it, and against aeronautics in general." He was pleased nonetheless that Earle and Hunsaker wanted to go ahead with the F-5. These men would also adopt an air log he invented which "everyone seems to think . . . solves the problem of ocean flight." On 9 September he approved designs for attaching two torpedoes to the F-5L and then went to Washington to "see about torpedoplane."[30] Earle was not ready for the experiment, however, until 30 October; Taylor was not ready until 4 November; and Benson did not approve until 5 November. It was the familiar story of too little and too late, for the Armistice was signed on 11 November.

In the May 1919 issue of the *Naval Institute Proceedings*, Henry Woodhouse praised Fiske's work on the torpedo plane.[31] Earle bridled and offered Woodhouse some corrections. He admitted that the British had produced a land-based torpedo plane and that the U.S. Navy had not come up with a seaplane capable of carrying a 1,000-pound torpedo. But the navy considered the torpedo plane useful merely for coastal defense, Earle said, and in no way considered it a revolutionary weapon.[32] Fiske, however, saw it as an offensive weapon for striking the ships of the High Seas Fleet which the Allies could not approach in any other way. Both the naval aircraft factory and Curtiss, he argued, could have produced planes needed to carry 2,000-pound torpedoes long before the end of the war. Said the *New York Times*, "The truth is that the Fiske invention was not taken seriously here in America. The British, Italians, and Germans had equipped planes with torpedoes. . . . But the Americans, who might have been ready with flotillas of torpedoplanes when they entered the war, were indifferent to the potentialities of their own countryman's invention and spent no time in experimenting—the old, old story."[33]

Unlike many other rear admirals, Fiske was not recalled to active duty during the war, yet postwar American naval aviation policy followed, in great part, principles he had underscored as early as 1910. When both Sims and the commander of the Atlantic Fleet, Henry T. Mayo, recommended encouraging torpedo plane work, Daniels approved. By the end of 1919, however, the British, with several carriers each capable of carrying twenty torpedo planes, had left the American navy far behind. The situation would never have developed had the Navy Department listened to Fiske. While the department failed even to acknowledge his efforts, on 1 August 1919 the Aero Club granted him its highest award—its Gold Medal—for inventing the torpedo plane. Both American and British historians give Fiske credit for keeping the idea of the torpedo plane alive during the war and for holding the F-5 tests. These in turn led to tests with the R-6 and, in 1920, to the development of the Martin torpedo bomber, the first aircraft specifically designed to handle torpedoes.[34]

Early in January 1922, the Curtiss Company turned over to the navy the Curtiss CT, a float hydroplane which, like other "torpedo" planes, could carry torpedoes or bombs or be used simply as a scout. On 11 January, the new chief of naval operations, Robert E. Coontz, asked Sims, now president of the Naval War College, for information on the tactics of torpedo planes. Informed by Fiske that torpedo plane squadrons had been established in the fleet, Sims gave Coontz the number and kinds of torpedoes available, adding that actual tests of torpedo planes could be expected in July.[35]

On 10 February 1922, Fiske called the attention of Rear Adm. William A. Moffett, first chief of the Bureau of Aeronautics (established in 1921), to his torpedo plane patent and alleged that Moffett was infringing upon it.

Fiske added that he had secured the patent entirely at his own expense and had conceived his invention "entirely apart from anything connected with any of my professional duties," even though he was at the time commanding a division of the Atlantic Fleet. Fiske suggested that a royalty of $500 be paid "for each complete apparatus; the foregoing to include the complete outfit for each torpedo-plane and the necessary spare parts therefore."[36] Thus began a ten-year battle which beautifully illustrates the vast amount of red tape that bound the government's bureaucracy.

By way of the chief of the Bureau of Ordnance, Charles McVay, Moffett asked the judge advocate general, Rear Adm. Julian L. Latimer, whether Fiske was entitled to royalties. It was McVay's opinion that since Fiske had patented his torpedo plane while on duty, the government could use the patent. Moreover, he was fairly sure that "the apparatus in current use did not infringe upon the claims of Fiske's patent."[37] If Fiske, however, had developed his invention outside of his official duty, the department "would not have a shop-right license thereunder." Nevertheless McVay would not recommend the payment of royalties to Fiske "until these questions are properly determined by a tribunal adequately qualified to pass upon these points."[38]

Fiske retorted that the bureau was infringing on his patent for the torpedo plane, which read:

> In combination with an air-ship, a torpedo of the self-controlled type, having an externally controllable device for starting the propelling mechanism of said torpedo, means for retaining said torpedo below said ship, and on said ship, means for operating said starting device and means for releasing said retaining means.

In sum, Fiske said, his invention—conceived in 1911 and patented in 1912—"constituted an embodiment of a wholly new conception." While the department "takes every advantage of it, [it] denies me all recognition as its inventor!" He enclosed a law brief on the case prepared by Ernest Wilkinson, a prominent patent attorney in Washington, and asked for a reconsideration of his claim.[39]

In reviewing Fiske's claim, Admiral Latimer believed that the navy had infringed only upon claim 3, the externally controllable device for starting the propelling mechanism of the torpedo.[40] Unconvinced, however, McVay demanded a legal interpretation. But he was unsure of exactly what Fiske wanted—credit and some payment for the invention, or a royalty on every torpedo plane, or a lump sum payment for relinquishing all past and future claims. If the last, McVay proposed offering "$5,000 as a reasonable settlement."[41] On 30 September the new secretary of the navy, Edwin Denby, offered Fiske $5,000 for his invention in keeping with the policy of the government "to encourage the making of beneficial suggestions and inventions by those connected with the Department."[42]

Fiske, told Denby (through Wilkinson) that the offer of payment for a beneficial suggestion was appreciated, but what he desired was acknowledgment of his "pioneer invention." When ordnance officers denied that Fiske's was a "pioneer invention," attorney Wilkinson retorted that Fiske should be acknowledged as the "inventor of this most important invention" and given some reimbursement for it—"in a small degree"—and not merely a bonus for a beneficial suggestion. Fiske, the attorney added, would grant a license to manufacture or transfer the patent to the department for a mere $25,000.[43] Denby said he would "have this matter inquired into and [would] write . . . more fully at a later date."[44]

To strengthen his client's claim, Wilkinson submitted to the Navy Department on 5 January 1923 a supplemental memorandum describing how Fiske had developed the "pioneer invention."[45] On 10 February, McVay cancelled his offer of $5,000 because the beneficial suggestion law applied only to the department's civil employees, adding that any rights under a patent could be recognized only after a legal decision was rendered and that legal action must be initiated by the claimant.[46] At Secretary Denby's direction, meanwhile, Latimer asked McVay to have his patent lawyers judge the validity of Fiske's patent "in order that the matter may be submitted to the Attorney General with [a] request for an opinion in the premises."[47]

On 14 November 1925, Fiske again protested the continued infringement of his patent on the torpedo plane and the department's failure to recognize him as the basic inventor of an important naval weapon. The protest, which went to the new secretary, Curtis D. Wilbur, asked why there had been such departmental inaction in response to his original protest, filed more than three years earlier.[48] Another year went by before Latimer sent Fiske's letter to Moffett for "comment and return."[49] Moffett replied on 12 January 1926 that he had taken official cognizance of the "alleged patent infringement" but had not been informed on any action taken in the matter by either Latimer or the chief of the Bureau of Ordnance, now Claude C. Bloch.[50] Bloch replied that nothing had occurred in the meantime to change the status of the Fiske case.[51] On 19 January, Fiske unofficially asked Secretary Wilbur, like Fiske, a Naval Academy graduate, why the department refused to give him credit for his invention. Could the secretary not get some action out of Latimer?[52] Wilbur said he would talk to Latimer.[53] Fiske, meanwhile, sent a three-page summary of his case directly to Latimer; on 13 March the judge advocate general advised Bloch that only one of Fiske's five claims was "apparently" being infringed by the department.[54]

Bloch disagreed, saying that all of Fiske's claims were invalid.[55] On 1 May, Wilbur asked the attorney general for an informal expression of opinion. The reply, dated 18 May 1926, held the patent invalid.[56]

On 20 November Wilkinson entered a suit in the Supreme Court of the District of Columbia against Secretary Wilbur, who was named "merely . . . as a government officer." Because Fiske could not sue the government directly, the only way to prove he had invented the torpedo plane was to bring action of "trespass on the case" against the individuals who had authorized or directed the infringement.[57] On 3 February 1927, the judge advocate general countered Fiske's attorney with a motion to dismiss Fiske's case and also entered a motion to require Fiske to amend his complaint brief to make it more definite. Wilkinson agreed to do so on 16 March.[58] When Judge William P. Stafford overruled the government's motion for dismissal, the case went to trial.[59]

At the trial, which lasted from 13 to 21 May 1929, Wilkinson represented Fiske and Harry C. Workman, the patent secretary in the Department of Justice, defended the government. Although some torpedo planes had been built earlier, Workman asked how many torpedo planes had been built between 20 November 1921 and 11 October 1928. He was told seven of one model (at a unit cost of $34,540) and fifty of another (each costing $16,108). On 2 July, Judge Stafford proposed having Moffett serve as the plaintiff who would represent all the other defendants in the case. In his decision Stafford ruled that Fiske had a right to bring his suit; the court had jurisdiction; the patent was valid; and the torpedo planes made and used by the navy did infringe on the patent. The judge found Moffett liable for damages amounting to $198,500.[60] After eighteen years, Fiske had won his battle for recognition.

Fiske laughed gleefully as he told reporters how the decision had gone and said he was extremely happy to have his rights sustained, even though there would be an appeal and the case might go to the Supreme Court. If overruled there, he could still take the case to the Court of Claims.[61]

Popular sympathy was with Fiske. He had been a gallant, distinguished, and honored officer while on active service. He had contributed without stint to the efficiency of the navy and continued to serve it even in retirement. The government was using many of his inventions without providing him recompense; nor was Fiske asking to be paid for them. In this case Fiske had, for many years, been the butt of envy, ridicule, and abuse; he fought, however, not only for himself but for all military inventors. Of course the government, not Moffett, should have been the defendant.[62] At a time of financial stringency and when plans were afoot for another disarmament conference, the United States could not overlook the relatively inexpensive and powerful weapon Fiske invented.

The case of *Moffett* v. *Fiske* was heard by the chief justice and three associates of the Court of Appeals of the District of Columbia on 8 March 1931. It was decided on 29 June that Fiske's patent was "invalid for inoperativeness." An inventor was not entitled to a patent, the court said, until he had embodied an idea in a useful physical contrivance, the novelty of which amounted to a discovery. Fiske had had merely a dream, the judges concluded,

> but a dream, like an idea, is not an invention, and cannot be patented until embodied in a physical contrivance making it practically useful. . . .
>
> Until the inventor has done this as a matter of reasonable legal certainty, and not as a matter of mere conjecture or prophetical possibility, he has given nothing to the public in return for the monopoly which he seeks by letters patent. . . .
>
> As we are of the opinion that the patent issued was invalid, for inoperativeness, and, in any event, that the United States was entitled to an irrevocable, but nonexclusive, license therein, the judgment is reversed, without costs, and the case remanded for further proceedings.[63]

On 26 October 1931, the Supreme Court refused to review Fiske's claim—and his case was dead.

17

VINDICATION BY INVESTIGATION, 1919–1921

On 14 February 1918, Bradley A. Fiske started work on his autobiography. His original draft ended with his experiences as a battleship division commander in early 1913, but at the suggestion of his publisher, the Century Company, he condensed the earlier parts and brought the story up to date, including his tribulations as aide for operations.[1]

These memoirs contain three major narratives. The first traces the change from the navy of wooden sailing vessels to that of steam, turbines, and steel, the change from smoothbores to high-powered steel rifles, and the development of gunnery as almost a science, thanks to his numerous inventions. The second theme deals with his trials as an inventor; and the third with his preparations for assuming ever higher positions in the service. Compared with those of such contemporaries as Adm. Sir Percy Scott, Grand Adm. Alfred von Tirpitz, and Adm. Reinhard Scheer, Fiske's memoirs glow with an aura of long-suffering patience and self-deprecation. All these highly placed naval officers agreed, however, that bad fighting was attributable to bad administration.

Jo Fiske died on 2 October 1919. As far as is known, she had never complained about Fiske's absences when he was ordered to distant duty. Several times she and their daughter Caroline followed him great distances just to be with him while his ship docked at this port or that—Hawaii, Manila, Shanghai, Yokohama. Jo filled their home with choice furnishings and often entertained Fiske and their friends, she at the piano while Caroline played the violin. During her last ten years while Jo was ill, sometimes critically, Fiske was at her bedside, and it may be recalled that he preferred to risk professional advancement by declining command of a battleship of the Great White Fleet rather than leave Jo for an extended time. Fiske lived with her for thirty-seven years; he would live twenty-three more years without her.[2]

From the armistice of November 1918 to the convening of the Washington Naval Disarmament Conference late in 1921, Fiske remained productive in many ways. He wrote two books, four articles, a number of book reviews, and various letters to newspaper editors.[3] Through research in optics and use of miniaturized printing, he invented a reading machine. He served as president of the Army and Navy Club of New York City and as president of the Naval Institute, where he tried to restore its *Proceedings*, divested of discussion of national and international issues by wartime censorship, to its normal lively and contentious style. In testimony before congressional committees he aired his views on what the navy should be doing and especially on what was being done to it during the postwar demobilization, retrenchment, and reformation at the hands of the Republicans (who won the congressional elections in 1918 and then the presidency in 1920). As a progressive reformer he continued to do battle against the "big smoke" —Secretary of the Navy Josephus Daniels, whose term would not end until March 1921—and the "smokescreen gang"—the conservative, or at least "obedient," naval officers who supported Daniels during the naval investigation hearings of 1920 and who remained obdurately opposed to the creation of a naval general staff.

On 30 September 1918, Burton J. Hendrick, an editor of *The World's Work*, asked William S. Sims to write about his part in the war. Sims replied that he was forbidden to talk about "mistakes of strategy, tactics, methods and organization." Alerted by various friends, however, to criticisms of him as a wartime commander, Sims succumbed. "I have no doubt . . . the . . . Republicans will begin an inquiry into the conduct of the war," he told William F. Fullam, commander of the Pacific Squadron. "If I am called to testify, you may be sure that I will not cover up any tracks." He also advised Fullam to read Fiske's memoirs, saying, "You will find it very diverting reading."[4]

Sims sent part of his book, *The Victory at Sea*, to Fiske, who noted in acknowledgment on 6 August 1920 that William S. Benson was being kept on as chief of naval operations by Daniels "because . . . he would not want you to come in and sweep out all his H[alf] A[ssed?] Sailor methods."[5] In a letter to the *New York Times* Fiske upheld Sims's efforts to avoid "the extreme unpreparedness for war of the United States Navy Department"; and in a review of Sims's book he stated that by waiting four months before adopting Sims's recommendations, Secretary Daniels postponed to the last possible moment saving the British from the "close call" of losing the war.[6]

In February 1919, Daniels appointed a board to consider the cases of all officers recommended to receive Medals of Honor, Distinguished Service Medals, and Navy Crosses. Upon finding that 68 percent of those recommended for a DSM had served only at desk jobs, he dropped some of them and added others who had lain the North Sea mine barrage or had served as naval armed guards. Since only 110 out of 500,000 enlisted men were granted awards, Daniels added thirteen DSMs and sixty-eight Navy Crosses for them.[7] Both Sims and Adm. Henry T. Mayo, commander in chief of the Atlantic Fleet, told him they were displeased, and Sims (followed by two other officers) declined the DSM awarded him on the ground that some of his recommendations were not followed. "Bully for you. You have done a fine thing," said Fiske, remarking, "On medals, [it is] not enough to reward for bravery; reward for excellence in knowledge of strategy. . . . I fancy this investigation will not be confined to medals. It must not be, more important things have been done (and not done) than awarding medals."[8] Sims rejoined that Fiske should "wait and see," adding, "something important is cooking."[9]

Chairman Carroll Smalley Page of the Senate Naval Affairs Committee established a subcommittee, headed by Frederick Hale, to ascertain the facts in the medals controversy. Partisanship dominated the hearings: the majority report by the three Republicans condemned most of Daniels's actions while the minority report by two Democrats upheld them.[10]

During the medals hearings, Senator Hale asked Sims to submit "any further correspondence with the Secretary of the Navy about the question of awards and their effect on the morale of the service." Sims furnished a letter to Daniels dated 7 January 1920 entitled "Certain Naval Lessons of the Great War." After the letter was read, Hale obtained authority to investigate the charges it leveled against the Navy Department. On 9 March he opened hearings which were to last until 28 May. While Daniels gathered data from the bureau chiefs, Rear Adm. Nathan C. Twining headed a pro-Sims group (which included Fiske and Fullam) that offered Hale questions for witnesses. In addition, Fiske tried to impress the Sims viewpoint on the publishers and editors of the *New York Sun*, the *New York Times*, the *New York Tribune*, and the *New York World*.[11]

In his letter to Daniels, Sims had documented errors of policy, tactics, strategy, and administration made by the Navy Department. Because of its faulty organization and failure to prepare for war while the nation was neutral, Sims charged, the navy "failed for at least six months, to throw [its] full weight against the enemy." During the most critical months of the U-boat campaign, from April to October 1917, he said, the department had violated the fundamental strategic principle of concentration of maximum force in the critical area of the conflict—the western approaches to the British Isles. Without the complete information Sims alone could have furnished from London, the department made plans that could not be carried out and also failed to cooperate wholeheartedly with the Allies. In his opening statement to the committee, moreover, Sims concluded that for the first six months at war the Navy Department had "cost the Allied cause 2,500,000 tons of shipping, 500,000 lives, and $15 billion."[12]

In his opening statement, Daniels attacked Sims in personal and political terms that applied to Fiske as well. When Hale asked various officers to send him suggestions on reorganizing the Navy Department, Daniels requested that Hale seek comments from those who opposed as well as those who, like Sims and Fiske, favored a general staff.[13] In cross-examination, Hale asked Daniels questions that involved Fiske's work during and subsequent to his tour as aide for operations. Hale asked whether the navy had a war plan against Germany, particularly a "thoroughly prepared" antisubmarine plan for the western approaches. Daniels hedged, saying he could not risk war by acting on Fiske's demands for preparedness while the nation remained neutral. By referring to the status of the navy on 7 April 1917, Hale showed that Fiske was closer to the truth than Daniels.[14]

Although testimony from some captains and an even larger number of admirals bore on whether the navy was ready on 6 April 1917, it often touched upon events which transpired while Fiske was aide for operations. On personnel matters as well as on war plans, Capts. Harris Laning and Leigh Palmer, leaders in the Bureau of Navigation during the war, and Joseph Taussig, senior wartime destroyer commander, upheld Sims.[15] Without mentioning Fiske, Capt. Charles P. Plunkett said that the prewar naval plans were defensive rather than offensive and confirmed that the navy was short of trained personnel.[16] Capt. Albert Grant added that no submarine or battleship had been ready for war and that battleships had served merely as schools to train men for the engineering and gunnery divisions of newly constructed ships and as armed guard crews for merchant ships. The only war service the battleships saw was as convey escorts during 1918.[17]

In order to answer Sims's charges, Admiral Mayo recalled his 1913 "gunboat duty" off Mexico which (as Fiske perennially had reminded Daniels) interfered with training and made impossible either the concentration of the fleet or necessary material maintenance. When the United States entered the war, Mayo testified, the Navy Department cannibalized his ships for men needed as armed guard crews and for other duties. By blaming the unpreparedness of the navy upon the neutrality policy followed from 1914 to 1917, the administration's failure to inform the navy of its foreign policies, and the faulty organization of the department, Mayo's testimony buttressed Fiske. He also supported Fiske by saying that Daniels amassed authority in his own hands and failed to decentralize control over details best left to military hands.[18]

Testifying on 31 March, Fiske summarized his work from 1910 until his retirement on 11 May 1915. He said that while in charge of the war plans section of the General Board (from December 1910 to August 1911), he found the plans to be "extremely meager, and did not embody, it seemed to me, even 1 per cent of what war plans should embody." A naval planning division was not created until August 1918; moreover, according to Fiske, not until it was divorced from administrative work in August 1919 did it become a real war planning division. Daniels, Fiske charged, was incapable of looking at the navy as a whole and concentrated primarily upon the enlisted men; he had been unable to get Daniels to ready the navy for war. Because Daniels refused to authorize him to prepare the navy for war, Fiske was, he said, little more than an adviser. Daniels refused to adopt an "administrative plan" that would merely supply a base from which war preparations could be made. Moreover, he cut Fiske's recommendations for appropriations for air power before the United States entered the war and did not ask for aviation funds until July 1917. As a result, the navy did little in the air during the war.

Although he sparked the creation of the Office of the Chief of Naval Operations, Fiske continued, Daniels succeeded in deleting the positions of officers necessary to draft war plans. Fiske noted, however, that after he had retired as aide for operations, Daniels approved the administrative plan and an Office of the Chief of Naval Operations. Because Daniels chose William Benson, who lacked interest in strategy, for the post, Fiske said he had tried to have officers detailed to work on war plans in that office. He arranged to testify before the naval committee of the House, on 24 and 26 March 1916, with the result that fifteen officers were provided in the naval act passed 29 August. Benson's failure to establish a war plans division until August 1918 meant that the navy fought the war without war plans.

Fiske was asked what the results had been of his battle for preparedness and improved discipline and morale. The answer was simple: "I had to get out." Asked if Daniels had acted promptly on matters Fiske took up with him, Fiske replied, "Not as a rule." The exception was with respect to the welfare of the enlisted men, but not with respect to an increase in their number. Fiske reported that if he mentioned preparing for war, Daniels would say, "Speak to me about this tomorrow, or next week." Had his services been engaged after the nation went to war? Absolutely not. At Senator Hale's suggestion, the letter of 1 August 1914 in which the General Board members at Newport recommended that Daniels prepare the navy for war and Fiske's subsequent work in bringing about the Office of Naval Operations were made part of the record.[19]

As an aide from February 1913 to February 1914, Fullam witnessed

Daniels's administrative methods. Despite Fiske's importunities, he testified, Daniels did nothing about increasing the number of men, or about organization, material, weapons, or aviation. "To my knowledge, [Fiske] forgot nothing sir." Fiske, he said, was instrumental in creating the Office of Chief of Naval Operations, "the one and only modern and effective feature of our naval organization"—but Daniels had emasculated the powers of its chief. Rather than following Fiske's advice to get the department and the fleet ready for war, Fullam testified that Daniels instead tried to make the navy "a great university."[20]

Although Rear Adm. Hugh Rodman was the first witness to disagree with Sims, he knew little about anything except that his battleships were short 20 percent of their men and that he went across the Atlantic without being furnished written plans or orders. Rodman said he did not consider the organization of the department satisfactory. He suggested entrusting the preparedness of the fleet and the execution of war plans to the chief of naval operations, rather than to the civilian secretary, and providing the former with a planning but not a general staff.[21] Like Rodman, Adms. Henry B. Wilson, Frank F. Fletcher, and Albert P. Niblack opted for a chief of naval operations to advise the secretary on preparing the navy for war and to execute war plans.[22] In contrast, Rear Adms. Joseph Strauss and Charles J. Badger emphatically denied Sims's charges.[23]

Capt. William V. Pratt, who served as aide and then assistant and general manager in Benson's office from February 1917 to January 1919, believed that Sims's letter of 7 January 1920 was directed more at the Office of Naval Operations than at the Navy Department. On the question of war plans, he referred negatively to Fiske's illustration—that is, the "ability to put your hand in a drawer and pull out a plan which at once throws us into war"—for otherwise one must accept the proposition that we were a militaristic nation anxious to take the offensive. He then took another swat at Fiske:

> There was a comment made by Admiral Fiske in which he submitted the plan under which the Office of Operations was to be organized, and he rather inferred that we had no plan up to the time, and no real plans section in the Office of Operations. . . . He does not know anything about it. We were there, doing the work, and we know what we are talking about. . . . I want to set at rest any doubt that may have arisen as to whether we had plans, as far as being capable of coping with the questions that came up.[24]

He confessed, however, that "there was not any real planning section in Operations; and that is why I say there is something the matter with the system." The creation of a planning section in the Office of Naval Operations would have "helped a great deal."[25]

Pratt was as fair a friend to Sims as he could be while remaining loyal to Benson, but Fiske told Sims he thought Pratt had kowtowed to Daniels by "defending a man who (he [Pratt] knows) would have brought the Navy to *ruin* before April 6, 1917,—if he had not been *prevented* from doing so by yours truly. . . ."[26]

Rear Adm. Josiah McKean was Benson's aide for material for three years and from January to June 1919, while Benson was in Europe, served as acting chief of naval operations. Blaming the Navy Department and Congress for the personnel shortages and material discrepancies existing in the fleet on 6 April 1917, he held that Sims's charges of unpreparedness were unfounded. Turning to "the most difficult subject in the whole outfit, that of aviation," he zeroed in on Fiske, saying:

> The dreaming of dreams as to air navigation, air battleships, cruisers, scouts, destroyers, torpedo planes, bombers, mine planters, etc., is easy. . . .
>
> Admiral Fiske as a fireside critic produced more aircraft on paper than he did actual aircraft as aid for operations.
>
> He had splendid ideas, if we could only have realized them. Nobody did.

Although he slighted all that Fiske had done for aviation as aide for operations and thereafter, McKean supported Fiske's demand that a secretary rely for military advice upon a single adviser who would be the chief of a naval general staff.[27]

When McKean finished his testimony, Sims wrote Fullam:

> It is a strong point in our favor that all of the witnesses recommended a reorganization of the Navy Department and more power to the military people. This is gall and wormwood to the man who is responsible for the present organization, and also [to] the Democrats in general, as this is a criticism of their administration.
>
> We are actually curious to see what Benson will have to say. . . .[28]

Rather than preparing himself to testify, Benson relied upon his memory and the testimony of Pratt and McKean. Upon assuming his new office, on 11 May 1915, he said he found nothing being done to prepare the navy for war. On 28 May Daniels had signed an administrative plan directing the bureau chiefs to report at stated intervals on their readiness, but Daniels never gave him definite instructions on preparing the navy for war. Moreover, Benson said, Daniels did not prepare for war while the nation remained neutral, with the obvious result that the navy was unprepared when it went to war. The fleet was purposely not concentrated, Benson explained, so that the ships scattered about the world could be in position to act against enemy raiders if war did occur. Once war started, he said, he would first defend the coasts of the United States, then "do everything we could to help them on the other side." With respect to naval organization, Benson dropped a bomb on Daniels by stating that the Office of Naval Operations not only "saved the day but that it should be given responsibility, under the Secretary, for preparing the Navy as a whole." It needed enough trained staff officers, he testified, to man a war plans section.[29]

Fullam wrote Sims about Benson's testimony:

> He has proved your case *absolutely!* . . . As for *Re-organization* his ideas go far beyond anything that we or Fiske or I have ever dared to suggest. He wants the Ch[ief] of Op[erations] to have about all the powers of the Sec[retary] and he suggests that he be (practically) a member of the President's cabinet. . . . The subcommittee is tired but the Republicans will be jubilant at Benson's disclosure, and admission. . . .[30]

Sims agreed.[31] Saying that Benson "has out-Fisked Fiske!" Fullam sent Benson's testimony "to *all* officers of the Navy and to many people in civil life as proof positive of the pusillanimous policies of Josephus."[32]

Fiske spent two days in early May 1920 in Washington. As he told Sims, he "dined at Hale's house on Monday, with him, . . . [and] Senators Keyes and Ball [Republicans on the sub-committee] and Fullam. We formed ourselves into a planning division, and devised a war plan to meet the situation *actually existing*. I think you will like it." Moreover, "Fullam and I had two long conferences [with a public relations man working for Hale] in getting ready the ammunition that Hale is to fire, and that Fullam is to fire himself. The *Un*easy boss will probably go on the stand Thursday or Friday. I don't see how he can escape Justice this time."[33]

Daniels decried Sims's attempt, made in his letter to the secretary dated 7 January 1920, to "curtail the power of the Secretary and remove the navy, as far as possible, from civilian control." And, he said, Fiske shared Sims's views. Daniels had Fiske's entire record investigated. On a sheet in his papers are references from Fiske's memoirs (published in 1919) which "show [Fiske's] opinion of himself on being military advisor to the Secretary of the Navy while aide" and the conclusion that Fiske had made money by selling his inventions to the navy. Thus primed, he charged that Fiske wanted to reduce the civilian secretary to a mere figurehead. With this objective, Daniels said, Fiske had "surreptitiously and secretly" proposed legislation for a chief of naval operations who "would have had the powers and authority of the Prussian chief of the admiralty staff, von Tirpitz, and the Kaiser himself combined in one."[34]

On his wine mess order of 1914, Daniels contradicted Fiske's testimony by saying that "it was preparedness in peace and demonstrated its wisdom in war." He never mentioned Fiske in connection with an extensive report Fiske gave on the naval aviation program. He alleged that Fiske had mentioned his refusal to add 19,600 men to the fleet only after Daniels had refused to approve Fiske's "plea to reorganize the Navy Department on plans 'made in Germany,'. . . and did not yield to his [Fiske's] repeated solicitations to make him commander-in-chief of the Atlantic Fleet." Moreover—and here Daniels clearly revealed his casuistry—Fiske's demand for 19,600 more men in 1914 was, the secretary said, a mere "drop in the bucket," for "when we got into the war we didn't need 20,000 more men, but nearly half a million. And we got them."[35]

Daniels testified that he had approved the administrative section for war plans and the Office of the Chief of Naval Operations, increased, reorganized, and exercised the fleet at war maneuvers and had added ships, officers, and men to the fleet—all in 1916, before the nation went to war. By taking personal credit for these steps, Daniels denied credit to Fiske.

On 10 May, Fiske jubilantly told Sims that he had won him the support of the *New York Times*.[36] On 17 May, Sims congratulated him for an interview entitled "Courage and Prudence" which appeared in the *Providence* (R.I.) *Journal*, saying that it "had attracted a great deal of attention and will do a considerable amount of good." Sims also praised Fiske's new book, *The Art of Fighting*.[37]

Fullam, meanwhile, warned Sims that Daniels had launched a mighty newspaper campaign against him and advised that "your rebuttal must be sensational." Fullam also wrote Senator Hale, on 20 May, to complain that Daniels had linked him (Fullam) with Fiske and Sims "as being a disciple of von Tirpitz and as favoring the Prussianizing of the United States Navy." Fullam continued, "These changes . . . have been widely published . . . greatly to my injury and humiliation as an officer of forty-seven years' service in the U.S. Navy." He therefore requested permission to appear before the committee "to give a full and truthful story of my work in connection with departmental organization and preparedness of the Navy for war, especially as my motives have been entirely patriotic."[38]

On 21 May, Hale asked Daniels for a schedule showing the plans of the General Board for war with Germany between 1 January and 6 April 1917. Under questioning, Daniels admitted that there was no special antisubmarine war plan. Hale then referred to Fiske's suggestion of an administrative section for war plans, calling for the bureaus to report quarterly on their preparedness. By referring to Fiske's memoirs, Hale refreshed Daniels's memory that Admiral Dewey had forwarded the suggestion and that Daniels had not wanted to discuss either that matter or the papers Fiske had sent him on "Meditations on Organization" and "Meditations on

Mobilization." Daniels's reply to Senator Hale was that Fiske talked to him often; because Fiske was to leave office in just a few days and a new chief of operations would soon be on board, Daniels had first "interned him," and then "let him go."[39]

"But that has nothing to do with this question," said Hale. Daniels could not recall Dewey bringing him Fiske's letter about the administrative plan. Hale noted that Fiske had offered the letter on 16 April 1917 and that Daniels signed it on 28 May, seventeen days after Fiske left office. Daniels finally remembered that Fiske had presented the letter and that he had signed it, but only after Benson took office. Hale thereupon charged that Fiske had brought the matter before Daniels two years, not two months, before the secretary approved it. Hale asked whether Fiske had lied in his memoirs. No, said Daniels, but he could not recall Dewey presenting Fiske's letter.

Hale then asked whether Daniels had studied department organization. Daniels replied that he had: having inherited a council of four aides, a "bad system," he had replaced it, he said, with the Office of the Chief of Naval Operations. He never would have given Fiske the powers he granted Benson, Daniels testified, because "what Admiral Fiske wanted . . . was that the Chief of Operations should control the Navy Department."[40] The chairman continued:

> Then it was upon your recommendation that the naval appropriation act of 1915 provided that there should be a Chief of Operations.[41]

In agreeing, of course, Daniels lied, and Hale proved it by using Fiske's memoirs to show that it was Fiske who had initiated the legislation. Daniels then backtracked and said that after he learned of Fiske's plan, he had it defeated in the Senate.

Daniels admitted that after reading in Fiske's memoirs how the Hobson bill was prepared, he had intended to get rid of Fiske "because . . . I had been bored by him long enough . . . so that when he began to send me in these long screeds, repetition, repetition, repetition, making him the big thing, I saw that he was a monumental egotist. Read his book. There has never a man in the world written a book of such shallow knowledge, of such monumental egotism."[42]

After Hale warned Daniels that he might ask Fiske to rebutt the charge that he attempted to "Prussianize" the navy, the chairman asked why Daniels had changed the Hobson plan, which called for a rear admiral to be chief of naval operations, to permit the appointment of a captain. Daniels replied that since Fletcher had declined the post and since most other admirals were on special duty, he settled on Benson as the best man, adding—with a great stretching of the truth—that Benson "was regarded by his fellow officers as one of the ablest strategists and tacticians."[43]

Hale then told Daniels that he had asked the following men to submit legislative suggestions for reorganizing the navy: Admirals Badger, Coontz, Fiske, Fletcher, Knight, McKean, Mayo, Rodman, Sims, Twining, and Wilson; Captains Laning and Pratt; Comdr. William S. Pye; and Assistant Secretary Roosevelt. Two admirals, Rodman and Wilson, said they had no recommendations. Hale invited Daniels to name anyone else. Daniels said the senator should ask all chiefs of bureaus and offices. Hale agreed and would then have the committee suggest that a board like the Moody-Mahan Board go over the recommendations and offer a report.

Under continued questioning by Hale, Daniels admitted that he had paid no attention to Fiske's repeated demands that the Navy Department be reformed and that the service be readied for war. Daniels was asked if he recalled talking with Fiske about his preparedness letter of 5 November 1914. Daniels said he did not. After introducing Fiske's letter in evidence, Hale asked Daniels if it refreshed his memory. It did not; nor did Daniels see how "all of this ancient history of grievances and grudges" touched on the question of naval preparedness. Hale suggested that Fiske's letter proved that Daniels had received adequate advice on preparing the navy for war. Daniels retorted that Fiske's letter was no "more important than his other 58 varieties. . . . At that time he was chiefly directing propaganda for reorganization and making trouble, and therefore I gave very little attention to his demands to reorganize the Navy."[44]

When Sims was recalled to testify on 27 May, he naturally found that the rest of the testimony supported the charges made in his letter of 7 January. He offered three major causes for the "distressing" condition of the navy prior to its entrance into the war and during the early months of the war:

> The faulty organization of the Navy Department.
>
> The policy governing the department's action previous to our entrance into the war and during the early months thereof.
>
> The failure of the responsible head of the department to take the action required, both before and after the outbreak of war, to meet the urgency of the situation, and to prepare the Navy for war, and to strike at once on the fighting front with all available forces.[45]

About 85 percent of the testimony given did not concern Sims's charges. Victor Blue in a letter to Daniels summarized the hearings' impact:

> The [3,445 pages of printed] testimony . . . seems to have narrowed

down to a question of Sims or the Navy. If one is exonerated the other is discredited.

While every one expects the Republican majority to decide in favor of Sims I cannot believe that they could be so short sighted as to make a decision which History would be compelled to record as a failure on [the] part of our navy and our country to do its full share in the World War.[46]

Sims did not force Daniels from the cabinet or obtain a reorganization of the Navy Department along the lines of a general staff. Although he proved there was room for improvement in the department, he failed to show that shortcomings stemmed from maladministration.

Fiske was in the hearing room on 27 May when Hale announced that both Fiske and Fullam had asked permission to rebut Daniels's assertions that they tried to "Prussianize" the navy. The committee agreed to receive their written statements. Hale read Fiske's letter, dated 28 May, to the committee. Its tenor may be gauged from the three concluding paragraphs:

> You know the various acts which I performed in order to get the organization established which later handled the Navy throughout the war. These are the acts for which the Secretary denounces me. Had I not performed them, the Navy would have gone into the war without the two principal agencies which the Secretary and his supporters have declared to you were vital—I mean, the office of Chief of Naval Operations and the administrative plan.
>
> Had I not done what I did, the Secretary himself would surely have been disgraced soon after we got into the war, for the unpreparedness of the Navy would then have burst suddenly on the people, and he would have become the object of their wrath.
>
> Instead of abusing me, I submit that the Secretary ought to thank me for saving not only the Navy but himself.[47]

In his reply, dated 2 June, Daniels spoke of Fiske's "absurd statements" and asserted that

> Fiske's plan of organization of the Navy was repudiated in the act of Congress and therefore had nothing whatever to do with the operations of the Navy in peace or war. . . . The preparation under the administrative plan owed nothing to him in conception or execution. His egotism . . . is monumental and his obsession that he was responsible for even a scintilla of naval efficiency is born of supervanity [sic] and has no basis to rest upon. He had nothing to do with any preparation for war.[48]

Second, Daniels said, Fiske did not apply for war duty until the war was fourteen months old. "His services were not needed then, and he was not called. . . . He would only have been a hindrance." Third, Daniels continued, as an "Obstacle to Operations," Fiske had burdened Daniels's life by "urging me to appoint him commander-in-chief of the Atlantic Fleet. . . . My sense of duty would not permit me to assign an officer so unfit for that duty. . . ." Fourth, Daniels charged, Fiske opposed "the policy of giving enlisted men an opportunity for education, and grew furious over my wine-mess order." Fiske had said he resigned as a protest against Daniels; in truth, the secretary explained, he resigned because another officer was chosen as the first chief of naval operations. Fiske sought to hold on to his position "and secretly and surreptitiously to 'bore from within' in a most disloyal manner."[49]

In his letter to the committee, dated 24 May, Fullam said he was honored to link his name with Fiske's and with others who demanded preparedness and reorganization and, in accordance with loyalty to their profession, stood squarely for principles regardless of personal disfavor. Officers like Fiske, Fullam wrote, simply wished to coordinate the work of the bureaus; they did not advocate diminution of the supreme authority of the secretary of the navy. Adms. Fletcher, Benson, Wilson, Rodman, Strauss, and McKean and Captain Pratt supported the Fiske-Fullam-Sims position that the chief of naval operations should have responsibility over all bureaus and other departmental agencies. These men were advocating what Sims had urged in 1908 and Fiske had recommended before that. Daniels replied that Fullam's complaints were typical of those who wished to air criticisms born of personal grievance.[50]

An appendix to the hearings contains the plans submitted for reorganizing the navy. By passing the problem to Congress, Roosevelt did not support Fiske on reorganization; Coontz, Mayo, Sims, and Fullam, however, did. Badger did not think a "radical" reorganization was needed; Fletcher favored restoring the aide system; and Knight supported the reformers. McKean had nothing to add, but Twining fully supported the reformers, as did Pratt, Laning, and Pye, with the last going a step further in seeking naval sponsorship of scientific research.[51] In sum, of the thirteen men who submitted suggestions, one—Roosevelt—effectively said nothing; one—McKean—said absolutely nothing; Badger was noncommittal; and Fletcher urged restoration of the aide system. The other nine supported Fiske.

Daniels, however, had spurned Fiske's advice. Following Fiske's resignation, he took credit for the reforms Fiske had suggested, particularly for the administrative plan, the Office of the Chief of Naval Operations, and the Naval Consulting Board. Unable to counter the testimony of Fiske and of other insurgents, "[Daniels] resorted to personal abuse and cowardly attacks," Fullam told Hale.[52] "What's the matter with Josephus?" Fiske asked Fullam, and then answered his own question, saying, "Oh—he's dead."[53]

Fiske was wrong. Nevertheless, the wounds inflicted during the hearings were deep and long-lasting; in some cases they were evident throughout the lifetime of the participants and supporters of both parties.

While Hale prepared his report, Daniels published articles upholding the readiness of the navy for war in 1917. As Fiske told Hale, Daniels thus contradicted the sworn statements of leading officers, misled the public, and discouraged those seeking an efficient navy.[54] Fiske also prodded Hale to issue his report.[55] Not until September 1921, however, with Daniels long out of office, did Hale issue a majority report, signed by the three Republicans on the committee, confirming most of Sims's contentions; two minority reports, written by the Democrats, rejected Sims's arguments. By this time the hearings were all but forgotten by the public. Suggestions for reorganizing the department overwhelmingly supported Fiske, yet any hope for constructive legislation had vanished. All Sims had accomplished was to force the Wilson administration to display its dirty linen to the world. Fiske and others believed that their campaign would spark a public demand for reform in naval administration; instead, the public looked upon the hearings as a battle between admirals, none of whom they knew, and between partisan committee members—just the kind of slugging match that could be expected in an election year. Moreover, some of Sims's complaints "appeared to many observers to reflect the parochial viewpoint of the commander of a single theater, the wounded ego of a proud man, or the visions of an Anglophile."[56] The 1920 elections, not the hearings, turned Wilson and Daniels out.

In 1921, an officer who had served on Sims's staff in London, Tracy B. Kittredge, published a book to support Sims and to discredit Daniels's testimony before Hale's committee. But it was so unabashedly biased as to be misleading. Although Fiske wrote its foreword, he tried to keep knowledge of the book from Sims. Sims, who knew about the book, admitted only that he read the galley proofs.[57] Fiske later told Sims that he would have preferred the title, *Naval Lessons of the Great War: A Review of the Criticisms by Admiral Sims of the Policies and Methods of Josephus Daniels*, to read simply *The Impeachment of Josephus Daniels*—"for it was *that*."[58] At any rate, in the foreword Fiske nailed his colors to the mast:

> This book is a record of official testimony given to Congress by navy officers under oath.
>
> It shows that the principal naval lesson of the war is the menace to the national honor and safety that was involved in committing the management of its navy to unworthy hands.
>
> The Secretary of the Navy should be a man of the highest order of ability, knowledge and foresight. This book shows that Secretary Daniels

was so far below this standard that the Navy would have been caught wholly unprepared when we entered the war, and would have been ineffective during the war, if certain navy officers had not sacrificed or endangered their positions, by putting through important measures, without his knowledge.

The Secretary of the Navy should be a man of the highest character. This book shows that Secretary Daniels, both in writing over his official signature, and in oral official testimony before Congressional Committees, made many statements about important naval matters within his cognizance, that were absolutely false.[59]

In seeking to defend Sims, Kittredge also vindicated Fiske by saying that the chief naval lessons of the Great War were those that Fiske had tried to teach Daniels prior to the war.

18

"KEEP YOUR POWDER DRY," 1919–1942

On 6 October 1920, William S. Sims, president of the Naval War College, expressed the hope that the Republicans would take office in March 1921 by writing William F. Fullam, "Only 140 odd days more!"[1] After the election, his hope realized, he told Bradley A. Fiske, "Gee Whiz! Holy Smoke! Great Scott! What do you think of the landslide? It is now up to the Republicans to make good with all the machinery in their hands. There must be a jail delivery of the time servers and incompetents and a new deal."[2] Fiske replied: "Gee Whiz. Holy Smoke. Great Scott. Sulking Moses. Caesar's Ghost. Uh-hell. What an a—— kicking!"[3] Two weeks later he added: "The next session of Congress will be *busy*, I fancy. As to the navy, the two main questions must be aeronautics and organization."[4] Although he wisely concluded not to broach the subject of reorganizing the navy until Josephus Daniels left office, Fiske told Sims, "let's get a Bureau of Aeronautics p.d.q.—as p.d.q. as possible. . . . If we don't get that Bureau next session, [Brigadier] General [William] Mitchell and a whole horde of politicians will get an 'Air ministry' established and the U.S. Navy will find itself lying in the street, and the procession marching over it."[5]

Fiske, Fullam, and Sims continued to criticize the "principal dignitaries" and those witnesses at the naval investigation hearings of 1920 who did not measure up to their expectations. They also opposed Daniels's proposal to appoint witnesses who had supported him to high positions before he left office, saying that leaders should be chosen from graduates of the Naval War College.[6] While Fiske tried to get Sen. Frederick Hale to see "the paramount importance of getting a thoroughly equipped Ch[ief of] Nav[al] Op[erations]," he got a promise from the prospective secretary of the navy, Edwin Denby, to make no important personnel changes until he had visited the Naval War College.[7] Fiske then wrote Sen. Henry Cabot Lodge "that the Navy needed an officer here of national standing, to keep the army from relegating us to the status of the Coast Survey." He asked Lodge to have Robert E. Coontz fired and get Sims appointed as chief of naval operations.[8] Lodge said that one could not fire a man who had a four-year appointment, and Sims sadly concluded that "it would be useless to try and do anything with the Navy as long as the smokescreen gang occupy all of the principal administrative positions."[9]

On 4 February 1921, the chairman of the House Naval Affairs Committee, Thomas S. Butler, began hearings on Pres. Warren G. Harding's proposal to call an arms limitation conference. Adms. Charles J. Badger, Coontz, and Sims all favored limiting arms "to some extent." Fiske not only favored completing the 1916 building program, but urged a great expansion of naval aviation and creation of a bureau of aeronautics. He declared that an aircraft carrier was superior to a battleship. Asked how he would alter the 1916 program, Fiske said he would substitute ten carriers for the ten battleships and would continue building the six battle cruisers. Although "Billy" Mitchell, head of the Army Air Service, wanted a united air service, Fiske said he knew of nothing "better calculated to wreck the defense of this country. . . . I think that would be absolutely fatal . . . to anything like naval efficiency."[10] In contrast, Daniels revealed his opinion of the power of aviation by volunteering to permit Mitchell to drop all the bombs he pleased on a vessel Daniels himself steered.[11]

Fiske testified before the Senate Naval Affairs Committee, repeating that aviation was "destined to bring revolution in warfare in comparison to which the revolution brought about by the invention of the gun was like a vaudeville performance."[12] While the General Board and the bureaus discounted aircraft and submarines in favor of battleships, Fiske, Sims, and Fullam pushed for "A Three Plane Navy"—one capable of operating effectively on, below, or above the sea.[13] Tests of aerial bombing against certain warships during June and July of 1921 increased their conclusions about carriers. "Intercontinental wars are difficult or impossible without big air and submarine forces," Sims told Fullam; those who opposed these views, said Fullam, suffered from "incurable battleshipitis."[14] During the summer of 1921, to bring the best knowledge on aviation matters before his student officers, Sims had Thomas T. Craven and Mitchell lecture on air power and had Fiske discuss the torpedo plane.[15]

Secretary Denby, who wanted a navy "equal to any other," supported the current building program, including two aircraft carriers, and opposed both a cabinet-level Department of Air and a unified military air service.[16] At hearings on a bill to establish a Bureau of Aeronautics within the Navy Department, Fiske strongly supported such a bureau; and even Daniels favored one. The bill passed without opposition and was approved July 12.

On 25 July, Harding commissioned Capt. William A. Moffett a rear admiral and appointed him as the bureau's chief. In the words of Lt. Comdr. Richard E. Byrd, "Flying stock went up in the Navy Department. With an Admiral to fight our battles we began to get things done."[17]

To Fiske's great displeasure, Denby kept on Daniels's "smokescreen gang" except for attrition through normal rotation or retirements. Furthermore, he transferred responsibility for the naval petroleum reserves in Wyoming and California to the Department of the Interior—and, thus, to exploitation by private interests. Although reductions in naval personnel caused him to decommission 376 ships in 1921 alone, Denby supported the conversion of the battle cruisers *Saratoga*, *Lexington*, and *Constellation* to carriers. He stopped work on six battleships and the other three battle cruisers. The Senate approved two carriers but the House disagreed and their provision was stricken.[18]

In a 1921 article entitled "The Warfare of the Future," Fiske traced advances made in man's ability to deliver destructive power: the galley gave way to the sailing ship and then to the steam ship, and mechanical contrivances increased the power and accuracy of naval guns; then came the airman with his torpedo and bomb. Fiske concluded that only time would tell whether this new combination would end the battleship era. But in any case aviation must be provided for the fleet.[19]

In another article, entitled "Defense of the Philippines with Airplanes" (also published in 1921), Fiske noted that when he had suggested aerial defense of the Philippines in 1910, aircraft were still in the experimental stage and he had won few converts. Since the Philippines could not be defended against Japan, he added, we must spend more money for aircraft, even if this meant engaging in an arms-building race.[20] In "The Relative Importance of the Philippines and Guam" (1921) Fiske favored using the Philippines as the site for an advanced base in the Pacific.[21] Soon thereafter he pleaded for a continuing program of research and development to be carried on by the cooperation of industrial corporations and inventors.[22]

In July 1921, Fiske was awarded an honorary LL.D. by the University of Michigan. Among eleven persons similarly honored was Sir Auckland Geddes, the British ambassador to the United States, who echoed Fiske in saying that it was "only the most optimistic dream that war will be no more."[23]

The Republicans elected in 1920 failed to fulfill Fiske's expectations for naval reorganization or sustained strength. They reduced naval appropriations, and competitive building by Great Britain and Japan greatly reduced the impact of the 1916 program. Conservatives in high naval positions declined to create a naval general staff or support naval aviation to the extent Fiske thought necessary. On the other hand, some progress was made: a

Bureau of Aeronautics was operating; attempts to pool all aviation in a single governmental department and to unify military aviation had been defeated; and students at the Naval War College were being taught the capabilities of air power. Fiske's book, the *Art of Fighting*, his articles, and letters to various editors also helped to educate the public, which in the end determined the nation's military policies. But would the public, tired of war, eager for tax reductions, and hoping to avoid a costly naval arms race, support additional defense or would they seek to obtain peace via arms reductions?

On 11 August 1921, President Harding invited nine nations to confer on naval disarmament and Far Eastern and Pacific problems. To insure Senate approval of the outcome of the Washington Conference, he chose Secretary of State Charles Evans Hughes to chair the American delegation and selected as its members one senator, a former senator, and a representative. Denby was completely overlooked; and only one naval officer from each nation acted as technical adviser to the subcommittees created to deal with naval armament and new weapons of warfare.

Fiske comforted Sims with his assessment that they were not chosen as delegates or members of the advisory committee because although they had helped win the Great War (one at the front, one at the rear), they were in bad graces at the Navy Department.[24] Sims replied that neither could "kick": having told the truth, they must accept their punishment. "However," Sims wrote, "I believe that you are exercising a very extensive influence upon the navy of the future, and I intend to do what I can in that line myself."[25] After reading an article by Fiske in the *New York American* headlined "United States Armament Policy a Disgrace," Sims added, "An officer who has your ability to write such things can do more good for the Navy and for the country than you could if you were on the active list even in a post of considerable authority."[26] Fiske retorted that he felt hurt because no one asked him for advice. He remarked, moreover, with evident reference to the Washington Conference, "It seems to me that Uncle Sam has the hot end of the poker and Japan the cool end." He thanked Sims, saying "I would rather have your good opinion than that of any other man."[27]

The American delegation to the Washington Conference was advised by a committee chaired by Adm. William L. Rodgers and included among others Coontz and Capt. William V. Pratt, a member of the General Board. The advisory board's report reflected Pratt's fairly strong internationalist views. Rodgers, however, also sounded out high-ranking officers and retired officers on twenty-one of the agenda items proposed for the conference.

Rodgers did not gather opinions, however, on Japan's proposal that the United States halt fortification of its Pacific islands. Foreseeing that American bases in the western Pacific would be major Japanese targets in time of war, Fiske was the only one of the twenty-four respondents to insist upon their importance.[28] He wrote Denby stressing the need to defend Guam and the Philippines with aircraft and in addition submitted three articles to the *North American Review* on the general subject of armaments and trade. When the articles were rejected, he called on the editors and was told that since the publisher was George Harvey, the U.S. ambassador to Great Britain, they could not print articles counter to administration policy.[29]

Harding and his delegation declined the advice naval officers offered at the Washington Conference. Harding halved the board's estimate of the number of ships the U.S. Navy should have; and on 12 November, Hughes boldly offered a plan for a ten-year shipbuilding holiday and a lowering of naval armaments by the scrapping of capital ships—thirty of them American, nineteen British, and sixteen Japanese. Most Americans approved, but Fiske characterized the plan as a sign of "decadence, . . . the first sign of decay in a nation long peaceful and wealthy."[30] He told the American delegates that allowing Japan 60 percent of the naval power of the United States and Great Britain precluded American defense of the Philippines, Guam, and Midway and Wake islands, even though they could be defended cheaply and adequately with aircraft, submarines, and in other ways. Japan could easily take the islands, but the United States would find it impossible to recapture them with the naval forces at hand or those contemplated.[31] Fiske thus gave a prophetic description of the events of World War II.

Among its other provisions, the Five-Power Naval Treaty, signed 6 February 1922, set relative limits on capital ships and carriers for Britain, United States, Japan, Italy, and France—at ratios of 5 : 5 : 3 : 1.75 : 1.75— and declared a moratorium on capital-ship building until 1931. In the Pacific, American, British, and Japanese fortifications and naval bases were to remain at the status quo. Hughes told Harding that the treaty "ends, absolutely ends, the race in competition in naval armament. At the same time it leaves the relative security of the great naval powers unimpaired. . . . No national interest has been sacrificed. . . ."[32] Outside of the Hearst chain, most of the press upheld the treaty. Pratt approved it,[33] but it was Fiske who reflected the unhappiness of most American naval officers, noting that the conference did not abolish war and that "nations foolish enough during peace to allow their national defense machine to get out of order paid for it bitterly when war came." Moreover, the U.S. Navy was not granted actual parity with Britain because although ship tonnages were equal, British personnel and ships were qualitatively superior. As for Japan, Fiske remarked that "to make war on [her] with the relative naval forces allotted by the Treaty would be an act of folly." Since Japan could not operate in the eastern Pacific, war would be fought in the western Pacific. The United States, however, had "no bases less than 6,000 miles away, except a most inadequate one in Hawaii, 4,000 miles away."[34] Fiske thus agreed with Fullam that the navy "emerged from the Washington Conference psychologically bruised and physically curtailed. Never before in their memory had naval men found their views so overwhelmingly rejected by public opinion."[35] In addition, Congress refused to build the navy up to strength or even to fund the modernization of older battleships, with the result that the navy was 104 ships and 19,406 men short of its treaty strength in 1925. Fiske, therefore, predicted that the nation would suffer from great inefficiency and financial waste if it should have to prepare for war suddenly. He accounted for the existing situation by the Jazz Age generation's mad race for money and pleasure.[36]

On 19 March 1924, when Curtis D. Wilbur succeeded Denby as secretary of the navy, best estimates put the naval ratios at 5:1:3, the material condition of the fleet was considered execrable, and the fleet was terribly short-handed. Wilbur demanded that the navy be built up to treaty strength. Congress refused. Several congressmen introduced bills calling for an investigation of reported naval weaknesses, but none of them passed.[37]

On 7 May 1924, the British prime minister, Ramsay McDonald, suggested holding a disarmament conference on aircraft and naval ships not affected by the Washington Conference. Perhaps because of a public letter dated 3 June in which Fiske warned him of the weak position of the United States in case of war in the Pacific, Wilbur retorted publicly that the United States should build the most powerful cruiser navy in the world. He thought that since they could not compete, other nations would agree to limit cruisers as they had battleships.[38]

Although Calvin Coolidge was ready to issue invitations to a conference, he also favored increasing appropriations for military aviation, and in this matter he had the backing of most naval veterans including Fiske, Sims, and Fullam.[39] In December 1924 Congress finally authorized eight 10,000-ton, 8-inch cruisers—particularly useful in covering the vast distances of the Pacific—and the modernization of old battleships. The renovation work, however, was not completed until the early 1930s.

Japan saw Coolidge's cruisers and the American fleet maneuvers projected for the Hawaiian area in 1925 as challenges to peace. Additionally irritated by the provision of the 1924 U.S. Immigration Act excluding Orientals, Japan reacted by laying down four large cruisers. As Fiske predicted, the armaments race shifted to cruisers and smaller ships; and he criticized Congress for showing the same indifference to the postwar navy as it had to the prewar navy. Keeping the navy up to the 5:5:3 treaty ratio, Fiske said, was like keeping religious sentiment alive, and he charged Congress with following a "suicidal policy."[40] Concerned about Japan's rising naval power, he wrote Wilbur saying that while war did not appear possible, the United States and Japan had different interests and noting that in the event of war, the American position would be "deplorable."[41] In various addresses Fiske also averred that American women had "effeminized" the nation and thus caused wars. As he should have expected, his remarks were utterly smashed in numerous editorials and he received many uncomplimentary letters written by female hands.[42]

Billy Mitchell was among the first to allege that aircraft could locate and destroy any kind of naval vessel under war conditions with a negligible loss of aircraft. Fiske felt, correctly, that the bombing tests conducted on the German battleship *Ostfriesland* in 1921 were deliberately designed by Mitchell to favor air power; furthermore, because the torpedo plane was not used, the public declared it a failure. Both American and British experiments showed that there was a greater probability of hitting a ship with torpedoes than with bombs. In American tests held during the summer of 1922, for example, seven of seventeen torpedoes hit the *Arkansas* and sent her to theoretical destruction.[43] Fiske also revealed that he had begun in 1919 to invent a method of exploding torpedoes beneath the hulls of ships. In 1921, however, when torpedo and ordnance officers showed no interest in his ignition system, he had obtained a patent on it and "put it on the shelf."[44] "It is a scheme of the utmost simplicity . . . and yet the Bureau [of Ordnance] seems paralyzed," he told Sims later. "It is acting as it did with the telescope sight, gunnery, training, and torpedoplane."[45]

In bombing tests, held 24 November 1924 on the modern battleship *Washington* which was being scrapped, the ship's partially completed protective deck defended her vitals against a 1,440-pound shell and a 2,000-pound bomb dropped from 4,000 feet. After three more bombs and two torpedoes hit her, she survived a three-day gale and was finally sunk by 14-inch shells from the *Texas*. As a result of this test, the Eberle board of the General Board told President Coolidge on 19 February 1925 that battleships could withstand an air attack and hence should remain the backbone of the fleet. The report thereby undermined Fiske's prediction that aviation would become dominant in sea warfare.[46]

A select House committee opened hearings into the operations of the United States Air Services on 9 October 1924. All went quietly until Mitchell glorified air power, arousing public interest in the hearings. In testifying, Fiske concurred with Sims, and also with Fullam, that Mitchell's demands for a unified air service should be denied. Secretary Wilbur agreed, and Coolidge's opposition to a unified air service quieted the controversy for a time.[47]

Samuel Johnson once referred to the "intellectual vulgarity" of those who derided others for opposing policies which later are proven wise. Fiske was guilty of "intellectual vulgarity" in several instances. The errors of those who had failed to prepare the nation for war grew ever larger in his mind, as did the part he played in urging and achieving preparedness, to the extent that he took credit for winning the war. Why, he asked, did the public not learn the most important lesson of history and realize that by opposing military spending they were making it ever more difficult to obtain adequate preparedness?[48] "In regard to Josephus the Execrable," he wrote Sims, "[Daniels] was merely the instrument and the hand that held the instrument was Wilson." He offered similar characterizations of William S. Benson and Victor Blue.[49]

At a meeting of the Foreign Policy Association held on 14 February 1925, Fiske asserted that economic competition was the greatest cause of war and that he was convinced that peace was not the noblest condition in which man could live. He saw Asia as a potential trouble spot because, he said, Japan held "trumps": "By merely threatening the Philippines, she could make these masses [of pacifists] insist on yielding to Japan's desires." Although Rabbi Stephen S. Wise praised Fiske because he "had stripped war of its romance and tinsel" by admitting that it was the result of commercial competition and economic rivalry,[50] Fiske was roundly criticized, especially by other men of the cloth, for daring to say that war rather than peace was the most noble condition of mankind. Undismayed, Fiske rejoined that affluence, except among the laboring class, was causing the disappearance of "the manly man and the womanly woman" who would support preparedness.[51]

In a number of addresses Fiske attacked pacifism, warned of Japanese and British commercial competition against the United States in the Far East, predicted that war would break out in the East, refurbished his preparedness plea, and called Woodrow Wilson a pacifist if not a physical coward.[52] In the July 1925 *Harper's*, he predicted that as a result of the Washington treaties the Japanese would encroach upon the open door in China. He warned the United States to be ever on guard against Japan's sinister designs and stated that Japan's encroachments would create an "emotional disturbance" that would lead to war.[53]

On 21 December 1926, Fiske spoke in New York City to representatives of fourteen patriotic organizations who met to decry the failure of Congress to maintain America's status in the Five-Power Naval Treaty. Predictably, he found the situation "full of peril for the nation."[54] At a meeting held on 29 January 1927 at the Republican Club, he charged that the delegates to the Washington Conference had deceived the people and had relinquished the nation's security. By some marvelous instinct, he predicted war with Japan in fourteen years—in 1941.[55]

Although naval officers represented the United States at the Geneva naval disarmament conference in 1927, Fiske favored additional arms limitations only if accompanied by American construction up to the ratios previously established.[56] The British and American delegates refused to give in to Japan's demands, especially on the issue of total cruiser tonnage and cruiser armament; and the conference foundered, said Fiske, because the naval delegates were no more able to reach agreement on the technical side than the statesmen were able to agree politically at Washington.[57] Fiske told the *New York Times* that the statesmen had erred "in regarding the matter as one of competition in armament, whereas it is basically one of competition in sea trade." To obtain and protect their sea trade, the British had defeated all of their rivals in turn—Spain, Holland, France, and Germany. The next rival, he averred, was the United States. The "rainbow chasers" at Washington gave away the security of the Philippines, Fiske charged, and permitted the British and Japanese to place the United States in a vulnerable position in the Pacific; and the Geneva Conference proved that the British and Japanese would not give up the advantages they had obtained at Washington.[58]

The collapse of the Geneva Conference prompted a revival of interest in naval affairs in Coolidge, in Congress, and in Wilbur. After Coolidge urged a "large" program in his annual message, Wilbur cut the General Board's recommendation of 107 ships to 71 and Representative Butler introduced the necessary bill on 24 December 1927. Even though 71 ships would not give the United States parity, antinavy and pacifist agitation was so great that the number was cut further in February 1928 to one carrier instead of five, fifteen rather than twenty-five cruisers, and pruned of destroyers and submarines. Known as the "15 Cruiser Bill," the legislation passed the House early in March 1928 and the Senate on 5 February 1929. Coolidge signed it on 13 February, only three weeks before Herbert Hoover became president. On 1 March, however, Coolidge signed a bill providing for the funding of only the first year of the program.

Fiske thought so highly of Hoover that he worked to help him win the presidential nomination in 1928. He told the Republican National Committee that pacifism was a "Democratic peril" and that he would cast his first ballot in a national election for Hoover on the grounds "that any person who voted for a Democratic President voted for the defeat of the United States in its next war and the economic ruin of the country."[59] After Hoover had been elected, Fiske warned him that the nation lacked a naval policy and advised that he build the navy up to the point where it could support national policy. Fiske, of course, had backed the wrong horse. Dismayed with the cruiser-building race following Geneva and facing the question of the replacement of old battleships in the depression year 1931, Hoover approved additional disarmament. He sent diplomats rather than naval officers to confer in London.

Again Fiske sought to educate the American public on the meaning of sea power, which was often confused with the fleet alone. Naval power, he said, was comprised of three elements—the fleet, the naval bases, and the merchant marine. At war, an enemy would seek out our Achilles heel, be it our bases or the merchant marine. To achieve parity with Britain, Fiske said, we must achieve parity in bases and in the merchant marine as well as in fleet strength; even if we could achieve parity with the British fleet, disarmament would leave us weaker than Great Britain.[60] He believed that the delegates to the London conference sought agreement on naval limits, not on national defense needs, that it was impossible for the United States to obtain parity with Britain, and that the heart of the matter lay in achieving a correct naval ratio with Japan.[61]

France and Italy subscribed to only relatively minor clauses of the London treaty, from which Japan gained parity in submarines and received improved ratios in destroyers and cruisers. The United States won parity with Britain in lesser ship replacements, but would have to spend about $1 billion to achieve that parity. Particularly disquieting to Fiske was an escalator clause providing that if nations not bound by the treaty began building in such a way as to endanger a treaty power, the ratios would no longer hold.[62]

Late in 1930, in reviewing the results of three disarmament conferences, Fiske said that by making political arguments instead of accepting the advice of the General Board, American statesmen had created a situation dangerous to future peace. On 27 October, Navy Day, he stated on a New York radio program (broadcast on WGBS) that building the navy up to treaty limits "is not a question of ethics or religion, but of statesmanship—of strategy."[63] Strategy should be determined by strategists and statesmen, Fiske argued, not by clergymen, college professors, and women of public influence who were ignorant of both statesmanship and strategy. Speaking on 17 February 1931 in New York over station WABC as a director of the National Security League (a post to which he had been elected in August 1927), Fiske said that the navy's greatest need was to receive a favorable attitude from American statesmen, who as a class failed "to tell the truth about the Navy."[64] Next, at Teachers College, Columbia University, in debate with Dr. Harry Elmer Barnes, who supported complete and wholehearted disarmament, Fiske cited the need for preparedness and strongly emphasized that "treaties aren't worth a dime when the drums begin to roll."[65]

Following the Kellogg-Briand Pact which "outlawed war," Fiske noted with alarm the Manchurian "incident" of 1931 and Japan's assault on Shanghai in January 1932. Speaking on the eve of his seventy-ninth birthday, he said that he was a genuine pacifist, not a "bogus" one. Wars, he explained, were caused by economic competition and could be avoided only if nations so balanced each other in military power that one feared to attack the other. Since 1922, he said, the American navy "has been too weak to meet Japan in the only places where we are apt to meet her—near her bases."[66] Since Hoover would not use military or economic measures against her, Fiske warned that Japan could as easily take the Philippines as Shanghai.[67] Even as the League of Nations Disarmament Conference was being held, he debated Rabbi Wise and John Haynes Holmes in Carnegie Hall, upholding the position "that continuous preparedness is necessary [for] the United States."[68]

The failure of another league disarmament conference, and Japan's withdrawal from the League of Nations and defiance of demands that she leave Manchuria, strengthened Fiske's determination to improve the military preparedness of the United States. He cautioned that nations did not have scruples about violating moral obligations when seeking their interests and that America could not trust paper pronouncements. How long would we remain short-sighted, he asked, and fail to prepare to defend our interests?[69] Late in 1934 he charged that the United States would be accused of fomenting an armaments race if it merely tried to improve its defense posture, and he had unkind words for the likes of Sen. Gerald P. Nye. When, Fiske asked, would the American people realize that diplomacy would work well only "if it is linked with bands of steel to strategy?"[70]

In 1935, Italy raped Ethiopia and Japan walked out of the second London Naval Disarmament Conference after denouncing the Five-Power Naval Treaty of 1922, effective 1936. With Hitler on the rise, it was also clear that no nation felt trammeled in its naval construction. On 13 September Fiske reiterated that moral forces for peace must have physical backing, that "force is that which moves or tends to move matter." Life was competition, he said; statesmen and businessmen daily fought battles for their national interests or trade. The United States should recall its unpreparedness for every war it had fought. Preparedness, he warned, prevented rather than provoked war: it was time to prepare.[71] His last known statement on the need for preparedness came on 19 September 1936, at the height of the Nye investigation into the "merchants of death"; Fiske's conclusion was that the United States remained unprepared because "politicians will not listen" to their military advisers.[72]

Despite Fiske's almost eighty-eight years, his 1942 article entitled "Air Power 1913–43" revealed that he kept up with current events and that his mind remained clear. One must ask whether the principles with respect to air power which he held in 1913 were still true.

While aide for operations, Fiske's opinions on aeronautics were sought by both officer and civilian colleagues. He obtained Daniels's permission to convene the first naval board ever to consider air power. Led by Capt. W. I. Chambers, the board recommended placing aircraft on battleships, establishing an aeronautical center at Pensacola, creating an aeronautic laboratory at the Washington Navy Yard, training pilots to fly over both land and water so they could be used in overseas expeditions, and creating a naval bureau of aeronautics. The Wilson administration had used bombers and torpedo planes defensively, had inadequately funded naval air power during 1914 and 1915, and had employed many qualified aviators in non-flying duties. During the Great War, however, Fiske learned much about aerial warfare from American and Allied fliers who had served in Europe. He witnessed the training of several Coast Patrol Units, and in the August 1917 issue of the *Naval Institute Proceedings* predicted the capabilities of air power in war.

By 1942, Fiske saw his predictions come true to the point that he could say that "the air arm dominates the war as a whole." Air power played a vital part in Germany's conquest of Western Europe and in Russia's defense against Germany. Japan proved the value of air power by sinking the battleship *Prince of Wales* and the battle cruiser *Repulse* in ninety minutes on 10 December 1941 using torpedo planes and bombers. Therefore, it was clear that "air power will threaten capital ships until there is available adequate air protection for naval units."

Fiske believed that the Japanese attacked Pearl Harbor to destroy American aircraft that otherwise would be sent to defend the Philippines. Heroic American resistance permitted the Japanese to accomplish only part of their objective. Similarly, the failure of the British to destroy the *Scharn-*

horst and the *Gneisenau* while they were at Brest for over eleven months spoke ill, particularly of the quality of their high-level bombing. He concluded that air power would progress more rapidly following 1942 than it had since 1940 and that "the air battles for the control of the Atlantic and the Pacific of the near future may dwarf the greatest battles held so far."[73]

Even while in retirement, Fiske continued to write and to experiment. In addition to serving as president of the U.S. Naval Institute until 1923 and after 1927 as a director of the National Security League, he produced between 1921 and 1942 a number of articles, a book, a magnetic torpedo-ignition system, and a reading machine. In 1931, after experimenting with optical apparatus for twelve years, he produced a rotary reading device he believed would ease eye strain. Like his reading machine, it passed strips, in this case fifty-six inches long, beneath a magnifying glass. The strips contained five thousand words on each side; twenty of them could contain a book of one hundred thousand words. The boon to the reader was that the magnified type was three times larger than ordinary type.

Fiske watched with dismay as the World War I navy was dismantled and the American people dropped their guard, embracing "normalcy" and the delights of the Jazz Age. He erred in believing that Republicans would do more for the navy than the Democrats, and he was more disappointed in Hoover than in Harding or Coolidge. He knew that officers on active duty were loath to voice complaints and that those who did so were punished. Of the few old insurgents still alive, Sims (who died in 1936) and Fullam (who died in 1926) continued to growl—unavailingly. The top naval leadership of the 1920s and 1930s was split: some favored a treaty navy sufficient to support the national interests; others, like Fiske, distrusted collective security and multilateral treaties. As a Mahanite, Fiske saw naval power as consisting of three elements—ships, bases, and the merchant marine—and objected to the reduction by the United States of any of them. Because of his experiences with Wilson and Daniels, Fiske keenly sensed the tendency of elected and administrative personnel to reject the advice of professional military advisers; he scoffed at American diplomats because they were too prone to be satisfied with any agreement, even if it sacrificed the national interests. Unfortunately, we have no record of what Fiske thought about the naval delegates who represented their countries at the London Naval Disarmament Conference of 1935; their lack of flexibility and unwillingness to compromise spelled failure.

Whether the continued operation of the naval treaty system would have postponed war remains unknown. Fiske was correct, however, in predicting that the naval treaties written between 1922 and 1935 made it extremely difficult for the United States to support its Far Eastern interests, especially in China, or for its navy to defend U.S. possessions west of Hawaii against Japan. He was also correct in predicting that war between the United States and Japan was inevitable. He often pointed out that the United States had been unprepared for every war it entered. The inefficient and costly war preparations which the United States made after the attack on Pearl Harbor fully justified his persistent demand that America "keep her powder dry."

19

A VERSATILE NAVAL OFFICER

There was nothing nautical in the background of Bradley A. Fiske's immediate family. His father was a minister, and young Fiske considered a career in the church or in law. But a visit by Fiske's maternal uncle made him decide (at the age of six, according to his memoirs) to become a naval officer. Although physically slight—he rarely weighed more than 125 pounds "dry"—he withstood the rigors of naval duties for forty-two years. Following graduation from the Naval Academy in 1874, he remained active in naval affairs for sixty-eight of his eighty-seven years, during the last twenty-two of these as an inventor, author, lecturer, and correspondent.

With the navy "almost comatose" and the chances for promotion slow, Fiske despaired of professional advancement and often thought about resigning. He was dissuaded by his friend, Park Benjamin, by his interest in adapting electricity to shipboard use, and by worries about his health. Fiske's climb up the rungs of the professional ladder was slow. Until he became a lieutenant commander, he served primarily as a watchstander when afloat and in ordnance work when ashore. As a lieutenant commander he served as the navigator and then acting executive officer of the gunboat *Petrel*, as executive officer of the monitor *Monadnock*, and as executive officer of the gunboat *Yorktown*. Following a tour of duty as inspector of ordnance, from 1900 to 1902, he was until 1904 the executive officer of the old battleship *Massachusetts*. As a commander he served primarily as inspector of ordnance at Cramp's shipyard in Philadelphia. Not until he reached the age of fifty-two years (in 1906) did he obtain his first command—the cruiser *Minneapolis*. Two short tours at Newport, one devoted to torpedo work the other largely to international relations and war planning, completed Fiske's formal education. To this education, however, were added the broadening influence of his very extensive travels, the year he spent on war planning with the General Board, and lessons learned in civil-military relations during his two years as aide for operations.

The senior officers who most greatly affected Fiske's thinking were

George Dewey, Stephen B. Luce, and Alfred T. Mahan. He idolized Admiral Dewey both as a fighter and as president of the General Board.[1] Admiral Luce impressed Fiske with his ideas on fleet training and on fleet and departmental organization. Mahan contributed greatly to Fiske's ideas on departmental organization and on the history and philosophy of sea power. The younger officers who most influenced Fiske were William S. Sims and William F. Fullam. And the civilians who helped build and develop his inventions were Park Benjamin, Frank J. Sprague, Elmer A. Sperry, and the managers of the Western Electric Company.

Forever the student, Fiske seriously studied science, technology, and history. He taught himself electrical engineering when we were just entering the age of electricity. He then worked on designs for the electrical plants aboard the first three cruisers of the "new navy" and for two years adapted electricity to their ordnance and gunnery. Despite the multitudinous tasks required of him as a regular sailor, Fiske produced so many novel mechanisms that he became the greatest naval inventor of his generation—perhaps in American history. Because the navy had no research and development program he turned to Western Electric and to the Sperry Company to help him develop instruments that would improve the habitability, safety, efficiency, and particularly the firing qualities of naval ships. With dogged industry he pursued an idea until it became a useful invention.

Between 1887 and 1896 he produced a boat detaching device, an electric log; an electric sounding machine; a flashing light for intership communications; an improved electrical insulator; an electric range finder; electrical gear for turning turrets and for raising and lowering their guns despite the roll of a ship; electric shell and ammunition hoists; a machine gun powered by compressed air; an electrical ship steering mechanism; a naval telescopic sight for recoiling as well as nonrecoiling guns; a range and position finder; an electric range transmitter; an electric range indicator; the stadimeter; an engine-order telegraph; a helm-angle indicator; a speed and direction indicator; a steering telegraph; after-steering; and an electrical semaphore signaling system. In addition he wrote a textbook on electrical engineering, adapted telephones to shipboard use, experimented with wireless radio communications between ships, and suggested a central shipboard gunfire-control station that would permit continuous-aim firing.

Fiske was not a specialist; instead, he thought in terms of systems. The best example is gunfire control: to the naval telescopic sight he added range finders, range keepers, a central plot room below deck, and a fire-control station aloft; and he provided electrical communications that tied the elements together. He was probably the first to attempt modern fire-control methods when, stadimeter in hand, he directed the fire of the *Petrel* in the Battle of Manila Bay on 1 May 1898.

Between 1896 and 1912, when he ended his career at sea, Fiske served aboard two monitors, a cruiser, and a battleship. As a captain he commanded a cruiser division; as a rear admiral he commanded a battleship division and was second in command of the Atlantic Fleet. On shore duty he served about five years as an inspector of ordnance and for a year served on the General Board. During these years he obtained patents for the wireless control of distant objects (patents that are still useful today), a turret range finder, apparatus to be furnished a ship's conning tower, a naval telescope pivoted at eye level, an improvement on the Morris Tube, and an improved electrical range finder. During his last five years of active duty, from 1911 to 1916, Fiske obtained a joint patent with Elmer Sperry on certain fire-control mechanisms that made possible continuous-aim battery fire. (The idea had come to him in 1888.) Ironically, after improving the firepower particularly of battleships, in 1912 he patented the torpedo plane, which did so much to make the battleship obsolete. During his last year of service, while rusticated at the Naval War College, Fiske devised means of breaking up the structural lines of ships and thus of deceiving enemy range finders. And, finally, while in retirement he produced a forerunner of microfiche—a reading machine that magnified the print on strips of paper—and also a rotary reading machine. Because he gave the navy some of his inventions and plowed the profits from many into still other projects, he probably just broke even financially as an inventor.

At this writing, no history of America's men of science includes Fiske. Nor is he included in the National Inventors' Hall of Fame established in 1972. Although his inventions in electrical engineering, optics, communications, gunnery, and aviation did not win him national fame, it is perhaps not too much to suggest that they nevertheless warrant giving him a most favorable niche in the history of naval inventors. His name has been perpetuated in the *Fiske* (DE-43), sunk by a U-boat in the Atlantic on 2 August 1944, and in the *Fiske* (DD-842), commissioned on 28 November 1945.

Until he was about forty-five, Fiske concentrated so intently on his naval work afloat and ashore, and on his inventions, that he failed to recognize the strategic implications of naval power. Thereafter his increasing awareness prompted him to write numerous essays on naval power and how naval officers could enhance it. He noted that naval officers, as engineers, rendered needed service. By not lifting their eyes from their mechanisms, however, he argued that they remained simply operatives. They should also think about naval organization, administration, tactics, and strategy; they should particularly consider organization because the secretary of the navy was almost always unversed in either science or strategy. Fiske's experiences in handling ship divisions, on the General Board, and especially as aide for operations gave him a vantage point—one denied others—for criticizing those in high naval offices. Throughout his remaining years of active duty and his long retirement, he stressed that the proper function of naval officers was to study war and the proper naval organization for war, to obtain the best material for the fleet, and to train men for war. By 1910, when he was a senior captain, Fiske ranked high among those who saw the importance of having as naval leaders men who understood the impact of new technology on tactics and strategy. This explains his efforts to establish proper organization and administration, to place Naval War College graduates in the highest naval positions, and to provide ships and aircraft that would give the navy the balanced forces it needed to support national policy.

By 1906, after thirty-two years of persistent battling with conservative administrators who declined or were slow to adopt his inventions, Fiske concluded that the bureau system produced poor ships. Moreover, responsibility for providing numbers and types of ships rested with congressmen--civilians who lacked technical and military knowledge; the strategic employment of the navy was directed by a civilian secretary untrained in physical science or the science of war. His solution to the problem was a naval general staff that would make the bureaus cooperate. On this issue he enjoyed the support of senior navy men—like Luce, Mahan, William Swift, George C. Remey, and Henry C. Taylor—of relative youngsters—like Sims, Fullam, Homer Poundstone, Albert L. Key, and Yates Stirling—and even of Pres. Theodore Roosevelt and Sec. William H. Moody. Because it lacked executive and administrative authority, the General Board, established in 1900, was not the answer. Nor was Fiske happy with the scattering of American naval ships overseas, for they could not be concentrated to meet and defeat an enemy fleet far at sea, as Mahan taught they should. Thus, Fiske felt, the efficient conduct of naval operations could come only through centralized direction by professional officers.

Fiske agreed that military power should remain subordinate to civilian power. He thought, however, that the secretary should accept the military advice given him and delegate authority to execute purely military matters; he should continue to determine policy and administer the civilian side of the department. In time of peace the secretary should prepare the navy for war with any potential enemy, always keeping in mind that naval power was relative and that he who stood still, lost ground in the ever-advancing technological race. Fiske advocated carrying out tactical fleet exercises so that officers could learn to work together and admirals could learn "admiralship." He urged too that officers be advanced to flag grade early, so that they might have time to learn and to serve in that grade. In 1905, Fiske wrote that the quality of American ships was poor, that American naval policy was uncertain, and that the naval officer corps lack cohesiveness and was denied the chance to contribute ideas for the construction of ships in which they would fight. If Fiske's ideas were acceptable to fellow line officers and reformers, they were an anathema to most naval secretaries, to Congress, and to the bureau chiefs.

Naval secretary Charles Bonaparte once admitted that the poor system of naval organization worked only because good men administered it. Although willing to reorganize the department "radically" so that the bureaus would cooperate under the direction of a military head responsible to the secretary, Bonaparte would not adopt a general staff nor give legal sanction to the General Board. "Why should the Army have a general staff and not the Navy?" asked Fiske. And why should Congress authorize the building of 13,000-ton ships when 16,000-ton battleships were already built and both Britain and Japan were working on 20,000-ton ships? Clearly, Fiske felt, a technically ignorant body was deciding against the professional judgment of leading naval officers. The military men finally had their way in 1906 when Congress failed to stipulate the tonnage for new construction and designs were prepared for 20,000-ton ships to match the British *Dreadnought*.

While the nation concentrated on the voyage of the Great White Fleet, Henry Reuterdahl called attention to "The Needs of the Navy" in *McClure's Magazine* for January 1908. Fiske sent his views on naval administration and organization to Sims, President Roosevelt's naval aide and the inspector of target practice. In part because of Luce and Mahan, Roosevelt looked into the reorganization of the Navy Department. The aide system recommended by both the Moody-Mahan board and the subsequent Swift board was adopted by Meyer in October 1909. While it did not provide a naval staff, it established a system of aides to serve collectively as the secretary's leading professional advisers.

Was Fiske disloyal in obtaining legislation to create the Office of the Chief of Naval Operations? He certainly violated *Navy Regulations* by meeting secretly with others, writing the necessary bill, and having it introduced by Rep. Richmond P. Hobson; he went through a period of agonizing indecision about resigning as aide for operations. Prudence told him to keep quiet, for he could, thus, remain in the highest professional billet in the navy and preserve his Establishment credentials. By resigning, even if on grounds of principle, he would rupture valued relationships and close friendships, perhaps tarnishing his image: the cost was great, the reward minimal. He would strike a blow for the security of the nation by revealing his profound disagreement with public policy. He was convinced by friends not to resign, and for a time he worked within the system, wondering meanwhile whether those who succeeded him would resign if the administration did not accept the reforms offered by naval progressives. When he finally did resign, Fiske received several congratulatory letters saying, in effect, "I wish I had your guts." An intrepid progressive, he also lived according to his professional and ethical principles. The only reason he could give for resigning was that he did so "for the good of the service." Moreover, rather than take credit for creating the Office of the Chief of Naval Operations, he attributed it and various other naval reforms to Admiral Luce, who began agitating for a naval staff in the mid 1870s. Luce, he said in an "appreciation" written after Luce's death in 1917, "taught the Navy . . . to think about the Navy as a whole."[2] Two years later, Fiske dedicated his memoirs to the memory of Luce, "who saw the light before others saw it and led the Navy toward it."

Fiske never achieved his supreme objective—an organization in which a professional naval officer administered the purely military functions and the civilian secretary directed the civil functions of the Navy Department. It is not too much to say, however, that he was one of the "fathers" of the Naval Consulting Board (established in 1915), of the Naval Research Laboratory (established in 1923), and of the National Security Council (established in 1947)—an outgrowth of his demands for a council of national defense.

Following his long struggle against inertia in the navy, be it opposition to adopting his inventions or ideas about administration and organization, Fiske became persona non grata to the highest civil and military leaders during his last years of active duty: among the former were Pres. Woodrow Wilson, Secretary of the Navy Josephus Daniels, Secretary of State William Jennings Bryan; among the latter were William S. Benson, and such bureau chiefs as Francis Ramsay, Charles O'Neil, and Ralph Earle.

Fiske clashed both personally and professionally with Daniels, who saw naval officers as aristocratic tyrants. The list of subjects on which they disagreed was long: legalizing the aide system and creating a naval general staff; reorganizing the department so that a professional man would handle its military matters; augmenting the number of officers sent to the Naval War College and placing only its graduates in high naval positions; providing annual fleet problems that involved the bureaus and the department as well as ships; increasing the number of officers and particularly of enlisted men; promoting younger officers to flag rank; adopting director systems for firing ships' guns; building up naval aviation and creating administrative machinery for it; and having the secretary determine policy and delegate to others the administration of details. Particularly irksome to Fiske were Daniels's abolition of the officers wine mess; his neglect of the navy's military work in favor of its moral and social aspects; Daniels's declining Fiske's advice in favor of that offered by Victor Blue and Albert G. Winterhalter; the secretary's distrust of naval officers and love for enlisted men; his opposition to the creation of a council of national defense and of a naval research program; his overturning recommendations by the General Board on the number and types of ships; his emphasis on educating the men to the detriment of their shipboard work and training; and his misunderstanding of Fiske's desire to become commander in chief of the Atlantic Fleet. As Fiske saw it, Daniels was "given absolute and uncontrolled power over a great machine he does not understand." Daniels's handling of the department, Fiske once told William C. Church, was "silly."

Tired of Fiske's persistence in seeking changes that augmented military power and derogated civilian direction of the navy, Daniels paid less and less attention to him, leaning more heavily upon such advisers as Blue and Winterhalter. And occasionally he did things without telling Fiske. Unable to win Daniels over, Fiske determined to appeal over his head to Congress and to the people. His bill creating the Office of the Chief of Naval Operations was emasculated by Daniels so as to keep control of the department in civilian hands; not until 1916 were assistants to write war plans provided the office. But the creation of the office marked the first major change in naval administration since the bureau system was established, and the provision of assistants made possible the eventual creation of a War Plans Division.

If, as Fiske said, Daniels failed to comprehend the "genius of the Navy," Secretary of State Bryan also failed to comprehend the "genius of statecraft." Compared with his counselors, John Bassett Moore and then Robert Lansing, Bryan was much too political and too moralistic. Untrained in diplomacy, he made such a shambles out of the foreign service, Fiske said, that naval officers made better diplomats than the diplomats did. Believing that the administration should determine policy and allow others to execute it, Fiske was chagrined that his ideas, which were supported by the General Board and by the army chief of staff, were not followed either with respect to the disposition of American naval forces during troubled times with Japan and Mexico or in preparing the navy for war after 1914. In fact, President Wilson prohibited military men from giving advice on national policy and, in addition, muzzled any expression of their views on the war. Instead of concentrating the fleet and preparing it for war, the administration dispersed its ships off Mexico, with still others supporting United States intervention in Haiti and in San Domingo. Fiske rather sneered at Congress, too, because it lacked a sufficient number of statesmen competent to vote on national and international questions and thus did not provide a navy adequate to support national policies. In the end, failing to impress his ideas upon Daniels, he turned to secret meetings with various trustworthy senators, representatives, reporters, and publicists and became, as the *New York Tribune* called him, Daniels's "severest critic." He became as well a hero to the Republican minority in Congress which was demanding additional preparedness.

Faithful to his principles, Fiske supported Sims against Daniels in the investigation into Sims's charge in 1920 that the Navy Department had been unprepared for war in 1917 and remained so for several months after the U.S. entered the war. William V. Pratt, who at the hearings had leaned more in support of Daniels than of Sims, concluded in a manuscript biography completed in 1939: "We entered the war unprepared. Let this be a lesson to us, but it is fair to say that never will a liberal state be [as] prepared for war as will . . . a totalitarian state." Furthermore, Pratt wrote, "Reviewing the war in the light of past war reflection, I think it correct to say, that the greatest naval weakness lay not in the fleet, but in the Department itself, due in part to our form of government." Fiske would have agreed with Pratt—thus far. But Pratt added that Sims had let his leg be pulled by the Republicans and that the real motives behind the hearings were political. Pratt apologized for Daniels, saying, "He did not know about the Navy but came to know and love it, and to get what was needed on the Hill."[3] Then he added a paragraph with which Fiske surely would have agreed:

> The weaknesses which I have tried to indicate above, did not invalidate the basic soundness of the Bureau system. Perhaps this system is correct, only there must be a controlling head, else the jealousies arising between bureaus, each striving for supremacy in the affections of the Secretary will cause a condition of affairs to raise which prevents cooperation and efficiency. . . . *Neither was the Secretary the proper person to wield the power which from the very nature of this must be wielded by a technical man.*[4]

Fiske had a keen perception of the relationships between the military and civilian aspects of government. He was far ahead of Daniels, for example, in calling for a council of national defense, a naval general staff, and a naval research and development program. His conception of the relationship between civilization and war was also better than that of Wilson, Bryan, and Daniels because he was a student both of history and of war.

It was not just that he had an appreciation of land power, and especially of air power, uncommon in a sailor; rather it was because he knew the history of the great military and naval leaders of all ages and of the methods they used to reach and implement critical decisions. Above all, he had a sense that economics had the greatest influence in making peace or war among nations. He believed that history was valid as an approach to understanding the past and that those ignorant of history were bound to repeat mistakes. Moreover, history was a practical study, a means to an end. He admitted that naval power was such a complex phenomenon that it was extremely difficult to define. His only objection to Admiral Mahan was that he wrote about "old history." As Robert Seager, a biographer of Admiral Mahan, told this writer, "Mahan was, essentially, an Age of Sail historian who never really understood, nor could he personally cope with 'the new naval monsters' (his words) of the Age of Steam and Steel."[5] For Fiske, history must account not only for the tremendous technological innovations that followed the Civil War but for the role played by economics and by finance. Fiske also felt that an absolute morality underlay all civilization. When morals became corrupted, war became a certainty. Affluence, he felt, made people soft; money bred greed; and greed caused war. Thus, the greatest cause of war was moral decadence.

Was Fiske the militarist Daniels thought? Fiske certainly wanted a professional officer placed in charge of all military naval matters, yet he concluded that he, himself, was not a militarist. Like most military men, he saw that both militarism and pacifism could lead to destruction. Fiske felt that until a world organization or international altruism abolished war and men so controlled their emotions that they no longer fought each other, rulers would continue to win more power, land, or wealth. Hence the United States must be like the strong man armed, for its security depended upon a sufficient measure of military and naval preparedness.

In an essay on the "Military Character," Sims enumerated characteristics against which any naval officer may be tested. Among them were: ardor, bravery, endurance, fortitude, decisiveness, combativeness, energy, caution, initiative, loyalty, responsibility, cheerfulness, foresight, and thoroughness. The Articles of the Government of the Navy state that "the Commanders of all fleets, squadrons, naval stations, and vessels belonging to the navy are required to show in themselves a good example of virtue, honor, patriotism, and subordination."[6]

While at the Naval Academy, Fiske sometimes overcompensated for his small stature by extroverted behavior. Thereafter, in circumstances in which a man's professional qualities rather than his physical size counted, he got along very well with his peers and superiors and displayed great pride in being a naval officer and great love of the naval profession. In addition, he had keen perceptions and a ready and agile mind. He possessed strong religious feelings, befitting a minister's son, and was fervently, unquestioningly patriotic. A very proud man, Fiske could also be opinionated and contentious, as his perpetual squabbling with Daniels revealed. Compared with Sims, however, who exuded a pugnacity that caused men to attend to him, Fiske was moderate, patient, and kind.

In his gunnery inventions, Fiske was the American counterpart of Sir Percy Scott. Yet Scott's biographer, Peter Padfield, suggests that Scott was better able than Fiske to influence his service:

> There were . . . officers in every navy with a natural scientific bent so strong that it resisted all efforts of contemporary naval education and wardroom ethos to submerge it. There were the men who provoked the second stage of the naval armaments revolution, when methods of aiming and fire control chased to catch up with ordnance engineering. Two of the most brilliant and effective of those were Bradley Fiske of the American and Percy Scott of the British service. Of the two Scott was the most [sic] influential for three main reasons: first, even though English he was more pushing and presumptuous than Fiske; second, he was the prime mover in a whole group of discontented gunnery enthusiasts whereas Fiske was at times almost alone in a far more hidebound and reactionary service than the British achieved at the height of their pomposity; third, the British service from 1888 onwards was constantly under pressure to maintain its assumed world superiority, and latterly bent all efforts to resisting the German threat, while the American service was quite convinced that it would never have to go to war and was simply maintained as a prestige and coast defence arm. So, while Scott's path was never easy, it was probably smoother than Fiske's.[7]

Padfield's reference to the "second stage of the naval armaments revolution" is further clarified by Fiske's comment on an article by Lt. William H. P. Blandy, USN. In "Director Firing a Century Ago," Blandy stated that director firing was used as early as 1829 when a British naval officer laid guns to a common angle of elevation, trained them to converge upon a point of known range and bearing, and fired them from a single station removed from the immediate vicinity of the guns. To Fiske, this was the first stage in the naval armaments revolution, and he took Blandy to task, showing how his own equipment included a technique for obtaining range and bearing and for firing while a ship was rolling.[8]

Fiske placed less emphasis on blind obedience and doctrine than on "intelligent cooperation," leaving a commander a reservoir of initiative to exercise in emergencies. On the other hand, while aide for operations he was both disobedient and disloyal to superior authority when, as a matter of principle, he went behind Daniels's back to obtain legislation creating an Office of the Chief of Naval Operations. Fiske may be excused only on the ground that his loyalty to superior authority was less than his loyalty to the mission of the navy—defense of the national interest. The most egregious example of his pride was his long and determined effort to obtain credit for inventing the torpedo plane.

As president of the U.S. Naval Institute from 1912 to 1923, Fiske was in an excellent position to impress his ideas upon that organization. Much of the actual work was done by the Board of Control and by the secretary-treasurer—Philip R. Alger, until his untimely death at the age of forty-seven in 1912, then Ralph Earle, Ernest J. King, and H. Kent Hewitt. Even though Sims, a good friend, once asked him to intercede with the Board of Control about publication of an article he had written, Fiske replied that he lacked any power over the board whatever. From 1914 to 1922, because of wartime censorship, the *Proceedings* lacked sparkle and published primarily technical articles.

Over the years, pressure built up among the institute's members that the chief of naval operations should be its president and that only active duty officers should serve as the organization's officers. Even though he was retired, however, the members continued to elect Fiske until he had served eleven years—longer than anyone else, a record that still stands.

Few of Fiske's naval contemporaries did as much writing as he. Austin M. Knight is best known for his text on seamanship, Fullam for several technical texts and various articles, and Sims for a respectable number of essays. As his heritage, Fiske left six books and 65 articles. He thus shares top honors for literary productivity with Mahan (who left twenty books and 145 articles), with Luce (who left three books and 58 articles), and with Dudley W. Knox, the perennial essayist who also wrote two books and edited many others.[9]

The quality of Fiske's literary work shows that he was no mere sabre rattler or "armed progressive," demanding a large navy for his own personal interest. His books include a text on electrical engineering, a history of inventions, a military history, a history of naval organization and operations, a history of his experiences in the Spanish-American War, and his memoirs. In none of these did he try to "sell" the navy even though his writings may have stimulated interest in naval affairs. Twenty-six of his articles deal with technical matters—electricity, signaling, navigation and gunnery instruments, shipbuilding, and aviation. He wrote one article on the Battle of Manila Bay and two on the Battle of Tsushima. Another article dealt with the rescue of a man at sea. He wrote articles of appreciation on George Dewey, Luce, Charles S. Sperry, and Theodore Roosevelt and one on the work and value of the U.S. Naval Institute. Not until 1907 did he write what may be considered a plan for a reorganized navy. Thereafter, he wanted a navy "superadequate" to support the nation's interests. Prohibited from commenting between 1914 and 1922 on the Great War, he nevertheless wrote copiously on naval strategy, tactics, logistics, and invention. After he learned the terms of the Washington Naval Treaty he persistently demanded that the navy be built up at least to treaty limits and thus not fall behind in relative power. Because he had retired in 1916, it is clear that Fiske battled thereafter neither for himself nor for the navy but for what he considered to be the national interest. What others might call "militarism" to him simply meant the law of life: nations, like man, needed strength to survive.

For a number of years following his retirement, Fiske summered in Jamestown, Rhode Island, and spent the rest of the year with his family in their New York City apartment. His care for Jo when she was ill reveals his great love for her. During the late summer of 1922 Fiske was hospitalized and recuperated at a nursing home. He then took a room at the Waldorf Astoria and fell in love with what he called "this comfortable but very expensive hostelry."[10] In 1926 he became a permanent guest of the hotel. He lived fretfully at the Commodore while the Waldorf was being rebuilt starting in 1931, then moved back in 1934 as one of the first, yet oldest, guests of the new institution. That same year, when he was eighty, a naval ball was given by the Naval Academy Graduates of New York in honor of Adm. David Foot Sellers, commander in chief of the United States Fleet. Amid the blue and gold decor of the Waldorf Astoria's grand ballroom, and to the tune of *Anchors Away*, Fiske—the oldest graduate of sixty Academy classes represented—led the march.

Fiske was in and out of his hotel a good deal until he reached almost eighty-five years old. He then made it his world. After breakfasting in his room he would dress, often in a sharply pressed blue suit, white shirt, and bow tie, and descend to an area called Peacock Alley. From an armchair reserved for him he spoke with other guests or friends who dropped by. He did a good deal of reading, often while smoking a cork-tipped cigarette, leaving only to have lunch and dinner until he retired for the night. Many remarked on how well he looked, for the clearness of his complexion, which he attributed to his father, belied his age. His favorite author, he said when interviewed in February 1942, was Charles Dickens, whom he called (with naval decisiveness) "the language's greatest writer." But he also enjoyed such fare as P. G. Woodhouse's *My Man Jeeves*. Asked if his theory about the torpedo plane was proven by the British carrier strike of 11 November 1940 at Taranto, in which a small number of bombers and torpedo planes scored hits on three Italian battleships, and more lately by the Japanese attack on Pearl Harbor, he admitted that it was. When asked how long the war would last, he answered, again with naval decisiveness, "How the hell would I know?" and returned to reading *Jeeves*.[11]

After being hospitalized in 1922, Fiske enjoyed good health until 1939, when he was treated, but not surgically, for a hernia. During the summer of 1940 his health began to fail rapidly, and for the next year and a half he was in the care of a male nurse. For his last two months he was confined to his room, where on 6 April 1942 he died at the age of eighty-seven. His only survivors were his daughter, Caroline Harper Fiske, and a sister living in Cleveland.

On 8 April, funeral services were held for Fiske in St. Thomas's Episcopal Church, where he and Jo had been married. With navy and Marine Corps enlisted men in attendance, the rector read Tennyson's *The Crossing of the Bar*, one of Fiske's favorite poems. Then, with a military escort at attention, about one hundred persons passed by his casket. Several men who had worked with Fiske on naval aviation matters served as honorary escorts, and three of the pioneer members of the National Aerial Coast Patrol Commission (which was organized with Fiske's assistance in 1915) served as escorts for services held in Washington.[12] On 10 April, following a short service in the Fort Myers Chapel, Fiske was laid to rest in Arlington National Cemetery with full military honors. So ended the life of a sailor, inventor, administrator, writer, and philosopher—a truly versatile naval officer.

NOTES

The following abbreviations have been used:

ADM	Admiral
AHR	*American Historical Review*
AN	*American Neptune*
ANJ	*Army and Navy Journal*
ANL	*Army and Navy Life*
APSR	*American Political Science Review*
ARR	*American Review of Reviews*
ARSN	*Annual Report of the Secretary of the Navy*
ASECNAV	Assistant Secretary of the Navy
BGEN	Brigadier General
BUAER	Bureau of Aeronautics
BUC&R	Bureau of Construction and Repair
BUEQ	Bureau of Equipment
BUNAV	Bureau of Navigation
BUORD	Bureau of Ordnance
CAPT	Captain
CDR	Commander
CH	*Current History*
COMMO	Commodore
CNO	Chief of Naval Operations
DAB	*Dictionary of American Biography*
ENS	Ensign
EW	*Electrical World*
GB	General Board of the Navy
GPO	Government Printing Office
IND	*Independent*
JAG	Judge Advocate General
JAH	*Journal of American History*

LCDR	Lieutenant Commander
LCOL	Lieutenant Colonel
LD	*Literary Digest*
LT	Lieutenant
LTJG	Lieutenant, junior grade
MA	*Military Affairs*
MDLC	Manuscript Division, Library of Congress
NAR	*North American Review*
NARG	National Archives Record Group
NHD:OA	Naval History Division, Operational Archives Branch
NWC	Naval War College
NWCR	*Naval War College Review*
ONI	Office of Naval Intelligence
PHR	*Pacific Historical Review*
RADM	Read Admiral
SA	*Scientific American*
SECNAV	Secretary of the Navy
USMC	United States Marine Corps
USNIP	*U.S. Naval Institute Proceedings*
VADM	Vice Admiral
WW	*World's Work*

CHAPTER 1

1. RADM Bradley A. Fiske, USN (RET), *From Midshipman to Rear-Admiral* (New York: Century Co., 1919), p. 4.
2. *Ibid.*, pp. 5–6.
3. Park Benjamin, *The Naval Academy: Being the Yarn of the American Midshipman* (New York and London: G. P. Putnam's Sons, 1900), pp. 299–300.
4. See *Regulations Covering the Admission of Candidates into the Naval Academy as Midshipmen, 1874–1875* (Annapolis, Md.: U.S. Naval Academy, 1874), p. 2; Benjamin, *Naval Academy*, pp. 350–85.
5. Benjamin, *Naval Academy*, p. 256.
6. *Annual Register of the United States Naval Academy at Annapolis, Md., for the Academic Year 1870–1871* (Washington: GPO, 1871), pp. 30–31.
7. Fiske, *From Midshipman*, p. 9.
8. *Ibid.*, pp. 10–14.
9. *Ibid.*, p. 23.
10. *Ibid.*, pp. 15–16; John Henry Wilson, *Albert A. Michelson: America's First*

Nobel Prize Physicist (New York: Messner, 1958), pp. 38–40.

11. Fiske, *From Midshipman*, p. 16.
12. *Ibid.*, pp. 16–18.
13. *Ibid.*, p. 18.
14. *Ibid.*, p. 19.

CHAPTER 2

1. Fiske, *From Midshipman*, pp. 20–31; Log, *Pensacola*, NARG 24.
2. Fiske, *From Midshipman*, pp. 23–24.
3. *Ibid.*, pp. 26–27, 37–38.
4. *Ibid.*, pp. 38–39.
5. *Ibid.*, p. 39.
6. *Ibid.*, pp. 39–40; Jeffers to Fiske, Nov. 18, 1878, NARG 74.
7. Fiske, *From Midshipman*, pp. 40–44.
8. ARSN, 1874, p. 84; see also ARSN, 1875, pp. 88–89.
9. ARSN, 1874, p. 215.
10. Fiske, *From Midshipman*, pp. 41–42; ARSN, 1875, pp. 93–98.
11. Fiske, *From Midshipman*, p. 45.
12. For the execrable condition of the fleet, see ARSN, 1874, pp. 9–13, 198–222; COMMO Foxhall A. Parker, USN, "Our Fleet Maneuvers in the Bay of Florida," USNIP 1 (Dec. 10, 1874): 163–76; RADM John R. Wadleigh, USN (RET), "The Best Was Yet To Be," *ibid.* 99 (Nov. 1973): 56–70.
13. ARSN, 1878, p. 96; Fiske, *From Midshipman*, pp. 46–48.
14. Fiske, *From Midshipman*, pp. 48–49.
15. *Ibid.*, pp. 49–50.
16. ARSN, 1879, pp. 116, 121–22; Fiske, *From Midshipman*, pp. 54–56. Apparently independently, Sir Percy Scott developed a similar signal lamp—in 1890; see "Scott's Flashing Signal Lantern," EW 16 (Sept. 13, 1890): 188.
17. Log, *Powhatan*, NARG 24.
18. Fiske, *From Midshipman*, pp. 60–61.
19. *Ibid.*, pp. 63–64. For the Harper family, see Eugene Exman, *The House of Harper: One Hundred and Fifty Years of Publishing* (New York: Harper and Row, 1967).
20. Fiske, *From Midshipman*, pp. 66–67.

CHAPTER 3

1. Fiske, *From Midshipman*, p. 71.

2. *Ibid.*, pp. 71–72.
3. *Ibid.*, p. 72.
4. See the review in EW 2 (Nov. 10, 1883): 175; and the unsolicited letter by Theodore F. Jewell, of the Naval Torpedo Station, *ibid.* 2 (Dec. 1, 1883): 231–32.
5. Fiske, *From Midshipman*, pp. 73–77.
6. ARSN, 1883, p. 412; ARSN, 1884, pp. 410–14, 437, 438.
7. Fiske to Sicard, Aug. 3, 1883, NARG 74.
8. Fiske, *From Midshipman*, p. 86.
9. ARSN, 1884, pp. 512–13.
10. W. D. Marks to Sicard, June 18, 1884; Sicard to Marks, June 19, 1884, NARG 74.
11. Fiske, *From Midshipman*, pp. 89–90. The genesis and arrangements for the exposition are explained in the issues of *Electrical World* from Dec. 22, 1883, through Sept. 20, 1884.
12. ARSN, 1884, pp. 509–12.
13. EW 6 (Nov. 21, 1885): 213; *ibid.* 6 (Nov. 28, 1885): 222–24.
14. Fiske, *From Midshipman*, pp. 82–84.
15. *Ibid.*, p. 85; Sicard to Fiske, Oct. 8, 17, 28, 1884, NARG 74.
16. Log, *Brooklyn*, NARG 24; to avoid having Fiske sent to sea, Sicard arranged to have Fiske serve briefly on the *Brooklyn*.
17. ARSN, 1888, pp. iv, viii; Fiske, *From Midshipman*, p. 97.
18. Fiske, *From Midshipman*, p. 97.
19. *Ibid.*, pp. 97–101.
20. Fiske to RADM S. B. Luce, Jan. 6, 1888, NHD:OA.
21. Fiske to Sicard, May 23, 1887, NARG 74.
22. Sicard to Fiske, June 3, 1887, *ibid.*
23. Fiske to Sicard, June 13, 1887, *ibid.*
24. Fiske to Sicard, June 27, 1887, *ibid.*
25. Fiske, *From Midshipman*, pp. 103–5.
26. Fiske to Sicard, Aug. 3, 1886, NARG 74.
27. Fiske to Sicard, Nov. 16, 28, 1886, *ibid.*
28. Fiske to Sicard, Nov. 11, 28, 1887; Sicard to Fiske, Dec. 2, 14, 1887, *ibid.*
29. Fiske to Sicard, Dec. 8, 1887, *ibid.*
30. Knight to William T. Sampson, Dec. 8, 1887, *ibid.*
31. Sicard to Fiske, Mar. 5, 1888, *ibid.*
32. Admiral Sir Percy Scott, Bart., *Fifty Years in the Royal Navy* (London: J. Murray, 1919), pp. 80–88; Peter Padfield, *Aim Straight: A Biography of Admiral Sir Percy Scott* (London: Hodder and Stoughton, 1966), pp. 79–81.
33. See, particularly, the extensive explanation of his plan in Fiske to Sicard, Feb. 22, 1888, NARG 74.

34. Fiske, *From Midshipman*, pp. 106–9.
35. Luce to Mahan, July 15, 1907, Mahan Papers, MDLC.

CHAPTER 4

1. Fiske, *From Midshipman*, pp. 111–14; 2d LT John W. Kennon, USMC, "U.S.S. Vesuvius," USNIP 80 (Feb. 1954): 183–88.
2. Wickes to SECNAV, Jan. 31, 1889, NARG 74.
3. Sicard to Fiske, Feb. 5, 1889; Fiske to Sicard, Feb. 13, 1889, *ibid.*
4. Wickes to Sicard, telegram, Feb. 20, 1889, *ibid.*
5. Sicard to James Fulton, Chief of Bureau of Provisions and Clothing, May 1, 1889, *ibid.*
6. Folger to SECNAV, May 15, 1888, NARG 45; Log, *Vesuvius*, June 7, 1890, NARG 24; Fiske, *From Midshipman*, pp. 114–16; Seaton Schroeder, RADM, USN (RET), *A Half Century of Naval Service* (New York and London: D. Appleton and Co., 1922), pp. 175–95; and the prize essay for 1894, "The U.S.S. Vesuvius, with Special Reference to Her Pneumatic Battery," USNIP 20, no. 1 (1894): 1–66.
7. Fiske, *From Midshipman*, p. 116.
8. *Ibid.*, pp. 117–18.
9. Professor P. R. Alger, USN, "Improvements in Ordnance and Armor in the Recent Past and Future," USNIP 23, no. 1 (1897): 125, 128, and "Naval Ordnance," *ibid.* 20, no. 3 (1894): 591–92; ENS Joseph Strauss, USN, "The Turrets of the New Battleships," *ibid.* 21, no. 4 (1895): 771–78.
10. "A Single Instrument Range Finder," SA 108 (Apr. 19, 1913): 360.
11. Charles O'Neil, Memorandum to the Chief BUORD, Oct. 15, 1889, NARG 74; Report on Range Finder on *Chicago*, Nov. 16, 1889, *ibid.*; Fiske, *From Midshipman*, p. 119.
12. Fiske, *From Midshipman*, pp. 109–10.
13. Wickes to Sicard, Nov. 22, 1889; Sicard to Wickes, Dec. 3, 1889, NARG 74.
14. Fiske, *From Midshipman*, pp. 119–21.
15. O'Neil to Sicard, Nov. 3, 1889, NARG 74.
16. The report, dated Feb. 26, 1890, is in *ibid*; see the illustrated article, "Lieutenant Fiske's Range and Position Finder," EW 15 (Feb. 8, 1890): 93–94.
17. LT Albert Gleaves, USN, "The Influence of Range-Finders upon Modern Ordnance, Gunnery, and Warship Construction," USNIP 18, no. 2 (1892): 259–64.
18. Report by LT S. H. May, LT H. O. Dunn, and ENS George Breed, NARG 74.
19. Schley to Chief BUORD, May 20, 1890, *ibid.*

20. Folger to Schley, May 28, 1890, *ibid.*
21. Fiske to Folger, July 21, 1890; Folger to Fiske, July 24, 1890, *ibid.*
22. Report dated July 23, 1890, *ibid.*
23. Folger to Fiske, Aug. 13, 1890, *ibid.*
24. Fiske to Folger, Aug. 15, 1890, *ibid.*
25. Folger to Fiske, Aug. 18, 1890, *ibid.*
26. *New York Times*, July 9, 1891, 4:2, cited in Fiske, *From Midshipman*, p. 124.
27. The report is in NARG 74; Fiske's italicized comment appears in *From Midshipman*, p. 124.
28. Dayton to Chief BUORD, July 8, 1891; Folger to Inspector in Charge of Naval Ordnance, Annapolis, June 30, 1891; Folger to Michelson, July 14, 1891, Jan. 19, 1892; Michelson to Folger, July 22, 1891; Joseph Brunnet, Acting Chief BUORD, to Michelson, Aug. 7, 1891, NARG 75.
29. Report by LTs Raymond P. Rodgers, H. S. Scheutze, and Austin M. Knight, Nov. 10, 1890, *ibid.*
30. Folger to Walker, Dec. 20, 1890, NARG 74.
31. *Ibid.*; the report was made by LT Sidney H. May.
32. Folger to Wickes, Jan. 11, 1892, *ibid.*
33. Wickes to Tracy, Jan. 15, 1891; Folger to Wickes, Jan. 11, 1892, *ibid.*
34. Fiske, *From Midshipman*, p. 119.
35. *Ibid.*, pp. 124–26.
36. *Ibid.*, p. 126.
37. Sir Percy Scott, Bart., *Fifty Years in the Royal Navy* (London: J. Murray, 1919), pp. 40–41.
38. See "Lieutenant Fiske's Position-Indicator," EW 15 (Mar. 8, 1890): 178; "The Fiske Electric Position-Finder," USNIP 18, no. 2 (1892): 310–15 (reprinted from *Iron Age*); "Lieutenant Fiske's Depression Position Finder," *ibid.* 19, no. 3 (1893): 314–17 (reprinted from *Electrical Engineer*, June 21, 1893).
39. LT Joseph Strauss, USN, "Telescopic Sights for Guns," *ibid.* 22, no. 79 (1896): 589–98.
40. Fiske, *From Midshipman*, p. 128.
41. *Ibid.*, pp. 131–32.
42. *Ibid.*, pp. 133–44.
43. *Ibid.*, pp. 145–60.
44. *Ibid.*, pp. 161–62.
45. ARSN, 1890, pp. 27–29; ARSN, 1891, pp. 38–43.
46. Winfield S. Schley, CAPT, USN, Commanding U.S.S.S. *Baltimore*, "Official Report on the Behavior of the U.S.S.S. *Baltimore*," USNIP 18, no. 2 (1892): 247–48.
47. Michelson to Folger, Jan. 21, Feb. 11, 15, 1892; Folger to Michelson, Feb. 13,

Oct. 4, 1892, NARG 74.

48. *Register of the Commissioned Officers of the United States Navy and Marine Corps* (Washington: GPO, 1888–98), passim; Fiske, *From Midshipman,* p. 162.

49. ARSN, 1893, pp. 25–28; ARSN, 1894, pp. 27–28; ARSN, 1895, pp. xxvii–xxviii; ARSN, 1896, pp. 19–35, 39–40; ARSN, 1897, pp. 39–40.

50. Fiske, *From Midshipman,* pp. 162–63. The description of Ramsay is from CAPT John M. Ellicott, USN, "Passing of the Cadet Engineers," USNIP 64 (Aug. 1938): 1131.

51. Log, *Baltimore,* Aug. 28, 1891, NARG 24.

52. Evans to SECNAV, in Letters to Navy Department from Commanding Officers of Vessels, NARG 313, Series 17, January 1892–July 1893.

53. See, in particular, Frederick B. Pike, *Chile and the United States, 1880–1962* (South Bend, Ind.: University of Notre Dame Press, 1963), pp. 66–70; Robley D. Evans, *A Sailor's Log: Recollections of Forty Years of Naval Life* (New York: D. Appleton Co., 1901), pp. 244–98.

54. Fiske, *From Midshipman,* pp. 167–68.

55. *Ibid.,* pp. 169–70. No amount of investigation by me, by friends who teach English or French literature, or by reference librarians has shed any light on the source of the name Algernon de Montmorenci. Fiske was frequently called "Jim" by his friends, a reference to the American financial speculator.

56. *Ibid.,* p. 171.

57. Evans to SECNAV, Mar. 31, 1892, NARG 313.

58. Log, *Yorktown,* NARG 45, OM, Box 412. *List of Vessels Boarded and Warned Against Sealing in the Bering Sea by United States and British Naval Vessels and United States Revenue Vessels, 1891 and 1892; Sea Log Book of the U.S. Revenue Cutter Rush, Captain W. C. Couson, Commanding,* NARG 45, OM, Box 415; *Routine Movements of U.S. Ships, 1871–1910, ibid.;* Evans to SECNAV, Aug. 1, 1891, Letters of Commanding Officers, NARG 313; Fiske, *From Midshipman,* pp. 173–78.

59. P. R. Alger, Professor of Mathematics, USN, "Improvements in Ordnance and Armor," pp. 126, 130–31; and "The Composition and Arrangement of Ships' Batteries," USNIP 23, no. 2 (1897): 229–48; Charles H. Cramp, "Mechanism of Modern Naval War: Necessity of Experience to Efficiency," *ibid.* 23, no. 4 (1897): 689–704; J. Bernard Walker, "The Fire Control Platform of a United States Battleship," SA 109 (Nov. 8, 1913): 363.

60. Fiske to Sampson, Mar. 8, May 2, 8, 31, 1893, NARG 74.

61. Cramp and Sons to Chief BUORD, Jan. 27, 1893, *ibid.*

62. Fiske, *From Midshipman,* p. 185.

63. E. M. Barton, "The Story of the Western Electric Co.," *Western Electric News* 1 (May 1912): 1–4; H. B. Thayer, President, "The Early Days of the

Company in New York," *ibid.* 1 (June 1912): 1–3; Western Electric Co., *Western Electric Company, 1869–1944* (New York: Western Electric Co., 1944); Frank H. Lovette, "Western Electric's First 75 Years: A Chronology," *Bell Telephone Magazine,* Winter 1944–45, pp. 271–87; "Memorandum by E. W. Rockafellow," typescript courtesy of Mrs. Young H. Quick, Western Electric Company.

64. Yates Sterling, RADM, USN (RET), *Sea Duty: The Memoirs of a Fighting Admiral* (New York: G.P. Putnam's Sons, 1939), pp. 105–6.
65. Correspondence between BUORD and Western Electric Company included the exchange of thirty-eight letters in 1894 alone; see NARG 74.
66. Log, *San Francisco,* NARG 24.
67. Fiske, *From Midshipman,* pp. 191–92.
68. *Ibid.,* pp. 192–97.
69. Caroline B. Hart and Louise Powers Benesch, comps., *From Frigate to Dreadnaught* (Sharon, Conn.: King House, 1973), p. 127; Lawrence F. Hill, *Diplomatic Relations Between the United States and Brazil* (Durham, N.C.: Duke University Press, 1932), pp. 274–81.
70. Log entries, May 7–9, 1894, *San Francisco,* NARG 24.
71. Thayer to Sampson, Oct. 1, 1894, NARG 74.
72. Sampson to Thayer, Jan. 3, 1895, *ibid.*
73. Glass to Sampson, Apr. 29, 1895, *ibid.*
74. Robley D. Evans to Sampson, May 18, 1895, *ibid.*
75. Fiske, *From Midshipman,* pp. 198–99.

CHAPTER 5

1. ARSN, 1894, pp. 239–40.
2. Fiske, *From Midshipman,* pp. 198–200.
3. Fiske to Sampson, Nov. 13, 1895, NARG 74.
4. Lennard to Sampson, Dec. 11, 1895, *ibid.*
5. Hichborn to SECNAV, Dec. 19, 1895, *ibid.*
6. Fiske, *From Midshipman,* pp. 201–2. At Sampson's request, Fiske also provided instructions for installing range indicators in ships (see Fiske to Sampson, Mar. 6, 17, 1896; Sampson to Fiske, Mar. 12, 1896, NARG 74).
7. Sampson to SECNAV, Jan. 4, 1896, NARG 74.
8. George Melville to SECNAV, Jan. 22, 1896, *ibid;* McAdoo to Sampson, Jan. 25, 1896, NARG 19.
9. Fiske, *From Midshipman,* pp. 202–3.
10. ARSN, 1897, pp. 9–10, 280.
11. Western Electric Co. to Sampson, Jan. 25, 1897; Sampson to Western Electric

Co., Feb. 17, 1897; Benjamin to Chief BUORD, May 26, 1897, Apr. 19, Nov. 18, 1899; Ernest Wilkinson to Chief BUORD, Oct. 27, 1898; O'Neil to SECNAV, Nov. 3, 8, 1898; Long to Chief BUORD, Nov. 12, 1898; Attorney General to SECNAV, Mar. 14, 1899, NARG 74.

12. Fiske, *From Midshipman*, p. 204.
13. *Ibid.*, pp. 205–6.
14. *Ibid.*, p. 206.
15. ARSN, 1895, p. 220.
16. *Ibid.*, p. 221.
17. Park Benjamin, "The Nerves of a War-ship," *Harper's New Monthly Magazine* 92 (Mar. 1896): 631–36.
18. Fiske, *From Midshipman*, p. 217.
19. *Ibid.*, pp. 218–19.
20. See CAPT H. C. Taylor, "Naval War College," USNIP 22 (1896): 429–46.
21. Fiske, *From Midshipman*, pp. 221–22; Ronald Spector, "Professors of War: The Naval War College and the Modern American Navy, 1884–1897" (Ph.D. diss., Yale University, 1967), pp. 10, 15, 27, 127; ARSN, 1894, pp. 28–30, 211; ARSN, 1895, pp. 754–55.
22. USNIP 22 (1896): 90–91; LCOL John C. Miller, USMC, "William Freeman Fullam's War with the Corps," *ibid.* 101 (Nov. 1975): 37–45.
23. Fiske, "Electricity in Naval Life," *ibid.* 22 (1896): 323–428.
24. *Ibid.*
25. *Ibid.*
26. ARSN, 1898, 1: 33–34.

CHAPTER 6

1. Fiske, *From Midshipman*, p. 224.
2. A. T. Mahan, "A Twentieth Century Outlook," *Harper's New Monthly Magazine* 95 (Sept. 1897): 521–33.
3. Alfred T. Mahan Papers, MDLC; see Mahan, *The Problem of Asia and its Effect upon International Relations* (Boston: Little, Brown, 1900).
4. Fiske, *From Midshipman*, pp. 229–32.
5. *Ibid.*, pp. 232, 237–38.
6. ARSN, 1898, 2:67.
7. CAPT Edward L. Beach, USN, "Manila Bay in 1898," USNIP 46 (Apr. 1920): 589; Bert B. Singman, "Eyewitness to History: A Participant's Memoirs of the Spanish-American War, Philippine Insurrection, Boxer Rebellion," typescript (U.S. Naval Academy Library, Annapolis, 1962), pp. 11–12.

8. Fiske, *From Midshipman*, pp. 242–45.
9. *Ibid.*, pp. 245–46; Bradley A. Fiske, *Wartime in Manila* (Boston: Gorham Press, 1913), pp. 15–16.
10. Fiske, *From Midshipman*, pp. 246–47; Fiske, *Wartime in Manila*, pp. 15–16.
11. Fiske, *From Midshipman*, p. 249; Fiske, *Wartime in Manila*, pp. 20, 21; ARSN, 1901, 2:652.
12. Fiske, *From Midshipman*, pp. 251–52; Fiske, *Wartime in Manila*, pp. 25–26; "Battle Casualties," NARG 45, HB, Box 1.
13. Fiske, *From Midshipman*, pp. 252–56; Fiske, *Wartime in Manila*, pp. 26–31.
14. Log, *Petrel*, May 3, 4, 1898, NARG 24; Fiske, *From Midshipman*, pp. 267–68; Fiske, *Wartime in Manila*, pp. 43–50.
15. "Report of Action at Manila Bay, May 1, 1898," ARSN, 1898, 2:69, 80–82.
16. Dewey to Long, May 15, 1898, *ibid.*, 2:69.
17. Fiske, *Wartime in Manila*, pp. 74–75.
18. Fiske, *From Midshipman*, pp. 270–73; Fiske, *Wartime in Manila*, pp. 106–12.
19. Fiske, *Wartime in Manila*, pp. 82–84, 113–14; "Narrative of Manila Campaign," comp. by CDR Nathan Sargent, USN, Nov. 10, 1904, NARG 45, OO, Box 17A, No. 3.
20. Fiske, *Wartime in Manila*, p. 99.
21. Log, *Petrel*, Aug. 9–10, 1898; E. P. Wood to Commander-in-Chief U.S. Naval Forces on Asiatic Station, Sept. 3, 1898, NARG 45, OM, Box 407; Sargent, "Narrative," pp. 135–38.
22. Fiske, *Wartime in Manila*, pp. 121–23.
23. Sargent, "Narrative," pp. 140–42; "Activities of the German Squadron in Manila Bay in 1898, told by Chief Boatswain Ernest Heilman," NARG 45, OO, Box 438. See also Thomas A. Bailey, "Dewey and the Germans at Manila Bay," AHR 45 (1939): 59–81.
24. Fiske, *From Midshipman*, pp. 276–80; Fiske, *Wartime in Manila*, pp. 129–31.
25. ARSN, 1898, 1:118.
26. Paolo E. Coletta, "The Peace Negotiations and the Treaty of Paris," in *Threshold to American Internationalism: Essays on the Foreign Policies of William McKinley*, Paolo E. Coletta, ed. (New York: Exposition University Press, 1970), pp. 129–30.
27. Log, *Petrel*, Sept. 26, 1898; Fiske, *From Midshipman*, pp. 284–85.
28. Wood to SECNAV, Nov. 30, 1898, NARG 45, OM, Box 414.
29. Log, *Monadnock*, Feb. 4, 5, 1899, NARG 24; CAPT H. E. Nichols, "Report of the Operations and Movements of the *Monadnock* from January 26, 1899 until June 9, 1899," dated June 9, 1899, to Commander-in-Chief U.S. Naval Forces on Asiatic Station, NARG 45, OM, Box 157.
30. Nichols, "Report"; Fiske, *From Midshipman*, pp. 302–3; Fiske, *Wartime in Manila*, pp. 206–8.

31. Fiske, *From Midshipman*, p. 306.
32. *Ibid.*, p. 316; Log, *Monadnock*, Jan. 26–June 9, 1898; Nichols, "Report."
33. Fiske to O'Neil, Jan. 30, 1899, NARG 74.
34. Fiske to O'Neil, Jan. 30, 1899; O'Neil to Fiske, Mar. 20, 1899; C. G. Van Nostrand to Western Electric Co., Mar. 20, 1900; O'Neil to Western Electric Co., Apr. 2, 18, 1900; Western Electric Co. to O'Neil, Mar. 21, Apr. 5, 21, 1900, *ibid.*
35. Log, *Yorktown*, NARG 24, end papers; Fiske, *Wartime in Manila*, p. 239.
36. Fiske, *From Midshipman*, pp. 317–20; Fiske, *Wartime in Manila*, p. 239.
37. Log, *Yorktown*, Aug. 23, 24, 26, 29, Sept. 21, Oct. 14, 1899; C. S. Sperry to Commander-in-Chief U.S. Naval Forces on Asiatic Station, Aug. 20, Nov. 30, 1899, NARG 45, OM, Box 411; Fiske, *From Midshipman*, pp. 32–33; Fiske, *Wartime in Manila*, pp. 243–54.
38. Watson to Fiske, Dec. 24, 1899, NARG 303; Fiske, *From Midshipman*, p. 336; Fiske, *Wartime in Manila*, p. 254.

CHAPTER 7

1. Fiske to Dewey, telegram, Feb. 15, 1901; Dewey to ASECNAV, Feb. 15, 16, 1901; Crowninshield, Memorandum for ASECNAV in the Case of LCDR Bradley A. Fiske, Feb. 16, 1901, NHD:OA.
2. Index to Letters Received, BUORD, 1900–1901, NARG 74.
3. *Ibid.*; ARSN, 1902, p. 501. Fiske explained his conception of a conning tower in USNIP 31 (Mar. 1905): 179–80.
4. Fiske, *From Midshipman*, p. 339.
5. *Ibid.*
6. *Ibid.*, p. 340; ARSN, 1903, pp. 608–10; Frederick Leslie Robertson, *The Evolution of Naval Armament* (London: H. T. Storey, 1968), pp. 291–93; Lloyd H. Chandler, "Automobile Torpedoes: Their Use and Probable Effectiveness," USNIP 29 (Sept. 1903): 903–4; "The New Turbine Torpedo of the United States Navy," *ibid.* 32 (Mar. 1906): 363–65 (reprinted from SA).
7. Fiske, *From Midshipman*, pp. 340–41. The watertight door system itself was devised by naval constructor Francis T. Bowles, USN. The electrical part of the system was worked out by Frank J. Sprague; see "Electrical Operation of Water-tight Bulkhead Doors," EW 34 (Dec. 9, 1899): 895–96.
8. A. S. Crowninshield to Western Electric Co., Nov. 28, 1899, NARG 45, EL; Western Electric Co. to BUEQ, Apr. 29, 1901; BUEQ to Western Electric Co., May 9, 1901, NARG 80, Box 510. See Also Fiske to W. S. Sims, Feb. 2, 1904, William S. Sims Papers, MDLC; Fiske, *From Midshipman*, p. 342;

Fiske, "The Signal Question Once More," USNIP 29 (Mar. 1903): 221–24; Fiske, "The Fiske Semaphore System," *ibid.* 29 (Sept. 1903): 679–98; Fiske, "War Signals," *ibid.* 29 (Dec. 1903): 931–34.

9. ARSN, 1902, p. 80; ARSN, 1903, pp. 21, 315, 373–74; ARSN, 1905, p. 319; Fiske, *From Midshipman*, p. 377; "Favorable Navy Reports on Wireless Telegraphy," EW 34 (Nov. 25, 1899): 820; "Wireless Telegraphy," USNIP 29 (Mar. 1903): 301–6.

10. Fiske, *From Midshipman*, pp. 343–44; Fiske, "A Naval Telescope and Mount," USNIP 29 (Sept. 1903): 699–700.

11. Fiske, *From Midshipman*, pp. 344–45.

12. See, for example, Commanding Officer *Brooklyn* to BUORD, Oct. 17, 1901; Commanding Officer *New York* to BUORD, Jan. 1, 1902, forwarded to SECNAV via BUNAV. These and many other similar reports are in NARG 45, BG, Boxes 110 and 111.

13. Fiske, *From Midshipman*, pp. 346–47.

14. Sims to his mother, Apr. 3, Aug. 19, Sept. 17, 1901; Sims to Bowles, Chief Constructor, Sept. 24, 1901, Sims Papers; Elting E. Morison, *Admiral Sims and the Modern American Navy* (Boston: Houghton Mifflin, 1942), pp. 79–80, 96–97; Sims, "Scott's (British) Device for Practicing at Loading Rapid-Fire Guns," with various endorsements, Nov. 5, 1901, NARG 45, Box 108.

15. Morison, *Sims*, pp. 87–89.

16. The idea was provided by Albert L. Key in Key to Sims, Apr. 29, 1905; Sept. 29, 1919, Sims Papers.

17. Morison, *Sims*, pp. 101–5.

18. Sims Papers.

19. Sims, "The Board on Construction and the Design of Battleships," Dec. 8, 1901, *ibid.*

20. Report of the Chief of BUORD, in ARSN, 1902, pp. 536–38.

21. *Ibid.*

22. These papers, with endorsements, are in NARG 45.

23. Morison, *Sims*, pp. 121–22.

24. Sims to Chief BUNAV, Feb. 6, 1903, NARG 45.

25. Elting E. Morison, *Men, Machines, and Modern Times* (Cambridge, Mass.: M.I.T. Press, 1966), p. 32.

26. "Electrical Appliances Massachusetts," received by the BUEQ, Feb. 21, 1899, NARG 19, Entry 1218.

27. Morison, *Sims*, pp. 131–34.

28. Fiske in Discussion Section, USNIP 30 (June 1904): 422–24.

29. The routine appears inside the cover of the log of the *Minneapolis*, of which

Fiske took command on June 4, 1906, and cannot be much different from that followed on the *Massachusetts*.

30. Fiske, *From Midshipman*, pp. 351–52; RADM Albert Gleaves, USN, *Life and Letters of Rear Admiral Stephen B. Luce, USN: Founder of the Naval War College* (New York and London: G. P. Putnam's Sons, 1925), pp. 134–48.
31. ARSN, 1903, pp. 683–84; Fiske, *From Midshipman*, pp. 353–54.
32. Fiske, *From Midshipman*, p. 355.
33. ARSN, 1901, 2:513; ARSN, 1903, p. 403.
34. Sims to LT W. P. Scott, USN, Nov. 4, 1903, Sims Papers; Fiske, *From Midshipman*, p. 360.
35. ARSN, 1903, p. 679.
36. Fiske, *From Midshipman*, p. 357.
37. *Ibid.*, pp. 361–63; RADM S. B. Luce, "An Address Delivered at the U.S. Naval War College, Narragansett Bay, Rhode Island, June 2, 1903," USNIP 29 (June 1903): 537–46.
38. Fiske, *From Midshipman*, pp. 363–66.
39. Fiske to Chief BUORD, Apr. 10, 1895, copy in Sims Papers.
40. Fiske, *From Midshipman*, p. 378.
41. *Ibid.*, pp. 378–80.
42. Morison, *Sims*, pp. 135–36; see also ARSN, 1904, p. 492.
43. Correspondence with BUORD by Fiske, Sims, Evans, J. B. J. Thompson, and Bristol for 1904, NARG 74; Hood to Sims, July 17, 1905, Sims Papers; Evans to SECNAV, Mar. 1, 1904, NARG 74.
44. See, for example, Acting Chief BUORD to Commander Caribbean Squadron, Pensacola, Feb. 29, 1904, NARG 45, Box 111.
45. Report of Chief BUORD, ARSN, 1907, p. 484; Sims, "Roosevelt and the Navy," *McClure's Magazine*, Nov. 1922, p. 37.
46. Morison, *Sims*, pp. 142–43; Sims, "Training Ranges and Long-Range Firing," USNIP 30 (Sept. 1904): 511–31.
47. Fiske to Chief BUORD, June 11, 1904, NARG 74, Entry 25.
48. Chief BUORD to Fiske, June 20, 1904, *ibid.*
49. Chief BUORD to Fiske, Mar. 29, 1905, *ibid.*
50. Moody to Commanders-in-chief, Commanders of Squadrons, Commanding Officers of Vessels, Feb. 18, 1905, NARG 45, BG, Box 111.
51. ARSN, 1904, p. 569.
52. Mason to SECNAV, July 11, 1905; Mason to SECNAV through BUEQ and BUC&R, Oct. 25, 1905; Mason to SECNAV, Oct. 26, 1905; Capps to Mason, Nov. 3, 1905, NARG 74, Entry 257.
53. Confidential: Report of Gunnery Information Obtained During a Visit to

England, June 1905; Sims to Roosevelt (personal), July 25, 1905; Fiske to Sims, Aug. 3, 1905, Sims Papers.

54. Report of a Board Convened by Order of the Secretary of the Navy, Nov. 21, 1905, to Consider the Fire-Control System of Vessels of the U.S. Navy, Dec. 21, 1905, *ibid.*

55. Fiske to Sims, Dec. 23, 1905, *ibid.*

56. Fiske to Sims, Jan. 11, 1906, *ibid.*

57. Mason to Converse, May 5, 1906, *ibid.*

58. Sims to Roosevelt, Oct. 22, 1906, *ibid.*

CHAPTER 8

1. Fiske, *From Midshipman*, pp. 370–71.

2. John D. Long, *The New American Navy*, 2 vols. (New York: Outlook Co., 1903), 2:182–86.

3. H. C. Taylor to Stephen B. Luce, June 22, 1896, Stephen B. Luce Papers, MDLC; Poundstone to Sims, June 21, Oct. 1, 1904, William S. Sims Papers, MDLC; H. C. Taylor, "The Fleet," USNIP 29 (Dec. 1903): 803; Paul T. Heffron, "Secretary Moody and Naval Administrative Reform, 1902–1904," AN 29 (Jan. 1969): 30–53.

4. Fiske, "American Naval Policy," USNIP 31 (Jan. 1905): 1–103. The second prize article for 1903, RADM S. B. Luce, USN, "The Department of the Navy: Naval Administration, III," USNIP 29 (Mar. 1903): 81–96, was equally critical of naval administration.

5. Sims to Fiske, Feb. 17, 1905, Sims Papers.

6. Fiske to Sims, Feb. 25, 1905, *ibid.*

7. Fiske to Sims, Mar. 18, 1905, *ibid.*

8. Fiske to Sims, Mar. 22, 1905, *ibid.*

9. Fiske, "The Civil and the Military Authority," USNIP 32 (Mar. 1906): 127–30.

10. ARSN, 1904, p. 7; ARSN, 1905, pp. 3, 369–70.

11. Sims to Roosevelt, n.d. [late 1905], Sims Papers.

12. ARSN, 1906, pp. 3–6, 29–43.

13. Mildred Dewey, Diary, Jan. 6, 8, 20, 27, 1906, George Dewey Papers, MDLC.

14. Fiske, "The Civil and Military Authority."

15. Sims to Bonaparte, Aug. 7, 1905, Sims Papers; Elting E. Morison, *Admiral Sims and the Modern American Navy* (Boston: Houghton Mifflin, 1942), pp. 156–57; LT Homer C. Poundstone, USN, "Size of Battleships for U.S. Navy," USNIP 29 (Mar. 1903): 1611–74, and "Proposed Armament for Type Battleship of U.S. Navy with Some Suggestions Relative to Armor

Protection," *ibid*. 29 (June 1903): 377–412; Naval Constructor Richard D. Gatewood, USN, "Approximate Dimensions for a Compromiseless Ship," *ibid*. 32 (June 1906): 571–84.

16. Fiske, "Compromiseless Ships," USNIP 31 (Sept. 1905): 549–53; Fiske, "Why Togo Won," *ibid*. 31 (Dec. 1905): 807–9; Fiske, "The Stadimeter in Fire Conrol," *ibid*. 31 (Dec. 1905): 973–74.
17. Fiske to Sims, May 3, 8, 1907, Sims Papers.
18. Sims, Memorandum on Fiske's Work, 1904–1907, n.d. [early 1907], *ibid*.
19. In *From Midshipman*, p. 379, Fiske said he took command on 10 March; the log of the *Minneapolis* shows that he actually came on board on 4 June, NARG 24.
20. Fiske, *From Midshipman*, pp. 384–85.
21. Log, *Minneapolis*, June 3–Sept. 20, 1906; Fiske, "An Unprecedented Rescue," USNIP 37 (Dec. 1910): 947–64, reprinted in Fiske, *From Midshipman*, pp. 385–93.
22. Fiske, *From Midshipman*, p. 396; Yates Stirling, RADM, USN (RET), *Sea Duty: The Memoirs of a Fighting Admiral* (New York: G. P. Putnam's Sons, 1939), pp. 112–13.
23. Fiske, "Fleet Telephony," USNIP 33 (Mar. 1907): 239–42.
24. Fiske, *From Midshipman*, pp. 400–401.
25. *Ibid*., pp. 402–3; Fiske, "The Horizometer," USNIP 33 (Sept. 1906): 1043–55.
26. Fiske, *From Midshipman*, pp. 406–7.
27. *Ibid*., pp. 406–9.
28. *Ibid*., pp. 409–11.
29. Evans to Board on Fire Control, Apr. 27, 1909, NARG 74.
30. Fiske, "Courage and Prudence," USNIP 34 (Mar. 1908): 277–308. See also Fiske, "Spotting and Range-Finding," *ibid*. 34 (June 1908): 655–61; "A Curious Fact about Spotting," *ibid*. 34 (Dec. 1908): 1297–98; Fiske, *From Midshipman*, pp. 411–13.
31. Fiske, *From Midshipman*, pp. 413–15; see *Alleged Structural Defects in Battle Ships of United States Navy*, Sen. Doc. no. 506, 60th Cong., 1st Sess. (Washington: GPO, 1908).
32. Fiske, "The Naval Profession," USNIP 33 (June 1907): 475–578.
33. *Ibid*.
34. *Ibid*.
35. Henry Reuterdahl, "The Needs of the Navy," *McClure's Magazine* 30 (Jan. 1908): 261–63; Roosevelt to Truman Handy Newberry, Jan. 20, Feb. 16, 1909; Roosevelt to George Edmund Foss, Feb. 1, 1909, Theodore Roosevelt Papers, MDLC; Morison, *Sims*, pp. 176–200.
36. *New York Times*, Mar. 3, 1908, 2:2, 3.

37. See, for example, "The Effort for an Efficient Navy," WW 17 (Jan. 1909): 11708.

38. See U.S. Congress, Senate, *Hearings Before the Committee on Naval Affairs, United States Senate, on the Bill S. 335, 1908* (Washington: GPO, 1908), Morison, *Sims*, pp. 185–99; Gordon Carpenter O'Gara, *Theodore Roosevelt and the Rise of the Modern Navy* (Princeton: Princeton University Press, 1943), pp. 41–45; and the editorials entitled "The Administrative Organization of the Navy Department," ANL 13 (July 1908): 1–4; (Aug. 1908): 129–33; (Sept. 1908): 260–64; (Oct. 1908): 349–54; (Nov. 1908): 426–30.

39. Sims to Mrs. Sims, June 23, 26, 29, 1908, Sims Papers.

40. "Report of Newport Conference: Battleship Design," NARG 45, AD12, Box 17; Morison, *Sims*, pp. 201–14; R. D. Walter, "The Newport Conference," ANL 13 (Oct. 1908): 365–70.

41. ANJ, Dec. 5, 1908.

42. Morison, *Sims*, pp. 217–23.

CHAPTER 9

1. Fiske, "To Adjust Range Finders Before Battle," USNIP 34 (Sept. 1908): 1043–44.

2. Report of Fleet Ordnance Officer to Commander-in-Chief Atlantic Fleet, Manila, Nov. 2, 1908; LCDR Ridley McLean to Commander-in-Chief Atlantic Fleet, Dec. 20, 1908, NARG 45.

3. Fiske, *From Midshipman*, pp. 415–16.

4. *Ibid.*, pp. 418–19; Log, *Tennessee*, Jan. 4–Aug. 28, 1909, NARG 24.

5. Fiske, *From Midshipman*, p. 429.

6. *Ibid.*, pp. 429–30.

7. *Ibid.*, pp. 432–34.

8. Fiske, "The Invention and Development of the Naval Telescope Sight," USNIP 35 (June 1909): 405–7.

9. *Ibid.*, pp. 407–24; Fiske, *From Midshipman*, pp. 435–38.

10. ASECNAV, 5th endorsement on Sub *Tennessee*: Captain B. A. Fiske Report on a Board on Turret Range Finder, Jan. 29, 1909, GB Letters 5:0453; ASECNAV to BUORD, Feb. 25, Mar. 3, 1909, NARG 80; GB to Navy Department, Feb. 24, 1909, GB Letters 5:0454.

11. Fiske, *From Midshipman*, p. 441.

12. *Ibid.*, pp. 446–49.

13. *Ibid.*, pp. 449–54.

14. *Ibid.*, p. 455.

15. *Ibid.*, pp. 431, 435; Fiske, "A Simple Electric Steering Gear," USNIP 35 (Jan. 1909): 263–66.
16. GB to SECNAV, Jan. 6, 1909, GB Letters 5:0379.
17. Report of Fleet Ordnance Officer to Commander-in-Chief Atlantic Fleet, C. S. Sperry, Oct. 1, 1908, NARG 45; Chief BUEQ to Chief BUORD, Nov. 18, 1908; BUC&R to BUORD, Jan. 1, 1909, with endorsement of Secretary Metcalf, NARG 74.
18. Sims to the President, Jan. 2, 1909; Mahan to Roosevelt, Jan. 13, 1909 (copy), William S. Sims Papers, MDLC.
19. Elting E. Morison, *Admiral Sims and the Modern American Navy* (Boston: Houghton Mifflin, 1942), pp. 246–48.
20. Copy of Sims's record, Feb. 23, 1909, Sims Papers.
21. Fiske, *From Midshipman*, p. 469.
22. Fiske's duty with the Special Squadron is described in the log of the *Tennessee*, and in Fiske, *From Midshipman*, pp. 458–75.
23. Fiske, *From Midshipman*, p. 475.
24. President GB to SECNAV, Oct. 14, 1910, NHD:OA, GB Records.
25. Senior Member Present to SECNAV, June 24, 1910, *ibid.*; Chief BUORD, Memorandum for Aide for Material, Correspondence of the Chief of BUORD, n.d. [Nov. 23, 1912], NARG 74.
26. Sperry to E. E. Capehart, Chief BUORD, Sept. 23, 1910; Chief BUORD to Sperry, Oct. 19, 1910; Sperry to BUORD, Aug. 22, Sept. 24, 29, 1910, NARG 74.
27. Fiske, *From Midshipman*, p. 479.
28. SECNAV to President NWC, copy to President GB, Nov. 16, 1910, GB Letters 7: Serial 425.
29. President GB to SECNAV, Mar. 13, 1911, *ibid.* 7: Serial 420–22.
30. W. L. Rodgers, Memorandum, Sept. 14, 1912, Report of Special Committee on War Plans, Enclosure A of Rodgers to Meyer, Oct. 19, 1911, *ibid.*
31. Fiske, *From Midshipman*, p. 478.
32. Wainwright, "The General Board," USNIP 48 (Jan. 1922): 189.
33. Fiske, "The General Board," *ibid.* 48 (May 1922): 635.
34. Fiske, *From Midshipman*, pp. 481–82, 511–13; Fiske, "The Relative Importance of Turret and Telescope Sight," USNIP 38 (June 1912): 595–602.
35. Fiske, "Naval Power," USNIP 37 (Sept. 1911): 683–736.
36. *Ibid.*, pp. 683–702.
37. *Ibid.*, pp. 703–5.
38. *Ibid.*, pp. 712–14.
39. *Ibid.*, pp. 714–19.
40. Fiske, *From Midshipman*, pp. 482–87.
41. *Ibid.*, p. 492.

42. *Ibid.*, pp. 493–97; Knox to Meyer, State Department Decimal File 839.00/453, National Archives, Washington.
43. Fiske, *From Midshipman*, p. 505.
44. *Ibid.*, pp. 507–11.
45. *Ibid.*, p. 513.
46. Fiske, "The Mean Point of Impact," USNIP 38 (Sept. 1912): 1001–36.
47. Fiske, *From Midshipman*, pp. 513–15.
48. *New York Times*, Oct. 13, 1912, VIII, 1.
49. Fiske, *From Midshipman*, p. 525.

CHAPTER 10

1. Organization of the Navy Department, Reports of the Swift Board, Oct. 11, 1909, NHD:OA GB Records, File 446; Wayne August Wiegand, "Patrician in the Progressive Era: A Biography of George von Lengerke Meyer" (Ph.D. diss., Southern Illinois University, 1974), pp. 239–52.
2. Sims to S. B. Luce, Dec. 13, 1909, William S. Sims Papers, MDLC; see also LCDR Needham L. Jones, USN, "Details of Navy Department Administration: Navy Department Policies," USNIP 40 (Mar.–Apr. 1914): 377–78; Weigand, "Meyer," p. 258.
3. Dewey to Hon. George Loud, House of Representatives, Jan. 31, 1910, George Dewey Papers, MDLC; see also Sims to Ridley McLean, June 6, Dec. 17, 1910, Sims Papers; "Secretary Meyer's Plan for the Reorganization of the Navy," SA 102 (Feb. 19, 1910): 158, "The Meyer Reorganization to Have a Fair Trial," *ibid.* 102 (Mar. 26, 1910): 254; Wiegand, "Meyer," pp. 258–67.
4. Sims to Ridley McLean, June 6, 1910, Sims Papers.
5. Fiske, Diary, Jan. 6, Feb. 8, 11, 1913. I have been able to locate only three of the great number of notebooks in which Fiske wrote his diary. One, covering the period Jan. 6, 1913, to Sept. 25, 1914, is in the Naval Academy Archives. The other two, covering the periods September 26, 1914, to March 5, 1917, and March 6, 1917, to September 18, 1918, respectively, are in the Manuscript Division, Library of Congress. Citations to the diaries will be made simply by date.
6. Sims to Fullam, Feb. 17, 1913, Sims Papers.
7. Jones to Albert Gleaves, Dec. 9, 1913, Albert Gleaves Papers, MDLC.
8. SECNAV to Aide for Operations, Personnel, Material, Inspections, Feb. 10, 1913 (copy to Dewey), Dewey Papers.
9. GB Proceedings, GB Records (hereafter cited as GB Proc.), Feb. 25, 1913, 5:31, 33.

10. "The Arkansas and Wyoming," SA 101 (Feb. 4, 1911): 114; "How Naval Guns Are Aimed," LD 49 (Sept. 26, 1914): 573; LCDR Thomas T. Craven, USN, "Hitting the Bull's Eye at Six Miles: Target Practice in the United States Navy," SA 109 (Feb. 14, 1914): 143–44.
11. Thomas T. Craven to Sims, Mar. 13, 1914 (two letters); Sims to Craven, Mar. 24, 1914, Sims Papers.
12. Daniels, Diary, Mar. 5, 1913, Josephus Daniels Papers, MDLC.
13. Fiske, Diary, Jan. 6, Mar. 5, 1913.
14. *Ibid.*, Mar. 5, 1913; Fiske, *From Midshipman*, pp. 530–31.
15. As recorded in Fiske, *From Midshipman*, p. 531.
16. Needham Jones to Gleaves, Apr. 4, 1914, Gleaves Papers.
17. Daniels to Wilson, Mar. (?), 1913, Daniels Papers; *Washington Post*, Mar. 11, Apr. 7, 11, 13, 14, 1913; ARSN, 1914, p. 9.
18. Dewey to the President, Apr. 11, 1913, Daniels to Dewey, Apr. 12, 1913, Wilson to Dewey, Apr. 16, 1913, Dewey Papers.
19. Fiske, Diary, Apr. 13, 1913; Fiske, *From Midshipman*, pp. 531–32.
20. Daniels to J. J. Adkins, May 27, 1913, Daniels Papers; "Making Over Our Sea Language," *The Nation* 96 (Apr. 24, 1913): 406–7.
21. Fiske, Diary, June 1, 1913.
22. Sims to Fullam, Mar. 21, 1913; Sims to Mrs. Sims, Apr. 15, 16, May 13, 1913; Sims to Fiske, June 30, 1913; Fiske to Sims, July 3, 1913, Sims Papers.
23. Fiske, Diary, June 24, 1913.
24. Elting E. Morison, *Admiral Sims and the Modern American Navy* (Boston: Houghton Mifflin, 1942), p. 285.
25. Yates Stirling, RADM, USN (RET), *Sea Duty: The Memoirs of a Fighting Admiral* (New York: G. P. Putnam's Sons, 1939), p. 133; see also *ibid.*, pp. 134–39.
26. ARSN, 1914, pp. 6–35.
27. Fiske, Diary, July 1, 1913.
28. Fiske to Daniels, Aug. 6, 1913, Daniels Papers.
29. Fiske, Diary, Aug. 1, 1913; Daniels to Fiske, Aug. 13, 1913, Daniels Papers.
30. GB Proc., Aug. 15, 1913, 5:145–46.
31. Fiske, Diary, Aug. 26, Sept. 7, 14, 15, 18, 19, 21, 22, 25, Oct. 1, 1913.
32. Fiske to Daniels, Aug. 22, 1913, Daniels Papers; Fiske to SECNAV, Aug. 26, 1913 (with enclosures), NARG 80.
33. Daniels to Fiske, Aug. 25, 1913, Daniels Papers.
34. Fiske to Church, Sept. 8, 1913, William C. Church Papers, MDLC.
35. Fiske, Diary, July 9, 1914; Josephus Daniels, "Training Our Bluejackets for Peace," IND 76 (Dec. 11, 1913): 490–92.
36. Frederick S. Harrod, "Enlisted Men in the United States Navy, 1899–1939" (Ph.D. diss., Northwestern University, 1973), p. 131.

37. Fullam to Daniels, Apr. 24, 1914; Fullam to Ridgely Hunt, Nov. 29, 1914, William F. Fullam Papers, MDLC.
38. "Aeronautics and Aviation in 1912," SA 108 (Jan. 11, 1913): 30; "Aviation Prophesy by Diagram," LD 46 (Feb. 1, 1913): 228.
39. Fiske to SECNAV, July 16, 1913, F. D. Roosevelt, Acting SECNAV, to GB, July 16, 1913, NARG 80; Secretary GB to Aide for Operations, July 31, 1913, GB Records.
40. CAPT W. I. Chambers, USN (RET), Memorandum re: "Aeronautics," Aug. 8, 1913, GB Records; Donald B. Duncan and H. M. Dater, "Administrative History of U.S. Naval Aviation," *Air Affairs: An International Quarterly* 1 (Summer 1947): 526–27.
41. GB Proc., Aug. 19, 22, 26, 1913, 5:147, 148, 150–51; Aid for Operations to SECNAV, July 16, 1913, with first endorsement by Acting SECNAV, GB to SECNAV, second endorsement on "Aid for Operations re development of airships for naval use," GB Proc., Aug. 30, 1913; President GB to SECNAV, Aug. 30, 1913, GB Records.
42. Fiske, Diary, Dec. 31, 1913; Archibald Turnbull, CAPT, USNR, and Clifford L. Lord, LCDR, USN, *History of United States Naval Aviation* (New Haven: Yale University Press, 1949), pp. 36–37.
43. Fiske to Church, Jan. 27, 1914 (with enclosure), Church Papers; "Reorganization of the Navy Personnel," SA 108 (Mar. 29, 1913): 282.
44. Fiske, Diary, May 12, 13, 1914; ARSN, 1914, pp. 144–45.
45. Daniels to Padgett, Feb. 20, 1914 (with enclosure), NARG 80.
46. Fiske, Diary, Mar. 8, 1914.
47. U.S. Congress, House, *Hearings before the Committee on Naval Affairs . . . , Sixty-fourth Congress, First Session, on Estimates Submitted by the Secretary of the Navy*, 3 vols. (Washington: GPO, 1916), 3:3621–23.
48. Frank Friedel, *Franklin D. Roosevelt: The Apprenticeship* (Boston: Little, Brown, 1952), pp. 221–22; Fiske, *From Midshipman*, pp. 577–78.
49. Kenneth S. Davis, *FDR: The Beckoning of Destiny, 1882–1928: A History* (New York: G. P. Putnam's Sons, 1971), pp. 310–11; Friedel, *Roosevelt*, pp. 90, 160–62, 172.
50. Fiske, Diary, May 21, 22, 26, 1914; GB Proc., May 22, 1914, 6:93.
51. Aid for Operations to SECNAV, May 27, 1914, NARG 80; Fiske, Diary, May 29, 1914.
52. Fiske, Diary, June 4, 1914.
53. *Ibid.*
54. Fletcher to Daniels, Jan. 13, 1914; telegram, Daniels to Fletcher, June 14, 1917, Daniels Papers; Fiske, Diary, June 4, 15, 18, 20, 1914.
55. Fiske to Fletcher, June 18, 1914 (copy), Dewey Papers.
56. Fiske, Diary, July 20, 1914; Fiske, *From Midshipman*, p. 545.

CHAPTER 11

1. Paolo E. Coletta, " 'The Most Thankless Task': Bryan and The California Alien Land Legislation," PHR 36 (May 1967): 163–87; "California Pertinax," IND 74 (Apr. 10, 1913): 792–93.
2. Bradley A. Fiske, Diary, Apr. 29, 1913.
3. *Ibid.*, Apr. 30, 1913.
4. NHD:OA, GB Records, Serial No. 425; GB Proc., May 6, 7, 1913, 5:88, 90; Fullam, Memorandum, 1913, William F. Fullam Papers, MDLC; Kenneth S. Davis, *FDR: The Beckoning of Destiny, 1882–1928: A History* (New York: G. P. Putnam's Sons, 1971), pp. 332–33.
5. Fiske to Daniels, May 13, 1913 (copy), Franklin D. Roosevelt Papers, MDLC; Fiske, Memorandum for SECNAV, May 14, 1913 (copy), Josephus Daniels Papers, MDLC.
6. Daniels, Diary, May 13, 1913, Daniels Papers; Leonard Wood, Diary, May 13, 1913, Leonard Wood Papers, MDLC; Frank Friedel, *Franklin D. Roosevelt: The Apprenticeship* (Boston: Little, Brown, 1952), pp. 223–24.
7. Aid for Operations to SECNAV, May 14, 1913 (copy), Daniels Papers.
8. Josephus Daniels, *The Wilson Era: Years of Peace, 1910–1917* (Chapel Hill: University of North Carolina Press, 1944), pp. 330–31; Davis, *FDR*, pp. 330–31; David F. Houston, *Eight Years with Wilson's Cabinet*, 2 vols. (Garden City, N.Y.: Doubleday, Page, 1926), 1:66. Leonard Wood's diary entry for May 16 reads in part: "Apparently Bryan and Daniels are against any degree of military preparedness whatever, and do not realize in any way the possible gravity of the situation, and the great disadvantage of failure to take reasonable precautions."
9. Fiske, Diary, July 18, 1913.
10. GB Proc., Aug. 26, Sept. 30, Oct. 28, Nov. 5, 1913, Mar. 31, Nov. 14, 1914, 5:156, 177, 198, 212, 225, 6:57.
11. *Ibid.*, Nov. 8, Dec. 4, 9, 1913, 5:234–38.
12. Jones to Gleaves, Nov. 25, 1914, Albert Gleaves Papers, MDLC.
13. Fiske, Diary, Feb. 2, 1913; Herman Hagedorn, *Leonard Wood: A Biography*, 2 vols. (New York and London: Harper and Brothers, 1931), 2:127–28; Paolo E. Coletta, *The Presidency of William Howard Taft* (Lawrence: University Press of Kansas, 1973), pp. 175–81.
14. See "What Are We Doing in Mexico?" IND 78 (May 4, 1914): 193–94.
15. Fiske, Diary, Feb. 22, Mar. 26, 1913.
16. Fiske to Sims, Nov. 18, 1913, Mar. 24, June 22, 1914; Sims to Fiske, Feb. 19, Sept. 2, 1914, William S. Sims Papers, MDLC.
17. Fletcher to Daniels, Feb. 4, 1914, Daniels Papers; Sims to Mrs. Sims, Nov. 17, Dec. 18, 1913, Sims Papers; Yates Stirling, RADM, USN (RET), *Sea Duty:*

The Memoirs of a Fighting Admiral (New York: G. P. Putnam's Sons, 1939), p. 146.

18. Fiske, Diary, Oct. 1, 1913; Lind to Bryan, Oct. 9, 10, 1913, William Jennings Bryan Papers, MDLC.
19. Leonard Wood, Diary, Oct. 15, 1913, Wood Papers; Hagedorn, *Wood,* 2:136.
20. Fiske to Church, William C. Church Papers, MDLC.
21. Fiske, Diary, Oct. 19, 1914; Hagedorn, *Wood,* 2:137.
22. Fiske, Diary, Nov. 5, 1913.
23. *Ibid.,* Nov. 26, 1913.
24. *Ibid.,* Jan. 9, 1914; Hagedorn, *Wood,* 2:139–40.
25. Fiske, Diary, Jan. 16, 1914.
26. *Ibid.,* Feb. 8, 1914.
27. *Ibid.,* Feb. 15, 1914.
28. Mayo to Zaragoza, Apr. 9, 1914, NARG 45; Fletcher to Daniels, Apr. 11, 1914, State Department Decimal File 812.00/1198, National Archives; Clarence A. Miller, American Consul at Tampico, "Political Conditions at Tampico including Repulsed Attack on Constitutionalists in April, the Tampico Flag Incident, Capture of Tampico, Exodus of Americans, etc.," n.d. [Apr. 1914], State Department Decimal File 812.00/12346.
29. Bryan to Wilson, Apr. 10, 1914, Woodrow Wilson Papers, MDLC; Fiske, Diary, Apr. 12, 1914.
30. Fiske, Diary, Apr. 13, 1914; see also Aid for Operations to SECNAV, Apr. 13, 1914 (2 letters), Wilson Papers.
31. Daniels to Wilson, Apr. 13, 1914, Wilson Papers; Fiske, Diary, Apr. 14, 1914; Robert E. Quirk, *An Affair of Honor: Woodrow Wilson and the Occupation of Veracruz* (Lexington: University of Kentucky Press, 1962), pp. 53–57.
32. Fiske, Diary, Apr. 14, 1914.
33. *New York Times,* Apr. 19, 1914, 1:5–6.
34. Dewey to Daniels, Apr. 18, 1914, NHD:OA, GB Records, File 425; GB Proc., Apr. 19, 1914; Richard D. Challener, *Admirals, Generals, and American Foreign Policy, 1898–1914* (Princeton: Princeton University Press, 1973), pp. 391–92.
35. Fiske, Diary, Apr. 19, 1914; Sims to Mrs. Sims, Apr. 19, 1914, Sims Papers.
36. Fiske, Diary, Apr. 20, 1914.
37. Wood, Diary, Apr. 20, 1914.
38. Fiske, Diary, Apr. 20, 1914.
39. Canada to Bryan, Apr. 21, 1914, State Department Decimal File 812.00/11564; *New York Times,* Apr. 21, 1914, 1:1–4.
40. Daniels to Fletcher, Apr. 21, 1914, Daniels Papers; Canada to Bryan, Apr. 21, 1914, State Department Decimal File 812.00/11594; Fiske, Diary, Apr. 21, 1914.

41. Fiske, Diary, Apr. 21, 1914.
42. *Ibid.*, Apr. 22, 1914.
43. *Ibid.*, Apr. 23, 1914.
44. *Ibid.*
45. *Ibid.*, Apr. 25, 1914.
46. Wilson to Dr. M. W. Jacobus, Apr. 29, 1914, in Ray Stannard Baker, *Woodrow Wilson: Life and Letters*, 8 vols. (Garden City, N.Y.: Doubleday, Page, 1927–39), 4:335.
47. Fiske, Diary, Apr. 26, 1914.
48. *Ibid.*, May 2, 1914.
49. *Ibid.*, May 12, 1914.
50. *Ibid.*, May 18, 20, 29, 1914.
51. *Ibid.*, June 2, 3, 5, 1914.
52. *Ibid.*, June 14, 1914.
53. "Our Evacuation of Veracruz," LD 49 (Dec. 15, 1914): 1104–5.
54. Fiske, Diary, May 6, 1914.
55. *Ibid.*, May 23, 1914.
56. *Ibid.*, June 2, 1914.
57. *Ibid.*, July 1, 1914; see also July 2, 21, 1914.
58. *Ibid.*, July 12, 1914.
59. F. D. Roosevelt to "Dearest Babs" (Mrs. Roosevelt), July 14, 1914, in Elliott Roosevelt, ed., *F.D.R.: His Personal Letters*, 4 vols. (New York: Duell, Sloan and Pearce, 1947–50), 2:223; Bryan to Wilson, July 18, 1914, Wilson Papers.
60. Paolo E. Coletta, *William Jennings Bryan*, vol. 2, *Progressive Politician and Moral Statesman, 1909–1915* (Lincoln: University of Nebraska Press, 1969), p. 202.
61. Fiske, Diary, July 25, 1914.
62. Bryan to Wilson, Jan. 7, 1915, Bryan Papers; Wilson to Bryan, Wilson Papers, Jan. 13, 1915, Wilson Papers.
63. Coletta, *William Jennings Bryan*, 2:336–44.
64. *Ibid.*, 2:207–8.

CHAPTER 12

1. NHD:OA, GB Proc., Aug. 1, 1914, 6:147–48, Aid for Operations to SECNAV (Operations), Aug. 1, 1914, Senior Member Present, GB, to SECNAV, Aug. 1, 1914, Knight to Dewey, Aug. 1, 1914, GB 420-1.
2. Fiske, Diary, Aug. 4, 1914.
3. *Ibid.*, Aug. 5, 7, 1914.

4. *Ibid.*, Aug. 5, 1914.
5. *Ibid.*, Aug. 6, 1914.
6. *Ibid.*, Aug. 9, 1914.
7. *Ibid.*, Aug. 7, 1914.
8. *Ibid.*, Aug. 12–14, 17, 1914.
9. *Ibid.*, Aug. 18, 19, 1914.
10. *Ibid.*, Aug. 26, 1914; Fiske, *From Midshipman*, pp. 547–48; Warner R. Schilling, "Admirals and Foreign Policy, 1913–1919" (Ph.D. diss., Yale University, 1954), pp. 80–83.
11. Elliott Roosevelt, ed., *FDR: His Personal Letters*, 4 vols. (New York: Duell, Sloan and Pearce, 1947–50), 2:233.
12. Roosevelt to Mrs. Roosevelt, *ibid.*, 2:238.
13. GB Proc., Sept. 8, 9, 1914, 6:161, 162; LCDR Zachariah Madison, Memorandum to GB, Sept. 8, 1914, GB 420-1; Kenneth S. Davis, *FDR: The Beckoning of Destiny, 1882–1928: A History* (New York: G. P. Putnam's Sons, 1971), pp. 375–76; Frank Friedel, *Franklin D. Roosevelt: The Apprenticeship* (Boston: Little, Brown, 1952), pp. 237–38; Roosevelt, *FDR: Letters*, 2:238.
14. Fiske, Diary, Sept. 1, 1914.
15. *Ibid.*, Sept. 8, 1914.
16. *Ibid.*, Sept. 9, 1914; GB Proc., Sept. 9, 1914, 6:162; Senior Member Present, GB, to SECNAV, Sept. 9, 1914, GB 420-1.
17. Fiske, *From Midshipman*, p. 550.
18. Fiske, Diary, Sept. 9, 1914; Organization and Operation of the Fleet, Sept. 16, 1914, GB 420.
19. Fiske, Diary, Sept. 15, 1914.
20. GB Proc., Sept. 18, 1914, 6:169.
21. Fiske, Diary, Sept. 26, 1914.
22. *Ibid.*, Sept. 18, 1914; Personnel of the Navy and Marine Corps, Aug. 7, 1914, GB 421.
23. Fiske, Diary, Sept. 28, 1914.
24. *Ibid.*, Sept. 29, 1914.
25. *Ibid.*
26. *Ibid.*, Oct. 2, 1914.
27. GB Proc., Oct. 1, 1914, 6:193–94.
28. Fiske, Diary, Oct. 6–9, 1914.
29. Ray Stannard Baker, *Woodrow Wilson: Life and Letters*, 8 vols. (Garden City, N.Y.: Doubleday, Page, 1927–39), 6:47; Charles Seymour, ed., *The Intimate Papers of Colonel House*, 4 vols. (Boston: Houghton Mifflin, 1926–28), 1:434–35, 2:1, 13; William W. Tinsley, "The American Preparedness Movement, 1913–1916" (Ph.D. diss., Stanford University, 1939), pp. 1–3, 7,

45–46; "The Armament Flurry in Congress," *The Nation* 100 (Jan. 21, 1915): 71.
30. Daniels, Diary, Jan. 24, 1915, Josephus Daniels Papers, MDLC.
31. "Our Unpreparedness for War," LD 49 (Oct. 31, 1914): 835–36; "The National Security Commission," SA 110 (Dec. 12, 1914): 486; "Hysteria and Common Sense," *ibid.* 110 (Dec. 19, 1914): 502.
32. Fiske, Diary, Oct. 18, 1914.
33. Josephus Daniels, *The Wilson Era: Years of Peace, 1910–1917* (Chapel Hill: University of North Carolina Press, 1946), p. 243.
34. Fiske, Diary, Oct. 23, 1914.
35. *Ibid.,* Oct. 21, 1914.
36. *Ibid.,* Oct. 21–22, 1914: E. H. Campbell to Fiske, Oct. 22, 1914, GB 420.
37. Fiske, Diary, Oct. 22, 1914; Fiske, *From Midshipman*, p. 553.
38. Fiske, Diary, Oct. 24, 1914.
39. Fiske, *From Midshipman*, p. 553; see also James Hewes, with commentary by Edward M. Coffman, "The United States Army General Staff, 1900–1917," MA 38 (Apr. 1974): 67–72.
40. Fiske, Diary, Oct. 26, 1914.
41. Fiske to Church, Oct. 27, 1914 (with enclosure), William C. Church Papers, MDLC.
42. Fiske, Diary, Oct. 29, 1914; Fiske, *From Midshipman*, p. 553.
43. Fiske, Diary, Oct. 31, 1914.
44. *Ibid.,* Nov. 3, 1914.
45. *Ibid.,* Nov. 5, 1914.
46. Daniels to Dewey, Nov. 4, 1914, Daniels Papers; GB Proc., Nov. 4, 1914, 6:222–24.
47. Fiske to Daniels, Nov. 9, 1914, in Fiske, *From Midshipman*, pp. 556–60.
48. Fiske, Diary, Nov. 5, 1914.
49. *Ibid.,* Nov. 7, 1914.
50. GB to Aid for Operations, Nov. 9, 1914, GB 420-1.
51. GB Proc., Nov. 10, 1914, 6:231–32.
52. Fiske, Diary, Nov. 10, 1914.
53. *Ibid.*
54. GB to SECNAV, Nov. 11, 1914, GB 421.
55. Fiske, Diary, Nov. 12, 1914.
56. GB Proc., Nov. 11, 12, 1914, 6:235–36.
57. *Ibid.,* Nov. 13, 1914, 6:238–39.
58. *Ibid.,* Nov. 16, 1914, 6:240.
59. *Ibid.,* Nov. 17, 1914, 6:244.
60. Fiske, Diary, Nov. 11, 1914.
61. Dewey to SECNAV, Nov. 17, 1914, GB 420-2.

62. Fiske, Memorandum for the General Board, Nov. 25, 1914, GB 420-2; GB Proc., Nov. 27, 1914, 6:254.
63. Yates Stirling, RADM, USN (RET), *Sea Duty: The Memoirs of a Fighting Admiral* (New York: G. P. Putnam's Sons, 1939), p. 158.
64. Fiske, *From Midshipman*, p. 550.
65. *Ibid.*, pp. 651–52.
66. Fiske, Diary, Dec. 8, 1914; Fiske, *From Midshipman*, p. 562.
67. ARSN, 1914, p. 52; Fiske, *From Midshipman*, p. 571.
68. Fiske, *From Midshipman*, p. 571.
69. U.S. Congress, House, Committee on Naval Affairs, *Hearings before the Committee on Naval Affairs of the House of Representatives, on Estimates Submitted by the Secretary of the Navy, 1915* (Washington: GPO, 1915), pp. 34–37, 281, 288.
70. *Ibid.*, p. 482.
71. *Ibid.*, p. 554.
72. *Ibid.*, pp. 560–61.
73. *Ibid.*, pp. 572–722.
74. Daniels to Fletcher, telegram, Dec. 15, 1914, Daniels Papers.
75. Fiske, Diary, Dec. 15, 1914; *Hearings, 1915*, pp. 921–95. Because of its wartime shipbuilding program, France ranked third in naval tonnage and the United States fourth. See "United States Navy Fourth in Tonnage," SA 112 (Feb. 6, 1915): 117; see also "The Navy—Our First Line of Defense: The Fleet as Authorized by Congress Far Below that Deemed Necessary by Its Naval Advisers," *ibid.* 112 (Feb. 6, 1915): 121–23.
76. Fiske, Diary, Dec. 12, 1914.
77. *Ibid.*, Dec. 16, 1914; Fiske, *From Midshipman*, pp. 563–64.
78. *Hearings, 1915*, pp. 999–1047.
79. *Ibid.*, pp. 1059–83.
80. Editorial, "Unexpected Testimony," *New York Times*, Dec. 18, 1914, 12:2.
81. Fiske, *From Midshipman*, p. 571; see also "Turning the Searchlight on the Navy's Flaws," LD 50 (Jan. 2, 1915): 1–3.

CHAPTER 13

1. U.S. Congress, House, Committee on Naval Affairs, *Hearings before the Committee on Naval Affairs of the House of Representatives, on Estimates Submitted by the Secretary of the Navy*, 3 vols. (Washington: GPO, 1915), 2:2911; *New York Sun*, Dec. 19, 1914, quoted in LD 50 (Jan. 2, 1915): 1–3; "Admiral Fiske's Opinion of Our Navy," ANJ 52 (Dec. 19, 1914): 502–3; "Deficiencies of our Navy," *ibid.* 52 (Jan. 9, 1915): 585–86.

2. Fiske, Diary, Dec. 21, 1914.
3. *Ibid.*, Dec. 25, 27, 28, 1914.
4. *Ibid.*, Dec. 29, 1914.
5. *New York Times*, Feb. 1, 16, 25, 1914; Walter E. Pittman, "Richmond P. Hobson: Crusader" (Ph.D. diss., University of Georgia, 1967), pp. 2–5, 12–14, 91, 101–4.
6. Fiske, Diary, Jan. 2, 1915.
7. *Ibid.*, Jan. 3, 1915.
8. *Ibid.*, Jan. 4, 1915.
9. *Ibid.*, Jan. 6, 1915.
10. *Ibid.*
11. William S. Sims Papers, MDLC.
12. *Ibid.*
13. Victor Blue, Acting, by direction of the Secretary, to Admiral of the Navy, Jan. 23, 1915, George Dewey Papers, MDLC.
14. Daniels to Fletcher, telegram, Jan. 23, 1915; Fletcher to Daniels, telegram, Jan. 26, 1915, Josephus Daniels Papers, MDLC.
15. Fiske, Diary, Jan. 9, 1915.
16. *Ibid.*, Jan. 28, 1915; "Navy Deficiency Told by Head of War College and Superintendent at Annapolis," *New York Times*, Jan. 26, 1915, 8:5.
17. Daniels, Diary, Jan. 26, 1915.
18. GB Proc., Oct. 28, Dec. 30, 1913, Mar. 31, June 23, Nov. 3, Dec. 29, 1914, Jan. 5, 19, 22, 1915, 5:198, 254, 6:130, 226, 270, 7:1, 6, 11.
19. *Ibid.*, Jan. 25, 26, 28, 1915, 7:15, 16, 24; Daniels to Dewey, Jan. 25, 1915, Daniels Papers; Fiske, Diary, Jan. 30, 1915; Fiske, *From Midshipman*, p. 572.
20. GB Proc., Jan. 30, Feb. 1, 2, 3, 6, 1915, 7:25, 29, 31, 36; Fiske, Diary, Feb. 6, 1915; Fiske, *From Midshipman*, pp. 572–73.
21. Fiske, Diary, Feb. 19, 1915; Fiske, *From Midshipman*, p. 575; Daniels to Swanson and Padgett, Feb. 19, 1915, NARG 80.
22. Fiske, *From Midshipman*, p. 575.
23. Fiske, Diary, Feb. 27, 1915.
24. Fiske, *From Midshipman*, p. 576.
25. *Ibid.*, pp. 569–70.
26. GB Proc., Mar. 5, 1915, 7:66.
27. Fiske, Diary, Mar. 7, 8, 1915.
28. Fletcher to Daniels, Mar. 20, 1915, Daniels Papers.
29. Sims to Mrs. Sims, Jan. 14, 1915, Sims Papers.
30. Knox to Sims, Mar. 10, 1915, *ibid.*
31. Knox to Sims, Feb. 16, 1915, *ibid.*
32. Fiske, *From Midshipman*, p. 577.
33. Dewey to SECNAV, Mar. 13, 1915, GB Records, no. 425, approved by Dan-

iels; GB Proc., Mar. 30, 1915, 7:91; Fiske, *From Midshipman*, p. 578.

34. Fiske, *From Midshipman*, pp. 578–79; copies of Fiske's two papers are in the William C. Church Papers, MDLC.
35. Fiske, *From Midshipman*, p. 579.
36. Fiske, Diary, Mar. 24, 1915.
37. Fiske, *From Midshipman*, pp. 580–81.
38. Fiske to Church, n.d. [probably early 1915], Church Papers.
39. ARSN, 1915, pp. 9–11; see Henry Beers, "The Development of the Office of the Chief of Naval Operations," MA 10 (Spring 1946): 40–68; *ibid*. 10 (Fall 1946): 10–38.
40. Sims to Mrs. Sims, Mar. 7, 1915, Sims Papers.
41. Fiske, Diary, Apr. 1, 1915.
42. *Ibid.*, Apr. 7–10, 1915.
43. *New York Times*, Apr. 11, 1915, 1:3.
44. *Ibid.*, Apr. 3, 1915, 1:1; Apr. 4, 1915, II, 12:4.
45. *Ibid.*, Apr. 4, 1915, III, 2:3; IV, 15:1.
46. Fiske, *From Midshipman*, pp. 581–83.
47. Sims to Mrs. Sims, Apr. 4, 1915, Sims Papers.
48. Cone to Sims, Friday (?), *ibid*.
49. Sims to Mrs. Sims, Apr. 13, 1915, *ibid*.
50. Fiske, Diary, Apr. 19, 1915; Fiske, *From Midshipman*, p. 584.
51. Fiske, Diary, Apr. 24, 1915.
52. Cronan to Sims, Apr. 22, 1915, Sims Papers.
53. [Elting E. Morison, ed.], *Naval Administration: Selected Documents on Navy Department Organization, 1914–1940* (Washington: Navy Department, 1945?), sect. II, p. 3.
54. McLean to Sims, Apr. 29, 1915, Sims Papers.
55. McLean to Fiske, Apr. 29, 1915, *ibid*.
56. Ernest J. King and Walter Muir Whitehill, *Fleet Admiral King: A Naval Record* (New York: Norton, 1952), p. 103.
57. Albert Gleaves Papers, MDLC.
58. Fiske, *From Midshipman*, p. 585.
59. *Ibid.*
60. BUORD to Navy Department, through BUC&R, July 16, 1915, NARG 19, Correspondence re Ships, 1916–1925.
61. U.S. Congress, Senate, *Hearings Before the Subcommittee of the Committee on Naval Affairs United States Senate*, 66th Cong., 2nd Sess., 2 vols. (Washington: GPO, 1921): 2:2741–44.
62. Fiske, Diary, May 11, 1915; Fiske, *From Midshipman*, pp. 585–86.
63. Burton J. Hendrick, "The Case of Josephus Daniels," WW 32 (1916): 281–96.
64. Roosevelt to "Dearest Babs," Nov. 9, 1916, in Elliott Roosevelt, ed., *FDR:*

His Personal Letters, 4 vols. (New York: Duell, Sloan and Pearce, 1947–50), 2:339.

65. Fiske, Diary, May 17, 1915.
66. Fiske, *From Midshipman,* pp. 587–88.
67. *Ibid.,* p. 588.
68. Fiske, Diary, May 21, 1915.
69. Roosevelt to Eleanor, Roosevelt, *FDR: Letters,* 2:270.
70. Sims to Cone, June 9, 1915, Sims Papers.
71. Frank Friedel, *Franklin D. Roosevelt: The Apprenticeship* (Boston: Little, Brown, 1952), pp. 251–52.

CHAPTER 14

1. Fiske, Diary, June 1, 1915.
2. Sims to Mrs. Sims, June 21, 1915, William S. Sims Papers, MDLC.
3. Sims to Mrs. Sims, Oct. 21, 1915, *ibid.*
4. *New York Times,* June 4, 1915, 1:3.
5. See, for example, Sims to Fiske, June 10, 1915, Sims Papers; editorial, *New York Times,* June 5, 1915, 8:1.
6. Church to Fiske, June 9, 1915; Fiske to Church, June 12, 1915, William C. Church Papers, MDLC.
7. Fiske to Church, June 16, 1915, *ibid.*
8. Fiske, Diary, June 13, 1915.
9. *Ibid.,* July 6–10, 1915; Fiske, *From Midshipman,* pp. 590–91.
10. Daniels to Fiske, Mar. 13, 1915, NARG 80.
11. Fiske, Diary, Dec. 5, 1915.
12. See, for example, "Rehabilitating the United States Navy," SA 113 (Oct. 30, 1915): 374.
13. Daniels to GB, Oct. 7, 1915, President GB to SECNAV, Oct. 12, 1915, GB 420-2.
14. See, for example, "The Insanity of Preparedness: An Interview with Congressman Kitchen," IND 84 (Nov. 20, 1915): 466–48; Arthur Capper, "The West and Preparedness," *ibid.* 85 (Jan. 10, 1916): 49–50.
15. Paolo E. Coletta, *William Jennings Bryan,* vol. 3, *Political Puritan, 1915–1925* (Lincoln: University of Nebraska Press, 1969), pp. 14–18; "The Defense Program Sagging," LD 52 (Jan. 16, 1916): 219–20; "President Rousing the Nation for Preparedness," *ibid.* (Feb. 5, 1916): 269–70.
16. Fiske, "Naval Strategy," USNIP 42 (Mar.–Apr. 1916): 387–408.
17. See editorial, "An Efficient Navy," *New York Times,* Dec. 4, 1915, 14:4.
18. Fiske, Diary, Dec. 25, 1915; Fiske, *From Midshipman,* pp. 595–96.

19. Fiske, Diary, Jan. 1, 1916.
20. *New York Times,* Jan. 5, 1916, 24:2.
21. Fiske, Diary, Jan. 6, 1916.
22. *New York Times,* Jan. 12, 1916, 4:4.
23. Fiske, Diary, Jan. 16, 1916.
24. *Ibid.,* Jan. 18, 1916.
25. *Ibid.,* Mar. 13, 1916; Fiske, *From Midshipman,* pp. 598–99.
26. Padgett to Daniels, Dec. 13, 1915; Daniels to Padgett, Dec. 15, 1915, Josephus Daniels Papers, MDLC; U.S. Congress, House, Committee on Naval Affairs, *Hearings before the Committee on Naval Affairs, House of Representatives, Sixty-fourth Congress, First Session, on Estimates Submitted by the Secretary of the Navy,* 3 vols. (Washington: GPO, 1916), 1:356–402.
27. *Hearings* (1916), 1:943–47.
28. *Ibid.,* 1:1401–3.
29. Fiske, Diary, Feb. 20, 1916.
30. *Hearings* (1916), 1:2272–418.
31. *Ibid.,* 2:2602–60.
32. *Ibid.,* 3:3136–49.
33. *Ibid.,* 3:3149–56.
34. Fiske, Diary, Mar. 19, 1916.
35. *Hearings* (1916), 2:2887–91.
36. *Ibid.,* 2:2891–99, 2903.
37. *Ibid.,* 2:2919.
38. *Ibid.,* 2:2921–28, 2970.
39. Fiske to Church, Mar. 28, 1916, Church Papers.
40. Fiske, *From Midshipman,* p. 600.
41. *Hearings* (1916), 3:3409–69.
42. *Ibid.,* 3:3409, 3431, 3462, 3466–71.
43. *Ibid.,* 3:3551–52, 3566, 3569–70.
44. *Ibid.,* 3:3655–58.
45. *Ibid.,* 3:3667, 3857–60.
46. McLean to Sims, Feb. 28, 1916, Sims Papers.
47. Sims to Reuterdahl, Feb. 28, 1916, *ibid.*
48. Sims to McLean, Mar. 14, 1916 (with enclosure); McLean to Roberts, May 18, 1916, copies in *ibid.*
49. McLean to Sims, Mar. 29, 1916, *ibid.*
50. Fiske to Sims, Mar. 31, 1916, *ibid.*
51. Fiske, Diary, Apr. 4, 1916; CAPT Damon T. Cummings, USN (RET), *Admiral Richard Wainwright and the United States Fleet* (Washington: GPO, 1962), p. 254.
52. Fiske to Church, Apr. 17, 18, 1916, Church Papers.

53. Fiske, *From Midshipman*, p. 604–6.
54. See *New York Times*, Apr. 13, 1916, 5:1.
55. Fiske, *From Midshipman*, p. 607.
56. Padgett to Fiske, Apr. 6, 1916, in *Hearings* (1916), 3:3859.
57. Fiske, Diary, Apr. 19, 1916; Fiske to SECNAV, Apr. 13, 1916, NARG 80; Daniels to Dewey, Apr. 12, 1916; Dewey to Daniels, Apr. 13, 1916, Daniels Papers; *New York Times*, Apr. 23, 1916, VIII, 4:5.
58. Fiske, Diary, July 19, 1916, Mar. 21, 1917; Fiske, *From Midshipman*, p. 635.
59. *New York Times*, Apr. 4, 1916, 9:1–3.
60. Fiske, *From Midshipman*, pp. 613–14.
61. *New York Times*, May 3, 1916, 5:2.
62. *Ibid.*, May 4, 1916, 3:5.
63. *Ibid.*, May 5, 1916, 10:2.
64. *Ibid.*, May 16, 1916, 12:4.
65. Fiske, *From Midshipman*, p. 616.
66. *Ibid.*, p. 617.
67. A copy of the speech may be found in the Daniels Papers.
68. Fiske, *From Midshipman*, p. 618.
69. Fullam to Sims, June 17, 1916, Sims Papers.
70. *New York Times*, June 12, 1916, 20:6.
71. Fiske, *From Midshipman*, pp. 618–19.

CHAPTER 15

1. Fiske, Diary, Dec. 2, 1916; Daniels to Fiske, Dec. 18, 1916, NARG 80.
2. Director of Gunnery Exercises and Engineering Performances to CNO, Mar. 29, 1917, NARG 38, File 210.
3. *New York Times*, June 14, 1916, 8:6; "Politics is the Foe of Preparedness: An Authorized Interview with Rear Admiral Bradley A. Fiske, USN," *New York Times*, Aug. 20, 1916, V:1.
4. Paolo E. Coletta, *William Jennings Bryan*, vol. 3, *Political Puritan, 1915–1925* (Lincoln: University of Nebraska Press, 1969), pp. 1–19.
5. Fiske, Diary, Aug. 29, 1916; Fiske, *From Midshipman*, p. 622.
6. Elting E. Morison, *Admiral Sims and the Modern American Navy* (Boston: Houghton Mifflin, 1942), p. 323.
7. *Ibid.*, p. 324.
8. Cronan, "The Greatest Need of the United States Navy," USNIP 42 (July–Aug. 1916): 1137–70.
9. Fiske, Diary, Sept. 21, Nov. 26, 1915, Dec. 7, 1916, Feb. 17, Oct. 18, 1917.
10. *Ibid.*, May 16, 1916.

11. *Ibid.*, May 31, 1916.
12. *Ibid.*, Sept. 20, 25, 1916.
13. *Ibid.*, Feb. 14, 1917.
14. *Ibid.*, Oct. 27, 1916.
15. "Submarine Warfare Off the American Coast," CH 5 (Nov. 1916): 223–24; Wellington Long, "The Cruise of the U-53," USNIP 92 (Oct. 1966): 86–96.
16. *New York Times*, Oct. 15, 1916, V, 2:1.
17. Fiske, Diary, Dec. 11, 1916.
18. LCDR Z. H. Madison, USN, "The Department Strategic Problem as a Drill for the Entire Naval Establishment," USNIP 42 (Nov.–Dec. 1916): 1793–1814.
19. See the report of the commander in chief, Atlantic Fleet, RADM Henry T. Mayo, in ARSN, 1916. On Nov. 8, 1916, Henry Mustin told his wife that "the aviation situation is too disgusting for words." (Mustin to Mrs. Mustin, Nov. 8, 1916, Henry Mustin Papers, MDLC.)
20. Fiske, Diary, Nov. 30, Dec. 18, 1916; Fiske, *From Midshipman*, pp. 626–27.
21. *New York Times*, Dec. 9, 1916, 9:1.
22. Fiske, "The Next Five Years of the Navy: What We Shall Get for the Billion Dollars We Shall Spend?" WW 33 (Jan. 1917): 256–73.
23. *Ibid.* 33 (Feb. 1917): 392–98.
24. Fiske, Diary, Dec. 18, 1916, Jan. 7, 1917; Fiske, *From Midshipman*, pp. 633–34; *New York Times*, Jan. 7, 1917, 12:1, Feb. 3, 1917, 2:3, Feb. 11, 1917, 1:5, Feb. 13, 1917, 10:2. Fiske repeated and enlarged these ideas in "Air Power," USNIP 43 (Aug. 1917): 1701–4, ending with the prophecy that some day a book would be written entitled *The Influence of Air Power on History*.
25. Daniels to Fiske, Mar. 22, 1917, NARG 80; Fiske, Diary, Mar. 26, 27, 29, 1917; *New York Times*, Mar. 29, 1917, 2:6.
26. Fiske, Diary, Feb. 1, 1917.
27. *Ibid.*, Feb. 5, 1917.
28. *Ibid.*, Feb. 17, 1917.
29. *Ibid.*, Feb. 25, 1917; Fiske to Daniels, Mar. 25, 1917, NARG 80.
30. Fiske, Diary, Mar. 5, 1915; *New York Times*, Mar. 7, 1917, 2:1.
31. Fiske, Diary, Apr. 6, 10, 1917.
32. Fiske, *From Midshipman*, pp. 640–41.

Chapter 16

1. Fiske to SECNAV, Mar. 25, 1917; F. D. Roosevelt, Acting, to Fiske, Mar. 29, 1917, Josephus Daniels Papers, MDLC; Fiske to William C. Church, Mar. 29, 1917, William C. Church Papers, MDLC.

2. Fiske, *From Midshipman*, pp. 642–43; and Diary, Apr. 16, 1917.
3. Park Benjamin, "The Flying Fish Torpedo: A New and Terrible Form of Attack on the High Seas or in Harbors," IND 80 (Nov. 2, 1914): 164–66.
4. Henry Woodhouse, *Textbook of Naval Aeronautics* (New York: Century Co., 1917), pp. 14–15.
5. Fiske to Daniels, Dec. 13, 1917, N. T. Newton to SECNAV, Jan. 18, 1918, NARG 72; SECNAV to CNO, Jan. 25, 1918; Pratt to Special Board on Anti-submarine Devices, Jan. 29, 1918; Special Board on Anti-submarine Devices to CNO, Feb. 11, 1918; CNO to Special Board on Anti-submarine Devices, June 28, 1918, NARG 80; Fiske, *From Midshipman*, p. 664.
6. Fiske, Diary, May 17, 19, 1917; Fiske, *From Midshipman*, p. 645.
7. Woodhouse, *Textbook on Naval Aeronautics*, pp. 23, 173.
8. Fiske, Diary, June 6, 15, 1917; Fiske, *From Midshipman*, pp. 646–47; "Professional Notes," USNIP 43 (July 1917): 1524–26.
9. Fiske, *From Midshipman*, pp. 647–49. For operations of British torpedo planes during the war, see Henry Albert Jones, *The War in the Air: Being the Story of the Part Played in the Great War by the Royal Air Forces*, 6 vols. (Oxford: At the Clarendon Press, 1922–27), 2:64–65, 4:55–58.
10. Fiske to Sims, June 20, Aug. 3, 1917; Sims to Fiske, July 11, 1917, William S. Sims Papers, MDLC.
11. Fiske, *From Midshipman*, pp. 651–53; see also "Military Aviation Abroad," IND 74 (Apr. 10, 1917): 839–40.
12. Fiske, Diary, July 13, 15, 19, 21, 25, 1917; "The Torpedo-plane in Future Naval Battles," in USNIP 46 (July 1920): 1130–31 (reprinted from *Flying*).
13. Fiske, Diary, Aug. 14, 1917; Fiske, *From Midshipman*, pp. 655–56.
14. Sims to Fiske, Aug. 21, 1917; Fiske to Sims, Sept. 10, 1917, Sims Papers.
15. Fiske, Diary, Aug. 21, 23, 24, Sept. 9, 1917; Fiske, *From Midshipman*, p. 656; *New York Times*, Sept. 7, 1917, 5:5.
16. Fiske, *From Midshipman*, p. 660. See Lord Northcliffe, "Is England Making Good?" IND 84 (Nov. 1915): 260–61, and Henry Lloyd George, *War Memoirs of Lloyd George*, 6 vols. (Boston: Little, Brown, 1933–37), 3:550–69.
17. Fiske, *From Midshipman*, p. 660.
18. CNO to BUORD, Oct. 8, 1917, NARG 80.
19. Fiske, Diary, Sept. 30, Oct. 1, 17, 26, 27, Nov. 14, 15, 19, 1917; Fiske to Daniels, Nov. 26, 1917; Daniels to Fiske, Nov. 28, 1917 (with enclosures), NARG 80.
20. Fiske, Diary, Nov. 28, 1917; Fiske, *From Midshipman*, pp. 662–63.
21. Fiske, *From Midshipman*, pp. 665–72. Fiske's ideas appeared at greater length in an essay entitled "Strategy, Tactics, Logistics and Invention," USNIP 43 (Dec. 1917): 2793–98.
22. Daniels to Fiske, Jan. 3, 1918; Fiske to Daniels, Jan. 12, 1918, NARG 80.

23. Sims to Fiske, Oct. 11, 1917, Sims Papers; Fiske, Diary, Jan. 11, 1918; Daniels to Fiske, Jan. 29, 1918, Daniels Papers; Fiske to BUORD and BUNAV, Jan. 31, 1918 (copies), Sims Papers.
24. Fiske, *From Midshipman*, p. 672.
25. Fiske, Diary, Jan. 24, 1918; Fiske, *From Midshipman*, pp. 673–74; Daniels to Fiske, Feb. 2, 9, 1918, NARG 80.
26. "H.C.S." in USNIP 44 (July 1918): 1733.
27. Fiske, Diary, Feb. 15, Mar. 8, 1918; Fiske, *From Midshipman*, pp. 674–75.
28. Fiske, Diary, May 21, 22, 1918; Fiske, *From Midshipman*, p. 676.
29. Daniels to Fiske, June 19, 1918; BUC&R to Sims, June 25, 1918; Sims to OPNAV, June 21, 1918; BUC&R to Sims, June 25, 1918; CNO (Aviation) to BUORD and BUC&R, July 1, 1918, NARG 72; Fiske to Daniels, June 21, 1918, NARG 80.
30. Fiske, Diary, July 19, Aug. 16, 20, 26, Sept. 10, 1918; Sims to OPNAV, Aug. 9, 1918; Sims to Fiske, Aug. 9, 16, 1918; Taylor to Manager of Naval Aircraft Factory, Aug. 17, 1918, Sims Papers; Sims to OPNAV, Aug. 9, 1918; J. C. Hunsaker to CNO (Aviation), Aug. 15, 1918, NARG 72.
31. Henry Woodhouse, "The Torpedoplane: A New Weapon Which Promises to Revolutionize Naval Tactics," USNIP 45 (May 1919): 743–52.
32. Earle, "Planning Navy Aviation Organization," USNIP 46 (May 1920): 765 (reprinted from ANJ 46 [Mar. 20, 1920]).
33. Editorial, "The Neglected Torpedoplane," *New York Times*, May 17, 1919, 12:3–4.
34. Archibald Turnbull, CAPT, USNR, and Clifford L. Lord, LCDR, USNR, *History of United States Naval Aviation* (New Haven: Yale University Press, 1949), p. 213; Gordon Swanborough and Peter M. Bowers, *United States Navy Aircraft Since 1911* (London: Putnam, 1968), pp. 98–100.
35. Fiske to Sims, Jan. 8, 1922, Sims Papers.
36. Fiske to Chief BUAER, Feb. 10, 1922, NARG 72.
37. Chief BUAER to JAG, via Chief BUORD, Feb. 20, 1922; Chief BUORD to JAG, Feb. 28, 1922, *ibid.*
38. JAG to BUORD, Apr. 1, 1922; BUORD to JAG, Apr. 17, 1922, *ibid.*
39. Fiske to Latimer, June 1, 1922 (with brief enclosed), *ibid.*; see also Ernest Wilkinson, "The Legal Rights of Naval Officers and Enlisted Men in Their Inventions," USNIP 50 (Aug. 1924): 1266–67.
40. JAG to BUORD, Aug. 21, 1922, NARG 80.
41. BUORD to JAG, July 8, 1922, *ibid.*
42. SECNAV to Fiske, Sept. 30, 1922, *ibid.*
43. Fiske to SECNAV, Nov. 6, 1922; Wilkinson to SECNAV, Dec. 15, 1922, *ibid.*
44. Denby to Fiske, Dec. 28, 1922, *ibid.*

45. Wilkinson to SECNAV, Jan. 5, 1923, *ibid.*
46. BUORD to JAG, Jan. 9, Feb. 10, 1923, *ibid.* Similar arrangements had been made by the army during World War I. When Wright and Curtiss continued to squabble over patent rights, the Aircraft Manufacturers Association was formed which took over the patents and paid $200 for each plane produced. See James J. Hudson, *Hostile Skies: A Combat History of the American Air Service in World War I* (Syracuse, N.Y.: Syracuse University Press, 1968), pp. 20–21.
47. JAG to Chief BUORD, Jan. 27, 1923, NARG 80.
48. Fiske to SECNAV, Nov. 14, 1925, *ibid.*
49. JAG to BUAER, Dec. 24, 1924, *ibid.*
50. *Ibid.*
51. Chief BUORD to JAG, Jan. 19, 1926, *ibid.*
52. Fiske to Wilbur, Jan. 20, 1926, *ibid.*
53. Wilbur to Fiske, Jan. 23, 1926, *ibid.*
54. JAG to BUORD, Mar. 13, 1926, *ibid.*
55. BUORD to JAG, Mar. 25, 1926, *ibid.*
56. Wilbur to Sargent, May 1, 1926; Sargent to Wilbur, May 18, 1926, *ibid.*
57. Wilkinson to Wilbur, Nov. 29, 1926, *ibid. Trespass on the case*: "The form of action at common law, adapted to the recovery of damages for some injury resulting to a party from the wrongful act of another, unaccompanied by direct or immediate force, or which is the indirect or secondary consequence of the defendant's act." (*Black's Law Dictionary*, 4th ed. [St. Paul, Minn.: West Publishing Co., 1951].)
58. Edward H. Campbell, Memorandum for RADM C. C. Bloch, RADM Charles B. McVay, RADM W. A. Moffett, Feb. 3, 1927, NARG 80.
59. Leo A. Rover, Assistant Attorney, to CDR R. A. Lavender, Mar. 16, 1927; JAG to Director of Naval Intelligence, Nov. 22, 1928; Office of the Attorney General to Wilbur, Nov. 23, 1928, *ibid.*
60. William D. Mitchell, Attorney General, to SECNAV, July 2, 1929; C. F. Adams to William D. Mitchell, July 5, 1929, NARG 80; *New York Times*, July 8, 1929, 3:2–3; "Admiral Fiske's Shore Victory," LD 102 (July 20, 1929): 12.
61. *New York Times*, July 5, 1929, 20:2.
62. Editorial, "Admiral Fiske's Torpedo Plane," *ibid.*, July 8, 1929, 18:3–4.
63. Moffett v. Fiske, 5061 F.2d 868-72 (1931).

CHAPTER 17

1. Fiske, Diary, Feb. 14, 1918.

2. Jo died intestate. On Nov. 9, 1930, her estate was appraised at $347,328; Fiske received $100,480 and Caroline, who remained unmarried, $218,961 (*New York Times*, Nov. 9, 1920, 31:1).

3. In addition to revising *The Navy as a Fighting Machine* (1918), Fiske wrote his memoirs (1919) and *The Art of Fighting: Its Evolution and Progress, with Illustrations from Campaigns of Great Commanders* (1920). His articles included "The United States Naval Institute," USNIP 45 (Feb. 1919): 197–200; "The [Theodore] Roosevelt Memorial," *ibid.* 45 (Aug. 1919): 1303–4; "The Warfare of the Future," *ibid.* 47 (Feb. 1921): 157–67; and "The Defense of the Philippines," NAR 213 (June 1921): 721–24. For the *New York Times* in 1920 he reviewed Lord John Fisher, *Memoirs, and Records*; John Jellicoe, *The Crisis of the Naval War*; and William S. Sims, *Victory at Sea.*

4. Sims to Hendrick, Oct. 14, Dec. 4, 1918; Fullam to Sims, Apr. 29, Oct. 4, Nov. 6, 1919; Sims to Fullam, Feb. 20, May 15, Oct. 1, Nov. 3, 8, 1919; Sims to Fiske, Feb. 7, 1919; W. V. Pratt to Sims, Mar. 10, 1919, William S. Sims Papers, MDLC.

5. Fiske to Sims, Aug. 6, 1919, *ibid.*

6. *New York Times*, Sept. 19, 1920, III, 3:1; Oct. 31, 1920, III, 4:1.

7. U.S. Congress, Senate, *Naval Investigation Hearings before the Subcommittee of the Committee on Naval Affairs, United States Senate, 66th Cong., 2d Sess.*, 2 vols. (Washington: GPO, 1921), 1:193 (hereafter cited as NIH).

8. Fiske to Sims, Dec. 23, 25, 1919, Jan. 6, 1920, Sims Papers.

9. Sims to Fiske, Jan. 10, 1920, *ibid.*

10. NIH, 1:194.

11. Fiske to Sims, Feb. 7, 10, 27, Apr. 15, 1920; Fullam to Sims, Jan. 19, 20, 1920; H. I. Cone to Harris Laning, Feb. 16, 1920, Sims Papers.

12. Sims's letter is available in his papers and in printed form in NIH, 1:1–9.

13. NIH, 2:1982, 2109–10, 2099–100, 2286–318.

14. Sims to Page for Hale, Jan. 23, 1920; Page to Sims, Jan. 28, 1920, Sims Papers; NIH 2:2929–44, 3080–138.

15. NIH, 1:375–516. I have at times violated the chronology of the hearings in order to deal topically with its various subjects.

16. *Ibid.*, 1:516–29.

17. *Ibid.*, 1:531–71.

18. *Ibid.*, 1:573–678.

19. *Ibid.*, 1:678–754.

20. *Ibid.*, 1:755–817.

21. *Ibid.*, 1:841–80.

22. *Ibid.*, 1:894–917.

23. *Ibid.*, 1:1050–80, 1089–142.

24. *Ibid.*, 1:1199–1200, 1356.
25. *Ibid.*, 1:1203, 1220–593; Sims to Pratt, June 1, 1920, Sims Papers. For Pratt career to 1920, see Gerald E. Wheeler, *Admiral William Veazie Pratt, U.S. Navy: A Sailor's Life* (Washington: Navy Department, Naval Histor Division, 1974), pp. 67–135.
26. Fiske to Sims, Apr. 25, 1920, Sims Papers.
27. NIH, 2:1617–773.
28. May 3, 1920, Sims Papers.
29. NIH, 2:1819–958.
30. May 6, 1920, Sims Papers.
31. Sims to Fullam, May 7, 1920, *ibid.*
32. Fullam to Sims, May 7, 11, 1920, *ibid.*
33. Fiske to Sims, May 5, 1920, *ibid.*
34. NIH, 2:2285–86, 2296, 2677, 2961.
35. *Ibid.*, 2:2449–58, 2693–2710, 2719, 2731, 2738–39, 2794.
36. Fiske to Sims, May 10, 1920, Sims Papers.
37. Sims to Fiske, May 17, 1920, *ibid.*
38. Fullam to Sims, May 11, 1920; Fullam to Hale, May 20, 1920, *ibid.*
39. NIH, 2:2856, 2589–60.
40. *Ibid.*, 2:2961–64.
41. *Ibid.*, 2:2964–68, 2970.
42. *Ibid.*, 2:2969–76.
43. *Ibid.*, 2:2988.
44. Sims to Hale, May 21, 1920, Sims Papers; NIH, 2:2302, 2731, 2739, 2792–9. 2821, 2991, 3038–46.
45. NIH, 2:2181–86; Cone to Sims, Apr. 12, 1920; Kittredge to Sims, Apr. 1. 1920, Sims Papers.
46. Blue to Daniels, May 18, 1920, Josephus Daniels Papers, MDLC.
47. NIH, 2:3370–71.
48. *Ibid.*, 2:3371–72.
49. *Ibid.*, 2:3371.
50. *Ibid.*, 2:3388–90.
51. *Ibid.*, 2:3391–95, 3407–10, 3414; Sims to Hale (with enclosure), May 1. 1920, Sims Papers.
52. Fullam to Hale, July 15, 1920, William F. Fullam Papers, MDLC.
53. Fiske to Fullam, Nov. 5, 1920, *ibid.*
54. Fullam to Sims, Apr. 20, 1920, Sims Papers.
55. Fullam to Sims, Apr. 21, 1920, Mar. 19, 1921, *ibid.*
56. Dean C. Allard, "Admiral William S. Sims and United States Naval Polic in World War I," AN 35 (Apr. 1975): 97–110.

57. Fiske to Sims, Nov. 10, 1920, Mar. 22, 1921; Sims to Fiske, Mar. 24, 1921, Sims Papers.
58. Fiske to Sims, Apr. 13, 1921, *ibid.*
59. Tracy B. Kittredge, *Naval Lessons of the Great War: A Review of the Criticisms by Admiral Sims of the Policies and Methods of Josephus Daniels* (New York: Doubleday, Page, 1921), p. vii.

Chapter 18

1. Sims to Fullam, Oct. 6, 1920, William F. Fullam Papers, MDLC.
2. Sims to Fiske, Nov. 4, 1920, William S. Sims Papers, MDLC.
3. Fiske to Sims, Nov. 6, 1920, *ibid.*
4. Fiske to Sims, Nov. 20, 1920, *ibid.*
5. *Ibid.*
6. Sims to Fullam, Nov. 12, 1919; Fullam to Sims, Feb. 8, Aug. 2, 1920; Plunkett to Sims, Oct. 11, 1920; H. I. Cone to Sims, Sept. 13, 1920, *ibid.*
7. Fiske to Sims, 2 telegrams, May 10, 1921, *ibid.*
8. Fiske to Sims, Mar. 15, 1921, *ibid.*
9. Sims to Fiske, Mar. 17, 1921, *ibid.*
10. U.S. Congress, House, *Hearings before the Committee on Naval Affairs of the House of Representatives on Sundry Legislation Affecting the Naval Establishment, 1920–1921* (Washington: GPO, 1921), pp. 692–704; *New York Times*, Feb. 5, 1921, 2:6; "Naval Aviation and a United Air Service," USNIP 47 (Apr. 1921): 5611–67; see also, William Mitchell, BGEN, Air Service, *Our Air Force: The Keystone of National Defense* (New York: L. P. Dutton Co., 1921).
11. "The New Menace to Sea Power," LD 70 (Aug. 6, 1921): 16–17.
12. U.S. Congress, House Appropriations Committee, *Hearings on Naval Appropriation Bill for 1922, 66th Cong., 3d Sess.* (Washington: GPO, 1921); *New York Tribune*, Jan. 23, 1921, VII, 2:1.
13. Sims to Fiske, Jan. 6, 10, Mar. 12, 1921; Fiske to Sims, Jan. 12, 1921; Fullam to Sims, Feb. 18, Mar. 21, 1921, Sims Papers; "Report of the Navy General Board," *Aviation* 10 (Feb. 14, 1921): 198–99.
14. Sims to Fullam, Aug. 1, 3, 1921; Fullam to Sims, Aug. 11, 1921, Fullam Papers.
15. Sims to Moffett, Sept. 19, 1921, Sims Papers.
16. "Secretary Denby Opposed to Unified Air Control," USNIP 47 (June 1921): 949–50; "American Aviation Policy," *ibid.* 47 (June 1921): 950–51.
17. Edward Arpee, *From Frigates to Flat-Tops: The Story of the Life and Achievements of Rear Admiral William Adger Moffett, U.S.N., "The*

Father of Naval Aviation," October 31, 1869–April 4, 1933 (Lake Forest, Ill.: privately printed, 1953), pp. 74–75, 84–86.

18. Cyril Godfrey Moran, "Sea Power: The Senate and the Air," USNIP 47 (Nov. 1921): 1676^4–76^{30}.

19. Fiske, "The Warfare of the Future," *ibid.* 47 (Feb. 1921): 157–67.

20. Fiske, "Defense of the Philippines with Airplanes," NAR 213 (June 1921): 721–24; *New York Times,* June 6, 1921, 12:3.

21. USNIP 47 (Nov. 1921): 1676^1–76^3.

22. "The Industrial Corporation and the Inventor," SA 105 (Nov. 18, 1921): 448–49; see also CDR C. S. McDowell, USN, "Naval Research," USNIP 45 (June 1919): 895–908.

23. *New York Times,* July 1, 1921, 12:7.

24. Fiske to Sims, Nov. 19, 1921, Sims Papers.

25. Sims to Fiske, Nov. 22, 1921, *ibid.*

26. Sims to Fiske, Dec. 10, 1921, *ibid.*

27. Fiske to Sims, Dec. 21, 1921, *ibid.*

28. Senior Member Present, GB, to Fiske, Aug. 25, 1921, NHD:OA, GB Records, GB no. 438.

29. Fiske to SECNAV, Sept. 9, 1921 (copy); Fiske to Sims, Sept. 22, 1921, Sims Papers.

30. *New York Times,* Nov. 12, 1921, 28:2.

31. *Ibid.,* Nov. 21, 1921, 14:1–2; Nov. 24, 1921, 18:7.

32. Thomas H. Buckley, *The United States and the Washington Conference, 1921–1922* (Knoxville: University of Tennessee Press, 1970), p. 172. Three other competent studies of the conference are Harold and Margaret Sprout, *Toward a New Order of Sea Power: American Naval Policy and the World Scene, 1918–1922* (Princeton: Princeton University Press, 1943); John C. Vinson, *The Parchment Peace* (Athens: University of Georgia Press, 1956); and Roger Dingman, *Power in the Pacific: The Origins of Naval Arms Limitation, 1914–1922* (Chicago: University of Chicago Press, 1976).

33. W. V. Pratt, "Naval Policy and the Naval Treaty," NAR 215 (May 1922): 590–99.

34. Fiske, "Strongest Navy: Reply to Wester-Weymss and Admiral Sims," CH 16 (July 1922): 556–63.

35. Fullam to Sims, Mar. 11, 1923, Sims Papers; see also William R. Braisted, *The United States Navy in the Pacific, 1909–1922* (Austin: University of Texas Press, 1971), p. 670.

36. Fiske to Fullam, May 28, 1923, Fullam Papers; *New York Times,* Oct. 6, 1923, 20:6.

37. ARSN, 1924, pp. 2, 3, 80; William King, "Condemnation of United States Naval Policy," CH 22 (May 1925): 167–77. Dudley W. Knox answered

Senator King in "Defense of the United States Naval Policy," *ibid*. 22 (June 1925): 339–44.

38. Fiske to Wilbur, June 3, 1924, copy in Sims Papers; the letter was also published in the *New York Tribune*. For Wilbur's reply, see USNIP 50 (Aug. 1924): 1320. See also ARSN, 1924, p. 2.

39. See U.S. Congress, House, *Hearings before the Select Committee of Inquiry into Operations of the United States Air Services*, 68th Cong., 2d Sess., 1924 (Washington: GPO, 1925).

40. *New York Times*, Jan. 20, 1924, 20:6; May 5, 1924, 15:3; May 26, 1924, 17:3; editorial, "Admiral Fiske's Alarms," *ibid*., June 4, 1924, 20:3.

41. Fiske to Wilbur, June 3, 1924, NARG 80.

42. Editorials, *New York Times*, Apr. 17, 1925, 25:3; Apr. 25, 1925, 20:4–5.

43. "Report of the Joint Board on Results of Aviation and Ordnance Tests Held During June and July 1921," reprinted in *Congressional Record*, 67th Cong., 1st Sess., 1921, pp. 8624–26; "Torpedo Planes 'Sink' the U.S.S. Arkansas," *Aviation* 13 (Oct. 12, 1922): 520; "Battleships vs Airplane," USNIP 50 (Dec. 1924): 2081–86; Harry H. Ransom, "The Battleship Meets the Airplane," MA 23 (Spring 1959): 21–27.

44. Fiske, "Torpedo Plane and Bomber," USNIP 48 (Sept. 1922): 1474–78.

45. Fiske to Sims, July 15, 1923, Sims Papers.

46. *New York Times*, Feb. 19, 1925, 1:5.

47. Sims to Fiske, Jan. 6, 1921, Sims Papers; Sims to Fiske, Mar. (?), 1921, quoted in Elting E. Morison, *Admiral Sims and the Modern American Navy* (Boston: Houghton Mifflin, 1942), p. 505; see also *Hearings . . . into Operations of the United States Air Services*.

48. Fiske, letter to editor, *New York Times*, Feb. 3, 1925, 12:7.

49. Fiske to Sims, June 23, 1925, Sims Papers.

50. *New York Times*, Feb. 15, 1925, 8:1. See also CAPT Yates Stirling, USN, "Some Fundamentals of Sea Power," USNIP 51 (June 1925): 889–918; Edward Eberle, "The Elements of Sea Power and the Future of the Navy," *ibid*. 51 (Oct. 1925): 1832–38; RADM William L. Rodgers, "Military Preparedness Necessary to the Economic and Social Welfare of the United States," *ibid*. 51 (Oct. 1925): 1845–57; CAPT Dudley W. Knox, USN (RET), "Sea Power and Pocket Books," *ibid*. 51 (Dec. 1925): 2231–41.

51. *New York Times*, Feb. 23, 1925, 19:2.

52. *Ibid*., Mar. 22, 1925, 2:2–3.

53. Fiske, "Limitation of Armaments," *Harper's* 151 (July 1925): 129–38; editorial, "Keeping the Peace in the Pacific," *New York Times*, July 23, 1925, 18:1.

54. *New York Times*, Dec. 22, 1926, 13:2.

55. *Ibid*., Jan. 30, 1927, II, 1:6.

56. *Baltimore Sun,* Dec. 16, 1924, Jan. 20, 1925; *Washington Evening Star,* Mar. 14, 1925; ARSN, 1924, p. 2.
57. L. Ethan Ellis, *Frank B. Kellogg and American Foreign Relations, 1925–1929* (New Brunswick, N.J.: Rutgers University Press, 1961), pp. 157–59; Gerald E. Wheeler, *Prelude to Pearl Harbor: The United States Navy and the Far East, 1921–1931* (Columbia: University of Missouri Press, 1963), pp. 131–50; "What the Failure of the Naval Conference Means," LD 94 (Aug. 20, 1927): 8–9; "How the Geneva Conference Hits Our Taxpayers," *ibid.* 94 (Aug. 27, 1927): 5–7.
58. Editorial, "Back to Direct Negotiations," *New York Times,* Aug. 5, 1926, 16:1; Fiske, letter to editor, *New York Times,* Aug. 8, 1927, 6:7.
59. *New York Times,* Oct. 5, 1928, 3:3.
60. Fiske, letter to editor, *New York Times,* July 21, 1929, 18:7.
61. *Ibid.,* Jan. 24, 1930, 3:6.
62. See, among others, Raymond G. O'Connor, *Perilous Equilibrium: The United States and the London Naval Conference of 1930* (Lawrence: University of Kansas Press, 1962), Stephen E. Pelz, *Race to Pearl Harbor; The Failure of the Second Naval Conference and the Onset of World War II* (Cambridge: Harvard University Press, 1974); Gerald E. Wheeler, *Admiral William Veazy Pratt, U.S. Navy: A Sailor's Life* (Washington: Navy Department, Naval History Division, 1974), pp. 159–86.
63. *New York Times,* Oct. 28, 1930, 6:1.
64. *Ibid.,* Feb. 18, 1931, 21:7.
65. *Ibid.,* Apr. 1, 1931, 20:2.
66. *Ibid.,* June 13, 1933, 31:3.
67. *Ibid.,* Feb. 14, 1932, 26:5.
68. *Ibid.,* Feb. 9, 1932, 4:5.
69. *Ibid.,* Feb. 28, 1933, 18:8; Oct. 1, 1933, 24:6.
70. *Ibid.,* Dec. 9, 1934, IV, 5:1–2.
71. Fiske, letter to editor, *New York Times,* Sept. 7, 1935, 22:7.
72. *Ibid.,* Sept. 17, 1936, 16:5.
73. Fiske, "Air Power, 1913–1943," USNIP 68 (May 1943): 686–94; see also Henry Woodhouse, "U.S. Naval Aeronautic Policies, 1904–1942," *ibid.* 78 (Feb. 1942): 161–75.

Chapter 19

1. Fiske, "Admiral Dewey: An Appreciation," USNIP 43 (Mar. 1917): 433–36.
2. Fiske, "Stephen B. Luce: An Appreciation," USNIP 43 (Sept. 1917): 1935–40.

3. Pratt, autobiography (typescript), pp. 2, 3, 7, William V. Pratt Papers, MDLC.

4. *Ibid.*, pp. 15–16, emphasis added.

5. Letter to the author, June 16, 1975.

6. Sims, "Military Character," USNIP 43 (Mar. 1917): 437–38.

7. Peter Padfield, *Guns at Sea* (London: Hugh Evelyn, 1973), p. 211.

8. For Blandy's article, see USNIP 46 (July 1920): 1089–95; for Fiske's comments, see "Director Firing a Century Ago," *ibid.* 46 (Sept. 1920): 1485–86.

9. See the annotated bibliography of Luce's writings in John D. Hayes and John B. Hattendorf, eds., *The Writings of Stephen B. Luce* (Newport, R.I.: Naval War College, 1975), pp. 163–235; John D. Hayes, "Dudley W. Knox, 1877–1960," USNIP 86 (Jan. 1960): 103–5. The information on Mahan was provided by Dr. Robert Seager in a letter to the author, June 23, 1975. Edwin A. Falk, in *Fighting Bob Evans* (New York: Cape and Smith, 1931), p. iii, acknowledged the "substantial assistance" Fiske gave in preparing the bibliography.

10. *New York Times*, June 22, 1934, 4:2–4.

11. *The New Yorker*, Feb. 7, 1942, pp. 10–11.

12. Artemus Gates to the author, Feb. 6, 1975; Robert A. Lovett to the author, May 8, 1975. See also Ralph D. Paine, *The First Yale Unit: The Story of Naval Aviation, 1916–1919*, 2 vols. (Cambridge, Mass.: Riverside Press, 1925).

SOURCES

Unpublished Materials

There is no collection of the letters Bradley A. Fiske wrote and received. Only three of his diaries have been discovered—two are in the Manuscript Division of the Library of Congress, and one is in the Archives of the U.S. Naval Academy. These cover the period from September 1914 to September 1918.

To supplement the diaries, I consulted the papers of naval officers Fiske knew: Reginald R. Belknap, William S. Benson (used with the permission of Benson's son, the late Commodore Howard H. J. Benson), Claude C. Bloch, Mark Lambert Bristol, Washington Irving Chambers, and Henry C. Mustin (used with the permission of a son, Vice Adm. Lloyd Mustin, USN [Ret.]). Bloch was chief of the Bureau of Ordnance when Fiske sued the navy over the patent on his torpedo plane. Bristol's, Chambers's, and Mustin's papers illustrate the growing pains of U.S. naval aviation. The papers of William F. Fullam, Dudley W. Knox, and particularly of William S. Sims detail Fiske's personal and official relationships with fellow naval officers. Occasional references to Fiske are also found in the papers of William D. Leahy, Stephen B. Luce, Alfred T. Mahan, Charles O'Neil, Hugo Osterhaus, William V. Pratt, William T. Sampson, Joseph Strauss, Henry C. Taylor, Richard Wainwright, and Harry E. Yarnell. All of these papers are housed in the Manuscript Division of the Library of Congress.

The diary of Mrs. George (Mildred E.) Dewey, which describes Admiral Dewey's tribulations as president of the General Board of the Navy, the Mary C. Powell Collection, which includes clippings (particularly from the *New York Herald*) on Fiske's early gunnery inventions, and the William C. Church Papers, containing a number of letters in which Fiske took the editor of the *Army and Navy Journal* into his confidence, may also be found in the Manuscript Division of the Library of Congress.

Particularly useful for establishing the political as well as the naval environment in which Fiske worked are the papers of William Jennings Bryan, Josephus Daniels, Lindley M. Garrison, Robert Lansing, Philander C. Knox, Richmond P. Hobson, William McKinley, William G. McAdoo, John Bassett Moore, Theodore Roosevelt, William Howard Taft, Woodrow Wilson, and Leonard Wood. These are also in the Manuscript Division of the Library of Congress. The George von Lengerke Meyer Papers, in the Navy Department Records at the National Archives, reveal a good deal about the administration of the Navy Department from 1909 to 1913. The William A. Moffett Papers, at the Naval Academy Library in Annapolis, detail the growing pains of U.S. naval aviation.

Fiske's relations with the Western Electric Company are described in various letters and copies of patents in the company's library. Fiske's relations with the U.S. Naval Institute are described in "Records of the Minutes of the Meetings of the Board of Control," kept in the institute's vault in Annapolis.

The most useful doctoral dissertations consulted were: Ernest Andrade, "United States Naval Policy in the Disarmament Era, 1921–1927" (Michigan State University, 1966); Edward H. Brooks, "The National Defense Policy of the Wilson Administration, 1913–1917" (Stanford University, 1950); Daniel J. Costello, "Planning for War: A History of the General Board of the Navy, 1900–1914" (Fletcher School of Law and Diplomacy, Tufts University, 1969); James Patrick Kelly, "The Naval Policy of Imperial Germany, 1900–1914" (Georgetown University, 1970); Jane L. Phelps, "The Public Life of Charles J. Bonaparte" (Georgetown University, 1959); Warner R. Schilling, "Admirals and Foreign Policy, 1913–1919" (Yale University, 1953); Ronald Spector, "Professors of War: The Naval War College and the Modern American Navy, 1884–1917" (Yale University, 1967); and Wayne August Wiegand, "Patrician in the Progressive Era: A Biography of George von Lengerke Meyer" (Southern Illinois University, 1974).

A significant master's thesis is Dean C. Allard, "The Influence of the U.S. Navy upon the American Steel Industry, 1880–1900" (Georgetown University, 1959).

OFFICIAL DOCUMENTS

The official story of naval activity is told in the *Annual Reports of the Secretary of the Navy*. I have read those published between 1874 and 1933. Those from 1874 to 1880 bemoan the low status of the navy; those from 1881 to 1898 speak largely of the "new navy"; and the appendix to the report of the Bureau of Navigation in the 1898 volume contains a superb record of the naval aspects of the Spanish-American War. The volumes for 1899 through 1901 address naval efforts devoted to suppressing the Filipino insurrection. The volumes for 1902 and 1903 deal in part with the supposed German threat in Venezuela. Meyer's reports emphasize the application of business management techniques to the navy and the reorganization of the department by means of the aide system. Daniels's reports from 1913 to 1915 emphasize his humanitarian, religious, and antimonopoly proclivities; those from 1915 to 1917 stress the belated preparedness crusade; those from 1917 to 1919 deal with the war effort; and those from 1919 to 1921 cover the postwar naval denouement. During the Harding, Coolidge, and Hoover years, the emphasis is on disarmament and economy.

Information about the curriculum and life at the Naval Academy was obtained from the academy's annual *Catalog*. Facts about naval officers of Fiske's generation are found in the U.S. Naval Academy's *Annual Register of the U.S. Naval Academy* (Annapolis: U.S. Naval Academy) and the annual *Register of the Commissioned and Warrant Officers of the United States Navy and Marine Corps* (Washington: GPO). Special publications that shed light on particular subjects pertinent to Fiske's career include: U.S. Department of the Navy, Bureau of Navigation, Office of Naval Intelligence, General Information Series no. 9, *Information from Abroad: A Year's Naval Progress* (Washington: GPO, published annually), and *Notes on the Spanish-American War*, 10 vols. (Washington: GPO, 1899); Lieutenant J. Grimes, USNR, "Aviation in the Fleet Exercises, 1911–1935," typescript (Washington: Office of the Chief of Naval Operations, 1943); U.S. Department of the Navy, *United States Naval Aviation, 1919–1970* (Washington: GPO, 1970); and USAF Historical Study no. 25, "Organization of Military Aeronautics, 1907–1935" typescript (Washington: AFCHO, HQ, USAF, 1937).

Among the congressional hearings into naval matters in Fiske's day, the most rewarding are: *Hearings before the Committee on Naval Affairs, 60th Cong., 2d Sess., U.S. Senate, on Bill S. 3335* (Washington: GPO, 1908); *Hearings before Committee on Naval Affairs of the House of Representatives on Estimates Submitted by the Secretary of the Navy, 1913* (Washington: GPO, 1913); *Hearings before the Committee on Naval Affairs of the House of Representatives, on Estimates Submitted by the Secretary of the Navy, 1915* (Washington: GPO, 1915); *Hearings before the Committee on Naval Affairs, House of Representatives, 64th Cong., 1st Sess., on Estimates Submitted by the Secretary of the Navy*, 3 vols. (Washington: GPO, 1916); *Hearings before the Committee on Naval Affairs of the House of Representatives* (Washington: GPO, 1919); *Naval Investigation: Hearings be-*

fore the Subcommittee of the Committee on Naval Affairs, U.S. Senate, 66th Cong., 2d Sess., 2 vols. (Washington: GPO, 1921); *Hearings before the Committee on Naval Affairs of the House of Representatives on Sundry Legislation Affecting the Naval Establishment, 1920-1921* (Washington: GPO, 1921); *Hearings before the Select Committee of Inquiry into Operations of the United States Air Services, House of Representatives, 68th Cong., 2d Sess., on Matters Relating to the Operations of the United States Air Services,* 6 vols. (Washington: GPO, 1925).

Also pertinent are: *Report of Joint Board on Results of Aviation and Ordnance Tests Held During June and July 1921, and Conclusions Reached* (Washington: GPO, 1921); and *U.S. Conference on Limitation of Armament* (Washington: GPO, 1922).

Of great value for Fiske's service as a member of the General Board in 1910 and as an ex-officio member while he was aide for operations from 1913 to 1915 are the General Board Records and the minutes published in the *Proceedings of the General Board* (Washington: Naval History Center, Operational Archives Branch). The report of the Swift Board, dated July 15, 1909, was published by the House of Representatives, Committee on Naval Affairs, as *Reports of a Board on the Organization of the Navy Department Convened by the Secretary of the Navy, July 15, 1909, Generally Known As the Swift Board Reports* (Washington: GPO, 1915).

The naval bible, of course, is *Navy Regulations.* An excellent collection of documents on naval administration and organization, with some commentary, is Elting E. Morison, *Naval Administration: Selected Documents on Navy Department Organization, 1915-1940* (Washington: Navy Department, 1945). Also of value is *The United States Navy—A Description of Its Functional Organization, Prepared by the Office of the Management Engineer, Navy Department, October 1952* (Washington: GPO, 1952).

Documents on Fiske's career in the National Archives in Washington may be found largely in the following Record Groups: RG 19, Bureau of Ships; RG 24, Records of Naval Officers and Ships' Logs; RG 38, Records of the Office of the Chief of Naval Operations; RG 45, Naval Records Collection of the Office of Naval Records and Library; RG 72, Records of the Bureau of Aeronautics; RG 80, General Correspondence of the Navy Department; RG 94, Records of the Naval War Board [1898]; RG 225, Joint Boards; RG 313, Records of Naval Operating Forces; and RG 405, Records of the U.S. Naval Academy. Unfortunately, no single file exists for the Office of the Aide for Operations; the correspondence of this office is scattered throughout RG 38, RG 45, and RG 80.

Selected diplomatic events were followed in the decimal files of the Department of State (also housed in the National Archives) and in pertinent volumes of the *Papers Relating to the Foreign Relations of the United States,* issued by the Department of State (Washington: GPO, 1898–1922).

Newspapers and Journals

Most metropolitan newspapers during Fiske's years paid some attention to naval affairs; those along the East Coast, such as the *Baltimore Sun,* the *New York American,* the *New York Herald,* the *New York Journal,* the *New York Sun,* the *New York Times,* the *New York Tribune,* the *New York World,* the *Philadelphia Evening Telegraph,* the *Washington Post,* and the *Evening Star,* provided good coverage not only of maritime matters but of what transpired in the Capital as well.

Republican newspapers, much more than Democratic ones, supported the naval building programs and an interventionist foreign policy from the term of President Arthur through that of Theodore Roosevelt. Conversely, Democratic papers supported Woodrow Wilson first on neutrality and then on preparedness. After Fiske's retirement, the *New York Times* gave him excellent coverage and printed many of his letters. While William F. Fullam wrote its "Quarterdeck" column, the *New York Tribune* reflected the demands of the large-navy school. William R. Hearst's *New York American,* like his many other journals, revealed an anti-British bias.

Views on changes within the navy have been ascertained from a number of magazines and journals. *The American Review of Reviews* and *Literary Digest* provided excellent summaries and editorial comment; the former, while under the editorship of Albert Shaw, was pronavy and expansionist in outlook. Pronavy sentiment also animated almost every issue of both the *Army and Navy Journal,* especially while it was edited by William C. Church, and the *Army and Navy Register.* The *U.S. Naval Institute Proceedings,* which I have read from 1874 to 1978, contains many articles critical of the navy. *Current History* is valuable for its in-depth coverage of issues. Accounts of naval affairs frequently grace the pages of *Atlantic Monthly, Forum, Harper's Magazine, North American Review,* and *World's Work.* Under the editorship of George Harvey, the *North American Review* was uproariously anti-Daniels. More specialized studies in naval matters appear in *American Neptune, Military Affairs,* and the *Scientific American.* While the *Independent* showed a religious bent and *The Nation* supported pacifism, *The Outlook* for years served as a mouthpiece for Theodore Roosevelt. Historical articles dealing with events of interest to Fiske were found also in the *Mississippi Valley Historical Review* (later *Journal of American History*), *American Historical Review, Pacific Historical Review,* and *The*

Electrical World (later *Electrical World* and *Electrical Engineer*). Aviation matters are covered in *Aerial Age, Aviation, Flying, Naval Aviation News,* and *U.S. Air Services.* Other magazines containing occasional items relevant to Fiske's career are *Harper's Weekly, Historian, McClure's Magazine, Mechanical Engineering, Newsweek, Saturday Evening Post, Sea Power,* and *Time.*

An extremely selective list of important (signed) articles in the magazines noted above and in others follows. Fiske's idea that economic determinism was a major cause of war is illustrated in Brooks Adams, "War as the Ultimate Form of Economic Competition," *USNIP* 29 (Sept. 1903): 829–82. Naval organization and administration are the burden of Park Benjamin, "The Proposed Navy General Staff," *Independent* 46 (Jan. 28, 1904): 201–3, and "The Reorganization of the Navy," *Independent* 67 (Dec. 16, 1909): 1384–87; Henry Beers, "The Development of the Office of the Chief of Naval Operations," *Military Affairs* 10 (Spring 1946): 40–68, *ibid.* 10 (Fall 1946): 10–38, *ibid.* 11 (Summer 1947): 88–99, and *ibid.* 11 (Winter 1947): 229–37; Caspar F. Goodrich, "Mr. Newberry's Naval Reforms," *North American Review* 191 (Feb. 1910): 155–57, *ibid.* (Mar. 1910): 340–45; John Hood, "Naval Policy: As It Relates to the Shore Establishment and the Maintenance of the Fleet," *USNIP* 40 (Mar.–Apr. 1914): 319–44; Needham L. Jones, USN, "The New Navy Regulations," *USNIP* 39 (Mar. 1913): 277–82, and "Details on Navy Department Administration: Navy Department Policies," *USNIP* 40 (Mar.–Apr. 1914): 377–88; Stephen B. Luce, "Naval Administration," *USNIP* 14 (June 1888): 561–88, "Naval Administration, II," *USNIP* 38 (Dec. 1902): 839–49, and "Naval Administration, III," *USNIP* 29 (Sept. 1903): 809–22; A. T. Mahan, "The U.S. Navy Department," *Scribner's Magazine* 33 (May 1903): 566–77; Martin Meadows, "Eugene Hale and the American Navy," *American Neptune* 22 (July 1962): 187–93; Elting E. Morison, "Naval Administration in the United States," *USNIP* 72 (Oct. 1946): 1303–13; J. A. Mudd, "The Reorganization of the Naval Establishment," *USNIP* 35 (Mar. 1909): 37–65; William L. Rodgers, "An Examination of the Testimony Taken by the Joint Committee of the Senate and House of Representatives in Regard to the Reorganization of the Navy," *USNIP* 20 (1893): 747–62, and "The Relations of the War College to the Navy Department," *USNIP* 38 (Sept. 1912): 835–50.

The following articles are helpful in understanding the gunnery problems Fiske tried to solve: Philip R. Alger, "Improvements in Ordnance and Armor in the Recent Past and Future," *USNIP* 23, no. 1 (1897): 125–40, "The Composition and Arrangement of Ships' Batteries," *USNIP* 23, no. 2 (1897): 229–48, "Errors of Gunfire at Sea," *USNIP* 26 (Dec. 1900): 575–92, "The Accuracy and Probability of Gunfire," *USNIP* 29 (Dec. 1903): 935–95, and "Gunnery in Our Navy: The Causes of Its Inferiority and Their Remedies." The last, although the prize-winning essay for 1903, was classified by the Bureau of Ordnance and never published. See also Stokely Morgan, "Electric Firing on Board Ship: Electric Primers and Firing Attachments," *USNIP* 20 (1894): 763–82; Joseph Strauss, "Telescope Sight for Guns," *USNIP* 22 (1896): 589–98.

Articles by Park Benjamin that deal with Fiske's inventions or support his demands for preparedness include: "The Nerves of the War-ship," *Harper's New Monthly Magazine* 92 (Mar. 1896): 631–36, "The Challenge of the Submarine," *Independent* 80 (Oct. 5, 1914): 13–17, "Germany's Navy —a Thorn in the Flesh," *Independent* 80 (Oct. 19, 1914): 96–98, "The Flying Fish Torpedo: A New and Terrible Form of Attack on the High Seas or in Harbors," *Independent* 80 (Nov. 2, 1914): 164–66, "Is Anything Wrong with the Navy?" *Independent* 82 (May 10, 1915): 241–44, and "Fiske Torpedoplane," *Independent* 90 (May 12, 1917): 281–82. A helpful summary is Henry Woodhouse's "Devices Invented by Admiral Fiske," *New York Times,* May 15, 1919, 3:3. Details on the ABCDs from a naval constructor's viewpoint are found in Francis T. Bowles, "Our New Cruisers," *USNIP* 9 (Sept. 1883): 595–631 (illustrated). George Harvey severely criticized Daniels's administration of the navy in "The Rt. Hon. Sir Josephus, N[orth] C[arolina] B[oy]: Our First Lord of the Admiralty," *North American Review* 201 (Apr. 1915): 481–500, and "Preparedness a Political Issue," *North American Review* 203 (Apr. 1916): 481–92. So did John Palmer Govit, "Much Ado About Daniels," *Harper's Weekly* 60 (May 8, 1915): 462–65, *ibid.* (May 15, 1915): 72–73; Burton J. Hendrick, "The Case of Josephus Daniels," *World's Work* 32 (July 1916): 281–96; Harry A. Austin, "U.S. Unprepared for War," *Forum* 51 (Apr. 1914): 526–34.

Problems associated with developing naval aviation are described in Washington Irving Chambers, "Aviation and Aeroplanes," *USNIP* 37 (Mar. 1911): 162–208, and "Aviation To-Day, and the Necessity for a National Aerodynamic Laboratory," *USNIP* 39 (Dec. 1912): 329–36; W. Geoffrey Moore, "The Seat of Your Pants Told You . . . ," *USNIP* 94 (June 1968): 82–94, describes the first British carrier landing, on August 2, 1917, by a Sopwith Pup on HMS *Furious.* Thomas T. Craven, USN, discusses the development of naval aviation in "Naval Aviation," *USNIP* 46 (Feb. 1920): 181–91, and "Naval Aviation and a United Air Service," *USNIP* 47 (Mar. 1921): 307–22. Also valuable on the subject are Hal Andrews, "Fifty Years of Naval Aircraft" (11 parts), *Naval Aviation News* (Feb.–Dec. 1961); Ashbrook Lincoln, "The United States Navy and the Rise of the Doctrine of Air Power," *Military Affairs* 15 (Fall 1951): 145–56; Edward G. Lowry, "The Three-Plane Navy," *Saturday Evening Post* 193 (June 11, 1921): 16–17; Roy

Campbell Smith, "Aircraft versus Battleships," *North American Review* 216 (Oct. 1922): 470–75; Adrian O. Van Wyen, "U.S. Naval Aviation in World War I" (in 18 parts), *Naval Aviation News* (Apr. 1967–Oct. 1968). Delightfully written but somewhat inaccurate is an article by the editors of *Sea Power*, "Fiske's Folly: Torpedo Planes," in *The Navy Reader*, edited by William Harrison Fetridge (Indianapolis: Bobbs-Merrill, 1943), pp. 137–41. An excellent overview of their subject is Donald B. Duncan and H. M. Dater, "Administrative History of U.S. Naval Aviation," *Air Affairs: An International Quarterly* 1 (Summer 1947): 526–39.

Support for Fiske's ideas on Navy Department reorganization is found in William P. Cronan, "The Greatest Need of the United States Navy: Proper Organization for the Successful Conduct of War," *USNIP* 42 (July–Aug. 1916): 1137–70; W. S. Crosley, "The Naval War College, the General Board, and the Office of Naval Intelligence," *USNIP* 39 (Sept. 1913): 965–74; Charles W. Cullen, "From the Kriegsacademie to the Naval War College: The Military Planning Process," *Naval War College Review* 22 (Jan. 1970): 6–18; and Yates Stirling, "Organization for Navy Department Administration: A Study of Principles," *USNIP* 39 (June 1913): 435–500, and "Bureaucracy Rules the Navy: The Absence of a General Staff Seriously Imperils the Value of Our Naval Forces," *Current History* 51 (Mar. 1940): 30–32. See also J. A. S. Grenville, "Diplomacy and War Plans in the United States, 1890–1917," *Royal History Society Transactions* (London) 11 (1961): 1–21.

John M. Ellicott visited all the Spanish ships and recorded his observations in "Effect of Gun-Fire, Battle of Manila Bay," *USNIP* 25 (June 1898): 323–34. Once converted to Fiske's viewpoint on the utility of range finders, Albert Gleaves wrote his conclusions about them in "The Influence of Range-Finders upon Modern Ordnance, Gunnery, and Warship Construction," *USNIP* 18, no. 62 (1892): 259–64. Fiske's range finder, shell-hoisting motors, and other early inventions are described by Hamilton Hitchins in "Electrical Equipment of Our Squadron of Evolution," *Electrical World* 17 (Jan. 31, 1891): 73–91, *ibid.* (Feb. 7, 1891): 97–99. Progress in the field may be followed in J. B. Murdock, "The Naval Use of the Dynamo Machine and Electric Light," *USNIP* 8 (Apr. 14, 1882): 343–86; George W. Dickie, "Auxiliary Engines and Transmission of Power on Naval Vessels," *Electrical World* 30 (Dec. 11, 1897): 699–700; Alton D. Adams, "Electric Auxiliary Machinery in the United States Navy," *USNIP* 25, no. 4 (1899): 956–63; and Alexander M. Charlton, "Electrical Division Aboard Ship," *USNIP* 45 (June 1919): 989–1108.

Articles by Dudley W. Knox that supported Fiske's opposition to naval disarmament include "A Defense of United States Naval Policy," *Current History* 22 (June 1925): 339–44, "Our 'Stake' in Sea Power," *USNIP* 53

(Oct. 1926) : 1087–89, and "The London Treaty and American Naval Policy," *USNIP* 57 (Aug. 1931): 1078–88. How Fiske devised the annual department-wide exercise is revealed by one of his "war staff," Z. H. Madison, "The Departmental Strategic Problems as a Drill for the Entire Naval Establishment," *USNIP* 42 (Nov.–Dec. 1916): 1793–814.

The disparagement of naval air power is evidenced by the army's William Mitchell, "Aviation over the Water," *American Review of Reviews* 62 (Oct. 1920): 391–98, and "Air Power vs. Sea Power," *ibid.* 63 (Mar. 1921): 273–77. William A. Moffett answered Mitchell in "Aviation Progress in America," *Current History* 17 (Feb. 1922): 775–82, and more particularly in "Air Service versus Air Force," *Forum* 75 (Feb. 1926): 179–85. Dudley W. Knox's answer to Mitchell may be found in Lester H. Brune, "Foreign Policy and the Air Power Dispute, 1919–1932," *Historian* 23 (Aug. 1961): 449–64, which is based on the Knox and Mitchell papers in the Library of Congress.

On the question of whether tonnage, the number and size of guns, or other factors should be used in measuring naval power, see Raymond G. O'Connor, "The 'Yardstick' and Naval Disarmament in the 1920's," *Mississippi Valley Historical Review* 45 (Dec. 1958): 441–63. William V. Pratt's internationalist outlook is revealed in "Naval Policy and the Naval Treaty," *North American Review* 215 (May 1922): 590–99, and "The Case for the Treaty Navy," *Current History* 18 (Apr. 1923): 1–5; his ideas received national coverage during the late 1930s and early 1940s when he wrote on naval matters for *Newsweek*.

Support for Fiske's warnings of American weaknesses in the Western Pacific following the Washington Conference is found in Gerald E. Wheeler, "The United States Navy and the Japanese 'Enemy'," *Military Affairs* 21 (Summer 1957): 61–74. There are several articles relevant to the naval disarmament conferences of the 1920s and 1930s: Thomas S. Butler, chairman of the House Committee on Naval Affairs, "America Misled by Five-Power Treaty," *Current History* 26 (Apr. 1927): 86–92, and "Don't Give Up the Ships," *North American Review* 224 (June 1927): 214–22; Burton French (a member of the House Naval Affairs Committee), "Naval Reduction: What It Means in Money," *Current History* 31 (Jan. 1930): 711–17, and "Our Navy: Shall We Build to the Limit?" *Saturday Evening Post* 204 (Oct. 31, 1931): 21–25; an address by Luke McNamee published as "The Navy and the 5-5-3 Ratio," *USNIP* 48 (July 1922): 1139–48; Franklin G. Percival, "The Cruiser Problem," *USNIP* 56 (May 1930): 387–99.

The development of naval science is traced in Green Fitzhugh, "Science and the Navy," *USNIP* 48 (Oct. 1922): 1697–706; Paul Foley, "The Naval Research Laboratory," *USNIP* 51 (Oct. 1925): 1925–32; Clyde S. McDowell,

"Naval Research," *Science* n.s. 49 (June 14, 1929): 607–9, and "Naval Research," *USNIP* 45 (June 1919): 895–908. Henry Woodhouse predicted great utility for the torpedo plane in "The Torpedoplane: A New Weapon Which Promises to Revolutionize Naval Tactics," *USNIP* 45 (May 1919): 743–52; twenty years later his predictions proved correct; see his "Torpedoplanes in World War II," *USNIP* 67 (Dec. 1941): 1750–64. See also articles by two naval aviators: C. DeWitt ["Duke"] Ramsey, "The Development of Aviation in the Fleet," *USNIP* 49 (Sept. 1923): 1395–417; Logan C. Ramsey, "The Torpedoplane's Advantage over the 'Naval Bomber," *Aviation* 31 (Apr. 1932): 179.

PERSONAL HISTORIES

Fiske's relations with his naval contemporaries are described in his autobiography, *From Midshipman to Rear-Admiral* (New York: The Century Co., 1919). For his relationship with his contemporaries, I have consulted autobiographies, biographies, and published letter collections. Neither James R. Soley, *Historical Sketches of the United States Naval Academy* (Washington: GPO, 1976), nor John D. M. C. Crane and James F. Kieley, *The United States Naval Academy: The First Hundred Years* (New York: McGraw-Hill, 1945), are as revealing as Park Benjamin, *The United States Naval Academy, Being the Yarn of the American Midshipman* (New York and London: G. P. Putnam's Sons, 1900). Edward Arpee, *From Frigates to Flat-Tops: The Story of the Life and Achievements of Rear Admiral William Adger Moffett, U.S.N., "The Father of Naval Aviation," October 31, 1869–April 4, 1933* (Lake Forest, Ill.: privately printed, 1953) is valuable. Progress made in ordnance work is detailed briefly in Wilbur R. Van Auken, *Notes on a Half Century of U.S. Naval Ordnance, 1880–1930* (Washington: George Banta, 1939). Reminiscences of military men that mention Fiske or illuminate his times are: Albert S. Barker, *Everyday Life in the Navy: The Autobiography of Albert S. Barker* (Boston: R. G. Badger, 1928); Charles E. Clark, *My Fifty Years in the Navy* (Boston: Little, Brown, 1917); Robert H. Coontz, *From the Mississippi to the Sea* (Philadelphia: Dorrance, 1930); George Dewey, *Autobiography of George Dewey: Admiral of the Navy* (New York: Charles Scribner's Sons, 1913), takes the story only up to 1899; Holden A. Evans, *One Man's Fight for a Better Navy* (New York: Dodd, Mead, 1940); Ruth Mitchell, *My Brother Bill: The Life of "Billy" Mitchell* (New York: Harcourt, Brace, 1953); Seaton Schroeder, *A Half Century of Naval Service* (New York and London: D. Appleton, 1922); Robert Seager II, *Alfred Thayer Mahan:*

The Man and His Letters (Annapolis: Naval Institute Press, 1977); Yates
Stirling, *Sea Duty: The Memoirs of a Fighting Admiral* (New York:
G. P. Putnam's Sons, 1939), and Henry Ariosto Wiley, *An Admiral from
Texas* (Garden City, N.Y.: Doubleday, Doran, 1934). A crewman on the
Petrel confirms her operations and Fiske's activities in the Battle of Manila
Bay: see Bert B. Singman, "Eyewitness to History: A Participant's Memories
of the Spanish-American War, Philippine Insurrection, Boxer Rebellion,"
typescript (U.S. Naval Academy Library, 1962).

Other personal or biographical accounts of value include: Damon T.
Cummings, *Admiral Richard Wainwright and the United States Fleet*
(Washington: GPO, 1962); Edwin A. Falk, *Fighting Bob Evans* (New
York: Jonathan Cape and Harrison Smith, 1931); Albert Gleaves, *The Life
and Letters of Rear Admiral Stephen B. Luce, U.S. Navy: Founder of the
Naval War College* (New York: G. P. Putnam's Sons, 1925); Hermann
Hagedorn, *Leonard Wood: A Biography*, 2 vols. (New York and London:
Harper and Brothers, 1931); Caroline Brownson Hart and Louise Powers
Benesch, comps., *From Frigate to Dreadnaught* [*Life of Willard H. Brownson*] (Sharon, Conn.: King House, 1973); John D. Hayes and John B.
Hattendorf, eds., *The Writings of Stephen B. Luce* (Newport: Naval War
College, 1975); Alfred F. Hurley, *Billy Mitchell: Crusader for Air Power*
(New York: Franklin Watts, 1964); Ernest J. King and Walter Muir
Whitehill, *Fleet Admiral King: A Naval Record* (New York: W. W.
Norton, 1952); Dorothy Michelson Livingston, *The Master of Light: A
Biography of Albert A. Michelson* (New York: Charles Scribner's Sons,
1973); Elting E. Morison's *Admiral Sims and the Modern American Navy*
(Boston: Houghton Mifflin, 1942) and *Turmoil and Tradition: A Study
of the Life and Times of Henry L. Stimson* (Boston: Houghton Mifflin,
1960); Hugh Rodman, *Yarns of a Kentucky Admiral* (Indianapolis: Bobbs-
Merrill, 1928); Sir Percy Moreton Scott, Bart., *Fifty Years in the Royal Navy*
(London: J. Murray, 1919); Ronald Spector, *Admiral of Empire: The Life
and Career of George Dewey* (Baton Rouge: Louisiana State University
Press, 1974); Gerald E. Wheeler, *Admiral William Veazie Pratt, U.S. Navy:
A Sailor's Life* (Washington: Navy Department, Naval History Division,
1974).

Among the autobiographies and biographies of political, literary, and
scientific figures, the most pertinent are: Ray Stannard Baker, *Woodrow
Wilson: Life and Letters*, 8 vols. (Garden City, N.Y.: Doubleday, Page,
1927–39), which is superseded in part by Arthur S. Link, *Wilson*, 5 vols.
(Princeton, N.J.: Princeton University Press, 1947–). Bonaparte's attempts to reorganize the navy are discussed in Joseph Bishop, *Charles Bonaparte: His Life and Public Services* (New York: Charles Scribner's Sons,

1922). Josephus Daniels told his story in a multivolume autobiography in which two volumes bear heavily on Fiske: *The Wilson Era: Years of Peace, 1910–1917* (Chapel Hill: University of North Carolina Press, 1944) and *The Wilson Era: Years of War and After, 1917–1923* (Chapel Hill: University of North Carolina Press, 1946). Superbly written is William Henry Harbaugh's *Power and Responsibility: The Life and Times of Theodore Roosevelt* (New York: Farrar, Straus and Cudahy, 1961). For Secretary Meyer, see Mark A. De Wolfe Howe, *George von Lengerke Meyer* (New York: Dodd, Mead, 1919). A superb biography is that of Thomas Parke Hughes, *Elmer Sperry: Inventor and Engineer* (Baltimore: Johns Hopkins Press, 1971). J. Gordon Vaeth in *Langley: Man of Science and Flight* (New York: Ronald Press, 1966) does for Langley what Orrin Dunlap does for Marconi in *Marconi: The Man and His Wireless* (New York: Macmillan, 1937). The outlook of William Jennings Bryan toward diplomacy, preparedness, war, and peace is covered in Paolo E. Coletta, *William Jennings Bryan*, 3 vols. (Lincoln: University of Nebraska Press, 1964–69), that of Taft in Coletta's *The Presidency of William Howard Taft* (Lawrence: University of Kansas Press, 1973), and that of McKinley in Coletta's edited collection, *Threshold to American Internationalism: Essays on the Foreign Policies of William McKinley* (New York: Exposition Press, 1970).

General Works

Very useful for revealing the attitude of Josephus Daniels and Theodore Roosevelt toward Bradley A. Fiske or naval problems with which Fiske was also concerned are: David Cronon, ed., *The Cabinet Diaries of Josephus Daniels, 1913–1921* (Lincoln: University of Nebraska Press, 1963); Henry Cabot Lodge, *Selections from the Correspondence of Theodore Roosevelt and Henry Cabot Lodge, 1884–1918*, 2 vols. (New York: Charles Scribner's Sons, 1925); and Elting E. Morison et al., eds., *The Letters of Theodore Roosevelt*, 8 vols. (Cambridge: Harvard University Press, 1951–54). The latest and best work of its kind is Myron J. Smith, Jr., ed., *American Naval Bibliography*, 5 vols. (Metuchen, N.J.: Scarecrow Press, 1972–74), especially volume 4, *The American Navy, 1865–1918* (1974), and volume 5, *The American Navy, 1918–1941* (1974). See also Myron J. Smith, Jr., ed., *World War I in the Air: A Bibliography and Chronology* (Metuchen, N.J.: Scarecrow Press, 1977).

For the characteristics of ships and aircraft I have relied on K. Jack Bauer, *Ships of the Navy, 1775–1969: Combat Vessels* (Troy, N.Y.: Rensselaer Polytechnic Institute, 1970); *Brassey's Naval Annual* (London and

New York: various publishers, 1886–1950); and *Jane's Fighting Ships* (London: A. Low, Marston, 1898–).

For a general understanding of science and especially of electrical engineering, ordnance, gunnery, and aviation in Fiske's day, the most useful studies are: Philip Rounseville Alger, *Groundwork of Practical Naval Gunnery* (Annapolis: U.S. Naval Institute, 1917); William Hannum Grubb Bullard, *Electricity on Ships* (Annapolis: U.S. Naval Institute, 1908) and *Naval Electricians Text and Hand Book* (Annapolis: U.S. Naval Institute, 1904, 1911); By the Officers of the Navy, *Ordnance and Gunnery: A Text-Book Prepared for the Use of the Midshipmen of the U.S. Naval Academy* (Annapolis: U.S. Naval Institute, 1899, 1903, 1910); Monte A. Calvert, *The Mechanical Engineer in America, 1830–1910: Professional Cultures in Conflict* (Baltimore: Johns Hopkins Press, 1967); Thomas K. Derry and Trevor J. Williams, *A Short History of Technology: From the Earliest Times to A.D. 1900* (Oxford: Clarendon Press, 1960); Percy Dunsheath, ed., *A Century of Technology* (London and New York: Hutchinson's Scientific and Technical Publications, 1951); A. Hunter Dupree, *Science in the Federal Government: A History of Policies and Activities to 1940* (Cambridge: Harvard University Press, 1957); Ralph Earle, ed., *Navy Ordnance Activities—World War 1917–1918* (Washington: GPO, 1920); Dennis Gabor, *Innovations: Scientific, Technological, and Social* (London: Oxford University Press, 1970); S. C. Gilfillan, *The Sociology of Invention* (Cambridge: M.I.T. Press, 1935, 1970); Edwyn Gray, *The Devil's Device: The Story of Robert Whitehead, Inventor of the Torpedo* (London: Seeley, Service, 1975); Samuel Haber, *Efficiency and Uplift: Scientific Management in the Progressive Era, 1890–1920* (Chicago: University of Chicago Press, 1974); Sir Arthur Hezlet, *Aircraft and Sea Power* (London: P. Davies, 1970), and *Electronics and Sea Power* (New York: Stein and Day, 1975); James J. Hudson, *Hostile Skies: A Combat History of the American Air Service in World War I* (Syracuse: Syracuse University Press, 1968); Jerome C. Hunsaker, "Forty Years of Aeronautical Research," in *Smithsonian Institution, Annual Report, 1955* (Washington, 1956), pp. 241–77; Henry Albert Jones, *The War in the Air: Being the Story of the Part Played in the Great War by the Royal Air Force*, 6 vols. (Oxford: Clarendon, 1922–37); James W. King, *The Development of Electrical Technology in the 19th Century*, Contributions from the Museum of History and Technology, Paper 30 (Washington, 1962); Dr. Franklin H. Martin, *Digest of the Proceedings of the Council of National Defense During the World War* (Washington: GPO, 1934); Elting E. Morison, *Men, Machines, and Modern Times* (Cambridge: M.I.T. Press, 1966) and *The War of Ideas: The United States Navy 1870–1890* (Colorado Springs: U.S. Air Force Academy, 1969); Peter Padfield, *Guns at Sea* (London: Hugh Evelyn, 1973); Oscar Parks, *British Battleships, Warrior to Vanguard, 1860–1950: A History of Design, Construction, and Armament* (London: Seeley, 1956); Taylor Peck, *Round-Shot to Rockets: A History of the Washington Navy Yard and U.S. Naval Gun Factory* (Annapolis: U.S. Naval Institute, 1949); Samuel Rappaport and Helen Wright, eds., *Engineering* (New York: New York University Press, 1963); Frederick Leslie Robertson, *The Evolution of Naval Armament* (London: H. T. Storey, 1968); Lloyd N. Scott, *Naval Consulting Board of the United States* (Washington: GPO, 1920); G. R. Simonson, ed., *The History of the American Aircraft Industry: An Anthology* (Cambridge: M.I.T. Press, 1968); Murray Frazer Sueter, *Evolution of the Submarine Boat, Mine and Torpedo, from the Sixteenth Century to the Present Time* (Portsmouth: Griffin and Co., 1907); Frederic Gordon Swanborough and Peter M. Bowers, *United States Navy Aircraft Since 1911* (London: Putnam, 1968); Sir Charles Percy Snow, *Science and Government* (Cambridge: Harvard University Press, 1961); Albert H. Taylor, *The First Twenty-Five Years of the Naval Research Laboratory* (Washington: Navy Department, 1948); Archibald Turnbull and Clifford L. Lord, *History of United States Naval Aviation* (New Haven: Yale University Press, 1949); and Henry Woodhouse, *Textbook of Naval Aeronautics* (New York: Century Co., 1917).

Fiske would have been less obsessed with the German naval staff if he could have read Larry Addington II, *The Blitzkrieg Era and the German General Staff, 1865–1914* (New Brunswick, N.J.: Rutgers University Press, 1971); Walter Gorlitz, *The German General Staff: Its History and Structure, 1657–1956*, trans. Brian Battershaw (London: Hollis and Carter, 1953); Holger H. Herwig, *Politics of Frustration: The United States in German Naval Planning, 1889–1941* (Boston: Little, Brown, 1976); and James Edward Sutton, "The Imperial German Navy, 1910–1914" (Ph.D. diss., Indiana University, 1953). Also pertinent are Carl-Axel Gemzell, *Organization, Conflict, and Innovation: A Study of German Naval Strategic Planning, 1888–1940* (Stockholm: Esselte Studium, 1973), and Holger H. Herwig, *The German Naval Officer Corps: A Social and Political History, 1890–1918* (Oxford: Clarendon, 1973).

Basic works that deal with the functions of the post–Civil War navy and the creation of the "new navy" are: Kenneth J. Hagan, *American Gunboat Diplomacy and the Old Navy* (Westport, Conn.: Greenwood Press, 1973); Walter Herrick, Jr., *The American Naval Revolution* (Baton Rouge: Louisiana State University Press, 1967); John D. Long, *The New American Navy*, 2 vols. (New York: Outlook Co., 1903); Harold and Margaret Sprout, *The Rise of American Naval Power, 1776–1918* (Princeton: Princeton University Press, 1939). Histories of the shift from sail to steam include Frank Marion Bennett, *The Steam Navy of the United States: A History of the Growth of the Steam Vessel of War in the U.S. Navy, and of the Naval Engineer Corps* (Pittsburgh: Nicholson, 1896), and P. W. Brock and Basil Greenhill, *Steam and Sail* (Princeton, N.J.: Payne Press, 1973).

Of the secretaries of the navy in Fiske's day, biographies have appeared on Bonaparte, Chandler, Daniels, Meyer, Tracy, and Whitney. For Daniels, see Joseph L. Morrison, *Josephus Daniels: The Small-d Democrat* (Chapel Hill: University of North Carolina Press, 1966); for Tracy, see Benjamin Franklin Cooling, *Benjamin Franklin Tracy: Father of the Modern American Fighting Navy* (Hamden, Conn.: Archon Books, 1973); for Whitney, see Mark D. Hirsch, *William C. Whitney: Modern Warwick* (New York: Dodd, Mead, 1948).

Among the best books that deal with U.S. naval activity in the Far East at the time of the Spanish-American War are Fiske's *Wartime in Manila* (Boston: Gorham Press, 1913) and French E. Chadwick, *The Relations of the United States and Spain: The Spanish-American War*, 2 vols. (New York: Charles Scribner's Sons, 1911). A brief but cogent study is Gordon Carpenter O'Gara, *Theodore Roosevelt and the Rise of the Modern Navy* (Princeton: Princeton University Press, 1943). A brilliant work is Howard K. Beale, *Theodore Roosevelt and the Rise of America to World Power* (Baltimore: Johns Hopkins Press, 1956).

On anti-Japanese sentiment in Fiske's day, see Akira Iriye, *Pacific Estrangement: Japanese and American Expansion, 1897–1911* (Cambridge: Harvard University Press, 1972); for Japan as a potential enemy, see Gerald E. Wheeler, *Prelude to Pearl Harbor: The United States Navy and the Far East, 1921–1931* (Columbia: University of Missouri Press, 1963). Important also are William R. Braisted's studies, *The United States Navy in the Pacific, 1897–1909* (Austin: University of Texas Press, 1958) and *The United States Navy in the Pacific, 1909–1922* (Austin: University of Texas Press, 1971).

For the numerous disarmament conferences of the 1920s and 1930s, see especially Thomas H. Buckley, *The United States and the Washington Conference, 1921–1922* (Knoxville: University of Tennessee Press, 1970); Dudley W. Knox, *Eclipse of American Sea Power* (New York: The Army and Navy Journal, 1922); Raymond G. O'Connor, *Perilous Equilibrium: The United States and the London Naval Conference of 1930* (Lawrence: University of Kansas Press, 1962); Stephen E. Pelz, *Race to Pearl Harbor: The Failure of the Second Naval Conference and the Onset of World War II* (Cambridge: Harvard University Press, 1974); Harold and Margaret Sprout, *Toward a New Order of Sea Power: American Naval Policy and the World Scene, 1918–1922* (Princeton: Princeton University Press, 1943).

For British naval affairs during Fiske's lifetime I have relied in part upon: Julian Corbett and Henry Newbolt, *History of the Great War, Based on Official Documents,* 5 vols. (London: Longmans, Green, 1920–31); Leslie Gardiner, *The British Admiralty* (Annapolis: U.S. Naval Institute, 1968); John Gooch, *The Plans of War: The General Staff and British Strategy, 1900–1916* (New York: Wiley, 1974); Arthur J. Marder, *From the Dreadnought to Scapa Flow: The Royal Navy in the Fisher Era, 1904–1919,* 4 vols. (New York: Oxford University Press, 1961–67); and Ernest Llwewellyn Woodward, *Great Britain and the German Navy* (Oxford: Clarendon, 1935). For information on naval strategy and tactics, in addition to the many works of Alfred Thayer Mahan, I have used Bernard Brodie, *A Guide to Naval Strategy,* 4th ed. (Princeton: Princeton University Press, 1958); Brodie's *Sea Power in the Machine Age,* 2d ed. (Princeton: Princeton University Press, 1943); and Giuseppe Fioravanzo, *Storia del pensiero tattico navale* (Rome: Italian Office of Naval History, 1973).

Information on civil-military relations has been garnered from: Samuel Huntington, *The Soldier and the State: The Theory and Politics of Civil-Military Relations* (Cambridge: Harvard University Press, Belknap Press, 1957); Morris Janowitz, *The Professional Soldier: A Social and Political Portrait* (Glencoe, Ill.: Free Press, 1960); and Walter Millis, *Arms and Men: A Study in American Military History* (New York: G. P. Putnam's Sons, 1956). A major work is that of Paul Y. Hammond, *Organizing for Defense: The American Military Establishment in the Twentieth Century* (Princeton: Princeton University Press, 1961).

THE WRITINGS OF BRADLEY A. FISKE

BOOKS

Electricity in Theory and Practice; or, The Elements of Electrical Engineering.
New York: D. Van Nostrand, 1887.

Wartime in Manila. Boston: Gorham Press, 1913.

The Navy as a Fighting Machine. New York: Charles Scribner's Sons, 1916.
A second edition appeared in 1918.

From Midshipman to Rear-Admiral. New York: Century Co., 1919.

The Art of Fighting: Its Evolution and Progress, with Illustrations from Campaigns of Great Commanders. New York: Century Co., 1920.

Invention: The Master-Key to Progress. New York: E. P. Dutton and Co., 1922.

ARTICLES

"The Electric Railway." *Popular Science Monthly* 24 (Apr. 1884): 742–51.

"The Naval Battle of the Future." *Forum* 9 (May 1890): 323–32.

"The Civilian Electrician in a Modern War." *Science* 16 (Oct. 24, 1890): 225–27.

"The Civilian Electrician in Modern War." *Electrical World* 16 (Nov. 1, 1890): 322–23.

"Electricity in Naval Life." *U.S. Naval Institute Proceedings* 22 (Sept. 1896): 323–428.

"Why We Won at Manila." *The Century Magazine,* n.s. 35 (Nov. 1898): 127–35.

"Range Finders." *U.S. Naval Institute Proceedings* 27 (June 1901): 432–34.

"A Useful Little Change in the Pelorus." *U.S. Naval Institute Proceedings* 27 (June 1901): 371–72.

"The Fiske Semaphore System." *U.S. Naval Institute Proceedings* 29 (June 1903): 679–98.

"A Naval Telescope and Mount." *U.S. Naval Institute Proceedings* 29 (June 1903): 699–700.

"War Signals." *U.S. Naval Institute Proceedings* 29 (Sept. 1903): 931–34.

"American Naval Policy." *U.S. Naval Institute Proceedings* 31 (Jan. 1905): 1–80.

"What America Has Learned from Togo." *Harper's Weekly* 49 (July 1, 1905): 938.

"Compromiseless Ships." *U.S. Naval Institute Proceedings* 31 (Sept. 1905): 549–53.

"The Stadimeter in Fire Control." *U.S. Naval Institute Proceedings* 31 (Dec. 1905): 973–74.

"Why Togo Won." *U.S. Naval Institute Proceedings* 31 (Dec. 1905): 807–9.

"The Civil and the Military Authority." *U.S. Naval Institute Proceedings* 32 (Mar. 1906): 127–30.

"The Horizometer." *U.S. Naval Institute Proceedings* 33 (Sept. 1906): 1043–55.

"Fleet Telephony." *U.S. Naval Institute Proceedings* 33 (Mar. 1907): 239–42.

"The Naval Profession." *U.S. Naval Institute Proceedings* 33 (June 1907): 475–578.

"Navigating without Horizon." *U.S. Naval Institute Proceedings* 33 (Sept. 1907): 955–57.

"Navigating without Horizon." *The Scientific American* 64 (Dec. 28, 1907): 405.

"Courage and Prudence." *U.S. Naval Institute Proceedings* 34 (Mar. 1908): 277–308.

"Spotting and Range-Finding." *U.S. Naval Institute Proceedings* 34 (June 1908): 655–61.

"A Fair Basis for Competition in Battle Practice." *U.S. Naval Institute Proceedings* 34 (Dec. 1908): 1189–98.

"A Curious Fact About Spotting." *U.S. Naval Institute Proceedings* 34 (Dec. 1908): 1297–98.

"An Unprecedented Rescue." *U.S. Naval Institute Proceedings* 36 (Dec. 1910): 957–64.

"Incorrect Adjustment of Range Finders." *U.S. Naval Institute Proceedings* 36 (Dec. 1910): 1069–70.

"Naval Power." *U.S. Naval Institute Proceedings* 37 (June 1911): 683–736.

"The Relative Importance of Turret and Telescope Sight." *U.S. Naval Institute Proceedings* 38 (June 1912): 595–602.

"The Mean Point of Impact." *U.S. Naval Institute Proceedings* 38 (Sept. 1912): 1001–36.

"The Diplomatic Responsibility of the United States Navy." *U.S. Naval Institute Proceedings* 40 (May–June 1914): 799–802.

"The Paramount Duty of the Army and Navy." *U.S. Naval Institute Proceedings* 41 (July–Aug. 1914): 1073–74.

"The Effectiveness of Skill." *U.S. Naval Institute Proceedings* 41 (Jan.–Feb. 1915): 67–70.

The Writings of Bradley A. Fiske

"The Mastery of the World." *North American Review* 202 (Oct. 1915): 517–26.

"Naval Principles." *North American Review* 202 (Nov. 1915): 693–701.

"Naval Preparedness." *North American Review* 202 (Dec. 1915): 847–57.

"Naval Policy." *North American Review* 203 (Jan. 1916): 63–73.

"Naval Defense." *North American Review* 203 (Feb. 1916): 216–26.

"Naval Strategy." *U.S. Naval Institute Proceedings* 42 (Mar.–Apr. 1916): 387–408.

"The Next Five Years of the Navy: What We Shall Get for the Billion Dollars We Shall Spend." *The World's Work* 33 (Jan. 1917): 256–75.

"The War's Most Important Hint to US: The Desirability of Invoking the Aid of Physical Science and the Genius of Invention." *The World's Work* 33 (Feb. 1917): 293–98.

"Admiral Dewey: An Appreciation." *U.S. Naval Institute Proceedings* 43 (Mar. 1917): 433–36.

"Naval Power and National Efficiency." *The Independent* 91 (July 21, 1917): 100.

"Air Power." *U.S. Naval Institute Proceedings* 43 (Aug. 1917): 1701–4.

"Stephen B. Luce: An Appreciation." *U.S. Naval Institute Proceedings* 43 (Sept. 1917): 1935–40.

"Strategy, Tactics, Logistics, and Invention." *U.S. Naval Institute Proceedings* 43 (Dec. 1917): 2793–98.

"The Future of the Torpedo Plane." *U.S. Naval Institute Proceedings* 44 (Jan. 1918): 137–43.

"The United States Naval Institute." *U.S. Naval Institute Proceedings* 45 (Feb. 1919): 197–200.

"The Roosevelt Memorial." *U.S. Naval Institute Proceedings* 45 (Aug. 1919): 1303–4.

"The Warfare of the Future." *U.S. Naval Institute Proceedings* 47 (Feb. 1921): 157–67.

"The Defense of the Philippines." *North American Review* 213 (June 1921): 721–24.

"Luxury and War." *North American Review* 215 (Jan. 1922): 28–31.

"Strongest Navy." *Current History Magazine* 16 (July 1922): 557–63.

"Torpedo Plane and Bomber." *U.S. Naval Institute Proceedings* 48 (Sept. 1922): 1474–78.

"Possibilities for Disarmament." *Annals of the American Academy of Political and Social Science* 120 (July 1925): 77–80.

"How We Shall Lose the Next War, and When." *The World's Work* 53 (Apr. 1927): 626–35.

"Pacifists and Militarists." *Woman Citizen*, n.s. 12 (Oct. 1927): 14–15 and (Dec. 1927): 38–39.

"Sperry's Contributions to the Naval Arts." *The Mechanical Engineer* 49 (1927): 111–12.

"Delusions of Pacifists." *Forum* 81 (Feb. 1929): 75–77.

"War and Peace." *Forum* 81, sup. 46 (Mar. 1929): xlvi.

"Air Power, 1914–1943." *U.S. Naval Institute Proceedings* 68 (May 1942): 686–94. (This article, written just before Fiske's death, was published posthumously.)

INDEX

Adder, 62
Aero Club of America, 187, 188, 189, 190–91, 193
Aeronautics, Bureau of, 214–15
After-steering, 91
Aguinaldo, Emilio, 56, 57, 59
Alabama, 44, 68
American Defense Society, 175, 176, 177, 184
American Range Finder Company. *See* Wickes, Edward
Ammunition hoist, electric, 42
Antilla, 126
Arkansas (BM-7) 81, 82, 86, (BB-33) 96, 103, 219
Atlanta, 17, 18, 19, 20, 23, 24

Badger, Charles J., 4, 100, 107, 112, 122, 124, 126, 134, 144, 145, 151, 168, 208, 210, 214
Baltimore, 23, 25, 27, 28, 29, 33, 34–35, 36, 37, 53, 54, 55
Barton, Enos, 38, 52
Battery fire, naval. *See* Continuous-aim battery fire
Battle of Manila Bay, 53–56
Benjamin, Park, 11–12, 46, 227, 228; and Fiske, 15, 98–99, 187; and Wickes, 44–45
Benson, William Sheperd, 4, 183, 188, 204–5, 210; as the first chief of naval operations, 158–59, 163, 168–69, 175, 184, 190, 191, 192, 199, 220, 232
Bloch, Claude C., 195–96
Blue, Victor, 104, 105, 108, 122, 123, 125, 138, 139, 140, 141, 142, 144, 152, 155, 167, 208–9, 220, 233

Bonaparte, Charles J., 78, 79, 231
Birmingham, 109, 110
Boston, 17, 18, 35, 53, 56
Bradley, John (maternal uncle), 3
Bradley, Susan Matthews (Mrs. William Allen Fiske), 3
Bristol, Mark, 72, 73, 109–10, 112, 135
Britten, Fred A., 166, 167, 169, 172
Brooklyn, 43, 44, 59, 63
Brownson, Willard Herbert, 4, 82
Bryan, William Jennings, 127, 128, 129, 136, 161, 186, 232, 233; and Mexico (1913–1915), 119, 121, 123, 124, 126
Bunce, Francis M., 19, 21
Bureau of Aeronautics, 214–15
Butler, Thomas S., 167, 214

Cabot, Godfrey L., 189–90
California, 90
Caperton, William B., 4, 129
Capitan Prat, 35
Carranza, Venustiano, 118, 122, 124, 126
Castilla, 54
Chadwick, French Ensor, 32, 70
Chambers, Washington Irving, 4, 109, 224
Charleston, 37, 40
"Check fire," 100
Chicago, 17, 23, 25, 26, 37, 53
Christina, 54
Church, William C., 107, 119, 136, 138, 140, 156, 163, 164, 170, 173
Cincinnati, 38, 41, 69
Colorado, 12, 13, (CA-7) 90
Concord, 53, 57
Cone, Hutch I., 151, 157, 161

Index

Index

213, 214, 216, 218, 220, 223, 228, 230, 236, 237; and Fiske, 79–80, 103, 151, 189–91; and naval administration, 66, 67; and naval general staff, 76, 77, 106, 168, 172; and naval gunnery, 64, 73, 104, 122; and the naval investigations hearings (1920), 200–212

Smith, Roy C., 136, 140, 159

Solace, 61

South Dakota, 92

Speed and direction indicator, 38, 46

Sperry, Charles S., 4, 60, 61

Sperry, Elmer A., 93, 100, 164, 228, 238

Sprague, Frank J., 18, 20, 21, 185, 228

Stadimeter, 38, 40–41, 42, 45, 46, 50, 54, 88

Steering gear, electric, 90–91

Stirling, Yates, 81, 106, 142, 143, 147, 157

Swift, William, 86, 114, 230

Taylor, David W., 152, 192

Taylor, Henry C., 4, 13, 22, 45, 48, 66, 67, 76, 230

Telescopic sight, 32–33, 35–36, 37, 39, 40, 42, 44–45, 50, 59, 65, 72, 79

Tennessee, 88–90, 91, 92, 95, 97

Terrible, 65

Texas, 38

Thayer, Harry B., 38, 45, 52, 60

Tillman, Benjamin R., 174, 177

Topeka, 63

Tracy, Benjamin F., 29, 33–34

Turret range finder, 60, 69, 70–71, 81, 82–83. *See also* Fire-control systems

Turret-turning gear, electric, 37, 41, 42, 43, 44, 51

U.S. Navy, 5–6, 11, 33; administration and personnel of, 33–34, 102, 150–54, 165, 175, 179, 185, 200–212, 214–15, 216–18, 221, 223; technological changes within, 11, 17, 19, 62–75, 83, 110; and World

War I, 154, 165, 177, 179–80, 185, 186

Utah, 93

Vermont, 90

Vesuvius, 23, 42

Virginia, 83

Wainwright, Richard, 91, 95, 97, 102, 112, 164, 173

Walker, John G., 15, 28

Washington, 90, 97, 98, (BB-47) 219

Watson, John C., 38, 39, 61

Wegman, Albert, 5, 6

Western Electric Company, 46, 47, 52, 63, 64, 67, 69, 70, 71, 228; and Fiske's inventions, 38, 40, 42, 60

West Virginia, 90

Wickes, Edward, 23–24, 28, 29, 44–45

Wilbur, Curtis D., 195–96, 218, 219, 221

Wilkinson, Ernest, 194–96

Wilson, Henry B., 203, 208, 210

Wilson, Woodrow, 105, 116, 130, 152, 160, 220, 232; and Germany, 184, 186; and Mexico, 118–26; and preparedness, 117, 131, 161–62, 165, 185

Winslow, Cameron McRae, 113, 124, 155, 158, 168, 177

Winterhalter, Albert G., 103, 108, 136, 138, 140, 141, 142, 143, 148, 151, 154, 155, 174, 233

Wireless telegraphy, 19, 50, 52, 63–64

Wood, Edward P., 51–56, 57, 58, 59

Wood, Leonard, 118, 119, 120, 123, 130

Woodhouse, Henry, 188, 192, 193

Wotherspoon, William W., 125, 134

Wyoming, 104

Yorktown, 32, 34, 35, 36, 37, 40, 45, 60, 61, 69, 89, 227

Ypiranga, 123, 124, 126

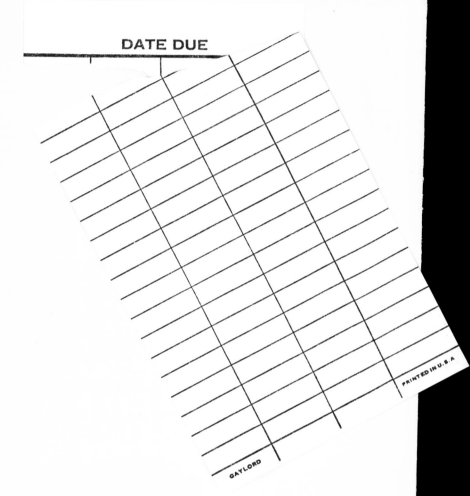

DATE DUE

GAYLORD

PRINTED IN U.S.A